Friedrich Nietzsche on Rhetoric and Language

David L. Mosley
Winter 1992
Goshen College

Friedrich Nietzsche on Rhetoric and Language

Edited and Translated
with a Critical Introduction by

Sander L. Gilman
Carole Blair
David J. Parent

New York   Oxford
OXFORD UNIVERSITY PRESS
1989

Oxford University Press

Oxford   New York   Toronto
Delhi   Bombay   Calcutta   Madras   Karachi
Petaling Jaya   Singapore   Hong Kong   Tokyo
Nairobi   Dar es Salaam   Cape Town
Melbourne   Auckland

and associated companies in
Beirut   Berlin   Ibadan   Nicosia

Published by Oxford University Press, Inc.
200 Madison Avenue, New York, New York 10016

Oxford is a registered trademark of Oxford University Press

Library of Congress Cataloging-in-Publication Data

Nietzsche, Friedrich Wilhelm, 1844–1900.
Friedrich Nietzsche on rhetoric and language : with the full text of his lectures on rhetoric
published for the first time / edited and translated, with a critical introduction, by Sander
L. Gilman, Carole Blair, David J. Parent.
p.   cm.
Bibliography: p.
Includes indexes.
ISBN 0-19-505159-9 (alk. paper).   ISBN 0-19-505160-2 (pbk. : alk. paper)
1. Rhetoric.   2. Languages—Philosophy.   I. Gilman, Sander L.
II. Blair, Carole.   III. Parent, David J.   IV. Title.
B3313.F69 1988
808—dc19

2 4 6 8 9 7 5 3 1

Printed in the United States of America
on acid-free paper

Preface

The first publication of Friedrich Nietzsche's complete lectures on rhetoric was made possible only with the cooperation of the Goethe-Schiller Archive of the National Research and Museum Organization of Classical German Literature, Weimar, and its director Karl-Heinz Hahn, who made the manuscripts available. We are also grateful for the new critical edition of Nietzsche's work edited by the late Mazzino Montinari and the late Giorgio Colli.

The volume was edited by Sander L. Gilman. The introduction was written by Carole Blair and Sander L. Gilman. The first section of the English translation of the lectures on rhetoric was done by Carole Blair and published in the journal *Philosophy and Rhetoric*. We are grateful to the editor of that journal, Professor Donald Verene, for his permission to republish the translation. The establishment of the entire German text was undertaken by Sander L. Gilman and David J. Parent. The second half of the translation of the lectures, as well as the translations of the texts in Part II, was done by David J. Parent (who received funding from two sources: Illinois State University and a 1984 NEH Summer Seminar at the University of California, Davis, under the directorship of James J. Murphy). The checking of the Greek texts was ably done by Fredericke Hohendahl.

Ithaca, New York   S.L.G.
July 1987

Contents

Nietzsche's Lectures on Rhetoric: Reading a Rhetoric Rhetorically

For rhetoric is the essence of Nietzsche's philosophy.
Hans Blumenberg, *Work on Myth*, 272.

Among Friedrich Nietzsche's early preserved writings are sets of lecture notes composed for his courses at the University of Basel. One such set of notes, those for a lecture series entitled "Rhetoric," is published here in its entirety in German and in translation. While the first seven sections of these notes were published in the Kröner (1912) and the Musarion (1922) editions of Nietzsche's works, the concluding nine sections have never been published, even in the more recent and extensive German-language editions of Nietzsche's works. The impact of the earlier sections of the lectures on rhetoric can be measured by their having been translated into French (by Philippe Lacoue-Labarthe and Jean-Luc Nancy) and into English by Carole Blair ("Lecture Notes"). These lectures form the center of a corpus of texts in which Nietzsche considered language and its function. Without a doubt the best known to date is the posthumously published essay, "On Truth and Lying in an Extra-Moral Sense," a new, complete translation of which appears in the present volume. In addition, the shorter unpublished essays on the "Origin of Language," "On the Poet," and "On Rhythm," never before translated into English, have been included to complete a volume of Nietzsche's nonaphoristic texts on the nature of human discourse.

Nietzsche's lectures on rhetoric have consistently been dated to 1874 by the editors of the fragmentary German publications of the lectures. The French translators argued it is more likely that the notes were composed in 1872. What is clear is that Nietzsche offered a series of lectures during the 1872–73 winter semester at the University of Basel on "The History of Greek Eloquence" (translated in the present volume). It has been assumed that these straightforward

lectures on the history of classical rhetoric are identical with the course of lectures which Nietzsche actually gave.

Nietzsche proposed a further course of lectures on classical rhetoric during the summer semester of 1874. Because of a lack of student interest they never took place, and the question of the relation between the two series of lectures has never been clarified. It was assumed that the more extensive notes were Nietzsche's preparation for the lecture series to have been held in 1874. It is a rare stroke of luck that Louis Kelterborn (who later became a writer under the name of Ludwig Wilhelm Kelterborn-Fischer [1853-1910]) was one of the two students who formed the audience for Nietzsche's lectures on classical rhetoric during the winter of 1872–73. He left us with a detailed account of the actual lectures:

> I had the luck to be able to be part of [Nietzsche's] career at the university, when, during the winter semester of 1872–73 I took a three-hour lecture course on the rhetoric of the Greeks and the Romans with him. As a citizen of Basel, I am still overcome with shame when I think that such an important faculty member only found two students, one of whom was a student of German, the other a student of law. And this was the only one of his announced courses which was actually held. No wonder that our beloved professor, whose health was already precarious, soon requested that we hear the rest of the lectures in his apartment. Thus we found ourselves three evenings a week in his familiarly elegant home for this lecture course. There we listened to him by lamplight and noted down the bon mots he dictated from his soft, red leather notebook. Here too he often stopped in the midst of a lecture, either to think or to give us time to process what we had heard. He was generous enough to offer us a beer, a Culmbacher, which he would drink out of a silver cup. From the size of my notes—eighty-four cramped quarto pages—one can imagine the rich content of the lectures, perhaps even more so from the following titles of the various subsections:
>
> 1. Introduction: Definition, history, bibliography; including the following important observations: "Classical education culminated in the ability to speak well." "The Hellene attempted to turn all of the occupations of life, even necessity and danger, into a game. He does not strictly separate truth and falsehood, is more talented in writing poetry and fiction, desires more to be persuaded than educated, and covers the necessity to speak with artistic drapery." "The Roman is more natural, dry, crude, however in him the worth of the individual personality remains more in the foreground."
> 2. The Division of Rhetoric (the didactic, epideictic, demonstrative, inventive; disposition, elocution, *memoria, actio*).

Even though the professor's lecture during each of the hours concentrated exclusively on the announced theme, there were still occasions, before or after the lectures, where we exchanged many a humorous or serious word with him on all sorts of topics. It is evident that I never once missed these lectures and still more evident was the professor's grade: "Attended with hard work and success, F.N." (Gilman, 1985, 111–12).

It is clear that the lectures as delivered (with beer and pretzels) were the text of the more extensive and theoretical lectures on rhetoric published here in their entirety for the first time. Evidently Nietzsche prepared two separate sets of notes, one on the history of classical rhetoric, which also formed the background for his appendix, the "Outline of the History of Eloquence," and one more original and extensive on the nature of rhetoric. It is clear that both lectures, when they discuss the history and substance of rhetoric, are derivative; Nietzsche borrowed material freely from Richard Volkmann's *Die Rhetorik der Griechen und Römer in systematischer Übersicht dargestellt.* He also drew heavily on the works of historians of rhetoric such as Gustav Gerber and Friedrich Blass. What is original is the centrality of rhetoric to Nietzsche's understanding of the formal functioning of language.

The notes bear Nietzsche's indelible mark in select portions, and they provide us a view of how Nietzsche conceived of ancient rhet-

oric, whether or not the conception was original with him. The notes constitute a significant work for a number of reasons, two of which we will address here. First, they provide an explicit and clear statement of Nietzsche's view of language. His focus on language has been explored to some degree since Kaufmann posited a need for a better understanding of Nietzsche's work in this area (495)[1]; however, the exploration has not been exhaustive, nor has it had access to the full range of implications of Nietzsche's most complete exposition on rhetoric.

The lecture notes have the further advantage of being clear and nonallegorical, a style that Nietzsche apparently reserved for his students. On the basis of portions of the notes, as well as on inferences drawn from Nietzsche's more widely known works, some writers have begun the task of demonstrating that the perspective on language found in these early fragments actually pervades Nietzsche's thought. It is this notion that we will develop first: that Nietzsche's philosophy can be reread productively with a more central place given to his conception of language.

The second issue addressed here will be Nietzsche's contribution to an understanding of rhetoric. This text in particular, and Nietzsche's philosophy in general, suggests that he shared many substantive concerns with contemporary rhetoricians. The claims that Nietzsche advanced are worth noting in their own right, but a secondary issue arises in considering Nietzsche's work in relation to the history of rhetorical studies: Nietzsche's historical impact upon the relationship between rhetoric and philosophy. If Ricoeur, Derrida, Foucault, and other contemporary European thinkers appear to address topics similar to those that modern rhetorical studies consider[2] it may be explained partially by the influence of Nietzsche's late-nineteenth-century reaction against philosophy. In reactions like it, rhetoric often seems to have displaced philosophy as the architectonic discipline of the humanities.[3] It is possible that Nietzsche, like the Sophists and the Italian Renaissance humanists, has been responsible for a historical reversal of the intellectual status (or possibly a reunion) of these two historically competitive fields. If Foucault is correct that the contemporary study of discourse will replace the intellectual centrality of, and focus upon, humanity, then we might profitably look to Nietzsche's thought as a watershed in this historical phenomenon.[4]

In examining both of these issues—the importance of language in

Nietzsche's philosophy and his potential contributions to the study of rhetoric—we concentrate our attention on the third section of the lecture notes. That in no way implies that other sections lack in interpretive value. However, this is a section that, more clearly than any other, departs from an expository presentation of classical rhetoric and presents a view that seems to be Nietzsche's own.

LANGUAGE IN NIETZSCHE'S PHILOSOPHY

The third section of Nietzsche's lectures on rhetoric offers what appears to be an early formulation of his view of perspectivism. (These views are most cogently explored in Nietzsche's manuscript "On Truth and Lying in an Extra-Moral Sense" [1873]). Nietzsche argued there that full and essential knowledge of the world cannot be had. Consciousness does not grasp things, but impulses or imperfect copies of things, and these impulses are represented only in images. The images are not the things but "the manner in which we stand toward them." Furthermore, the impulses gained through sensation and experience themselves are signs. Because of that, "language is rhetoric," for it conveys an attitude or opinion, a partial view rather than an essential knowledge of the thing. Thus, there is "no unrhetorical 'naturalness' of language. . . . the language itself is the result of audible rhetorical arts," and rhetoric "is a further development, guided by the clear light of understanding, of the artistic means which are already found in language." So, for Nietzsche, the partial or partisan nature of rhetoric is a further, conscious refinement of that quality as it already exists in natural language. Language, the very material of perception and experience, is inherently partial, and therefore perspectival.

But Nietzsche went one step further in demonstrating the perspectival nature of language. He argued that all words or signs are tropes, and because of their tropic nature as partial, transferable, and reversible they present an imperfect knowledge. First, because "language never expresses something completely but displays only a characteristic which appears prominent," language is a synecdochic or partial representation of things. Second, because words can be assigned new meanings metaphorically, they demonstrate a transferability that is not true of the things represented. Furthermore, since signs can substitute cause and effect metonymically, language reverses the nature of the things or procedures as they actually exist. These characteris-

tics of language, according to Nietzsche, become institutionalized or conventionalized in the actual language practices and common usage of a society.

This view of language anchors the ethical and epistemological perspectivism advocated by Nietzsche, as well as its connection to the will to power. Because our ethics and knowledge are grounded in language use, they always are partial; there are no absolute truths, for our experience and knowledge are linguistically based.

Consider, for example, Nietzsche's statement in *Beyond Good and Evil* (sec. 108): "There are no moral phenomena at all, but only a moral interpretation of phenomena." Given Nietzsche's position in the earlier lecture notes, the morality attached to a phenomenon is a matter of perspective. And the perspective is derived from and represented by signs. It is, therefore, partial, transferable, and reversible. And any divergent perspective would be grounded in the same way, through language. Consequently, no perspective could have an essential, philosophical priority over any other.

Similarly, Nietzsche argued that knowledge, our own understanding, is shaped by language:

> The whole notion of an 'inner experience' enters our consciousness only after it has found a language that the individual *understands*—i.e., a translation of a situation into a *familiar* situation—: 'to understand,' naively put, merely means: to be able to express something old and familiar (Schlechta, 3:805, quoted in de Man, *Allegories*, 108).

Thus knowledge and ethics are functions of language as we bring it to bear in our perceptions and experiential stances. There is no absolute ethic or universal knowledge system; there are only linguistically based perspectives.

Nietzsche was fairly clear about the relationship of these perspectival interpretations and the all-important will to power. In *The Will to Power*, Nietzsche suggested that to interpret a thing was to become master of it (sec. 643). And, in an earlier section, he argued that the categories created by language, which are accepted as the grounds of knowledge and morals, are interpretations, "in the sense of a will to power" (sec. 589). The interesting conclusion, of course, is that Nietzsche's philosophy too is grounded in interpretation. But he seems to have done other philosophies one better, for in interpreting language itself, in advancing his perspectival interpretation of it, Nietzsche, by his own analysis, would have achieved a mastery of

language, and by extension a mastery of knowledge and morals. Ijsseling summarizes magnificently:

> In his view rhetoric is, on the one hand, an effect and on the other hand, an expression of the will to power. There should be no misunderstanding here. In attempting to show that existing philosophy is rhetorical he undoubtedly intends to unmask the pretensions of philosophy. In no way, however, does he plan to construct a non-rhetorical philosophy over and against this existing philosophy. Even his own philosophy is also rhetorical and purposely intended to be an excellent example of rhetoric (108).

So, in examining the very foundations of "knowledge" and "morality," Nietzsche is able to transcend the conventional versions of both, and he is able to assert the primacy of the will to power as a governing principle, by insisting on the mediating role of rhetoric. But, this position has specific, tactical implications.

Human thought is inherently limited by the capacities and constraints of language. In Nietzsche's words,

> ... we think *only* in the form of language. ... we cease to think when we refuse to do so under the constraint of language; we barely reach the doubt that sees this limitation as a limitation. Rational thought is interpretation according to a scheme that we cannot throw off (*Will to Power*, sec. 522).

Because of this necessary captivity of thought in language, thought is characterized by an abstractness and historicity that further limit its capacity. As Nietzsche argued in *The Will to Power*, the historicity of language, and therefore of thought, poses a constraint:

> Philosophers ... have trusted in concepts as completely as they have mistrusted the senses: they have not stopped to consider that concepts and words are our inheritance from ages in which thinking was very modest and unclear (sec. 409).

The implication, of course, is that concepts can never be more sophisticated than the language in which they are portrayed. Nor can they be more concrete than the nature of their formation in language. Nietzsche described this "problem" clearly: "Finally, concepts, possible only when there are words—the collecting together of many images in something invisible but audible" (*Will to Power*, sec. 506). But if we hark back to the earlier lecture notes, in which Nietzsche argued that the rhetorical is a further development of the means

already present in language, it is possible to infer that a sophisticated rhetorical practice is a method for developing a sounder conceptual, intellectual, and moral base. Certainly, it would never certify a true knowledge or moral base, but it would give its user a higher degree of power or mastery over concepts.

Whether or not Nietzsche's early and late works can be so intimately intertextualized is certainly an issue that qualifies these speculations and one that deserves more inquiry than is possible here. At the very least, however, Nietzsche's early concentration on language and rhetoric draws our attention more specifically to those concepts as they appear in his later writings. And if it is not to be concluded finally that language is Nietzsche's ultimate means of departure from the isolated world of nihilism and its denial of our ability to know, we at least are able to more legitimately pose the question of what part language does play in Nietzsche's philosophy. Paul de Man seems to agree:

> We can legitimately assert therefore that the key to Nietzsche's critique of metaphysics—which has, perhaps misleadingly, been described as a mere *reversal* of metaphysics or of Plato—lies in the rhetorical model of the trope or, if one prefers to call it that way, in literature as the language most explicitly grounded in rhetoric (*Allegories*, 109).

Like de Man, it is our position that rhetoric is of tremendous concern in the interpretation of Nietzsche's philosophical writings. These early lecture notes, together with Nietzsche's later references to the power of language, lead us to conclude, with Ijsseling (106), that

> Rhetoric has an extremely important role in Nietzsche's analysis of the structure of philosophy and the function of philosophical speech, in the genealogical detection of the factors responsible for the factum of philosophy and in the question of the precise nature of formulation and interpretation. One can even say that the problem of rhetoric has been a decisive influence on his thought and that much of his 'philosophical' terminology is derived from the classical rhetorical tradition. This also applies to the so-called '*will to power*.'

This position also leads us to consider Nietzsche's relationship to the systematic study of rhetoric.

NIETZSCHE AND THE STUDY OF RHETORIC

Based on textual evidence, it is possible only to speculate about the impact of rhetorical principles on Nietzsche's philosophical per-

spective. One can, however, argue for an extensive consideration of Nietzsche's work in the context of rhetorical studies, for this is a matter of advocacy rather than interpretation. To argue that Nietzsche deserves no consideration by rhetoricians is no longer possible, despite the fact that his work has been all but ignored in this area.[5] A number of possible explanations of this oversight will be advanced later. At this point, though, it is possible to argue that Nietzsche is a figure strongly deserving of attention in a systematic study of rhetoric. That Nietzsche's view of language and rhetoric helped to shape his entire philosophy is itself an argument in favor of such a study. But there are a number of others as well.

First and most obvious, Nietzsche has provided, in the early lecture notes, a commentary on classical rhetoric that displays an unusual depth and range of familiarity with classical sources. Though his work is largely derivative, the selection, arrangement, and placement of the subject matter are of his choosing, and his sensitive treatment of classical rhetoric is well worth examining. It is instructive to note, too, Nietzsche's de-emphasis of Plato and Aristotle in the notes, a departure from the emphasis—common among the contemporary histories of classical theory—upon the "inventive" rhetorics of antiquity.[6] Nietzsche's emphasis is more distinctly on Ciceronian rhetoric, projecting its greater concern with style.

Nietzsche's stress on the stylistic canon suggests a second justification for reconsidering his work in light of contemporary rhetoric. Modern rhetorical studies have, in essence, merged the classical *officia* of *inventio* and *elocutio* in their emphasis upon the inventive and epistemological character of language.[7] The widespread and enthusiastic reception in rhetorical studies of I. A. Richards's and Kenneth Burke's works is strong evidence of the modern marriage of style and invention. Nietzsche's work appears to be a late-nineteenth-century forerunner of this phenomenon.

In fact, Nietzsche actually went a great deal further than contemporary rhetoricians have been willing to go. He not only placed language at the forefront of his rhetorical theory, but used its enhanced philosophical position to launch a full-scale attack on logic and rationality, a step rhetoricians apparently have been loath to take, despite their current fascination with the world of symbols, sometimes at the expense of considering reasoning or strategies of argumentation.[8]

The similarities remain. Though Nietzsche's case for a systematic study of language is more radical than that advanced by current

scholars of rhetoric, his work parallels the growing contemporary interests of this group with regard to language in general, particularly tropes, and more specifically the master tropes.[9] His work and theirs advocate further investigation of the primary figures as well as the minor forms to develop a philosophical view of the nature of language and thought.

Even more important than Nietzsche's anticipation of the twentieth-century focus upon language, but also related to it, are his almost prophetic statements on rhetoric's relation to knowledge. Among the more prominent issues in contemporary rhetoric, perhaps the single most important is the controversy over rhetoric's epistemic status.[10] Those who are party to the issue argue variously about the types of knowledge that rhetoric creates; whether there are forces other than rhetoric at work in creating knowledge, particularly a reinforcive or constitutive objective reality; and whether or not this knowledge is "real" knowledge or an informed or consensual opinion or *doxa*.[11] The issues addressed by the various writers essentially distill to the relation between linguistic and nonlinguistic phenomena, between words and things.

Nietzsche's view is mirrored, to some degree, in the position on "perspectivism" taken by Cherwitz and Hikins, but they, unlike Nietzsche, posit an independent realm of reality or truth and argue for "treating consciousness as a phenomenon which *itself* emerges when an entity of a particular type (e.g., a human being) stands in a particular *relation* to other entities." ("Perspectivism," 258). Cherwitz and Hikins's version of perspectivism, based on the formulations of Evander McGilbary, parts company with Nietzsche's in its postulate that "In experience there is presented to us, directly, a world of phenomena largely independent of our attitudes, beliefs, and values" ("Perspectivism," 251). Obviously this runs counter to Nietzsche's position that there is no *direct* experience of reality possible. The only other real similarity between the Cherwitz and Hikins stance and Nietzsche's position is their agreement that knowledge is social; Cherwitz and Hikins, following John Stuart Mill, argue that knowledge is consensual ("John Stuart Mill"). Nietzsche's stance differs, though the result may be similar; knowledge is social for Nietzsche, precisely because it is shaped by the inherently social phenomenon of language.

Nietzsche's view bears a closer resemblance, in general terms, to those of Brummett and Scott, especially in the subjectivist claims

made in the third section of the lecture notes and in this conclusion in *The Gay Science* (sec. 354):

> ... it seems to me as if the subtlety and strength of consciousness always were proportionate to a man's (or animal's) *capacity for communication*, as if this capacity in turn were proportionate to the *need for communication*.... Consciousness is really only a net of communication between human beings; it is only as such that it had to develop; a solitary human being who lived like a beast of prey would not have needed it.... In brief, the development of language and the development of consciousness (*not* of reason but merely of the way reason enters consciousness) go hand in hand.

Nietzsche's view of knowledge, like Brummett's for example, is intersubjectivist to the extent that it is dependent upon language, a socially held and conventionalized phenomenon. It is in their ethical implications that the two views differ most. Brummett contends that "Truth which is rhetorically made encourages choice and awareness of alternative realities" ("Process," 40). Nietzsche, of course, argued the opposite, suggesting that at least in most cases we tend to rigidify and dogmatize our moral perspectives.

Nietzsche's connection of the capacity for communication with the degree of human need for it seems to resemble the stance assumed by Burke, and in turn by Gregg,[12] that human ability to communicate is a function of need, although Nietzsche's version leaves out the teleological sense that Burke emphasizes ("Definition," 17–18). It is particularly revealing to compare the following statement from Burke's "Definition of Man" with the principles Nietzsche articulated throughout his many discussions of language:

> In responding to words, with their overt and covert modes of persuasion ..., we like to forget the kind of relation that really prevails between the verbal and the nonverbal. In being a link between us and the nonverbal, words are by the same token a screen separating us from the nonverbal—though the statement gets tangled in its own traces, since so much of the "we" that is separated from the nonverbal by the verbal would not even exist were it not for the verbal (or for our symbolicity in general ...) (5)

In fact, Nietzsche's formulation of the language-knowledge relationship appears to contain aspects of all of these contemporary views.

Determining where Nietzsche stands precisely in regard to this modern controversy is not so important here as simply demonstrat-

ing that his writings do have commentary to add to the rhetoric-epistemology issue. Given the tremendous import of that issue in rhetorical studies, Nietzsche's writings take on a new significance.

Last, and certainly not less important than the other justifications
for incorporating Nietzsche into the historical *oeuvre* of rhetoric, is
a historiographic concern. It has been a fairly commonly held view
that rhetoric was a moribund and silent field during the nineteenth
century, at least after the last edition of Richard Whately's *Elements
of Rhetoric* in 1846. I. A. Richards, for example, reported in a widely
quoted statement that rhetoric "may perhaps be said to end with
Archbishop Whately" (5). Nietzsche's writings may be considered, in
one sense, a single counterexample among many, illustrating this historical blunder. Blair ("Archeological Critique," 114–16) discusses
the conspicuous lack of historical attention granted to nineteenth-
century thinkers who studied rhetoric. Even Freud, Bentham, Mill,
and Kierkegaard, who quite clearly raised issues pertinent to the
study of rhetoric, have been given scant attention by historians of
rhetoric (Jaffe). And the nineteenth century has not received the
same degree of attention from historians of rhetorical theory as have
even the Middle Ages,[13] a rather arid period of rhetorical thought to
say the least. But Nietzsche's work, most prominently these lecture
notes, is a strident denial of the traditional wisdom regarding the
silence of rhetoric in the past century.

Foucault's historical rendering of Nietzsche, however, offers not
only an explanation for this historical blunder, but also a more
urgent rationale for a rhetorical study of Nietzsche's writings, as well
as those of other nineteenth-century figures. Foucault has claimed
that Nietzsche was a central figure in an epistemological transformation that ultimately will shift the attention of the human sciences
almost exclusively toward studying discourse and language.[14] But if
that transformation began in the last century, and primarily occurred
in Europe, its beginnings would have been easily overlooked. Heidegger, Gadamer, Derrida, Ricoeur, Lacan, Foucault, and others, all
of whom share an interest in language, and all of whom were influenced profoundly by Nietzsche,[15] have become pivotal figures in the
study of rhetoric.[16] And, in fact, the writings of these more contemporary European thinkers, together with other forces, have helped to
shape a new and growing interdisciplinary interest in rhetoric
(Simons; Lyne; Nelson and Megill).

Given these developments, it may be fair to argue that Nietzsche's

thought is central to a historical transformation that is still taking shape. If that is borne out, and only a more systematic historical investigation could provide such confirmation, there is ample reason to focus a great deal of intellectual energy upon Nietzsche's rhetorical concerns. It is not inconceivable that Nietzsche's work has been largely responsible for a twentieth-century revival of rhetoric as a systematic field of thought that is increasingly removed substantively from its Platonic and Aristotelian ancestry.

NOTE ON THE TEXT

The lecture notes on rhetoric are edited from the manuscript held in the former Nietzsche Archive (now part of the Goethe-Schiller Archive) in Weimar. The text is transcribed as it stands in the manuscript. Illegible words are noted by [?]. The texts in Part II were translated from the Musarion edition, except for Nietzsche's essay "On Truth and Lying in an Extra-Moral Sense," which has been compared with the new Colli/Montinari edition.

NOTES

1. A number of studies have reflected this interest. The essays in the Allison anthology are good examples. So too are Schacht, and de Man, "Nietzsche's Theory of Rhetoric."
2. See Harvey's discussion for a review of the potential impact of Nietzsche on the rhetorical thought of contemporary French thinkers.
3. For a general discussion of the relation between rhetoric and philosophy see McKeon. Seigel and Ijsseling both address the issue historically. Seigel, in particular, demonstrates the changing intellectual predominance of one field over the other in his history of the relation between rhetoric and philosophy during the Renaissance.
4. Foucault, *Order of Things* (303–43). Specifically he argues that "Language did not return into the field of thought directly and in its own right until the end of the nineteenth century. We might even have said until the twentieth, had not Nietzsche the philologist—and even in that field he was so wise, he knew so much, he wrote such good books—been the first to connect the philosophical task with a radical reflection upon language" (305).
5. There are rare exceptions. See, for example, McGuire.
6. The emphasis upon invention is largely due to a focus upon Aristotle. Black's and Charles J. Stewart's discussions reflect the centrality in the

twentieth century of research on Aristotle's *Rhetoric*. Also, Ehninger discusses the emphasis upon invention in the study of classical rhetoric in his essays on George Campbell. See also Kennedy, *Art of Persuasion* (82–114), and *Classical Rhetoric* (60–85).

7. For excellent and explicit discussions of the shift away from considering style and invention as separable to the view of symbol use and choice as inventional, see Ehninger's introduction to *Contemporary Rhetoric* (9–10) and his "A Synoptic View" (452–53). Hauser's discussion of metaphor in a section of his book entitled "Topical Thinking" illustrates this contemporary merger of invention and style (63–65).

8. There are any number of examples of this phenomenon. Richards shifts attention away from logical function to language. Burke's emphasis does the same, though he allows for study of logical structures, for example, in his notion of syllogistic form (*Counter-Statement*, 124). Perhaps the most current and prominent example is Fisher's "narrative paradigm," a perspective that he introduces explicitly as a departure from a "rational world paradigm." Fisher's work, however, also exemplifies the refusal to dispose of rationality altogether in that he retains a "good reasons" posture to maintain narrative fidelity and probability (10).

9. See Burke, *Grammar* (503–17), and Grassi. Also see Ricoeur, *Rule*, and his "Post-Critical Rhetoric." Ehninger notes this focus on language (Editor's Introduction, 9–10), as does Gregg (*Symbolic Inducement*) in his first-chapter characterization of contemporary views of rhetoric.

10. The importance of this issue has been noted frequently. Leff, for example, in his review of recent theoretical works in rhetorical theory, argues that the epistemology issue is the most central one for rhetorical study. Also see Leff and Procario.

11. For a sample of the positions on the rhetoric-epistemology issue, see the works of Brummett; Carleton; Cherwitz; Cherwitz and Hikins; Croasmun and Cherwitz; Farrell; Gregg; Orr; and Scott. Reviews of this literature can be found in Gregg, "Rhetoric and Knowing," as well as in Leff, and in Leff and Procario.

12. See Burke, "Definition." Also see Gregg, *Symbolic Inducement*.

13. For a thorough discussion of medieval rhetoric, see Murphy.

14. See Foucault, *Order of Things* (303–43).

15. See Heidegger's studies of Nietzsche. Note too Gadamer's assessment that "the philosophical situation of our century . . . finally goes back to Nietzsche's critique of consciousness." (*Philosophical Hermeneutics*, 119). Said describes parts of Derrida's project as "affirmatively Nietzschean" (207). Ricoeur and Lacan are both influenced by Nietzsche also, but less so, and far less than Foucault. Dreyfus and Rabinow point out that "all of the seeds of Foucault's work of the 1970s can be found in this discussion of Nietzsche" (106). But Foucault's works of the 1980s

also seem to reflect this Nietzschean influence. See "Preface to *The History of Sexuality*, Volume II." Also see the interviews with Foucault: "Polemic" and "Politics."

16. That these thinkers are becoming more important in the study of rhetoric is apparent in Blair, "The Statement"; Glynn; Harvey; Hyde; Hyde and Smith; Marassi; and John Stewart, among others, whose works focus explicitly on issues of importance to rhetoric. For works by Foucault that have the most direct bearing on rhetoric, see *Archeology* and "Nietzsche." See also works by Derrida; Gadamer, *Truth and Method*; Heidegger, *Being and Time*; and Ricoeur, *Interpretation Theory*.

WORKS CITED

Allison, David B., ed. *The New Nietzsche: Contemporary Styles of Interpretation*. New York: Delta, 1977.

Black, Edwin. *Rhetorical Criticism: A Study in Method*. New York: Macmillan, 1965.

Blair, Carole. "An Archeological Critique of the History of Rhetorical Theory: Beyond Historical-Critical Dualism in the Analysis of Theoretical Discourse." Diss., Pennsylvania State U, 1983.

———. "The Statement: Foundation of Foucault's Historical Criticism." *Western Journal of Speech Communication* 51 (1987): 364–83.

———. trans. "Nietzsche's Lecture Notes on Rhetoric: A Translation." *Philosophy and Rhetoric* 16 (1983): 94–129.

Blass, Friedrich. *Die griechische Beredsamkeit in dem Zeitraum von Alexander bis auf Augustus*. 3 vols. Berlin: Weidmann, 1865.

Brummett, Barry. "A Defense of Ethical Relativism as Rhetorically Grounded." *Western Journal of Speech Communication* 45 (1981): 286–98.

———. "On to Rhetorical Relativism." *Quarterly Journal of Speech* 68 (1982): 425–30.

———. "Some Implications of 'Process' or 'Intersubjectivity': Post-Modern Rhetoric." *Philosophy and Rhetoric* 9 (1976): 21–51.

Burke, Kenneth. *Counter-Statement*. 2nd ed. Berkeley: University of California Press, 1968.

———. "Definition of Man." In *Language as Symbolic Action: Essays on Life, Literature, and Method*. Berkeley: University of California Press, 1966. 3–24.

———. *A Grammar of Motives*. Berkeley: University of California Press, 1969.

Carleton, Walter M. "What is Rhetorical Knowledge: A Response to Farrell —and More." *Quarterly Journal of Speech* 64 (1978): 313–28.

Cherwitz, Richard A. "Rhetoric as a 'Way of Knowing': An Attenuation of the Epistemological Claims of the 'New Rhetoric.'" *Southern Speech Communication Journal* 42 (1977): 207–19.

———. and James W. Hikins. "John Stuart Mill's *On Liberty*: Implications for the Epistemology of the New Rhetoric." *Quarterly Journal of Speech* 65 (1979): 12–24.

———. "Rhetorical Perspectivism." *Quarterly Journal of Speech* 69 (1983): 249–66.

Croasmun, Earl, and Richard A. Cherwitz. "Beyond Rhetorical Relativism." *Quarterly Journal of Speech* 68 (1982): 1–16.

de Man, Paul. *Allegories of Reading: Figural Language in Rousseau, Nietzsche, Rilke, and Proust.* New Haven: Yale University Press, 1979.

———. "Nietzsche's Theory of Rhetoric." *Symposium: A Quarterly Journal in Modern Foreign Literatures.* Syracuse: Syracuse University Press, 1974. 33–51.

Derrida, Jacques. *Of Grammatology.* Trans. Gayatri Chakravorty. Baltimore: Johns Hopkins University Press, 1974.

———. *Writing and Difference.* Trans. Alan Bass. Chicago: University of Chicago Press, 1978.

Dreyfus, Hubert L., and Paul Rabinow. *Michel Foucault: Beyond Structuralism and Hermeneutics.* 2nd ed. Chicago: University of Chicago Press, 1983.

Ehninger, Douglas. Editor's Introduction. *Contemporary Rhetoric: A Reader's Coursebook.* Glenview, IL: Scott, Foresman, 1972. 1–14.

———. "George Campbell and the Revolution of Inventional Theory." *Western Speech* 15 (1950): 270–76.

———. "George Campbell and the Rhetorical Tradition: A Reply to LaRusso." *Western Speech* 32 (1968): 276–79.

———. "A Synoptic View of Systems of Western Rhetoric." *Quarterly Journal of Speech* 61 (1975): 448–53.

Farrell, Thomas B. "Knowledge, Consensus, and Rhetorical Theory." *Quarterly Journal of Speech* 62 (1976): 1–14.

——— "Social Knowledge II." *Quarterly Journal of Speech* 64 (1978): 329–34.

Fisher, Walter R. "Narration as a Human Communication Paradigm: The Case of Public Moral Argument." *Communication Monographs* 51 (1984): 1–22.

Foucault, Michel. *The Archeology of Knowledge and the Discourse on Language.* Trans. A. M. Sheridan Smith. New York: Harper Torchbooks, 1972.

——— . "Nietzsche, Genealogy, History." In *Language, Counter-Memory, Practice: Selected Essays and Interviews by Michel Foucault.* Ed. Donald

F. Bouchard. Trans. Donald Bouchard and Sherry Simon. Ithaca: Cornell University Press, 1977. 139–64.

——. *The Order of Things: An Archeology of the Human Sciences.* Trans. Alan Sheridan. New York: Vintage Books, 1973.

——. "Polemics, Politics, and Problematizations: An Interview with Michel Foucault." Trans. Lydia Davis. In Rabinow. 381–90.

——. "Polemics and Ethics: An Interview." Trans. Catherine Porter. In Rabinow. 373–80.

——. "Preface to *The History of Sexuality*, Volume II." Trans. William Smock. In Rabinow. 333–39.

Gadamer, Hans-Georg. *Philosophical Hermeneutics.* Trans. David E. Linge. Berkeley: University of California Press, 1976.

——. *Truth and Method.* Trans. Garrett Barden and John Cumming. New York: Crossroad, 1982.

Gerber, Gustav. *Die Sprache als Kunst.* Bromberg: Mittler'sche Buchhandlung, 1872.

Gilman, Sander L., ed., *Begegnungen mit Nietzsche.* 2nd ed. Bonn: Bouvier Verlag Herbert Grundmann, 1985.

——. ed., *Conversations with Nietzsche.* Trans. David J. Parent. New York: Oxford University Press, 1987.

Glynn, Stephan. "Beyond the Symbol: Deconstructing Social Reality." *Southern Speech Communication Journal* 51 (1986): 125–41.

Grassi, Ernesto. *Rhetoric as Philosophy: The Humanist Tradition.* University Park: Pennsylvania State University Press, 1980.

Gregg, Richard B. "Rhetoric and Knowing: The Search for Perspective." *Central States Speech Journal* 32 (1981): 133–44.

——. *Symbolic Inducement and Knowing: A Study in the Foundations of Rhetoric.* Columbia: University of South Carolina Press, 1984.

Harvey, Irene E. "Contemporary French Thought and the Art of Rhetoric." *Philosophy and Rhetoric* 18 (1985): 199–215.

Hauser, Gerard A. *Introduction to Rhetorical Theory.* New York: Harper and Row, 1986.

Heidegger, Martin. *Being and Time.* Trans. John Macquarrie and Edward Robinson. New York: Harper and Row, 1962.

——. *Nietzsche.* Trans. Frank A. Capuzzi. Ed. David Farrell Krell. 4 vols. New York: Harper and Row, 1979–84.

Hyde, Michael J. "Jacques Lacan's Psychoanalytic Theory of Speech and Language." Rev. *Quarterly Journal of Speech* 66 (1980): 96–108.

——, and Craig R. Smith. "Hermeneutics and Rhetoric: A Seen but Unobserved Relationship." *Quarterly Journal of Speech* 65 (1979): 347–63.

Ijsseling, Samuel. *Rhetoric and Philosophy in Conflict: An Historical Survey.* Trans. Paul Dunphy. The Hague: Martinus Nijhoff, 1976.

Jaffe, Samuel. "Freud as Rhetorician: Elocutio and the Dream-Work," *Rhetoric* 1 (1980): 42–69.

Kaufmann, Walter. *Nietzsche: Philosopher, Psychologist, Antichrist.* 4th ed. Princeton: Princeton University Press, 1974.

Kennedy, George A. *The Art of Persuasion in Greece.* Princeton: Princeton University Press, 1963.

———. *Classical Rhetoric and Its Christian and Secular Tradition from Ancient to Modern Times.* Chapel Hill: University of North Carolina Press, 1980.

Lacoue-Labarthe, Philippe, and Jean-Luc Nancy, trans. "Friedrich Nietzsche, Rhétorique et Langage." *Poetique* 2 (1971): 99–130.

Leff, Michael C. "In Search of Ariadne's Thread: A Review of the Recent Literature on Rhetorical Theory." *Central States Speech Journal* 29 (1978): 73–91.

———, and Margaret Organ Procario. "Rhetorical Theory in Speech Communication." *Speech Communication in the 20th Century.* Ed. Thomas W. Benson. Carbondale: Southern Illinois University Press, 1985. 3–27.

Lyne, John. "Rhetorics of Inquiry." *Quarterly Journal of Speech* 71 (1985): 65–73.

Marassi, Massimo. "The Hermeneutics of Rhetoric in Heidegger." *Philosophy and Rhetoric* 19 (1986): 79–98.

McGuire, Michael. "The Ethics of Rhetoric: The Morality of Knowledge." *Southern Speech Communication Journal* 45 (1979): 133–48.

McKeon, Richard. "The Uses of Rhetoric in a Technological Age: Architectonic Productive Arts." *The Prospect of Rhetoric.* Ed. Lloyd F. Bitzer and Edwin Black. Englewood Cliffs, NJ: Prentice Hall, 1971. 44–63.

Murphy, James J. *Rhetoric in the Middle Ages: A History of Rhetorical Theory from Saint Augustine to the Renaissance.* Berkeley: University of California Press, 1974.

Nietzsche, Friedrich. *Beyond Good and Evil.* Trans. Walter Kaufmann. New York: Vintage, 1966.

———. *The Gay Science.* Trans. Walter Kaufmann. New York: Vintage, 1974.

———. "Rhetorik." *Nietzsche's Werke.* Vol. 3, part 2. Ed. Otto Crusius. Leipzig: Alfred Kroner Verlag, 1912. 237–68.

———. "Rhetorik." *Gesammelte Werke.* Vol. 5, Lectures 1872–1876. Munich: Musarion Verlag, 1922. 287–319.

———. *Werke in drei Banden.* Ed. Karl Schlecta. 3 vols. Munich: Carl Hanser, 1954–1956.

———. *The Will to Power.* Trans. Walter Kaufmann and R. J. Hollingdale. Ed. Walter Kaufmann. New York: Vintage, 1968.

Nelson, John S., and Allan Megill. "Rhetorics of Inquiry: Projects and Prospects." *Quarterly Journal of Speech* 72 (1986): 20–37.

Orr, C. Jack. "How Shall We Say: 'Reality is Socially Constructed through Communication?'" *Central States Speech Journal* 29 (1978): 263–73.

Rabinow, Paul, ed. *The Foucault Reader*. New York: Pantheon, 1984.

Richards, I. A. *The Philosophy of Rhetoric*. London: Oxford University Press, 1936.

Ricoeur, Paul. *Interpretation Theory: Discourse and the Surplus of Meaning*. Fort Worth: Texas Christian University Press, 1976.

———. *The Rule of Metaphor: Multi-Disciplinary Studies of the Creation of the Meaning in Language*. Trans. Robert Czerny with Kathleen McLaughlin and John Costello. Toronto: University of Toronto Press, 1975.

———. "Toward a 'Post-Critical Rhetoric'?" *Pre/Text* 5 (1984): 9–16.

Said, Edward W. *The World, the Text, the Critic*. Cambridge: Harvard University Press, 1983.

Schacht, Richard. *Nietzsche*. London: Routledge and Kegan Paul, 1983.

Scott, Robert L. "On Viewing Rhetoric as Epistemic." *Central States Speech Journal* 27 (1976): 258–66.

Seigel, Jerrold E. *Rhetoric and Philosophy in Renaissance Humanism: The Union of Eloquence and Wisdom, Petrarch to Valla*. Princeton: Princeton University Press, 1968.

Simons, Herbert W. "Chronicle and Critique of a Conference." *Quarterly Journal of Speech* 71 (1985): 52–64.

Stewart, Charles J. "Historical Survey: Rhetorical Criticism in Twentieth America." *Explorations in Rhetorical Criticism*. Ed. G. P. Mohrmann, Charles J. Stewart, and Donovan J. Ochs. University Park: Pennsylvania State University Press, 1973.

Stewart, John. "Speech and Human Being: A Complement to Semiotics." *Quarterly Journal of Speech* 72 (1986): 55–73.

Volkmann, Richard. *Die Rhetorik der Griechen und Römer in systematischer Uebersicht dargestellt*. Berlin: Ebeling and Plahn, 1872.

Whately, Richard. *The Elements of Rhetoric*. Ed. Douglas Ehninger. Carbondale: Southern Illinois University Press, 1963.

I

DARSTELLUNG DER ANTIKEN RHETORIK
(1872–73)

I. BEGRIFF DER RHETORIK

Die ausserordentliche Entwicklung derselben gehört zu den spezifischen Unterschieden der Alten von den Modernen: in neuerer Zeit steht diese Kunst in einiger Nichtachtung,[1] und wenn sie gebraucht wird, ist auch die beste Anwendung unserer Modernen nichts als Dilettanterei und rohe Empirie. Im Allgemeinen ist das Gefühl für das an sich *Wahre* viel mehr entwickelt: die Rhetorik erwächst aus einem Volke, das noch in mythischen Bildern lebt, und noch nicht das unbedingte Bedürfnis nach historischer Treue kennt: es will lieber überredet als belehrt sein, und auch die *Nothdurft* des Menschen in der gerichtlichen Beredsamkeit soll zur freien Kunst entfaltet sein. Sodann ist es eine wesentlich *republikanische* Kunst: man muss gewohnt sein, die fremdesten Meinungen und Ansichten zu ertragen und sogar ein gewisses Vergnügen an ihrem Widerspiel empfinden: man muss ebenso gerne zuhören als selbst sprechen, man muss als Zuhörer ungefähr die aufgewandte Kunst würdigen können. Die Bildung des antiken Menschen kulminirt gewöhnlich in der Rhetorik: es ist die höchste geistige Bethätigung des gebildeten politischen Menschen—ein für uns sehr befremdlicher Gedanke! Am deutlichsten spricht Kant, *Kritik der Urtheilskraft*, p. 203:

> Die redenden Künste sind Beredsamkeit und Dichtkunst. Beredsamkeit ist die Kunst, ein Geschäft des Verstandes als ein freies Spiel der Einbildungskraft zu betreiben, Dichtkunst ein freies Spiel der Einbildungskraft als ein Geschäft des Verstandes auszuführen. Der Redner also kündigt ein Geschäft an und führt es so aus, als ob es bloss ein Spiel mit Ideen sei, um die Zuhörer zu unterhalten. Der Dichter kündigt bloss ein unterhaltendes Spiel mit Ideen an, und es kommt doch so viel für den Verstand heraus, als ob er bloss dessen Geschäfte zu treiben die Absicht gehabt hätte.

Damit ist das Spezifische des hellenischen Lebens charakterisirt: alle Geschäfte des Verstandes, des Lebensernstes, der Noth, selbst der Gefahr noch als Spiel aufzufassen. Die Römer sind lange Zeit in der

DESCRIPTION OF ANCIENT RHETORIC
(1872–73)

I. THE CONCEPT OF RHETORIC

The extraordinary development of the concept of rhetoric belongs to the specific differences between the ancients and moderns: in recent times, this art stands in some disrepute,[1] and even when it is used, the best application to which it is put by our moderns is nothing short of dilettantism and crude empiricism. Generally speaking, the feeling for what is *true* in itself is much more developed: rhetoric arises among a people who still live in mythic images and who have not yet experienced the unqualified need of historical accuracy: they would rather be persuaded than instructed. In addition, the *need* of men for forensic eloquence must have given rise to the evolution of the liberal art. Thus, it is an essentially *republican* art: one must be accustomed to tolerating the most unusual opinions and points of view and even to taking a certain pleasure in their counterplay; one must be just as willing to listen as to speak; and as a listener one must be able more or less to appreciate the art being applied. The education of the ancient man customarily culminates in rhetoric: it is the highest spiritual activity of the well-educated political man—an odd notion for us! Kant makes the clearest statement of this (*Kritik der Urteilskraft*):

> The arts of speech are rhetoric and poetry. Rhetoric is the art of transacting a serious business of the understanding as if it were a free play of the imagination; poetry that of conducting a free play of the imagination as if it were a serious business of the understanding. Thus the orator announces a serious business, and for the purpose of entertaining his audience conducts it as if it were a mere play with ideas. The poet promises merely an entertaining play with ideas, and yet for the understanding there inures as much as if the promotion of its business had been his one intention.[2]

What is unique to Hellenistic life is thus characterized: to perceive all matters of the intellect, of life's seriousness, of necessities, even of danger, as play. For a long period of time, the Romans are natu-

Rhetorik Naturalisten, vergleichsweise trocken und derb. Aber die aristokratische Würde des römischen Staatsmanns, seine vielseitige juridische Praxis geben die Farbe: gewöhnlich waren ihre grossen Redner mächtige Partei*führer*, während die griechischen Redner im Interesse von Parteien sprachen. Das Bewusstsein der individuellen Würde ist römisch, nicht griechisch. Auf ihre Auffassung der Rhetorik passt mehr, was Schopenhauer W.a.W. u. V. II 129 sagt:

> Beredsamkeit ist die Fähigkeit, unsere Ansicht einer Sache oder unsere Gesinnung hinsichtlich derselben, auch in Anderen zu erregen, unser Gefühl darüber in ihnen zu entzünden und sie so in Sympathie mit uns zu versetzen: dies alles aber dadurch, dass wir, mittels Worten, den Strom unserer Gedanken in ihren Kopf leiten, mit solcher Gewalt, dass er den ihrer eigenen von dem Gange, den sie bereits genommen, ablenkt und in seinen Lauf mit fortreisst. Dies Meisterstück wird um so grösser sein, je mehr der Gang ihrer Gedanke vorher von dem unserigen abwich.

Hier wird das beherrschende Uebergewicht der einzelnen Persönlichkeit betont, im Sinn der Römer, bei Kant das freie Spiel bei Geschäften des Verstandes, im Sinne der Griechen.

Im Allgemeinen aber sind alle Neueren in ihren Definitionen ungenau, während durch das ganze Alterthum hindurch der Wetteifer um die richtige Definition der Rhetorik hingeht, und zwar unter Philosophen und Rednern. Alle chronologisch zusammengestellt von Spengel, Rh. Mus. 18 p. 481. Darnach bei Rich. Volkmann, Rhetorik, Berlin 1872. Diejenigen, welche der Strenge der Definition auswichen, suchten wenigstens das τέλος, officium, des Redners zu bestimmen. Dies ist das πείθειν, dicendo peresuadere, es war schwierig, dies in den ὁρισμός aufzunehmen; denn die Wirkung ist nicht das Wesen der Sache: und zudem bleibt das Ueberreden bei den besten Reden mitunter aus. Die Sikuler Korax und Tisias sagen ῥητορική ἐστι πειθοῦς δημιουργός: bei den Dorern hat das Wort δημιουργός eine höhere Bedeutung als bei den Ioniern "Schöpferin," "Walterin": die höchsten obrigkeitlichen Personen in den dorischen Staaten heissen so (*dort* nur "Gewerbetreibende"). Ebenso Gorgias und Isokrates, der es mit πειθοῦς ἐπιστήμη prosaischer umschreibt.

ralists in rhetoric, comparatively dry and coarse. But, the aristocratic dignity of the Roman statesman and his versatile juridical practice add color; the Romans' eminent orators usually were powerful party *leaders*, whereas the Greek orators spoke in the interest of private parties. The awareness of individual dignity is Roman, not Greek. What Schopenhauer says is more suited to the conception of the former (*Die Welt als Wille und Vorstellung,*):

> Eloquence is the faculty of stirring up in others our view of a thing, or our opinion regarding it, of kindling in them our feeling about it, and thus of putting them in sympathy with us; and all this by our conducting the stream of our ideas into their heads by means of words, with such force that this stream diverts that of their own thoughts from the course already taken, and carries this away with it along its own course. The more the course of their ideas differed previously from ours, the greater will be this masterly achievement.[3]

Here, the commanding dominance of the individual personality, in the sense of the Romans, is stressed; whereas in Kant, the free play in the business of the understanding, in the sense of the Greeks, is emphasized.

Generally speaking, the moderns are inaccurate in their definitions, whereas the competition over the correct definition of rhetoric goes on throughout the whole of antiquity, and specifically among philosophers and orators. All of this has been compiled chronologically by Spengel (*Rh. Mus.*, 18, 481), and later by Richard Volkmann (*Rhetorik*).[4] Those who avoided giving a strict definition have at least sought to determine the orator's *telos* or *officium* [task or office]. This is the *peithein, dicendo persuadere* [persuasion]: it was difficult to incorporate this into the *horismos* [definition] because the effect is not the essence of the thing, and furthermore, persuasion does not always take place even with the best orator. The Sicilians Corax and Tisias say that *rhētorikē esti peithous dēmiourgos* [rhetoric is a craftsman (maker) of persuasion]; among the Dorians, the word *dēmiourgos* [craftsman, maker] has a higher meaning than the words "maker" or "manager" have among the Ionians: the most authoritative persons in the Doric states were so named (*there*, only "artisans"). And the same holds for Gorgias and Isocrates,[5] the latter paraphrasing it more prosaically as *peithous epistēmē* [knowledge of persuasion].

Plato hat einen grossen Hass auf sie: er bezeichnet sie als eine Geschicklichkeit ἐμπειρία χάριτός τινος καὶ ἡδονῆς ἀπεργασίας und ordnet sie zusammen mit der Kochkunst ὀψοποιική, der Putzkunst κομμωτική und Sophistik der κολακεία unter (Gorgias p. 463). Dagegen giebt es auch Spuren einer anderen Auffassung der Rhetorik. Rud. Hirzel, "Ueber das Rhetorische und seine Bedeutung bei Plato," Leipzig 1871. Im Phaedr. p. 239 E ff. wird gefordert, der Redner solle mit Hülfe der Dialektik über alle Dinge klare Begriffe erwerben, damit er im Stande ist, dieselben immer zweckdienlich darzustellen. Er soll sich in den Besitz des Wahren setzen, um auch über das Wahrscheinliche zu gebieten und so seine Zuhörer täuschen zu können. Dann wird gefordert, dass er die Leidenschaften seiner Hörer zu erregen und dadurch über sie zu herrschen verstehe. Dazu müsse er eine genaue Kenntniss der menschlichen Seele haben und die Wirkung aller Redeformen auf das menschliche Gemüth kennen. Die Bildung einer wirklichen Rede*kunst* setzt also eine sehr tiefe und umfassende Vorbildung voraus: dabei ändert sich nichts an der Voraussetzung, dass es die Aufgabe des Redners sei, mit Hülfe des Wahrscheinlichen seine Hörer zu überreden. Freilich erklärt Sokrates 273E, dass wer einmal diese Höhe des Wissens erreicht hat, sich nicht mit der niedrigen Aufgabe begnügen wird: das höhere Ziel ist dann "Mittheilung des erworbenen Wissens an Andere." Der Wissende kann also sowohl ῥητορικός als διδακτικός sein. Das eine Ziel ist nur viel höher: doch soll nicht jede Anwendung der Rhetorik ausgeschlossen sein: nur ja nicht ernsthafter Lebensberuf! Im Politikos 304D spricht er die διδαχή der Rhetorik ab und weist ihr die Aufgabe zu, πλῆθος und ὄχλου διὰ μυθολογίας zu überreden. So schildert Plato nun auch den wahren Philosophen Sokrates, bald wissenschaftlich belehrend, bald populär-rhetorisch. Der *mythische* Bestandtheil der Dialoge ist der rhetorische: der Mythus hat das Wahrscheinliche zum Inhalt: also nicht den Zweck, zu belehren, sondern eine δόξα bei den Zuhörern zu erregen, also zu πείθειν. Die Mythen gehören zur παγκάλη παιδιά: die rhetorischen ebenso wie die schriftlichen Compositionen sind nur zum Vergnügen angefertigt. Die Wahrheit lässt sich weder in schriftlicher noch in rhetorischer Form aussprechen. Das Mythische und das Rhetorische wird angewandt, wenn die Kürze der Zeit keine wissenschaftliche Belehrung zulässt.

Plato has a strong dislike for it; he labels it as a skill, *empeiria charitos tinos kai hēdonēs apergasias* [experience in a certain outward grace and pleasure in expression (making or producing)], and subordinates it to *kolakeia* [flattery], together with the art of cooking [*opsopoiikē*], the art of embellishment [*kommōtikē*], and Sophistry (*Gorgias*, p. 463). In contrast, there are vestiges of another view of rhetoric (see Rudolph Hirzel, *Über das Rhetorische und seine Bedeutung bei Plato*, Leipzig, 1871). In the *Phaedrus* (239e),[6] it is claimed that the orator should acquire clear ideas of all things with the help of dialectic, so that he is always in the position to represent them suitably. He should set himself in possession of that which is true in order to have command of what is probable as well, so that he is able to deceive his audience. Then, it is required that he know how to inspire the passions of his audience, and to be master of them by this means. To that end, he must have accurate knowledge of the human soul and be acquainted with the effects of all forms of discourse upon the human mind. The development of a true *art* of speaking, therefore, presupposes a very profound and extensive education. This, by no means, affects the assumption that it is the task of the rhetor to persuade his audience with the help of what is probable. Indeed, Socrates declares (273e) that whoever has once reached this summit of knowledge will not be content with humble tasks: the higher goal is then "communication of the acquired knowledge to others." He who knows can be *rhētorikos* [rhetorical] as well as *didaktikos* [apt in teaching]. The one goal is merely a higher one; yet not every employment of rhetoric need be suspended. Nevertheless, it obviously cannot be a serious occupation in life! In the *Statesman* (304d), he denies rhetoric the *didachē* [teaching] and assigns to it the duty of persuading *plēthos* [the multitudes] and *ochlou dia mythologias* [mobs through the telling of myths]. It is also in this way that Plato depicts the true philosopher, Socrates, as sometimes instructing academically, and at others being rhetorical in a popular fashion. The *mythic* component in the dialogues is the rhetorical: the myth has the probable for its content, and therefore not the aim of instruction, but one of inspiring a *doxa* [opinion] in one's audience, thus to *peithein* [persuade]. The myths belong to *pankalē paidia* [a good childish game]: the rhetorical, just as with written compositions, is fabricated only for amusement. The truth can be articulated neither in a written nor in a rhetorical form. The mythical and the rhetorical are employed when the brevity of time allows for no scientific instruc-

Das Anrufen von Zeugen ist ein rhetorischer Kunstgriff; ebenso werden die platonischen Mythen durch Berufung auf Zeugen eingeführt. Höchst merkwürdig Republ. 376E: hier unterscheidet er zwei Arten von Reden, solche, die die Wahrheit enthalten, und solche, welche lügen: zu letzteren gehören die *Mythen*. Er hält sie für berechtigt und tadelt Homer und Hesiod nicht deshalb, dass sie gelogen, sondern dass sie es nicht in der rechten Weise gethan. Ebenso spricht er es 389B geradezu aus, dass die Lüge unter Umständen den Menschen nütze und es den Herrschern erlaubt sein müsse, sich ihrer zum Wohl ihrer Mitbürger zu bedienen. So führt er III 414B einen vollständigen Mythus ein, um eine bestimmte Ansicht in den Seelen sciner Bürger zu begründen, und er scheut zu diesem Zweck die Lüge als rednerisches Mittel nicht.—Die Polemik Platos gegen das Rhetorische richtet sich einmal gegen die schlechten Zwecke der populären Rhetorik, sodann gegen die ganz rohe und ungenügende unphilosophische Vorbildung der Redner. Auf philosophischer Bildung ruhend, zu guten Zwecken, d.h. zu Zwecken der Philosophie verwendet, lässt er sie gelten.

Wir haben nur *zwei* alte Werke über Rhetorik, alle anderen mehrere Jahrhunderte später. Die eine, die *rhetorica ad Alexandrum*, hat nichts mit Aristoteles zu thun, sondern ist wohl das Werk des Anaximenes; s. Spengel, Philolog. 18, p. 604. Sie ist rein zu praktischem Gebrauche, ganz unphilosophisch, im Wesentlichen nach der Lehre des Isokrates. Keine Definition der Rhetorik, nicht einmal der Name ῥητορική.

Rein philosophisch und höchst einflussreich für alle späteren Begriffsbestimmungen die *Rhetorik* des Aristoteles. ῥητορικὴ δύναμις περὶ ἕκαστον τοῦ θεωρῆσαι τὸ ἐνδεχόμενον πιθανόν, "alles mögliche Wahrscheinliche und Ueberzeugende" [Aristot. rhet. I 2]. Also weder ἐπιστήμη noch τέχνη, sondern δύναμις, die aber zu einer τέχνη erhoben werden könne. Nicht das πείθειν, sondern das, was man für eine Sache vorbringen könne: gleich einem Arzt, der einen Unheilbaren pflegt, könne auch der Redner eine missliche Sache verfechten. Alle späteren Definitionen halten an diesem κατὰ τὸ ἐνδεχόμενον πείθειν fest (gegen die sicilische Definition). Sehr wich-

tion. The appeal to witnesses is an artificial rhetorical device, in the same way that the Platonic myths are introduced by means of appealing to witnesses. *The Republic* (376e ff.) is extremely striking: here he distinguishes two kinds of speaking, those which contain the truth and those which deceive, *myths* belonging to the latter. He holds myths to be valid, and he blames Homer and Hesiod not for having lied, but for not having lied in the right fashion. In the same way, he says clearly in 389b that lying is useful for human beings under certain circumstances, and that it must be permitted rulers to use for the benefit of their fellow citizens. For instance, he introduces a complete myth in 3, 414b, in order to establish a specific opinion in the minds of the citizens, and he does not avoid the lie as a rhetorical means for this purpose.

Plato's polemic against the rhetorical is directed sometimes against the base goals of popular rhetoric, and sometimes against the entirely crude and insufficient, unphilosophical preparatory training of rhetors. He holds rhetoric to be legitimate when it rests upon philosophical education, and provided it is used for good aims, i.e., those of philosophy.

We have only *two* classical works on rhetoric, all others appearing many centuries later. The first, the *Rhetorica ad Alexandrum*, has nothing to do with Aristotle, but is likely to have been the work of Anaximenes (see Spengel, *Philolog.*, 18, 604).[7] It is purely for practical usage; it is wholly unphilosophical, essentially following the doctrine of Isocrates. No definition of rhetoric is given, and the name *rhētorikē* is never used.

[The second, which is] purely philosophical and most influential for all later conceptual determinations of the concept, is the *Rhetoric* of Aristotle: *rhētorikē dynamis peri hekaston tou theōrēsai to endechomenon pithanon* [rhetoric is the power (faculty, ability) to observe all possible means of persuasion about each thing], "all that is feasibly probable and convincing" (Aristotle, *Rhetoric*, 1, 2). Thus, it is neither *epistēmē* [knowledge in a scientific sense] nor *technē* [art or craft], but *dynamis* [power (faculty or ability)], which, however, could be elevated to a *technē*. It is not the *peithein* [persuasion], but that which one can advance for a cause, which is its object: the rhetor can defend a difficult cause, just as a physician who cares for an incurable patient. All later definitions hold firmly to this *kata to endechomenon peithein* [persuasion according to all available means] (as opposed to the Sicilian definition). The universal *peri*

tig das universale περὶ ἕκαστον, auf alle Disciplinen anwendbar. Eine rein formale Kunst. Endlich wichtig das θεωρῆσαι: darauf hat man den Vorwurf gemacht, er habe nur die inventio, nicht elocutio dispositio memoria pronuntiatio aufgenommen. Aristoteles will wahrscheinlich den Vortrag nicht als essentiell, sondern nur als Accidens betrachtet wissen: denn er denkt an das Rhetorische in Büchern (wie er auch die Wirkung des Dramas von der Aufführung unabhängig denkt und deshalb nicht das sinnliche Erscheinen auf der Bühne in die Definition aufnimmt). Es genügt τὸ ἐνδεχόμενον πιθανόν zu erkennen, zu schauen: dass dies Erkannte irgendwie darzustellen ist, *liegt bereits in πιθανόν*: nun ist selbst jedes *Kunstmittel* der pronuntiatio auf diesem *pithanon abhängig* zu machen. Nur eben das λέγειν ist nicht nothwendig.

Nun kommen Jahrhunderte erbitterten Schulkampfes in den Rhetoren- und Philosophen-Schulen. Die Stoiker bezeichnen sie Laert. D. VII, 42, τήν τε ῥητορικὴν ἐπιστήμην οὖσαν τοῦ εὖ λέγειν περὶ τῶν ἐν διεξόδῳ λόγων καὶ τὴν διαλεκτικὴν τοῦ ὀρθῶς διαλέγεσθαι περὶ τῶν ἐν ἐρωτήσει καὶ ἀποκρίσει λόγων. Wichtig diese Verwandtschaft der Rhetorik und der Dialektik: gleichsam eine ausgedehnte Eristik, obwohl dieser Begriff zu eng ist. Aristot. Topik I, 12 sagt, man behandle eine Sache philosophisch nach der Wahrheit, dialektisch nach dem Schein oder Beifall, nach der Meinung, der δόξα Anderer. Dasselbe liesse sich von der Rhetorik aussagen. Beide unter den Begriff zu fassen: *die Kunst, Recht zu behalten in Rede und Unterredung*: εὖ λέγειν! Das lässt sich gegen die Aristotelische Definition einwenden: die Dialektik erscheint als eine Unterrubrik der Rhetorik.

Man bemüht sich nun, eine Definition zu finden, in der die Theile der Beredsamkeit zu erkennen sind, da man Aristoteles vorwarf, er bezeichne nur die inventio. Inventio und elocutio, als die wichtigsten Faktoren vereinigt Quint. 2, 15, 37: qui recte sentire et dicere rhetorices putaverunt (ὀρθῶς γνῶναι καὶ ἑρμηνεῦσαι). Die dispositio (τάξις) hinzugefügt bei Rufus: ἐπιστήμη τοῦ καλῶς καὶ πειστικῶς

hekaston [about each thing], applicable to all disciplines, is very important. It is a purely formal art. Finally, the *theōrēsai* [to contemplate (consider, observe)] is important: that he took up only the *inventio* here, and not the *elocutio, dispositio, memoria,* and *pronuntiatio,* has been the source of objection. Aristotle probably wishes delivery to be viewed, not as essential, but only as something incidental: for he views the rhetorical as one finds it in books (just as he also thinks the effect of drama to be independent of the performance, and thus does not take up the physical presence on stage in its definition). It is sufficient to know *to endechomenon pithanon* [all available means of persuasion] to see that what is known must also be presented somehow *and is already contained* in *pithanon* [calculated to persuade]; that is why every *artificial means* of the *pronuntiatio* is to be made equally *dependent* upon this *pithanon*. Even the *legein* [speaking] is not essential.

Now come centuries of embittered academic struggles in the schools of the rhetoricians and philosophers. The Stoics characterize it (Diogenes Laertius, 7, 42):

> *tēn te rhētorikēn epistēmēn ousan tou eu legein peri tōn en diexodōi logōn kai tēn dialektikēn tou orthōs dialegesthai peri tōn en erōtēsei kai apokrisei logōn.* [And rhetoric is scientific knowledge of speaking well about matters (words, propositions) in detailed narrative, and dialectic is correct (just, true) discussion about matters in question and answer].

The connection of rhetoric and dialectic is significant; almost an extended eristic, although that conception is too narrow. Aristotle (*Topics*, 1, 12) says that one treats a subject philosophically with respect to truth; dialectically, according to the appearance or approval, i.e., according to the *doxa* [opinion], of others. One could say the same thing about rhetoric. Both can be comprehended as the *art of being victorious in discourse and conversation: eu legein* [to speak well]! One can object to the Aristotelian definition in that dialectic here seems to be a subspecies of rhetoric.

One strives now to find a definition in which the components of eloquence can be distinguished, because Aristotle has been reproached for designating only invention. *Inventio* and *elocutio* are combined as the most important factors by Quintilian (2, 15, 37): *qui recte sentire et dicere rhetorices putaverunt (orthōs gnōnai kai hermēneusai)* [those who held that the aim of rhetoric is to perceive and articulate rightly]. The *dispositio* (*taxis*) is added to these by Rufus: *epistēmē tou kalōs kai peistikōs diadesthai ton logon* [scientific

διαθέσθαι τὸν λόγον. Theodorus Gadareus bei Quint. 2, 15, 21 hat vier Theile: ars inventrix et iudicatrix et nuntiatrix decente ornatu (griechisch wohl τέχνη εὑρετικὴ καὶ κριτικὴ καὶ ἑρμηνευτικὴ μετὰ πρέποντος κόσμου). Endlich alle fünf Quint. 5, 10, 54: id aut universum verbis complectimur ut rhetorice est bene dicendi scientia, aut per partes ut rhetorice est recte inveniendi et disponendi et eloquendi cum firma memoria et cum dignitate actionis scientia. Man sieht, wie das εὖ λέγειν der Stoiker allmählich umschrieben wird. Sodann wurde an Stelle des aristotelischen περὶ ἕκαστον, wie es scheint, durch den höchst einflussreichen Hermagoras (nicht lange vor Cicero lebend) gesetzt: ἐν πολιτικῷ πράγματι: um philosophische Untersuchungen sowie speziell fachwissenschaftliche auszuschliessen. Darunter werden verstanden die allen Menschen innewohnenden Begriffe von dem, was gut, recht und schön ist, die einer besonderen Lehre nicht bedürfen: κοιναὶ ἔννοιαι im Gegensatz eines speziellen Studiums oder Handwerks. Der platonische Protagoras giebt Aufschluss, was man unter der ἀρετὴ πολιτική eines Mannes verstand.

Nach den zwei griechischen Lehrbüchern des Anaximenes und des Aristoteles folgen lateinische Bearbeitungen der Rhetorik: auctor ad Herennium und Ciceros Schriften. Als Ersterer gilt jetzt Cornificius: in seinen Thatsachen berührt er nur die sullanische Zeit [. . .]. Ciceros *de inventione* (II Bücher) eine Jugendarbeit ganz nach griechischen Quellen: der Auctor ad Herennium hier viel benutzt, doch macht Cicero im Allgemeinen alles schlechter als jener. Die in späterem Alter (698) geschriebenen Bücher *de oratore* hält er nach Form und Inhalt für sehr wichtig: die Hauptpersonen, Crassus und Antonius, drücken nur die Ueberzeugung des Verfassers aus. Er eifert gegen die trivialen gewöhnlichen Lehrbücher (darunter z. B. der auctor ad H. gehört). In der Person des Antonius belehrt er uns, wie er seine Reden technisch ausarbeitete: in der des Crassus entwirft er das

knowledge of rightly and persuasively binding up the word (argument)]. Theodorus of Gadara, cited in Quintilian (2, 15, 21) has four parts: *ars inventrix et iudicatrix et nuntiatrix decente ornatu* [art which discovers and judges and expresses with duly proportioned elegance] (in Greek, probably *technē heuretikē kai kritikē kai hermēneutikē meta prepontos kosmou* [art inventive and critical and interpretative with a manner befitting ornamentation]).[8] Ultimately, all five are found in Quintilian (5, 10, 54):

> *id aut universum verbis complectimur, ut rhetorice est bene dicendi scientia: aut per partes, ut rhetorice est recte inveniendi et disponendi et eloquendi cum firma memoria et cum dignitate actionis scientia* [Such a definition is either stated in general terms, such as Rhetoric is the science of speaking well, or in detail, such as Rhetoric is the science of correct conception, arrangement, and utterance, coupled with a retentive memory and a dignified delivery].

One can see how the *eu legein* [good speaking] of the Stoics becomes gradually defined. Then, the Aristotelian *peri hekaston* [about each thing] is replaced by *en politikōi pragmati* [in political affairs], by the most influential author Hermagoras (living not long before Cicero), so as to exclude philosophical investigations as well as those of the special branches of learning. By this, one understood those concepts, found in all human beings, which are concerned with what is good, right, and beautiful, and for which special instruction is not necessary: *koinai ennoiai* [common knowledge] in contrast to a special study or skill. Plato's Protagoras elucidates what was understood by the *aretē politikē* [political virtue] of man.

After the two Greek textbooks of Anaximenes and Aristotle, come Latin treatises on rhetoric: *Auctor ad Herennium* and Cicero's writings. Today, Cornificius is held to be the author [of the *ad Herennium*]; as far as data are concerned, he only touches upon the time of Sulla [. . .]. Cicero's *De Inventione* (two books) is a youthful work, entirely following Greek sources: the *Auctor ad Herennium* is used extensively here; yet generally speaking, Cicero usually is worse than the former. Cicero considers the book which he wrote much later in life, *De Oratore*, to be very important, as far as form and content are concerned. The leading characters, Crassus and Antonius, express only the beliefs of the author. He zealously opposes the customary trivial textbooks (of the general class to which the *Auctor ad Herennium* belongs, for example). In the person of Antonius, he instructs us how he drafts his speeches technically; in the person of

höhere Bild des philosophischen Redners (etwa das Idealbild Platons). Aber er hat nie den Gegensatz des wahren Philosophen und des Redners begriffen, gegen Aristoteles ist sein Buch roh und unerspriesslich.—Der Brutus ist eine συναγωγὴ Ῥωμαίων ῥητόρων. Charakterzeichnung der berühmten Redner Roms, unschätzbar. Der *Orator* behandelt nur einen Theil der Rhetorik: C. findet den perfectus orator in der elocutio. Die *Topik*, eine Gelegenheitsschrift an den Trebatius, geht aber über ihr Ziel, eine Topik zu sein, hinaus.

II. EINTHEILUNG DER RHETORIK UND DER BEREDSAMKEIT

Die ältesten τέχναι, vor Isokrates, enthielten nur Anleitung zur Abfassung von Prozessreden. Diese Beschränkung auf die *gerichtliche* Beredsamkeit tadelt Isokrates in orat. XIII 19 und fügt die berathende Beredsamkeit hinzu. Diese beiden Gattungen kennt allein Anaximenes. Aristoteles fügt das genus demonstrativum ἐπιδεικτικόν hinzu, zum deliberativum und iudiciale. Dem *Stoffe* nach zerfällt die Beredsamkeit also in drei genera caussarum, genus δικανικόν συμβουλευτικόν ἐπιδεικτικόν (auch πανηγυρικόν und ἐγκωμιαστικόν genannt). Die gerichtliche will anklagen oder vertheidigen, die berathende will zu etwas antreiben oder von etwas abmahnen, die epideiktische hat zu loben oder zu tadeln.

Grosser Kampf dagegen: als Suasorien und Controversien aufkamen, gab es zwei Arten der Beredsamkeit. Thatsächlich γένος πραγματικόν in negotiis und γένος ἐπιδεικτικόν in ostentatione positum. Für beide vier Unterarten εἶδος δικανικόν (wirkliche oder fingirte Controversien), γένος συμβουλευτικόν (wirkliche in Rathsversammlungen oder vor dem Volke gehaltene berathende oder imitierte Suasorien, Lob-und Tadelreden, γένος ἐγκωμιαστικόν (mit den invectivae) und γένος ἐντευκτικόν Gelegenheitsreden, namentlich Begrüssungs- und Abschiedsreden. Andere stellten als viertes genus das ἱστορικόν dazu: wohl gemeint die rhetorisirende Geschichtsschreibung, wie sie durch die Schule des Isokrates namentlich bei Theopomp hervortritt. Auf diesem Wege weitergehend zählten einige an 30 Gattungen auf (Eintheilung der gesammten kunstmässigen Prosa).

Crassus, he sketches the nobler picture of the philosophical rhetor (nearly the ideal conception of Plato). But he never understood the opposition of the true philosopher and the orator. His book is crude and distasteful compared to that of Aristotle. The *Brutus* is a *synagōgē Rhōmaiōn rhētorōn* [collection of Roman orators], a characterization of the renowned Roman orators; inestimable. *De Oratore* treats only a part of rhetoric: Cicero locates the *perfectus orator* in *elocutio.* The *Topics*, a work written for a special occasion and addressed to Trebatius, goes beyond its goal of being a topology.

II. THE DIVISION OF RHETORIC AND ELOQUENCE

The oldest *technai* [handbooks on rhetoric], written before Isocrates, contained instruction for the composition only of forensic speeches. Isocrates finds fault with this restriction to *forensic* eloquence (*Orat.*, 13, 19)[9] and adds the deliberative eloquence. Anaximenes knows only these two types. Aristotle adds the *genus demonstrativum, epideiktikon*, to the *deliberativum* and *iudiciale.* Therefore, according to the *content*, eloquence consists of three *genera caussarum, genus dikanikon* [judicial], *symbouleutikon* [deliberative], and *epideiktikon* [epideictic] (also called *panēgyrikon* [panegyric] and *encōmiastikon* [encomium]). The forensic is intended to accuse or defend; the deliberative, to persuade toward something or to dissuade from something; the epideictic, to praise or blame.

There is an important contention to the contrary: as *suasoriae* and *controversiae* came into use, there were two sorts of eloquence: in fact, *genos pragmatikon* [the practical (active) class] *in negotiis*, and *genos epideiktikon* [the epideictic (for display) class] *in ostentatione positum.* For both, there were four subspecies: *eidos dikanikon* [legal class] (real or contrived controversies); *genos symbouleutikon* [deliberative class], *suasoriae* actually presented in council meetings or before the public, or imitated ones; praising or blaming speeches, *genos encōmiastikon* [class of encomia] (together with the *invectivae*); and *genos enteuktikon* [incidental class], speeches for special occasions, especially welcoming and farewell speeches. Others added *historikon* [history] as the fourth of the *genera*: in all likelihood, they meant the rhetorical writing of history, as it became prominent through Isocrates' school, particularly with Theopompus. Continuing in this manner, some have counted up to thirty *genera* (to constitute a classification of all artistically correct prose).

Die Philosophen haben eingetheilt in θέσις und ὑπόθεσις. Erstere betrachtet die Sache an sich und ganz allgemein, letztere wie sie unter gegebenen Umständen in die Erscheinung tritt. Das Allgemeine zu bestimmen, ist Sache der Philosophie, das Spezielle fällt der Rhetorik anheim. Die drei genera haben die Philosophen der ὑποθέσις untergeordnet. Nur die Stoiker setzen das demonstrativum unter die θέσις, das nämlich macht die grösste Mühe und der gemeinen Praxis ist es sehr unbequem. Die Stoiker theilen:

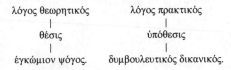

Das sind die Gattungen der Reden. In allen diesen Gattungen hat nun der Redner eine *fünffache* Thätigkeit zu zeigen: 1. *Erfindung* inventio εὕρεσις, 2. *Anordnung* dispositio τάξις, 3. *Ausdruck* elocutio λέξις, 4. *Gedächtnis* memoria μνήμη, 5. *Vortrag* pronuntiatio oder actio ὑπόκρισις. Erst allmählich ist diese Wahrheit allgemein anerkannt worden: jedenfalls erst *nach* Anaximenes und Aristoteles. Bei ihnen fehlen ὑπόκρισις und μνήμη (bei Aristoteles ganz consequent, da er die Leserede als Typus anerkennt). Vor allem aber war die stoische Eintheilung zu überwinden νόησις εὕρεσις διάθεσις *intellectio inventio dispositio; etenim caussa proposita primum intellegere debemus, cuius modi cuassa sit, deinde invenire quae apta sint caussae, tum inventa recte et cum ratione disponere.* Streit darüber, ob es ἔργα τοῦ ῥήτορος oder ἔργα τῆς ῥητορικῆς seien. Quint. 3, 3 11. Νόησις wird erklärt: *intellegendum primo loco est, thesis sit an hypothesis; cum hypothesis esse intellexerimus i.e. controversiam,*

The philosophers classified [prose] into *thesis* and *hypothesis*. The first regards the subject matter in itself and in very general terms; the latter, as the matter appears in given circumstances. It is the task of philosophy to determine the general; the particular falls to rhetoric. The philosophers subordinated the three *genera* to the *hypothesis*. Only the Stoics placed the *demonstrativum* under the *thesis*, because it causes the most difficulty, and because its general practice is very uncomfortable. The Stoics distinguish:

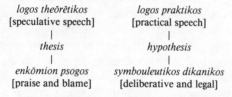

logos theōrētikos	*logos praktikos*
[speculative speech]	[practical speech]
thesis	*hypothesis*
enkōmion psogos	*symbouleutikos dikanikos*
[praise and blame]	[deliberative and legal]

These are the genera of speech. In all these types, the rhetor now has to perform a *fivefold* activity: (1) invention, *inventio, heuresis*. (2) disposition, *dispositio, taxis*. (3) expression, *elocutio, lexis*. (4) memory, *memoria, mnēmē*. (5) diction, *pronuntiatio* or *actio, hypokrisis*. This truth was generally acknowledged only gradually, at least only *after* Anaximenes and Aristotle. *Hypokrisis* and *mnēmē* were missing in their works (this is entirely consistent in Aristotle, in that he admitted the oral reading as prototype). Above all, the Stoic classification was to be overcome:[10] *noēsis* [understanding], *heuresis* [invention], *diathesis* [disposition or composition], *intellectio, inventio, dispositio: etenim caussa proposita primum intellegere debemus, cuius modi caussa sit, deinde invenire, quae apta sint caussae, tum inventa recte et cum ratione disponere* [understanding, invention, disposition; and indeed we ought first to understand the case which has been set forth, of what mode the case is, then we should invent what is suitable to the case, and then arrange what has been invented in a correct and systematic way]. There was dispute on the point, whether it was to be *erga tou rhētoros* [the work of a rhetorician] or *erga tēs rhētorikēs* [the work of rhetoric (the art)]. In Quintilian (3, 3, 11),[11] *noēsis* [intellect] is explained as follows:

intellegendum primo loco est, thesis sit an hypothesis; cum hypothesis esse intellexerimus, i.e., controversiam, intellegendum erit an consistat; tum ex qua specie sit; deinde ex quo modo; deinde cuius status; postremo cuius figùrae [In the first place, we must understand whether it is a thesis or hypothesis; if we should understand it as an hypothesis, that is, as

intellegendum erit an consistat; tum ex qua specie sit; deinde ex quo modo; deinde cuius status; postremo cuius figurae. Zur εὕρεσις gehört nun ἐνθύμημα und παράδειγμα. Zur διάθεσις *gehört* τάξις und οἰκονομία.—Die älteste Theilung scheint aber die Zweitheilung zu sein, z. B. bei Isokrates: die Auffindung oder enthymematische Umformung des gegebenen Stoffes und die Darstellung dieser eigenen ἐνθυμήματα. Also inventio und elocutio. Dionys von Halikarnass, der sich oft an Isokrates anschliesst, hat die Zweitheilung: λέξις und πρᾶξις Form und (meistens gegeben) Inhalt. Bei seiner Beurtheilung der Autoren unterscheidet er den πραγματικὸς χαρακτήρ vom λεκτικός und spricht von πραγματικαὶ und λεκτικαὶ ἀρεταί. Der πραγματικὸς τόπος zerfällt in die παρασκευή (wie εὕρεσις) und οἰκονομία (als χρῆσις τῶν παρεσκευασμένων); der λεκτικὸς τόπος zerfällt in die ἐκλογὴ τῶν ὀνομάτων und die σύνθεσις τῶν ἐκλεγέντων. Die *zweiten* Abschnitte handeln also von Anordnung (οἰκονομία) und Composition (σύνθεσις) der Rede und sind die wichtigeren.

Die Herrschaft über die fünf Theile der Rede kommt durch dreierlei zu Stande, durch φύσις natürliche Anlage, durch τέχνη theoretische Anleitung, ἄσκησις oder μελέτη Uebung. Diese Dreiheit zuerst von Protagoras aufgestellt. Vereinigt im Anfange von pro Archia poeta: Si quid est in me ingenii, indices, quod sentio quam sit exiguum, aut si qua exercitatio dicendi, in qua me non infitior mediocriter esse versatum, aut si huiusce rei ratio aliqua ab optimarum artium studiis ac disciplina profecta, a qua ego nullum confiteor aetatis meae tempus abhorruisse etc.

controversy, then it will be necessary to understand whether it holds *status*, then of which species it is, then of which mode, then of which status, and finally of which figure].

Enthymēma [enthymeme] and *paradeigma* [example] now belong to the *heuresis* [invention]. *Taxis* [disposition] and *oikonomia* [arrangement] belong to the *diathesis* [composition].

But, the dichotomy seems to be the oldest division; for example, in Isocrates, one finds the discovery or enthymematic recasting of a given subject matter and the proper recasting of this *enthymēmata* [argumentation], thus *inventio* and *elocutio*.[12] Dionysius of Halicarnassus, who often conforms to Isocrates, has the dichotomy: *lexis* [speaking] and *praxis* [the result], form and content (the latter mostly given). In his evaluation of the authors, he distinguishes the *pragmatikos charaktēr* [practical (systematic) character] from the *lektikos* [ability to speak (style)] and speaks of *pragmatikai* [deliberations on matters of fact] and *lektikai aretai* [virtues of speaking (style)]. The *pragmatikos topos* [factual topic] is divided into *paraskeuē* [preparation] (as *heuresis* [invention] and *oikonomia* [arrangement] (as *chrēsis tōn paraskeuasmenōn* [the employment of things having been prepared]); the *lektikos topos* [speaking ability (stylistic) topic] is divided into the *eklogē tōn onomatōn* [choice of words] and the *synthesis tōn eklegentōn* [combination of the words being chosen]. The second division in each case, therefore, deals with disposition (*oikonomia*) and composition (*synthesis*) of the speech, and is the most important.[13]

The mastery over the five elements of speech is gained in three ways, through *physis*, natural ability, through *technē*, theoretical instruction, or through *askēsis* or *meletē*, practice. This triad was set forth first by Protagoras. They are combined at the beginning of [Cicero's] *Pro Archia Poeta* (1, 1) as follows:

Si quid est in me ingenii, iudices, quod sentio quam sit exiguum, aut si qua exercitatio dicendi, in qua me non infitior mediocriter esse versatum, aut si huiusce rei ratio aliqua ab optimarum artium studiis ac disciplina profecta, a qua ego nullum confiteor aetatis meae tempus abhorruisse ... [Whatever talent I possess (and I realize its limitations), whatever be my oratorical experience (and I do not deny that my practice herein has been not inconsiderable), whatever knowledge of the theoretical side of my profession I may have derived from a devoted literary apprenticeship (and I admit that at no period of my life has the acquisition of such knowledge been repellent to me). . .].

III. VERHÄLTNISS DES RHETORISCHEN ZUR SPRACHE

"Rhetorisch" nennen wir einen Autor, ein Buch, einen Stil, wenn ein bewusstes Anwenden von Kunstmitteln der Rede zu merken ist, immer mit einem leisen Tadel. Wir vermeinen, es sei nicht *natürlich* und mache den Eindruck des Absichtlichen. Nun kommt sehr viel auf den Geschmack des Urtheilenden an und darauf, was ihm gerade "natürlich" ist. Im Allgemeinen erscheint uns, die wir rohe Sprachempiriker sind, die ganze antike Litteratur etwas künstlich und rhetorisch, zumal die römische. Das hat auch darin seinen tieferen Grund, dass die eigentliche Prosa des Alterthums durchaus Widerhall der lauten *Rede* ist und an deren Gesetzen sich gebildet hat: während unsere Prosa immer mehr aus dem *Schreiben* zu erklären ist, unsere Stilistik sich als eine durch *Lesen* zu percipirende giebt. Der Lesende und der Hörende wollen aber eine ganz andere Darstellungsform, und deshalb klingt uns die antike Litteratur "rhetorisch": /d.h. sie wendet sich zunächst ans Ohr, um es zu bestechen./ Ausserordentliche Ausbildung des rhythmischen Sinnes bei Griechen und Römern, im Hören des Gesprochenen, bei ungeheurer fortwährender Uebung.—Es steht hier ähnlich wie bei der Poesie—wir kennen Litteraturpoeten, die Griechen wirkliche Poesie ohne Vermittlung des Buches. Wir sind viel blasser und abstrakter.

Es ist aber nicht schwer zu beweisen, dass was man als Mittel bewusster Kunst "rhetorisch" nennt, als Mittel unbewusster Kunst in der Sprache und deren Werden thätig waren, ja, dass die *Rhetorik eine Fortbildung der in der Sprache gelegenen Kunstmittel* ist, am hellen Lichte des Verstandes. Es giebt gar keine unrhetorische "Natürlichkeit" der Sprache, an die man appelliren könnte: die Sprache selbst ist das Resultat von lauter rhetorischen Künsten. Die Kraft, welche Aristoteles Rhetorik nennt, an jedem Dinge das heraus zu finden und geltend zu machen, was wirkt und Eindruck macht, ist zugleich das Wesen der Sprache: diese bezieht sich ebensowenig wie die Rhetorik auf das Wahre, auf das *Wesen* der Dinge, sie will nicht belehren, sondern eine subjektive Erregung und Annahme auf Andere übertragen. Der sprachbildende Mensch fasst nicht Dinge oder Vorgänge auf, sondern *Reize*: er giebt nicht Empfindungen wieder, sondern sogar nur Abbildungen von Empfindungen. Die Empfindung, durch einen Nervenreiz hervorgerufen, nimmt das Ding nicht selbst auf: diese Empfindung wird nach aussen hin durch

III. THE RELATION OF THE RHETORICAL
TO LANGUAGE

We call an author, a book, or a style "rhetorical" when we observe
a conscious application of artistic means of speaking; it always
implies a gentle reproof. We consider it to be not *natural*, and as
producing the impression of being done purposefully. Obviously,
very much depends on the taste of the one who passes judgment and
upon what he prefers to call "natural." In general, all ancient literature, above all the Roman literature, appears to be somewhat artificial and rhetorical to us, who are unrefined speech empiricists. This
has a deeper reason also, in the fact that the true prose of antiquity
is an echo of public *speech* and is built upon its laws, whereas our
prose is always to be explained more from *writing*, and our style presents itself as something to be perceived through *reading*. He who
reads, and the one who hears, desire wholly different presentational
form, and this is the reason that ancient literature seems "rhetorical"
to us; viz., it appeals chiefly to the ear, in order to bribe it. Among
the Greeks and Romans, one finds an extraordinary development of
the sense of rhythm, as far as listening to the spoken word is concerned. [This was achieved] through an enormously persistent practice. The situation here is similar to that in poetry—we are
acquainted with literary poets; the Greeks had real poetry without
the mediation of the book. We are much more pale and abstract.

But, it is not difficult to prove that what is called "rhetorical," as
a means of conscious art, had been active as a means of unconscious
art in language and its development [*Werden*], indeed, that the *rhetorical is a further development*, guided by the clear light of the understanding, of *the artistic means which are already found in language*.
There is obviously no unrhetorical "naturalness" of language to
which one could appeal; language itself is the result of purely rhetorical arts. The power to discover and to make operative that which
works and impresses, with respect to each thing, a power which Aristotle calls rhetoric, is, at the same time, the essence of language; the
latter is based just as little as rhetoric is upon that which is true, upon
the essence of things. Language does not desire to instruct, but to
convey to others a subjective impulse and its acceptance. Man, who
forms language does not perceive things or events, but *impulses*: he
does not communicate sensations, but merely copies of sensations.
The sensation, evoked through a nerve impulse, does not take in the
thing itself: this sensation is presented externally through an image.

ein Bild dargestellt: es fragt sich aber überhaupt, wie ein Seelenakt durch ein Tonbild darstellbar ist? Müsste nicht, wenn vollkommen genaue Wiedergabe stattfinden sollte, vor allem das Material, in welchem wiedergegeben werden soll, dasselbe sein, wie dasjenige ist, in dem die Seele arbeitet? Da es nun aber ein Fremdes ist—der Laut—, wie kann da Genaueres herauskommen als ein *Bild*? Nicht die Dinge treten ins Bewusstsein, sondern die Art, wie wir zu ihnen stehen, das πιθανόν. Das volle Wesen der Dinge wird nie erfasst. Unsere Lautäusserungen warten keineswegs ab, bis unsere Wahrnehmung und Erfahrung uns zu einer vielseitigen, irgendwie respektabeln Erkenntniss der Dinge verholfen hat: sie erfolgen sofort, wenn der Reiz empfunden ist. Statt der Dinge nimmt die Empfindung nur ein *Merkmal* auf. Das ist der *erste* Gesichtspunkt: *die Sprache ist Rhetorik*, denn sie will nur eine δόξα, keine ἐπιστήμη übertragen.

Als wichtigstes Kunstmittel der Rhetorik gelten die *Tropen*, die uneigentlichen Bezeichnungen. Alle Wörter aber sind an sich und von Anfang an, in Bezug auf ihre Bedeutung, Tropen. Statt des wahren Vorgangs stellen sie ein in der Zeit verklingendes Tonbild hin: die Sprache drückt niemals etwas vollständig aus, sondern hebt nur ein ihr hervorstechend scheinendes Merkmal hervor. Wenn der Rhetor "Segel" statt "Schiff," "Welle" statt "Meer" sagt, so ist das die *Synekdoche*, ein "Mitumfassen" trat ein; aber dasselbe ist doch, wenn δράκων Schlange heisst, eigentlich die "glänzend blickende" oder serpens die kriechende; aber warum heisst serpens nicht auch Schnecke? Eine einseitige Wahrnehmung tritt ein für die ganze und volle Anschauung. In anguis bezeichnet der Lateiner die Schlange als constrictor; die Hebräer nennen sie die Zischelnde oder die Sichwindende oder die Verschlingende oder die Kriechende.—Die zweite Form des Tropus ist die *Metapher*. Sie schafft die Wörter nicht neu, sondern deutet sie um. Z. B. bei einem Berg redet sie von Koppe, Fuss, Rücken, Schlünde, Hörner, Adern; πρόσωπον Gesicht, mit νεώς das Vordertheil, χείλη Lippen, mit ποταμῶν Flussufer, γλῶσσα Zunge, auch Mundstück der Flöte; μαστός Brust, auch Hügel. Die Metapher zeigt sich in der Bezeichnung des Geschlechtes, das genus im grammatischen Sinn ist ein Luxus der Sprache und reine Metapher. Dann Uebertragung vom Raume auf die Zeit, "zu Hause," "Jahraus," von der Zeit übertragen auf Causalität, qua ex re, hin-

But, the question of how an act of the soul can be presented through a sound image must be asked. If completely accurate representation is to take place, should the material in which it is to be represented, above all, not be the same as that in which the soul works? However, since it is something alien—the sound—how then can something come forth more accurately as an *image*? It is not the things that pass over into consciousness, but the manner in which we stand toward them, the *pithanon* [power of persuasion (plausibility; also a thing producing illusion)]. The full essence of things will never be grasped. Our utterances by no means wait until our perception and experience have provided us with a many-sided, somehow respectable knowledge of things; they result immediately when the impulse is perceived. Instead of the thing, the sensation takes in only a *sign*. That is the *first* aspect: *language is rhetoric*, because it desires to convey only a *doxa* [opinion], not an *epistēmē* [knowledge].

The *tropes*, the nonliteral significations, are considered to be the most artistic means of rhetoric. But, with respect to their meanings, all words are tropes in themselves, and from the beginning. Instead of that which truly takes place, they present a sound image, which fades away with time: language never expresses something completely but displays only a characteristic which appears to be prominent to it [language]. If the rhetor says "sail" instead of "ship," "waves" instead of "sea," the *synecdoche,* "an encompassing," has taken place; but it is the same when *drakōn* is called snake, actually "that which looks shiny," or *serpens,* that which crawls; but why is *serpens* not also snail? A partial perception takes the place of the entire and complete intuition. By *anguis*, the Latins designate snake as *constrictor*; the Hebrews call it that which hisses or winds or creeps.

The second form of the *tropus* is the metaphor. It does not produce new words, but gives a new meaning to them. For example, with regard to a mountain, it speaks of summit, foot, ridge, gorge, horns, veins; *prosōpon*, face, in connection with *neōs* [ship], means the front or the prow; *cheilē*, lips, in connection with *potamōn* [rivers], means riverbanks; *glōssa* [tongue], also means the mouthpiece of the flute; *mastos*, breast, also means hill. Metaphor also appears in the designation of the gender; *gender*, in the grammatical sense, is a luxury of language and pure metaphor. Then, there is also the transposition from place to time: "*zu Hause*" [at home], "*Jahraus*" [during the

cinde, ὅθεν, εἰς τί.—Eine dritte Figur ist die *Metonymie*, Vertauschung von Ursache und Wirkung; wenn z.b. der Rhetor "Schweiss" für
"Arbeit" sagt, "Zunge" statt "Sprache." Wir sagen "der Trank ist bitter" statt "er erregt in uns eine Empfindung der Art"; "der Stein ist
hart," als ob hart etwas anderes wäre als ein Urtheil von uns. "Die
Blätter sind grün." Auf Metonymie zurück geht die Verwandtschaft
von λεύσσω und lux luceo, color (Decke) und celare. μήν mensis
mânôt ist der "Messende," nach einer Wirkung benannt.—In
summa: die Tropen treten nicht dann und wann an die Wörter
heran, sondern sind deren eigenste Natur. Von einer "eigentlichen
Bedeutung," die nur in speziellen Fällen übertragen würde, kann gar
nicht die Rede sein.

Ebensowenig wie zwischen den eigentlichen Wörtern und den Tropen ein Unterschied ist, giebt es einen zwischen der regelrechten
Rede und den sogannten *rhetorischen Figuren*. Eigentlich ist alles
Figuration, was man gewöhnlich Rede nennt. Die Sprache wird ge-
schaffen von den einzelnen Sprachkünstlern, festgestellt aber dadurch, dass der Geschmack der Vielen eine Auswahl trifft. Die einzeln Wenigen reden σχήματα, ihre virtus vor Vielen. Dringen sie
nicht durch, so beruft sich Jeder ihnen gegenüber auf den usus und
spricht von Barbarismen und Solöcismen. Eine Figur, welche keine
Abnehmer findet, wird Fehler. Ein von irgend einem usus angenom-
mener Fehler wird eine Figur. Die Freude an *Gleichklängen* gilt auch
bei den ῥήτορες, τὰ ἴσα σχήματα, zu denken an die παρισώσεις des
Gorgias. Aber über das Maass ist grosser Streit: der Eine ist da ent-
zückt, wo der Andere widrige Fehler empfindet. Luther tadelt als
neue Wörter beherzigen, erspriesslich. Sie sind durchgedrungen,
ebenso wie "furchtlos" seit Simon Dach, "empfindsam" seit der
Uebersetzung von Yoriks empfindsamer Reise 1768. "Umsicht" als
Uebersetzung von circumspectio von 1794, "Leidenschaft" erst seit
Ch. Wolf nach πάθος. Aber die Formen der Enallage, Hypallage,
Pleonasmus sind bereits im Werden der Sprache, des Satzes thätig;
die gesammte Grammatik ist das Produkt dieser sogenannten figurae
sermonis.[2]

whole year]; the transposition from time to causality: *qua ex re, hinc inde, hothen, eis ti* [whence, until what; thus, whence to (or for) what].

A third figure is the *metonymy*, the substitution of cause and effect; for example, when the rhetor says "perspiration" for "work," "tongue" for "language." We say "the drink is bitter," instead of "it excites a particular sensation of that kind in us"; "the stone is hard," as if hard were something other than a judgment on our part. "The leaves are green." The relationships of *leussō* [to look] and *lux, luceo* [light, to shine], *color* [cover] and *celare* [to conceal], also go back to metonymy. *Mēn, mensis, mânôt* [moon, month] is the measuring, named from the perspective of the effect.

In sum: the tropes are not just occasionally added to words but constitute their most proper nature. It makes no sense to speak of a "proper meaning" which is carried over to something else only in special cases.

There is just as little distinction between actual words and tropes as there is between straightforward *speech* and *rhetorical figures*. What is usually called language is actually all figuration. Language is created by the individual speech artist, but it is determined by the fact that the taste of the many makes choices. Only very few individuals utter *schēmata* [figures] whose *virtus* [virtue, worth] becomes a guide for the many. If they do not prevail, then everyone appeals to the common *usus* [use, practice] in their regard, and speaks of barbarism and solecism. A figure which finds no buyer becomes an error. An error which is accepted by some *usus* or other becomes a figure. The delight in the *similarity of sound* is also of value to the *rhētores*: *ta isa schēmata* [the same figures], think of the *parisōseis* [balanced (or equal) clauses] of Gorgias. But there is great dispute over the degree: for the one is delighted where the other experiences disgusting errors. Luther condemns "*beherzigen*" [to take heart] and "*erspriesslich*" [profitable] as new words. They prevailed anyway, just as "*furchtlos*" [fearless] prevailed since Simon Dach; "*empfindsam*" [sentimental] since the translation of Yorik's *Sentimental Journey* (1768); "*Umsicht*" [circumspection] as a translation for *circumspectio* in 1794; "*Leidenschaft*" [passion] for *pathos*, only since Christian Wolff. But the forms of enallage, hypallage, and pleonasm are already active in the development [*Werden*] of language and the proposition; the whole grammar is the product of this so-called *figurae sermonis*.[14]

IV. REINHEIT, DEUTLICHKEIT UND ANGEMESSENHEIT DER ELOCUTIO

Von "Reinheit" ist nur die Rede bei einem sehr entwickelten Sprachsinn eines Volkes, der vor allem in einer grossen Societät, unter den Vornehmen und Gebildeten sich festsetzt. Hier entscheidet sich, was als provinziell, als Dialekt und was als normal gilt, d.h. "Reinheit" ist dann positiv der durch den usus sanktionirte Gebrauch der Gebildeten in der Gesellschaft, "Unrein" alles, was sonst in ihr auffällt. Also das _Nicht-Auffällige,_ ist das Reine. An sich giebt es weder eine reine noch eine unreine Rede. Sehr wichtiges Problem, wie sich das Gefühl für die Reinheit allmählich bildet, und wie eine gebildete Gesellschaft _wählt,_ bis sie das ganze Bereich umschrieben hat. Offenbar verfährt sie hier nach unbewussten Gesetzen und Analogieen; eine Einheit, ein einheitlicher Ausdruck wird erreicht: wie einem Volksstamm ein Dialekt genau entspricht, so einer Societät ein als "rein" sanktionirter Stil.—In Perioden eines Sprachwachsthums ist von "Reinheit" nicht die Rede: nur bei einer abgeschlossenen Sprache. Barbarismen, häufig wiederholt, gestalten endlich die Sprache um: so bildete sich die κοινὴ γλῶσσα, später die byzantinische ῥωμαϊκὴ γλῶσσα, endlich das gänzlich barbarisirte Neugriechisch. Wie viel Barbarismen haben daran gearbeitet, um aus dem Lateinischen die romanischen Sprachen zu bilden. Und durch diese Barbarismen und Solöcismen kam es zu gutem, sehr gesetzmässigem Französisch!

Das καθαρὸν τῆς λέξεως allgemeines Erforderniss: nicht nur grammatische Correktheit, sondern auch richtige Wahl der Worte. Aristot. Rhet. III 5 sagt: ἀρχὴ τῆς λέξεως τὸ ἑλληνίζειν. Die späteren Redner gehen im reinen _Atticismus_ bis zur Manierirtheit. Bei Cornific. IV 12, 17 wird ebenso die latinitas betont—welche die Rede freihält von Solöcismen, syntaktischen Verstössen, und Barbarismen, Verstössen gegen die Formenlehre (das Wort von der athenischen Colonie Σόλοι in Cilicien, besonders schlechtes Griechisch Strabo XIV p. 663). Die Barbarismen sind folgende: 1. πρόσθεσις: z.B. Σωκράτην für Σωκράτη relliquiae als "adiectio litterae"; 2.

IV. PURITY, CLARITY, AND APPROPRIATENESS OF THE *ELOCUTIO*

[One speaks of] "purity" only in connection with a people's highly developed sense of language, which, in a large society, establishes itself, above all, among the aristocratic and educated. Here it is decided what is to be considered as provincial, as dialect, and as normal; viz., "purity," then, is positively the customary usage of the educated in society, which received its sanction through the *usus*, and the "impure" is everything else which attracts attention in it. Thus, the "*not-striking*" is that which is pure. There is neither a pure nor an impure speech in itself. A very important question arises of how the feeling for purity gradually is formed, and of how an educated society *makes choices*, to the point at which the whole range has been defined. It evidently acts according to unconscious laws and analogies here: a unity, a uniform expression is achieved; "pure," sanctioned style corresponds to a high society in the same way that a dialect corresponds to a limited group of a people.

In periods of language growth, [one cannot speak of] "purity" of speech; [it is spoken of only with reference] to an established language. Barbarisms, repeated frequently, finally transform the language; thus the *koinē glōssa* [common language, (koine Greek)] arose, later the Byzantine *rōmaikē glōssa* [Roman language ("Roman" Greek)], and finally the completely barbarized new Greek. Who knows how many barbarisms have worked in this way to develop the Roman language out of Latin? And, it was through these barbarisms and solecisms, that the good rule-bound French came about!

The *katharōn tēs lexeōs* [purity (clarity)] has as a general requisite not only grammatical correctness, but also the proper selection of words. Aristotle (*Rhetoric*, 3, 5), says: *archē tēs lexeōs to hellēnizein* [the beginning (first cause) of speaking is speaking Greek]. In pure *Atticism*, the later orators go to the point of affectation. Cornificius (4, 12, 17), equally stresses *latinitas* [pure Latin style]—that which keeps the speech free of solecisms, syntactical errors, and barbarisms, violations of the accidence[15] (the word from the Athenian colony, *Soloi*, noted for especially bad Greek—Strabo, 14, 2, 28). The barbarisms follow:

1. *prosthesis* [addition (of a letter or syllable)]: for example, *Socratēn* for *Socratē* [Socrates], *relliquiae* [for *reliquiae*—relic] as "*adiectio litterae*" [addition of letters].

ἀφαίρεσις: Ἑρμῆ statt Ἑρμῆν pretor für praetor als "detractio litterae"; 3. ἐναλλαγή: z. B. ἠδυνάμην für ἐδυνάμην als immutatio litterae, si litteram aliam pro alia pronuntiemus ut arvenire pro advenire; 4. μετάθεσις: δρίφον für δίφρον transmutatio litterae Evandre statt Evander; 5. συναλοιφή: ὁ θάτερος statt ὁ ἕτερος bei Menander, weil die Crasis θάτερον nur das Neutrum betreffen kann; 6. διαίρεσις: z.B. Δημοσθένεα statt Δημοσθένη; 7. κατὰ τόνον: z.B. βουλῶμαι für βούλομαι; 8. κατὰ χρόνους: z.B. steteruntque comae; 9. κατὰ πνεῦμα: z.B. αὔριον statt αὔριον omo für homo, chorona für corona. Dann zweite Gattung: Solöcismen,[3] dritte Gattung die ἀκυρολογία, Verstösse gegen die Synonymik. Die Unterscheidung geht auf die Stoiker zurück.

Die ἀκυρολογία ist die Hauptsünde gegen die *Deutlichkeit*, dadurch dass sie die proprietas der Worte vernachlässigt. Unter proprietas im rhetorischen Sinne der Ausdruck zu verstehen, der eine Sache am vollständigsten bezeichnet, quo nihil inveniri potest significantius. Besonders Lysias wird gerühmt, er habe seine Gedanken stets durch κύριά τε καὶ κοινὰ καὶ ἐν μέσῳ κείμενα ὀνόματα ausgedrückt und doch, beim Vermeiden des Tropus, seinem Gegenstand Schmuck, Fülle und Würde erwiesen. Die Dunkelheit entsteht durch Gebrauch veralteter Wörter und Ausdrücke,[4] auch entlegener ter-

2. *aphairesis* [removal (of initial or other letters)]: for example, *Hermē* instead of *Hermēn* [Hermes], *pretor* for *praetor* [leader], as "*detractio litterae*" [taking away letters].

3. *enallagē* [interchange (of letters)]: for example *ēdynamēn* for *edynamēn* [switch of eta for epsilon], as *immutatio litterae* [substitution], *si litteram aliam pro alia pronuntiemus* [if we pronounce one letter for another], like *arvenire* for *advenire* [to arrive].

4. *metathesis* [transposition (of letters)]: *driphon* for *diphron* [sent], *transmutatio litterae* [transmutation of letters], *Evandre* instead of *Evander.*

5. *synaloiphē* [contraction of two syllables]: *ho thateros* instead of *ho heteros* [the other one] by Menander, because the *crasis thateron* [the other, another] can only refer to the neuter.

6. *diairesis* [dividing one syllable into two]: for example, *Dēmosthenea* instead of *Dēmosthenē.*

7. *kata tonon* [stretched down or broadened (vowels)], for example, *boulōmai* for *boulomai* [use of omega in the former, omicron in the latter].

8. *kata chronous* [against (bad) times or quantities of syllables]: for example *stetĕruntque comae* [the second syllable in *steterunt* would normally contain a long vowel sound].

9. *kata pneuma* [against (bad) breathings]: for example *haurion* [with rough breathing or "h" sound] instead of *aurion* [with smooth breathing, no "h"], *omo* for *homo* [man], *chorona* for *corona* [garland].

Then came the second type, solecisms,[16] and the third type, the *akyrologia* [incorrect phraseology], violation of the study of synonyms. The distinction originated with the Stoics.

The *akyrologia* [incorrect phraseology] is the cardinal sin against *clarity*, in that it neglects the *proprietas* [propriety] of words. By *proprietas,* in the rhetorical sense, one understands that expression which most completely signifies an object, *quo nihil inveniri potest significantius* [the employment of words with the maximum of significance (Quintilian, 8, 2, 9)]. Lysias especially is praised for always having expressed his ideas through *kyria te kai koina kai en mesōi keimena onomata* [both proper and ordinary words established in common (use)],[17] and yet, while avoiding the *tropus*, having given his subject matter adornment, fullness, and dignity. The obscurity originates in the employment of antiquated words and expressions,[18]

mini technici, durch unübersichtliche Länge, durch verschränkte Wortstellung, durch Einschiebsel und Parenthesen, ἀμφιβολίαι die ἀδιανόητα (wo hinter klaren Worten ein ganz anderer versteckter Sinn liegt). Der Redner muss nicht nur dafür sorgen, dass man ihn verstehen kann, sondern dass man ihn verstehen _muss_. Schopenhauer Parerga II, 436f.: "Dunkelheit und Undeutlichkeit ist allemal und überall ein sehr schlimmes Zeichen. Denn in 99 Fällen unter 100 rührt sie her von der Undeutlichkeit des Gedankens, welche selbst wiederum fast immer aus einem ursprünglichen Missverhältniss, Inconsistenz und also Unrichtigkeit desselben entspringt." "Die, welche schwierige dunkle verflochtene zweideutige Reden zusammensetzen, wissen ganz gewiss nicht recht, was sie sagen wollen, sondern haben nur ein dumpfes, nach einem Gedanken ringendes Bewusstsein davon: oft auch wollen sie sich selber und Anderen verbergen, dass sie eigentlich nichts zu sagen haben."—"Wie jedes Übermaass einer Einwirkung meistens das Gegentheil des Bezweckten herbeiführt, so dienen zwar Worte, Gedanken fasslich zu machen; jedoch auch nur bis zu einem gewissen Punkt. Ueber diesen hinaus angehäuft, machen sie die mitzutheilenden Gedanken wieder dunkler und immer dunkler ... Jedes überflüssige Wort wirkt seinem Zweck entgegen: wie Voltaire sagt, "das Adjektiv ist der Feind des Substantivs," "das Geheimniss, langweilig zu sein, ist, alles zu sagen." "Immer noch besser, etwas Gutes wegzulassen, als etwas Nichtssagendes hinzuzusetzen." "Alles Entbehrliche wirkt nachtheilig."

Das dritte Erforderniss der Darstellung ist _Angemessenheit_ des _Ausdrucks_, oratio probabilis eine Rede, die nicht weniger noch mehr sei, als recht ist; die λέξις müsse πρέπουσα sein, sagt Arist. Rhet. III 2. Vermeidung gewisser Fehler nöthig: 1. κακέμφατον oder αἰσχρολογία (durch zufällige Trennung oder Verbindung von Silben kommen Obscenitäten zum Vorschein, cum notis hominibus loqui, cum Numerio fui). 2. ταπείνωσις oder humilitas, durch die die Grösse oder Würde einer Sache beeinträchtigt wird, saxea est verruca in summo montis vertice. Ein Mörder darf nicht als nequam,

also through obscure technical terms, through tortuous length, through confused word order, through insertions and parentheses, *amphiboliai* [double meaning], and the *adianoēta* [unintelligible] (where a completely different, concealed sense lies behind clear words). The orator must not only take care that one is able to understand him, but that one must understand him. Schopenhauer (*Parerga*, 2, 436f.) says:

> Obscurity and indistinctness are always and above all a bad symptom. For in 99 cases out of 100, it originates from the vagueness of thought, which itself almost always arises in turn from its fundamental inadequacy, inconsistency, and even falsehood.
>
> They who compose difficult, obscure, involved, ambiguous speeches, almost certainly do not really know what they want to say, but have only a vague awareness of the thought for which they struggle: also, they often want to conceal from themselves and others that they actually have nothing to say.
>
> Just as each excess brings about an effect, which usually is the opposite of the one intended, in the same way, words indeed serve to make thoughts comprehensible, however only up to a point. Accumulated beyond this, they make the thoughts to be communicated more and more obscure.... Each superfluous word operates to the contrary of its purpose: as Voltaire says, "the adjective is the enemy of the substantive," and "the secret of being boring is to say everything." "It is always better to omit something good than to add something which says nothing." "Everything which is superfluous is counterproductive."[19]

The third requisite of the presentation is *appropriateness* of the *expression, oratio probabilis* [language which is acceptable], a speech which is no more nor less than correct; the *lexis* [style] must be *prepousa* [conspicuously fitting], according to Aristotle (*Rhetoric*, 3, 2). It is necessary to avoid certain errors:

1. *kakemphaton* [vulgarity] or *aischrologia* [obscenity] (obscenities come to the surface through accidental separation or connection of syllables, *cum notis hominibus loqui* or *cum Numerio fui*).[20]
2. *tapeinōsis* [humility (lowness) of style], through which the magnitude or dignity of a thing will be injured, *saxea est verruca in summo montis vertice* [there is a rocky wart upon the mountain's brow]. A murderer cannot be labeled as a *nequam* [scamp], nor could someone who had a liaison with a courtesan be labeled as *nefarius* [villainous].

jemand, der mit einer Hetäre ein Verhältniss hat, nicht als nefarius bezeichnet werden. 3. Die μείωσις, hier fehlt etwas an der Vollständigkeit. 4. Die ταὐτολογία, die Wiederholung desselben Wortes oder desselben Begriffes. 5. Die συνωνυμία, die Wiederholung des eben Gesagten mit anderen Ausdrücken. 6. Die ὁμοιολογία, Mangel jeglicher Abwechslung, Monotonie. 7. Die μακρολογία, longior quam oportet sermo. 8. Pleonasmus, cum supervacuis verbis oratio oneratur. Unser "Flickwort" ist παραπλήρωμα. Cicero redet bei den asiatischen Rednern von complementa numerorum. 9. περιεργία supervacua operositas. 10. κακόζηλον eine verkehrte Affektation, der Stil erscheint als "gemacht" (das was wir "rhetorische" oder poetische Prosa nennen), entsteht aus der Neigung, den Stil blühend zu machen: dahin gehört aber auch das Frostige τό ψυχρόν (Arist. Rhet. III 3) im Gebrauch dichterischer Composita, glossematischer Ausdrücke, überflüssiger Epitheta und zu weit hergeholter Metaphern. 11. τὸ ἀνοικονόμητον, schlecht disponiert. 12. ἀσχήματον, schlecht angewandte Figuren. 13. κακοσύνθετον, schlecht gestellt. Der σαρδισμός ist Vermischung der Dialekte (Attisch mit Dorisch, Ionisch, Aeolisch). Dann die Vermischung der Stilarten, des Erhabenen mit Niedrigem, Alten mit Neuem, Poetischen mit Gewöhnlichem. Um passend zu sprechen, muss man nicht nur auf das sehen, was nützt, sondern auch auf das, was sich geziemt. Apologie des Sokrates darnach zu beurtheilen.—Manche von diesen vitia kommen nun auch als Zierden, als Steigerungen später, unter der Rubrik des ornatus, vor.

Es kommt ferner darauf an, für wen und bei wem man spricht, zu welcher Zeit, an welchem Ort, für welche Sache. Anders der bejahrte Redner, anders der junge Mann. Bewundernswerth Lysias, sich bei seinen Reden nach dem Charakter der Redenden zu richten, ebenso

3. The *meiōsis* [diminution]: here, something is wrong with regard to completeness.
4. The *tautologia* [tautology]: the repetition of the same word or of the same idea.
5. The *synōnymia* [synonymy]: the repetition of what has already been said with other expressions.
6. The *homoiologia* [uniformity of style]: lack of any variation; monotony.
7. The *makrologia* [long speech], *longior quam oportet sermo* [the use of more words than are necessary].
8. *Pleonasmus, cum supervacuis verbis oratio oneratur* [Pleonasm, when we overload our style with a superfluity of words]. Our "expletive" is *paraplērōma*. With respect to the Asiatic orator, Cicero speaks of *complementa numerorum* [filling out the rhythm].
9. *periergia, supervacua operositas* [overelaboration].
10. *kakozēlon* [using bad, affected style], a perverse affectation; the style appears to be "affected" (that which we call "rhetorical" or poetical prose). It originates from the inclination to make the style florid: in the use of the poetical *composita* [constructions], glossy expressions, superfluous epithets, and overly far-fetched metaphors; the cold *to psychron* [frigid style] belongs to this also (Aristotle, *Rhetoric*, 3, 3).
11. *to anoikonomēton* [unarranged], badly disposed.
12. *aschēmaton* [formless, without arrangement], poorly used figures.
13. *kakosyntheton* [ill-composed], badly placed.

The *sardismos* [mixing of dialects] is a mixture of the Attic with Doric, Ionian, and Aeolian dialects; then the mixture of stylistic types, of the lofty with the vulgar, old with new, poetic with usual. In order to speak appropriately, one must not only pay attention to what is useful, but also to what is suitable. The *Apology* of Socrates is to be judged accordingly.[21]

Many of these *vitia* [faults] also appear as ornaments, later as enhancements, under the rubric of the *ornatus* [ornamentation].

It is a matter of importance to observe for whom, and among whom, one speaks, at which time, at which place, and for what cause. It is different for the aged rhetor and for the young man. Lysias is admirable in that he adjusts his speeches to the character of the

nach den Zuhörern und dem Gegenstande. Dionys. de Lys. iudic. 9 p. 245. Manche an sich lobenswerthe Eigenschaften können unpassend erscheinen—in einem Prozess auf Leben und Tod ist zu grosse Sorgfalt des Stils und Kunst der Komposition nicht erlaubt. Die epideiktische Beredsamkeit verlangt viel mehr Schmuck als die gerichtliche. Die scharfe Scheidung der genera im Ausdruck führte sogar zur Manier: Quint. III 8, 58 klagt, dass einige Deklamatoren bei der Suasoria einen schroffen Anfang affektiren, eine eilige und aufgeregte Rede, im Ausdruck den cultus effusior, um in allen Stücken von der Gerichtsrede abzuweichen.—Also in summa: Reinheit und Deutlichkeit überall; alles aber modificirt nach dem Charakteristischen von Ort, Gelegenheit, Sprechenden, Zuhörenden—das Stilgefühl, welches in jedem Falle einen modifizirten Ausdruck verlangt: etwas wie in der Musik der gleiche Rhythmus eines Tonstücks durchgeht, unverletzt: innerhalb desselben aber die zartesten Modifikationen nöthig sind. Der charakteristische Stil ist das eigentliche Kunstbereich des Redners: hier übt er eine freie *plastische* Kraft, die Sprache ist für ihn ein bereites Material. Hier ist er nachahmender Künstler, er redet ähnlich wie der Schauspieler aus einer fremden Person oder einer ihm fremden Sache heraus: hier liegt der Glaube zu Grunde, das Jeder in seiner eigensten Manier seine Sache am besten führt, d.h. am überzeugendsten wirkt. Dabei empfindet der Zuhörer die Natürlichkeit, d.h. die unbedingte Angemessenheit und Einheitlichkeit: während er, bei jeder Abweichung davon, die Künstlichkeit empfindet und dann misstrauisch gegen die vertretene Sache wird. Die Kunst des Redners ist, nie eine Künstlichkeit merken zu lassen: daher der charakteristische Stil, der aber erst recht ein Produkt der höchsten Kunst ist: wie die "Natürlichkeit" des guten Schauspielers. Der wahre Redner redet aus dem ἦθος der von ihm vertretenen Person oder Sache heraus: er erfindet die besten Apologieen und Argumente (wie sie gewöhnlich nur der Egoismus findet), die überredendsten Worte und Manieren: das Merkwürdige an ihm ist, dass er durch Kunst, durch ein Vertauschen der Personen und durch darüber schwebende Besonnenheit alles das findet und sich zu Nutze macht, was der beredteste Anwalt jedes Menschen und jeder Partei, der Egoismus, nur zu finden vermag. Es ist eine Vertauschung des ego wie bei dem Dramatiker. Goethe betont, dass alle bei Sophokles auftretenden Personen die besten Redner sind; denn wenn jede ge-

speaker, as well as to the listeners and to the subject (Dionysius of
Halicarnassus, *Lys. iudic.* 9, p. 245).[22] Many qualities which are
praiseworthy in themselves can appear to be unsuitable—in a trial
of life and death, it is not justifiable to give too great attention to the
style and art of composition. The epideictic oratory demands much
more decoration than does the forensic. The sharp separation of the
genera even led to mannerism in the expression: Quintilian (3, 8, 58)
complains that in the case of the *suasoria*, some declaimers affected
a rough beginning, a hurried and excited speech, the *cultus effusior*
[cultivated extravagance] in the expression, in order to depart in
every way from the forensic speech.

Therefore, in sum, purity and clarity everywhere; but all modified
according to the characteristics of place, occasion, speakers, and listeners—the feeling for style, which demands a modified expression,
is approximately the same as in music [in which] the same rhythm
goes through a musical composition unimpaired, but within which
the most delicate modifications are necessary. The characteristic
style is the proper domain of the art of the orator: here he practices
a free *plastic* art; the language is his material which has already been
prepared. Here, he is an imitative artist; he speaks like an actor who
plays a role unfamiliar to him or in an unfamiliar situation: here, the
belief is basic that each manages his object best, i.e., works most con-
vincingly in his own manner. It is in this way that the listener perceives the naturalness, viz., the absolute appropriateness and unifor-
mity, whereas with each deviation from the natural, he perceives the
artificiality and becomes distrustful about the matter presented. The
art of the orator is never to allow artificiality to become noticeable:
hence, the characteristic style which, however, is all the more a product of the highest art, just like the "naturalness" of the good actor.
The true orator speaks forth from the *ēthos* of the persons or things
represented by him: he invents the best apologies and arguments (in
the manner in which only egoism usually finds them), the most per-
suasive words and manners; what is remarkable about him is that,
through art, through an interchange of persons, and through a prudence which hovers over them, he finds and turns to his advantage
what the most eloquent lawyer of each person and each party,
namely egoism, only is able to discover. It is an exchange of egos, as
with the dramatist. Goethe claims that, in Sophocles, all publicly
appearing persons are the best orators, for when each has spoken,

sprochen, hat man immer den Eindruck, dass ihre Sache die ge-
rechteste und beste ist. Das ist eben die Wirkung des charakteristischen Stils, durch den Sophokles, zur Reife gelangt, sich
auszeichnete, nach seinem eigenen Zeugniss.

V. DIE CHARAKTERISTISCHE REDE IM VERHÄLTNISS ZUM SCHMUCK DER REDE

Im Munde dessen, der für sich oder eine Sache redet, muss die
Rede ganz angemessen und natürlich erscheinen: man muss also an
die Kunst der Vertauschung nicht erinnert werden, weil sonst der
Zuhörer misstrauisch wird und überlistet zu werden fürchtet. Es
giebt also, auch in der Rhetorik, eine "Nachahmung der Natur," als
Hauptmittel zu überzeugen: nur wenn der Sprechende und seine
Sprache einander ädaquat sind, glaubt der Zuhörer an den *Ernst* und
die *Wahrheit* der vertretenen Sache; er erwärmt sich für den Redner
und *glaubt* an ihn—nämlich dass er selbst an seine Sache *glaubt*, also
redlich ist. Die "Angemessenheit" geht also auf einen moralischen
Effekt hinaus, Deutlichkeit (und Reinheit) auf einen intellektuellen:
verstanden will man werden, als redlich will man gelten. Die "Reinheit" ist schon eine halb künstlerische Beschränkung des Charakteristischen; denn in dem Munde vieler würden, zur vollen Täuschung,
auch Solöcismen und Barbarismen nöthig sein (zu erinnern an die
Art, wie Shakespeare Pförtner und Ammen auftreten lässt, *Kilissa* in
den Choephoren). Das Charakteristische wird also einmal gebrochen
durch Uebertragung in die *gebildete* Sprachsphäre. Zweitens durch
das allgemeine Erforderniss vom "Schmuck der Rede." Dieser ist
aus der *agonalen* Neigung der Alten zu erklären—alles öffentliche
Auftreten des Individuums ist ein Wettkampf: dem Kämpfer aber
ziemen nicht nur starke, sondern auch *glänzende* Waffen. Nicht nur
angemessen, sondern schön muss man die Waffen handhaben, nicht
nur zu siegen, sondern "elegant" zu siegen, ist Erforderniss bei einem
agonalen Volke. Ausser dem Eindruck der "Redlichkeit" soll auch
der Eindruck der *Ueberlegenheit*, in der Freiheit, Würde, Schönheit
der Form des Kampfes, hervorgebracht werden. Das eigentliche
Geheimniss der rhetorischen Kunst ist nun das *weise* Verhältniss
beider Rücksichten, auf das Redliche und auf das Künstlerische.
Ueberall, wo die "Natürlichkeit" nackt nachgeahmt wird, fühlt sich
der künstlerischer Sinn der Zuhörer beleidigt, wo dagegen rein ein
künstlerischer Eindruck erstrebt wird, wird leicht das moralische

one always has the impression that his cause was the most just and the best. It is precisely the force of the characteristic style, through which Sophocles distinguished himself after he had come to maturity, according to his own testimony.

V. THE TYPICAL SPEECH IN RELATION TO THE EMBELLISHMENT OF SPEECH

The speech must appear to be appropriate and natural in the mouth of a person who speaks for himself or for a thing: thus, one must not be reminded of the art of substitution,[23] because the listener will be distrustful and will fear being deceived. Therefore, in rhetoric, there is also an "imitation of nature" as a basic means to persuade. The listener will believe in the *earnestness* of the speaker and the *truth* of the thing advocated only if the speaker and his language are adequately suited to one another: he takes a lively interest in the speaker and *believes* in him—that is, that the speaker himself *believes* in the thing, and thus is *sincere*. Therefore, "appropriateness" aims at a moral effect, clarity (and purity) at an intellectual one: one wants to be understood, and one wishes to be considered sincere. "Purity" already is a half-artistic delimitation of what is typical; for in the mouths of many, solecism and barbarism also would be necessary for a full illusion (just recall the manner in which Shakespeare allows porters and nurses to appear, or the *Kilissa* [Sicilian woman] in the *Choephori* [732]). Therefore, what is typical is broken down first by means of transference into the *cultured* domain of language, and second, through the general requisite of the "embellishment of the speech." This is to be explained from the ancients' *agonale* [competitive] tendency—all public appearance of the individual is a contest: however, not only strong weapons, but also *brilliant* ones, are suited to the combatant. One must handle the weapons not just suitably, but also beautifully; to win "elegantly," not just to be victorious, is required among a people with a sense for competition. In addition to the impression of "being reasonable and sincere," the impression of being *superior*, in freedom, dignity, and beauty of the form of the contest, must also be produced. The real secret of the rhetorical art is now the *prudent* relation of both aspects, of the sincere and the artistic. Whenever the "naturalness" is imitated nakedly, the artistic sense of the listeners will be offended; in contrast, wherever a purely artistic expression is sought, the moral con-

Zutrauen des Zuhörers gebrochen. Es ist ein Spiel auf der Grenze des Aesthetischen und Moralischen: jede Einseitigkeit vernichtet den Erfolg. Die ästhetische Bezauberung soll zu dem moralischen Zutrauen hinzukommen, beide sollen sich nicht aufheben: die admiratio des Kämpfers ist ein Hauptmittel des πιθανόν. Cicero schreibt an Brutus: nam eloquentiam, quae admirationem non habet, nullam iudico. Er sagt De orat. III 14, 52 s. [. . .]: "Niemals ist ein Redner darum bewundert worden, weil er lateinisch sprach: kann er das nicht, so wird er ausgezischt und kaum für einen Menschen, geschweige für einen Redner gehalten. Noch niemand hat den gepriesen, der so redete, dass die Anwesenden ihn verstehen konnten, sondern den verachtet, der das nicht konnte. Wer also erschüttert die Menschen? Wer fesselt die staunenden Blicke? Wem tönt Beifall? Wer ist so zu sagen der Gott unter den Menschen? Wer deutlich, wer zusammenhängend, wer mit reicher Fülle und strahlender Pracht der Sachen und der Worte redet und dabei fast in dichterischen Rhythmen sich bewegt—das ist's, was ich schön nenne. Wer zugleich sich so weit mässigt, als es die Würde der Sachen und Personen verlangt, von dem sage ich, dass er das Lob eines angemessenen Vortrags verdient." Hier erscheint das *Charakteristische* fast als eine Einschränkung des *Schönen*:[5] während gewöhnlich das Schöne als Einschränkung des Charakteristischen betrachtet wird. Sehr schön sagt der Autor des dialog. de orator. c. 22:[6] "Ich verlange vom Redner, wie von einem wohlhabenden und stattlichen Hausvater, dass das Haus, in dem er lebt, nicht nur gegen Regen und Wind schütze, sondern auch Sinne und Augen erfreue, dass er sich ein Hausgeräth schaffe, nicht nur zur Befriedigung der nächsten Bedürfnisse, sondern dass auch Gold und Edelgestein in seinen Schränken liege, das man bisweilen in die Hand nehmen und anschauen mag." Die Abwesenheit jedes Schmuckes wird c. 23 keinesfalls als Zeichen voller Gesundheit angesehen; es gebe trübselige und von jeder Anmuth entblösste Redner, die ihre geistige Frische, von der sie so viel Wesens machen, nicht aus einer starken Organisation, sondern durch eine Hungerkur gewinnen. "Den Aerzten gefällt aber das physische Dasein einer Gesundheit nicht, die man durch ängstliche Sorgsamkeit erwirbt; nicht krank sein, genügt durchaus nicht: wakker, lustig, froh soll der Mensch sein. Wo man nur das Wohlbefinden zu rühmen weiss, da ist die Kränklichkeit nicht ferne." Die Schön-

fidence of the listener will be shaken. It is a playing at the boundary
of the aesthetic and moral: any one-sidedness destroys the outcome.
The aesthetic fascination must join the moral confidence; but they
should not cancel one another out: the *admiratio* [admiration] of the
combatant is a basic means of the *pithanon* [persuasion]. Cicero
writes to Brutus: *nam eloquentiam, quae admirationem non habet,
nullam iudico* [eloquence which evokes no admiration is, in my
opinion, unworthy of the name].[24] He says, in *De Oratore* (3, 14, 52):

> ... nobody ever admired an orator for correct grammar, they only laugh
> at him if his grammar is bad, and not only think him no orator but not
> even a human being; no one ever sang the praises of a speaker whose
> style succeeded in making his meaning intelligible to his audience, but
> only despised one deficient in capacity to do so. Who then is the man
> who gives people a thrill? whom do they stare at in amazement when
> he speaks? who is interrupted by applause? who is thought to be so to
> speak a god among men? It is those whose speeches are clear, explicit
> and full, perspicuous in matter and in language, and who in the actual
> delivery achieve a sort of rhythm and cadence—that is, those whose
> style is what I call artistic. Those who manage this same artistry as the
> relative importance of the facts and persons concerned directs, deserve
> to be applauded on the score of the sort of distinction that I designate
> appropriateness and suitability of style.

Here what is *typical* appears almost as a restriction on the beautiful:[25]
although the beautiful is usually considered as a restriction of what
is typical. The author of the *Dialogue on Orators* says it well (22):[26]

> My own view is that the orator, like a prosperous and stately house-
> holder, ought to live in a house that is not only wind- and weather-
> proof, but pleasing also to the eye; he should not only have such fur-
> nishings as shall suffice for his essential needs, but also number among
> his belongings both gold and precious stones, so as to make people want
> to take them up now and again, and gaze with admiration.

The absence of any decoration (23) is never viewed as a sign of complete health; it is said that there are pitiable rhetors, deprived of any
grace, and even the intellectual vivacity of which they boast they owe
not to a sturdy constitution, but to a starvation diet.

> Why, in dealing with the human body, doctors have not much to say in
> praise of the patient who only keeps well by worrying about his health.
> It is not enough not to be ill; I like a man to be strong and hearty and
> vigorous. If soundness is all you can commend in him, he is really next
> door to an invalid.

heit gilt ihm gewissermaassen als die Blüthe der Gesundheit, c. 21: "es ist mit der Rede, wie mit dem menschlichen Körper: sie ist nur dann schön, wenn die Adern daran nicht hervortreten, die Knochen nicht zu zählen sind, wenn vielmehr gesundes gutes Blut die Glieder füllt, schwellende Muskeln bildet und auch über die Nerven die Röthe breitet und alles schön darstellt." Andererseits macht Cicero de oratore III 25, 98 ss. darauf aufmerksam, wie an die grösste Sinnenlust der grösste Ueberdruss angrenzt: es sei also grosse Gefahr mit dem ornatus verknüpft. Die Rede muss Schatten und Ruhepunkte darbieten, einmal, damit keine Abstumpfung eintrete, sodann, damit die Lichtseiten hervortreten (wie Hamann sagt: "Deutlichkeit ist die richtige Vertheilung von Licht und Schatten").

Die allgemeinen Eigenschaften des ornatus beschreibt Quint. VIII c. 3, 61: ornatum est, quod perspicuo ac probabili plus est—also eine Steigerung (oder Modifikation) der Eigenschaften der Deutlichkeit und des Angemessenen. Die grammatische Correctheit lässt sich nicht steigern, aber modificiren, durch Ausdrucksweisen, die von dem Herkömmlichen zwar abweichen, aber doch berechtigt sind und angenehme Abwechslung bringen (z.B. alterthümliche Formen und Ausdrücke). Die sogenannten grammatischen Figuren gehören hierher. Dann Abweichen von der proprietas durch die Tropen. Die Deutlichkeit zu steigern durch Anwendung von Bildern und Gleichnissen, oder ausdrucksvolle Kürze oder Amplifikation. Dann Sentenzen und Figuren als Kunstmittel der Rede, zur Verstärkung des Angemessenen.—Aber aller Schmuck muss männlich kräftig und würdig sanctus sein, frei von weibischer Leichtfertigkeit und falscher Schminke. Obwohl hier das Grenzgebiet zwischen Tugenden und Fehlern sehr klein ist. Dies gilt besonders im Betreff der numeri orationis: die Alten verlangten auch für die ungebundene Rede fast Verse: zum Athemholen nämlich Schlusspunkte, die nicht nach Ermüdung, nicht nach Interpunktionszeichen, sondern nach dem numerus einzufügen seien. Diese numeri stehen wieder in Verbindung mit der modulatio der Stimme. Dabei gilt aber ein wirklicher *Vers* durchaus als Fehler. Damit hängt dann wieder der Bau der Periode zusammen. Besonders wichtig sind die Anfänge und die Schlüsse der Perioden, diese fallen am stärksten ins Ohr.

Beauty means almost the same to him as the blossom of health (21):

> it is with eloquence as with the human frame. There can be no beauty
> of form where the veins are prominent, or where one can count the
> bones: sound healthful blood must fill out the limbs, and riot over the
> muscles, concealing the sinews in turn under a ruddy complexion and
> a graceful exterior.

On the other hand, Cicero (*De Oratore*, 3, 25, 98), points out how
the highest sensual pleasure borders on the highest disgust: thus,
there would also be greater danger associated with the *ornatus*. The
speech must offer shade and rest points, first, to avoid the occurrence
of dullness, and also to make the bright sides become prominent (as
Hamann says: "clarity is the right distribution of light and
shadow").[27]

Quintilian described the general qualities of the *ornatus* (8, 3, 61):
"*ornatum est, quod perspicuo ac probabili plus est*" [the ornate is
something that goes beyond what is merely lucid and acceptable]—
thus an enhancement (or modification) of the qualities of clarity and
appropriateness. Grammatical correctness cannot be enhanced, but
modified, through modes of expression which deviate from the traditional ones, but which are yet justified and bring about an agree-
able modification (ancient forms and expressions, for example). The
so-called grammatical figures belong to this [group]. Then, there are
the deviations from the *proprietas* by means of the tropes. These are
to increase the clarity through the use of images and comparisons, or
highly expressive brevity or amplification. Then, aphorisms and figures, as artistic means of speech, may strengthen its appropriateness.

But all embellishment must be masculinely powerful and dignified, *sanctus* [pure], free from effeminate frivolity and false cosmetic.
Here, though, the boundary region between virtue and vice is very
narrow. This matters in regard to the *numeri orationis* [rhythm of
speaking] especially: the ancients almost demanded verses, even for
prosaic speech; namely periods to allow for breathing, to be placed
according to the *numerus* and not according to fatigue or to punctuation marks. These *numeri* are again connected with the *modulatio*
[rhythmical measure] of the voice. But, in this case, a real *verse* is
considered definitively as an error. And, it is with this that the construction of the period is closely connected. The beginnings and end-
ings of the periods are especially important; these strike the ear most
strongly.

Der Schmuck also verlangt die Uebertragung des Angemessenen in eine höhere Sphäre von Schönheitsgesetzen, er ist Verklärung des Charakteristischen, einmal durch Ausscheidung des minder Edlen im Charakteristischen, sodann Steigerung des Edlen und Schönen, der grossen Züge des Charakteristischen. Er ist höhere Natur, im Gegensatz zu einer gemeinen Natürlichkeit, Nach- und Umbildung, im Gegensatz zur Nachahmung und Nachäffung.

VI. MODIFIKATION DER REINHEIT

Da die Dichter (sagt Arist. Rhet. III 1) trotz gewöhnlicher Gedanken durch den Reiz ihrer Sprache zu solchem Ruf gelangt zu sein schienen, war die erste Rede eine poetische, und auch jetzt noch glauben die meisten Ungebildeten, dass diese Art Redner am schönsten sprächen. Gorgias wollte der Rede einen ähnlichen Reiz verleihen, wie ihn die Dichter besassen: er erkannte das Gesetz des Isokrates nicht an, dass sie sich nur der gewöhnlichen Worte zu bedienen hätten. Er wurde der Erfinder der grossartigen und poetisirenden Redegattung, die besonders von Thucydides ausgebildet wurde. Thucydides liebt, nach Dion. von Halic., die λέξις ἀπηρχαιωμένη und γλωσσηματική. Seine Sprache ist die für öffentliche Verhandlungen damals in Athen nicht mehr gebräuchliche: er hielt sich an das Verschwindende, wie an den altattischen Dialekt mit seinem πράσσω, ξύν, ἐς, τετάχαται, u.s.w. Thucydides fühlte, dass die gemeine Sprache weder ihm noch seinem Thema angemessen sei. In neuen und eigenthümlichen Formen, in ungebräuchlichen Constructionen thut er seine Herrschaft über die Sprache dar. Bei Rednern, die durch ihre Reinheit und Schlichtheit berühmt sind, ist der Gebrauch veralteter Worter γλῶσσαι sehr selten, ebenso der der Neubildungen πεποιημένα und Composita διπλᾶ oder σύνθετα. Werden sie gebraucht, dann an gehobenen Stellen. Es verräth eine mangelhafte technische Durchbildung, wenn seltene Wörter beliebig, ohne bestimmten Zweck, wie bei Andocides, verwendet werden: der Stil wird buntscheckig. (Hier finden sich Reminiscenzen an die Sprache der Tragiker.) Sehr viel Bewusstsein hat Antiphon, der Würde erstrebt, auch durch Alterthümlichkeit, z. B. σσ: während schon

Embellishment, thus, requires that one carry over appropriateness into a higher sphere of laws of beauty; it is a transfiguration of what is typical, first, through the elimination of the less noble in what is typical, and then, through an enhancement of the noble and beautiful, which are important traits of what is typical. Embellishment is a higher nature, in contrast to the common naturalness; reproduction and transformation, in contrast to imitation and mimicry.

VI. MODIFICATION OF PURITY

Because the poets (according to Aristotle, *Rhetoric*, 3, 1) seemed to have attained such a reputation through the charm of their language, in spite of their ordinary ideas, the first speech was a poetic one. And, even now, most educated people believe that this kind of orator speaks most beautifully. Gorgias wanted to lend to speech a charm similar to that which the poets possess:[28] he did not accept the law of Isocrates, that they had to make use of only ordinary words. He became the inventor of the grand and poetic type of speech, which would be perfected, especially by Thucydides. According to Dionysius of Halicarnassus, Thucydides loved the *lexis apērchaiōmenē* [style having just become completely ancient] and *glōssēmatikē* [(style) fattened with obsolete words].[29] His language was [such that] it was no longer in use for public discussions in Athens in those days: he held on to what was disappearing, such as the old Attic dialect with its *prassō* [to achieve or accomplish (later *prattō* in Attic)], *xyn* [with (harsher pronunciation of *syn*)], *es* [into or to (old Attic form of *eis*)], *tetachatai* [(from *tassō*) to draw up in order of battle], and so forth. Thucydides felt that the common language was appropriate neither to him nor to his theme. He displayed his command of the language in new and peculiar forms, and in unusual constructions. The use of antiquated words, *glōssai*, is very rare with orators who were famous for their purity and simplicity, and so were new constructions, *pepoiēmena*, and *composita dipla* or *syntheta* [compound or composite constructions]. When they are used, it is always in elevated passages. It betrays a deficient technical education when rare words are used arbitrarily, without decided aim, such as in the case of Andocides: the style becomes variegated. (Reminiscences of the language of the tragic poets are found here.) Antiphon sought dignity very consciously, also through the ancient usage, *ss*,

Pericles sich dem modernen Dialekt in öffentlichen Reden anbequemte und die Komödie beweist, wie man zu Antiphon's Zeiten öffentlich im Volke sprach. In seiner τέχνη waren Vorschriften über Bildung neuer Worte gegeben. Innerhalb der Grenze der Deutlichkeit schmückt er die Rede mit allen Reizen des Neuen und Ungewöhnlichen. Viele ἅπαξ λεγόμενα. Dann die Substantivirung der Neutra von Participien und Adjectiven.—Bei den Römern beginnt die Neigung zum archaistischen Ausdruck mit der Kaiserzeit, nachdem Sallust das Beispiel gegeben hat, und steigert sich sehr schnell. Schon Augustus macht (Sueton Aug. 86) dem Tiberius in einem Briefe Vorwürfe ut exoletas interdum et reconditas voces aucupanti. Seneca sagt von seinen Zeitgenossen ep. 114, 13: multi ex alieno saeculo petunt verba: duodecim tabulas loquuntur. Gracchus illis et Crassus et Curio nimis culti et recentes sunt, ad Appium usque et ad Coruncanium redeunt. Es war ein Reizmittel für einen verdorbenen Geschmack. Cicero wurde als Schädiger der echten latinitas angesehen; das Harmonische war verhasst. Sehr wichtige Periode für die Erkenntnis des Archaischen: viel aus Gellius zu gewinnen. Fronto ist der dümmste und frechste Vertreter. Von dieser krankhaften Phase ist ganz das Verhältniss zum Archaischen in der klassischen Periode zu unterscheiden. Die festen termini sind: latinitas (ausgeschieden das Ausserlateinische), urbanitas (ausgeschieden alles Plebejische und Provinzielle im Lateinischen). Die patavinitas, die Asinius Pollio dem Livius vorwarf, war ein Fehler gegen die urbanitas. Im Allgemeinen wird jedes insolens verbum gemieden: Caesar (nach Macrobius I, 5, 4): tamquam scopulum sic fuge insolens verbum. Cicero de oratore III 25, 97: moneo ut caveatis ne exilis ne inculta sit oratio vestra, ne vulgaris, ne obsoleta. Varro bewahrt mit Bewusstsein das Archaische, Sallust mit Affektation. Cic. de orat. III 38, 153, der sehr

for example [as in *prassō* rather than *prattō* (above)—Trans.], while Pericles already had adapted himself to the modern dialect in public speeches, and the comedy proves how one spoke publicly among the people in Antiphon's time. In his *technē*, he gave formulae concerning the formation of new words. Within the limitation of clarity, he decorated his speech with all the charms of the new and unusual. [One finds] many *hapax legomena* [things being said once only], as well as the neuter of the participle and adjectives as nouns.

The preference for the archaic expression begins with the Romans in the time of the Empire, with Sallust providing the example, and it then increases very quickly. Augustus reproaches Tiberius in a letter *ut exoletas interdum et reconditas voces aucupanti* [for sometimes hunting up obsolete and pedantic expressions] (Suetonius, *Augustus*, 86). Seneca speaks of his contemporaries (*Letters*, 114, 13):

> *multi ex alieno saeculo petunt verba: duodecim tabulas loquuntur. Gracchus illis et Crassus et Curio nimis culti et recentes sunt, ad Appium usque et ad Coruncanium redeunt.* [Many orators hark back to earlier epochs for their vocabulary, speaking in the language of the Twelve Tables. Gracchus, Crassus, and Curio, in their eyes, are too refined and too modern; so back to Appius and Coruncanius.]

It was a stimulus for a spoiled taste. Cicero was considered to be the originator of damage to the genuine *latinitas*; the harmonious was hated. This was a very important period for our understanding of the archaic, with much to be gained from Gellius. Fronto is the stupidest and most insolent representative. The relation to the archaic in the classical period is to be entirely separated from this pathological phase. The fixed *termini* [boundaries] are: *latinitas* (that which was not Latin was excluded), *urbanitas* [urbane, refined] (all that is plebeian and provincial in Latin was excluded). The *patavinitas* [dialect of Padua], for which Asinius Pollio reproached Livy,[30] was an error against *urbanitas*. In general, each *insolens verbum* [unusual word] was avoided. Caesar said (according to Macrobius, 1, 5, 4): *tamquam scopulum sic fuge insolens verbum* [I should avoid a rare and unusual word as I would a rock]. Cicero (*De Oratore*, 3, 25, 97) says: *moneo ut caveatis ne exilis, ne inculta sit vestra oratio, ne vulgaris, ne obsoleta* [I warn you to avoid an impoverished and uncultivated style, and expressions that are vulgar or out of date]. Varro preserves the archaic consciously, Sallust with affectation. Cicero (*De Oratore*, 3,

vor dem Archaischen in der *Rede* warnt, sagt aber doch, am rechten Orte gebraucht, gebe es der Rede einen grossartigen Anstrich; er werde sich nicht scheuen zu sagen qua tempestate Poenus in Italiam venit, oder proles suboles oder fari nuncupare, non rebar opinabar.[7] Verständig Quint. I 6, 39ff., eine Rede sei fehlerhaft, si egeat interprete, daher seien verba a vetustate repetita zwar, sofern sie Majestät mit Neuheit verbinden, vortrefflich, aber opus est modo ut neque crebra sint haec neque manifesta, quia nihil est odiosius affectatione, nec utique ab ultimis et iam oblitteratis repetita temporibus, qualia sunt topper et antegerio et exanclare et prosapia et Saliorum carmina vix sacerdotibus suis satis intellecta. Das Wort ἀρχαϊσμός kommt vor bei Dionys. de compos. verbor. c. 22. Dann auch ἀρχαίζω ἀρχαιολογεῖν ἀρχαιοειδές, auch ἀρχαϊκὸν κάλλος.

Die Neubildungen πεποιημένα ὀνόματα, nova fingere. Cicero hat de orat. III 38, 152 inusitatum verbum aut novatum, und im orator c. 24 nec in faciendis verbis audax et parcus in priscis. Neologismus ist kein griechisches Wort, ebensowenig wie Monolog, Biographie. Die Griechen waren viel freier und kühner darin. Quint. sagt: Graecis magis concessum est qui sonis etiam et affectibus non dubitaverunt nomina aptare, non alia libertate quam qua illi primi homines rebus appellationes dederunt. Bei den Römern war es

38, 153), who warns strongly against the archaic in *speech*, says, however, that it would give the speech a grand coloring if used in the right place; he would not be afraid to say *qua tempestate Poenus in Italiam venit* [what time the Carthaginian came into Italy], *prolem* [offspring], *sobolem* [progeny], *effari* [utter], *nuncupare* [pronounce], *non rebar* [I did not deem], or *opinabar* [I opined].[31] It is, thus, understandable that Quintilian (1, 6, 39ff.) says that a speech is defective *si egeat interprete* [if it requires an interpreter], thus, *verba a vetustate repetita* [archaic words], inasmuch as they combine majesty with novelty, are indeed excellent, but:

> *opus est modo, ut neque crebra sint haec neque manifesta, quia nihil est odiosius adfectatione, nec utique ab ultimis et iam oblitteratis repetita temporibus, qualia sunt "topper" et "antegerio" et "exanclare" et "prosapia" et Saliorum carmina vix sacerdotibus suis satis intellecta* [such words must be used sparingly and must not thrust themselves upon our notice, since there is nothing more tiresome than affectation, nor above all must they be drawn from remote and forgotten ages: I refer to such words as "*topper*" (quite), "*antegerio*" (exceedingly), "*exanclare*" (to exhaust), "*prosapia*" (a race), and the language of the Salian Hymns now scarcely understood by its own priests].

The word *archaismos* [old-world charm] appears with Dionysius (*De Composita Verborum*, 22), and then also *archaizō* [to copy the ancients (in language)], *archaiologein* [to use an old-fashioned style], *archaioeides* [old-fashioned], and *archaikon kallos* [old-fashioned beauty (of style)].

Novel constructions, *pepoiēmena onomata, nova fingere.* Cicero (*De Oratore*, 3, 38, 152) speaks of *inusitatum verbum aut novatum* [rare words or new coinages], and in the *Orator* (24), *nec in faciendis verbis audax et parcus in priscis* [to not be bold in coining words and sparing in the use of archaisms]. "Neologism" is no more a Greek word than "monologue" and "biography." The Greeks were much freer and bolder in this. Quintilian says:

> *Graecis magis concessum est, qui sonis etiam quibusdam et adfectibus non dubitaverunt nomina aptare, non alia libertate quam qua illi primi homines rebus appellationes dederunt* [the coining of new words is more permissible in Greek, for the Greeks did not hesitate to coin nouns to represent certain sounds and emotions, and in truth they were taking no greater liberty than was taken by the first men when they gave names to things].[32]

bedenklich. Celsus verbot es dem Redner ganz. Cicero hatte Glück mit den Übertragungen philosophischer termini. beatitas und beatitudo von ihm gebildet de nat. deor. I 34, 95 mit den Worten: utrumque omnino durum, sed usu mollienda nobis verba sunt. Sergius Flavius hat ens und essentia gebildet, doch beruft sich wegen des zweiten Wortes Seneca ep. 58, 6 auf Cicero und Papirius Fabianus. Reatus ist zuerst von Messalla, munerarius von Augustus aufgebracht, bald im allgemeinen Gebrauch, piratica fanden die Lehrer Quintilians noch anstössig. Cicero hielt favor und urbanus für neu, er tadelte piissimus (von Antonius gebraucht, ganz gebräuchlich in der silbernen Latinität). breviarium statt summarium erhält in der Zeit Senecas Eingang. obsequium hielt Cicero für eine Neubildung des Terenz (doch schon bei Plautus und Naevius). Cervix singularisch zuerst von Hortensius. Quintilian giebt dann die Vorschrift: si quid periculosius finxisse videbimur, quibusdam remediis praemuniendum est "ut ita dicam," "si licet dicere," "quodam modo," "permittite mihi sic uti." Nach welchen Gründen sich die Aufnahme von Neologismen entscheidet, ist nicht zu bestimmen. Horaz ars poet. 60 vergleicht den Wandel der Wörter mit dem Wechsel des Lebens, ja, es scheint noch willkürlicher und zufälliger zuzugehen v. 70:

> multa renascentur quae iam cecidere, cadentque quae nunc sunt in honore vocabula, si volet usus, quem penes arbitrium est et ius et norma loquendi.

Bei den späteren Griechen überwuchern besonders die Neubildungen von Compositionen. Lobeck redet darüber im Phrynichos p.

With the Romans, it was objectionable. Celsus entirely prohibited the rhetor from making use of it. Cicero had success with the transposition of philosophical *termini: beatitas* and *beatitudo* [happiness, blessedness] are introduced by him in *De Natura Deorum*, 1, 34, 95), with the words: *utrumque omnino durum, sed usu mollienda nobis verba sunt* [and either is certainly a hard mouthful, but words have to be softened by use. Sergius Flavius introduced *ens* [thing] and *essentia* [essence], but with respect to the second word, Seneca (*Letters*, 58, 6) refers to Cicero and Papirius Fabianus. *Reatus* [the accused in a legal case] was used first by Messalla; *munerarius* [belonging to a gladiatorial exhibition] was introduced by Augustus, and then soon came into general use; the teachers of Quintilian still found *piratica* [piracy] scandalous. Cicero believed *favor* [favor, goodwill] and *urbanus* [of or belonging to the city, urbane] to be new; he reproved *piissimus* [superlative of *pius*, meaning pious] (used by Antonius, and wholly normal in the latinity of the silver age); *breviarium* [summary] was introduced in place of *summarium* in the time of Seneca. Cicero believed *obsequium* [compliance] to be a new construction by Terence (but it was already used by Plautus and Naevius). *Cervix* [neck] was used first in the singular by Hortensius. Quintilian then gave the formula:

> *si quid periculosius finxisse videbimur, quibusdam remediis praemuniendum est: Ut ita dicam. Si licet dicere, Quodam modo, Permittite mihi sic uti* [If, however, one of our inventions seems a little risky, we must take certain measures in advance to save it from censure, prefacing it by phrases such as "so to speak," "if I may say so," "in a certain sense," or "if you will allow me to make use of such a word"].[33]

The reasons according to which the admission of neologisms is defined cannot be determined. Horace (*Ars Poetica*, 60), compares the alteration of words with the variation in life: it even appears to be more arbitrary and fortuitous there [than in life] (70):

> *multa renascentur quae iam cecidere, cadentque quae nunc sunt in honore vocabula, si volet usus, quem penes arbitrium est et ius et norma loquendi* [Many terms that have fallen out of use shall be born again, and those shall fall that are now in repute, if Usage so will it, in whose hands lies the judgment, the right and rule of speech].

With the later Greeks, the new constructions of compositions became especially overrun. Lobeck speaks of it in *Phrynichos* (600).[34]

600. Der wunderbare Prozess einer Auswahl der Sprachformen geht immer fort. Man hat gefunden, dass unter den wilden und rohen Volksstämmen Sibiriens, Afrikas und Siams schon zwei oder drei Generationen hinreichen, um das ganze Ausschen ihrer Dialekte zu verändern. Missionäre in Centalafrika versuchten die Sprache wilder Stämme niederzuschreiben und machten Sammlungen aller Wörter. Nach zehn Jahren zurückkehrend, fanden sie dieses Wörterbuch veraltet und unbrauchbar. In litterarischen Zeiten geht es langsamer, doch muss Goethe, während eines langen Lebens, eine ausserordentliche mehrmalige Neufärbung und Abänderung des Stils gemerkt haben. Wir stehen jetzt unter dem Einflusse des übermässigen Zeitungslesens, besonders nach dem Jahre 1848. Man muss sorgsamer als je sein, wenn unsere Sprache nicht allmählich den Eindruck der Gemeinheit machen soll.

VII. DER TROPISCHE AUSDRUCK

Cic. de orat. III 38, 155 sagt, die metaphorische Redeweise ist von der Nothwendigkeit im Drang der Armuth und Verlegenheit erzeugt, nachmals aber gesucht worden wegen ihrer Anmuth. "Wie die Kleidung zuerst, um die Kälte abzuwehren, erfunden, nachmals auch zum Schmuck und zur Veredlung des Körpers gebraucht wurde, so entsprang der Tropus aus Mangel und wurde häufig gebraucht, wenn er ergötzte. Selbst die Landleute reden von den Augen der Reben,[8] gemmare vites, luxuriem esse in herbis, laetas segetes, sitientes agri. Metaphern sind gleichsam geliehenes Gut, das man anderwärts nimmt, weil man es selbst nicht hat." Gegensatz der κυριολογία κυριολεξία κυριωνυμία und der τροπικὴ φράσις. Oder proprietas und improprium (ἄκυρον). Quintil. VIII 2,3 bezeichnet einmal als proprietas die niedere volksmässige, von der man nicht immer abweichen könne, da man nicht für alles passende Ausdrücke habe, z.B. müsse man iaculari auch sagen, wenn pilis geworfen werde, lapidare, wenn glebis oder testis. Dergleichen abusio oder κατάχρησις sei nothwendig. Sodann ist ihm proprietas auch die Urbedeutung der

The wondrous process of choosing new forms of language always continues. It has been found that among the savage and uncultured Siberian, African, and Siamese races of people, two or three generations are sufficient to change the whole appearance of their dialects. Missionaries in central Africa attempted to write down the language of savage tribes and made collections of all their words. Returning after ten years, they found this collection to be antiquated and useless. In literary eras, it goes more slowly, yet Goethe, during his long life, must have noticed an extraordinary and repeatedly new coloring and alteration of style. We are standing now under the influence of the extravagant reading of newspapers, especially since 1848. One must be ever more careful that our language not gradually make an impression of vulgarity.

VII. THE TROPICAL EXPRESSION

Cicero (*De Oratore*, 3, 38, 155) says that the metaphorical manner of speaking was engendered from necessity, found in the distress of poverty and embarrassment, but sought after for its grace. "Just as clothing was invented first to protect against the cold, and afterward was used for the decoration and refinement of the body, the *tropus* originated from deficiency and became commonly used when it was pleasing. Even the country folk speak of the 'eyes of the vine,'[35] *gemmare vites* [jewelled vines], *luxuriem esse in herbis* [luxurious herbage], *laetas segetes* [rich crops], and *sitientes agri* [thirsty fields]. Metaphors, in which you take what you have not got from somewhere else, are a sort of borrowing."[36] There is an opposition between the *kyriologia* [proper meaning of a word], *kyriolexia* [use of literal expressions], *kyriōnymia* [use of proper names], and the *tropikē phrasis* [figurative expression], or the *proprietas* and *improprium (akyron)* [incorrect usage]. Quintilian (8, 2, 3) first labels the low and popular as *proprietas,* from which one cannot always depart, and which does not always contain proper expressions for everything; "for example, the verb *iaculari* is especially used in the sense of 'to throw a javelin,' whereas there is no special verb appropriated to the throwing of a ball or a stake. So, too, while *lapidare* has the obvious meaning of 'to stone,' there is no special word to describe the throwing of clods or potsherds. Hence abuse or *katachrēsis* of words becomes necessary. . . .The second sense in which the word propriety is used occurs when there are a number of things all called by the

Wörter, z.B. vertex sei eigentlich contorta in se aqua, dann quidquid aliud similiter vertitur, dann die pars summa capitis (propter flexum capillorum), dann id quod in montibus eminentissimum. Die eigentlichen Bedeutungen erscheinen so als die älteren, schmucklosen. Dagegen richtig Jean Paul, Vorschule der Aesthetik: "Wie im Schreiben Bilderschrift früher war als Buchstabenschrift, so war im Sprechen die Metapher, insofern sie Verhältnisse und nicht Gegenstände bezeichnet, das *frühere* Wort, welches sich erst allmählich zum *eigentlichen Ausdrucke* entfärben musste. Das Beseelen und Beleiben fiel noch in Eins zusammen, weil noch Ich und Welt verschmolz. Daher ist jede Sprache in Rücksicht geistiger Beziehungen ein Wörterbuch erblasster Metaphern." Die Alten konnten sich die Kunst nur als eine bewusste vorstellen; die nichtkünstlerischen Metaphern—in quo proprium deest—schrieben sie (wie Quintil.) den indoctis ac non sentientibus zu. Obwohl auch der feine Mann sich oft nicht zu helfen weiss.[9] Also aus Verlegenheit und Dummheit entstehen die volksthümlichen Tropen, aus Kunst und Wohlgefallen die rednerischen. Ganz falscher Gegensatz. In gewissen Fällen ist die Sprache zu Uebertragungen gezwungen, weil Synonyma fehlen, in anderen Fällen sieht es aus, als triebe sie Luxus: dann vornehmlich, wenn wir die Uebertragungen mit den eher gebräuchlichen Ausdrükken vergleichen können, erscheint die Uebertragung als freies Kunstschaffen, die usuelle Bezeichnung als das "eigentliche" Wort.

Als Bezeichnung für Uebertragung hatten die Griechen zuerst (z. B. Isokrates) μεταφορά, auch Aristoteles. Hermogenes sagt, dass bei den Grammatikern noch μεταφορά heisse, was die Rhetoren τρόπος nannten. Bei den Römern ist tropus angenommen, bei Cicero noch translatio immutatio, später auch motus mores modi. Ueber Zahl und Unterarten der Tropen gab es erbittert Streitigkeiten: man kam zu 38 und mehr Arten. Wir besprechen Metapher, Synecdoche, Metonymie, Antonomasie, Onomatopoiie, Katachrese, Metalepsis,

"Uebertragung – transmission"

same name: in this case, the original term from which the others are derived is styled the proper term. For example, the word *vertex* means a whirl of water, or of anything else that is whirled in a like manner: then, owing to the fashion of coiling the hair, it comes to mean the top of the head, while finally, from this sense it derives the meaning of the highest point of a mountain. All these things may correctly be called *vertices*, but the proper use of the term is the first."[37] The proper meanings, therefore, seem to be the older, plainer ones. On the other hand, and correctly, Jean Paul (*Vorschule der Aesthetik*) says:[38]

> Just as in writing, where writing with hieroglyphics was older than writing with the letters of the alphabet, so it was that in speaking, the metaphor, insofar as it denotes relationships and not objects, was the *earlier* word, which had only to fade into the *proper expression*. The besouling and the embodiment still constituted a unity, because I and world were still fused. Thus, with respect to spiritual relationships, each language is a dictionary of faded metaphors.

The ancients could understand art only as conscious presentation; the inartistic metaphors—*in quo proprium deest* [when there is no literal term]—they attributed (according to Quintilian) to the *indoctis ac non sentientibus* [uneducated, and unconscious employment].[39] Yet, the cultivated man often was also unable to help himself.[40] Thus, the popular tropes originated from embarrassment and stupidity, the rhetorical tropes from art and delight. This is an entirely false contrast. In certain cases, language is forced to use metaphors because synonyms are missing, and in other cases, it seems as if it employs luxury: the metaphor appears as a free artistic creation, and the usual signification appears as the "proper" word, especially in the cases when we can compare the metaphor to the earlier, usually employed expression.

The Greeks first signified the metaphorical use by *metaphora* (Isocrates and Aristotle, for example). Hermagenes says that the grammarians still called *metaphora* what the rhetoricians called *tropos*. With the Romans, *tropus* became generally accepted, although in Cicero [we still find] *translatio* [translation], *immutatio* [alteration], and later, *motus* [movement], *mores* [usages], *modi* [modes]. There were embittered disputes over the number and subspecies of the tropes; one came to thirty-eight kinds or more. We will speak about metaphor, synecdoche, metonymy, antonomasia,

Epitheton, Allegorie, Ironie, Periphrasis, Hyperbaton, Anastrophe, Parenthesis, Hyperbel. Ueber die logische Berechtigung dieser Arten will ich nichts sagen; man muss aber die Ausdrücke verstehen. Die *Metapher* ist ein kürzeres Gleichniss, wie wiederum das Gleichniss als μεταφορὰ πλεονάζουσα bezeichnet wird. Cic. de orat. III 40, 159s. findet es verwunderlich, dass die Menschen bei dem grössten Reichthum an eigentlichen Ausdrücken doch die Metapher lieber haben. Es rühre wohl daher, weil es ein Beweis von Geistesstärke sei, das vor den Füssen Liegende zu überspringen und nach dem weit Entfernten zu greifen. Vier Fälle werden unterschieden: 1. Von zwei belebten Dingen setzt man das eine für das andere ("Scipio ist von Cato gewöhnlich 'angebellt' worden," Hund für Mensch). 2. Unbelebtes für anderes Unbelebtes Verg. Aen. VI,1: classi inmittit habenas. 3. Unbelebtes für Belebtes, z.B. wenn Achill ἕρκος 'Αχαιῶν genannt wird. 4. Belebtes für Unbelebtes, z. B. Cic. pro Lig. c. 3, 9: quid enim Tubero, tuus ille districtus in acie Pharsalica gladius agebat? cuius latus ille mucro petebat? qui sensus erat armorum tuorum? Aristot. Poetik c. 21 unterscheidet dagegen: eine Metapher ist die Uebertragung eines Wortes, dessen gewöhnliche Bedeutung eine andere ist, entweder von der Gattung auf die Art oder von der Art auf die Gattung oder von der Art auf die Art oder nach der Proportion.[10] Uebertragung von der Gattung auf die Art z.B. "dort ruht mir das Schiff" a 185, denn im Ankerplatz sein ist eine Art des Ruhens. Von der Art auf die Gattung: "schon tausende von edlen Thaten hat Odysseus verrichtet", ω 308 ἦ δὴ μυρί' 'Οδυσσεὺς ἐσθλὰ ἔοργεν denn die tausende sind viele, und der Dichter gebraucht hier jenen Ausdruck im Sinne "viele." Von der Art auf die Art: "mit dem Erze das Leben wegschöpfend," und "mit dem unverwüstlichen Erze wegschneidend," hier steht wegschneiden für schöpfen, dort schöpfen statt wegschneiden, beides sind Arten des Wegnehmens. Nach der Proportion: "wie das Alter zum Leben, so verhält sich der Abend

onomatopoeia, catachresis, metalepsis, epithet, allegory, irony, periphrasis, hyperbaton, anastrophe, parenthesis, and hyperbole. I will not speak about the logical justification of these types, but we must understand the expressions.

The *metaphor* is a shortened simile, as the simile is designated as *metaphora pleonazousa* [metaphor being exaggerated]. Cicero (*De Oratore*, 3, 40, 159ff.) finds it astonishing that men still prefer metaphors even though they have the vast riches of proper expression available. It seems to be a consequence of the fact that to leap over that which is lying before one's feet and to seize that which is far away is taken to be a proof of a strong spirit. Four cases will be distinguished:

1. Of two living things, one is put in place of the other ("Scipio is usually 'barked at' by Cato." Dog replaces man.)
2. A lifeless thing replaces another lifeless thing; for example, Virgil (*Aeneid*, 6, 1): *classi inmittit habenas* [he gave his fleet the rein].
3. A nonliving thing replaces a living thing; for example, when Achilles was called *herkos Achaiōn* [the defense (wall) of the Achaeans].
4. A living thing replaces a nonliving thing; for example Cicero (*Pro Ligurio*, 3, 9): *Quid enim tuus ille, Tubero, destrictus in acie Pharsalica gladius agebat? Cuius latus ille mucro petebat? Qui sensus erat armorum tuorum?* [What was that sword of yours doing, Tubero, the sword you drew on the field of Pharsalus? Against whose body did you aim its point? What meant those arms you bore?].

In contrast, Aristotle (*Poetics*, 21) distinguishes in this way: a metaphor is the carrying over of a word whose usual meaning is something else, either from the genus to the species, from the species to the genus, from species to species, or according to proportion.[41] Carrying over from the genus to the species: for example, "here stands my ship" (*Odyssey*, 1, 185; 24, 308), for being at anchor is a species of standing. From the species to the genus: "Odysseus has already performed thousands of noble deeds" (*Iliad*, 2, 272): *ē dē myri' Odysseus esthla eorgen*), for the word "thousands" stands for "many," and the poet uses the former expression here in the sense of "many." From species to species: "drawing off his life with the bronze," and "severing with the tireless bronze." First, "drawing off" stands for "severing," and then "severing" for "drawing off," and both are species of "taking away." According to proportion: "as old age is to life,

zum Tage, also kann man den Abend das Alter des Tages nennen und das Alter den Abend des Lebens." Streng genommen, bleibt nur diese vierte Art übrig κατὰ τὸ ἀνάλογον. Denn das Erste ist keine Metapher (das Ungenauere steht für das Genauere, nicht das Uneigentliche für das Eigentliche), die dritte Art ist nicht klar. Die zweite Art hat es nur mit engeren und weiteren Begriffssphären eines Wortes zu thun.

Ein übermässiger Gebrauch von Metaphern verdunkelt und führt zum Rätselhaften. Sodann, da es der Vorzug der Metaphern ist, einen sinnlichen Eindruck zu machen, so muss man alles Unanständige meiden: Cicero giebt de orat. III 41 die Beispiele: castratam morte Africani rem publicam, stercus curiae Glauciam. Quintilian tadelt den Vers des Furius Bibaculus: "Juppiter hibernas cana nive conspuit Alpes."

Synecdoche. Nach einem wesentlichen Theile wird der Begriff von domus bezeichnet, wenn man es tectum nennt: tectum aber ruft die Vorstellung des domus hervor, weil in der Wahrnehmung, auf welcher diese Wörter beruhen, beide Dinge zugleich auftreten: cum res tota parva de parte cognoscitur, aut de toto pars. In der Sprache sehr mächtig, wie ich schon ausführte. Bopp, Vergl. Gramm. T. II p. 417 vertheidigt die Ansicht, dass das griechische Augment ursprünglich identisch mit dem α privativum sei, d.h. dass es die Gegenwart verneine und so die Vergangenheit bezeichne. Die Sprache drückt niemals etwas vollständig aus, sondern hebt überall nur das am meisten hervorstechende Merkmal hervor: freilich ist die Negation der Gegenwart noch keine Vergangenheit, aber die Vergangenheit ist wirklich eine Negation der Gegenwart. Ein Zahn-habender ist noch kein Elephant, ein Haar-habender noch kein Löwe, und dennoch nennt das Sanskrit den Elephanten dantín, den Löwen kesín. Der Gebrauch ist natürlich für Dichter noch freier als für Redner: die Rede verträgt mucro als Schwert, tectum als Haus, aber nicht puppis als Schiff. Am meisten zulässig die freie Anwendung des numerus, z.B. Romanus für Romani, aes aurum argentum für eherne, goldene und silberne Gefässe, gemma ein aus Edelstein gefertigtes Gefäss. ἀλώπηξ Fuchspelz totum pro parte, ἐλέφας Elfenbein, χελώνη Schuldkrot, κόμαι Χαρίτεσσιν ὁμοῖαι (für Χαρίτων κόμαις). Oder

so evening is to day; thus, one can call evening the old age of the day, or old age the evening of life."[42] Taken strictly, only this fourth type, *kata to analogon* [according to proportion], remains, for the first is not a metaphor (the less precise stands for the more precise, not the improper for the proper). The third type is not clear. The second kind is concerned only with narrower and broader conceptual spheres of a word.

An excessive use of metaphor obscures and leads to enigmas. Thus, since it is preferable that one make a sensible expression, one must avoid all that is improper in using metaphors. Cicero (*De Oratore*, 3, 41, 164) gives the examples: *castratam morte Africani rem publicam* [the state was gelded by the death of Africanus], and *stercus curiae Glauciam* [Glaucia, the excrement of the Senate house]. Quintilian censures the verse of Furius Bibaculus:[43] "*Juppiter hibernas cana nive conspuit Alpes*" [Jove with white snow the wintry Alps bespewed].

Synecdoche. The concept of *domus* [house] is signified by an important part, when one calls it *tectum* [roof], but *tectum* evokes the representation of *domus* because both things appear together in the perception [upon which] both words depend: *cum res tota parva de parte cognoscitur, aut de toto pars* [the whole is known from a small part or a part from the whole].[44] It is very powerful in language, as I have already demonstrated. Bopp (*Vergleichende Grammatik*, 2)[45] defends the view that the Greek augment was originally identical with the *alpha privativum*, i.e., that it denied the present tense and thus signified the past tense. Language never expresses something completely, but stresses the most outstanding characteristic; of course, the negation of the present tense is still not the past tense, but the past tense really is a negation of the present tense. A "possessor of teeth" is still not an elephant, and a "possessor of hair" is still not a lion, yet Sanskrit calls the elephant *dantín* [tooth], and the lion *kesín* [long-haired].[46] Naturally, the usage is still freer for poets than for orators: speech tolerates *mucro* [point] for sword, *tectum* [roof] for house, but not *puppis* [stern] for ship. The most admissible is the free use of the *numerus*; for example, *Romanus* [Roman] for *Romani* [Romans], *aes* [bronze], *aurum* [gold], and *argentum* [silver], for bronze, gold, and silver vessels, and *gemma* [jewel] for a vessel made of precious stones. *Alōpēx* [fox], fur of a fox, *totum pro parte* [whole for part], *elephas* [elephant], ivory, *chelōnē* [tortoise], tortoise shell, *komai Charitessin homoiai* [hair (plural) like (the same as) the

Choeph. 175 Chor ποίαις ἐθείραις; Electra αὐτοῖσιν ἡμῖν κάρτα προσφερὴς ἰδεῖν. Dahin gehört auch das von Huhnken bezeichnete genus loquendi quo quis facere dicitur, quod factum narrat, z. B. Homerus Venerem sauciat sagitta humana.

Metonymia, Setzung eine Hauptwortes für ein anderes, auch ὑπαλλαγή. eius vis est, pro eo quod dicitur, causam propter quam dicitur, ponere. In der Sprache sehr mächtig: die abstrakten Substantiva sind Eigenschaften in uns und ausser uns, die ihren Trägern entrissen werden, und als selbständige Wesen hingestellt werden. Die audacia bewirkt, dass Männer audaces sind; im Grunde ist das eine Personifikation, wie die der römischen Begriffsgötter Virtutes Cura u.s.w. Jene Begriffe, die lediglich unserer Empfindung ihr Entstehen verdanken, werden als das innere Wesen der Dinge vorausgesetzt: wir schieben den Erscheinungen als *Grund* unter, was doch nur Folge ist. Die Abstrakta erregen die Täuschung, als seien *sie* jenes Wesen, welches die Eigenschaften bewirkt, während sie nur in Folge jener Eigenschaften von uns bildliches Dasein erhalten. Sehr lehrreich der Uebergang der εἴδη in ἰδέαι bei Plato: hier ist die Metonymie, Vertauschung von Ursache und Wirkung, vollständig. In der jetzigen Bedeutung von "alt" ist Ursache und Wirkung vertauscht, eigentlich "gewachsen." Pallida mors, tristis senectus, praeceps ira. Die erfundenen Dinge werden nach ihren Erfindern, die unterworfenen nach ihren Unterwerfern genannt. Neptunus Vulcanus, vario Marte pugnare. Homerische Helden als typische Repräsentanten ihrer Fertigkeiten. Automedon für "Fuhrmann," die Aerzte Machaones.

Antonomasia est dictio per accidens proprium significans. Statt eines Eigennamens ein ihn kennzeichnendes Epitheton. Romanae eloquentiae princeps für Cicero, Africani nepotes als Bezeichnung

Graces] for *Charitōn komais* [hair (plural, i.e., hairs)]. Or *Choephori* (175, Chorus): *poiais etheirais* [well-made locks?]; Electra: *autoisin hēmin karta prospherēs idein* [our own (locks are) very much similar to behold]. The *genus loquendi quo quis facere dicitur, quod factum narrat* [the genre of speech in which someone is said to be the perpetrator of the deeds that he reports], which Ruhnken mentions, also belongs to this;[47] for example, *Homerus Venerem sauciat sagitta humana* [Homer wounded Venus with a human arrow].

Metonymy, the placement of one noun for another, also called *hypollagē* [an interchange, exchange], *cuius vis est, pro eo quod dicitur causam propter quam dicitur ponere* [the substitution of the cause for which we say a thing in place of the thing to which we refer].[48] It is very powerful in speech: the abstract *substantiva* are qualities inside us and around us, which are torn away from their substrata and set forth as independent essences. The *audacia* [courage] causes men to be *audaces* [courageous]; at bottom, this is a personification, like that of the Roman concept-gods, such as Virtutes, Cura, etc. These concepts, which owe their origin only to our experiences, are proposed *a priori* to be the intrinsic essences of the things: we attribute to the appearances as their cause that which still is only an effect. The *abstracta* evoke the illusion that they themselves are these essences which cause the qualities, whereas they receive a metaphorical reality only from us, because of those characteristics. The transition from the *eidē* [originally, shape or form of that which is seen] to *ideai* [ideal forms] by Plato is very instructive; here, metonymy, the substitution of cause and effect, is complete. In the present meaning of "*alt*" [old], literally "*gewachsen*" [grown], cause and effect are exchanged. *Pallida mors* [pale death], *tristique senectus* [sad old age], *praecipitem iram* [headlong anger], are examples.[49] Things invented will be named after their inventors; those things that are subjugated will be named after their conquerors. *Neptunus* [the sea], *Vulcanus* [fire], *vario Marte pugnatum est* [they fought with varying success], are examples. Homer's heroes [are named] as typical practitioners of their skills: Automedon for "wagoner," Machaones for physicians.

Antonomasia est dictio per accidens proprium significans [Antonomasia is diction signifying a property by means of an accidental trait]. A characteristic epithet is used instead of a proper name, for example *Romanae eloquentiae princeps* [the prince of Roman eloquence] for Cicero; *Africani nepotes* [Africanus' nephews] for the Gracchi.

der Gracchen. *Onomatopoiia* est dictio ad imitandum sonum vocis confusae ficta, ut cum dicimus hinnire equos, balare oves, stridere vaccas(?), et cetera his similia. *Catachresis* wird nur als tropus betrachtet, wenn zu ihrer Einführung keine Noth besteht (wie bei "silberner Hufeisen"). Cicero führt an grandis oratio pro longa, minutus animus pro parvo. Dann häufig in der Vertauschung der Sinnesthätigkeiten κτύπον δεδόρκα, Aeschylus. Sept. 99. Beispiele bei Lobeck Rhemat. S. 333ff. παιὰν δὲ λάμπαι, bei Soph.; Il. II 127 λεύσσω παρὰ νηυσὶ πυρὸς δηίοιο ἰωήν (das Brausen, das Geschrei); Soph. Aj. 785 ὅρα ὁποῖ᾽ ἔπη θροεῖ. Anders Hesiod, Erg. 612: βότρυας χρὴ δεῖξαι ἠελίῳ δέκα τ᾽ ἤματα καὶ δέκα νύκτας. *Metalepsis* transsumptio sehr künstlicher tropus λέξις ἐκ συνωνυμίας τὸ ὁμωνύμον δηλοῦσα, wie wenn Odyss. O 299 die νῆσοι ὀξεῖαι θοαί heissen. θοόν und ὀξύ ist synonym (nämlich κάτα τήν κίνησιν), Homonym aber mit ὀξύ sind die νῆσοι ὀξεῖαι (die Spitzinseln in der Nähe Anatoliens). Quintilian interpretiert: est enim haec in metalepsi natura ut inter id quod transfertur et in quod transfertur, sit medius quidam gradus, nihil ipse significans, sed praebens transitum. Wenn Cicero sus für Verres sagt, so steht dazwischen ein verres, nicht als Namen sondern als Thier. Eustath. findet eine metalepsis, Il. Θ 164 ἔρρε κακὴ γλήνη für ἔρρε ὃ δειλὸν κοράσιον. Denn κόρη Mädchen und κόρη Augapfel sind homonym, aber κόρη und γλήνη synonym. *Epitheton.* Die Dichter, sagt Quintil. bedienen sich der Epitheta in reichem Masse, ihnen ist es genug wenn sie überhaupt nur zu ihren Hauptwörtern passen, beim Reden dürfen sie nur angewandt werden, wenn ohne dieselben etwas fehlen oder weniger gesagt sein

Onomatopoiia est dictio ad imitandum sonum vocis confusae ficta, ut cum dicimus hinnire equus, balare oves, stridere vaccas (?)[50] *et cetera his similia* [Onomatopoeia is diction made to imitate the sound of a blurred voice, as when we say that the horse neighs, the sheep bleat, the cows moo, and other things of this sort].

Catachresis is regarded as a trope only when there is no need to introduce it (as in "silver horseshoe"). Cicero cites *grandis oratio* [lengthy speech] for *longa* [long], *minutus animus* [meagre spirit] for *parvo* [small]. Then [it appears] frequently in the confusion of sensory activities: *ktypon dedorka* [he saw the noise], Aeschylus (*Sept.,* 99). Examples in Lobeck (*Rhemat.,* pp. 333ff.) include: *paian de lampai* [the chanted prayer rings clear] in Sophocles. (*Iliad,* 16,[51] 127): *leusso para nēusi pyros dēioio iōēn* [Lo, I see by the ships the rush of consuming fire] (the noise, the screams). Sophocles (*Ajax,* 785): *hora hopoi epē throei* [look at what words he is thrusting around]. Differently, Hesiod (*Erga,* 611–12): *botruas chrē deixai ēeliōi deka t' hēmata kai deka nyktas* [One has to expose the grapes to the sun for ten days and nights].

Metalepsis (transumptio) is a very artificial trope, *lexis ek synōnymias to homōnymon dēlousa* [a word that reveals a homonym from synonyms], as when in *Odyssey* (15, 299) the *nēsoi* [islands] are called *oxeiai thoai* [sharp peaks], *thoon* [sharp] and *oxy* [pointed] are synonymous (namely *kata tēn kinēsin* [virtually]). The *nēsoi oxeiai* (the pointed islands not far from Anatolia), however, are homonymous with *oxy* [sharp]. Quintilian interprets:

> *est enim haec in metalepsi natura ut inter id quod transfertur et in quod transfertur, sit medius quidam gradus, nihil ipse significans, sed praebens transitum* [It is the nature of *metalēpsis* to form a kind of intermediate step between the term transferred and the thing to which it is transferred, having no meaning in itself, but merely providing a transition].[52]

When Cicero says *sus* [pig, sow] for *Verres*, the connecting link is a *verres* [pig, boar], not as a name but as an animal.[53] Eusthathius finds a metalepsis in *Iliad* (8, 164): *erre kakē glēnē* [away, weak girl!] for *erre ō deilon korasion* [away, O cowardly maiden!]. For *korē*, girl, and *korē*, eyeball, are homonyms, while *korē* [eyeball] and *glēnē* [eyeball] are synonymous.

Epithet. The poets, Quintilian says, use epithets abundantly, as long as they fit their nouns; but in oratory they may be used only when otherwise something would be missing or less would be said.

würde. *Allegoria*, inversio aut aliud verbis, aliud sensu ostendit, aut etiam interim contrarium: die erstere Gattung die eigentl. Allegorie, die letztere die Ironie. Virg. Georg. II 542: et iam tempus equum fumantia solvere colla, d.h., das Gedicht zu beendigen. Oder Horaz od 1, 14: O navis, referent in mare te novi fluctus. *Rein* wird die Allegorie in der Rede selten angewandt, meist mit apertis gemischt (mit nicht allegorischen Bestandtheilen), rein z.B. Cicero: hoc miror, hoc queror quemquam hominem ita pessum dare velle, ut etiam navem perforet, in qua ipse naviget. Cic. pro Murena 17, 35: quod enim fretum, quem Euripum tot motus, tantas tam varias habere putatis agitationes, commutationesque fluctuum, quantas perturbationes et quantas aestus habet ratio comitiorum? Man muss sich hüten, nicht aus dem Bilde zu fallen: viele, sagt Quintil., fangen mit Sturm an und hören mit Feuer oder Einsturz auf. Das *Räthsel*, eine ganz dunkle Allegorie, ist in der Rede unstatthaft. Das passende Grammatikenbeispiel: mater me genuit, eadem [*sic*] mox gignitur ex me (Wasser—Eis—Wasser). *Ironie* illusio: Die Worte besagen gerade das Gegenteil von dem, was sie zu besagen scheinen. Als Arten der Ironie unterscheidet Quintilian σαρκασμός (plena odio atque hostilis irrisio) μετὰ σεσηρότος τοῦ προσώπου λεγόμενος (mit zum grinsenden Lachen verzogenem Gesicht, Lat.: exacerbatio), ἀστεϊσμός (eine witzige Selbstironie) μυκτηρισμός und χλευασμός die auf andere gerichtete Ironie. In der Form eines leisen Spotts geben sie den χαριεντισμός. Dann die ἀντιφρασις eine λέξις διὰ τοῦ ἐναντίου ἢ παρακειμένου τὸ ἐναντίον παριστῶσα χωρὶς ὑποκρίσεως. Il. O, 11

Allegory, (inversio) aut aliud verbis, aliud sensu ostendit, aut etiam interim contrarium [either presents one thing in words and another in meaning, or else something absolutely opposed to the meaning of the words]:[54] the first type is allegory in the strict sense, the second is irony, Virgil (*Georgics*, 2, 542) *et iam tempus equum fumantia solvere colla* ['tis time to loose our horses' streaming necks], i.e., to end the poem. Or Horace (*Odes*, 1, 14): *O navis, referent in mare te novi fluctus* [O ship, new waves will bear thee back to sea].[55] Allegory is seldom used in *pure form* in discourse, usually mixed with *apertis* (nonallegorical components), purely, e.g., Cicero:

> *hoc miror, hoc queror quemquam hominem ita pessum dare velle, ut etiam navem perforet, in qua ipse naviget* [What I marvel at and complain of is this, that there should exist any man so set on destroying his enemy as to scuttle the ship on which he himself is sailing].[56]

Cicero (*Pro Murena*, 17, 35):

> *quod enim fretum, quem Euripum tot motus, tantas tam varias habere putatis agitationes, commutationesque fluctuum, quantas perturbationes et quantas aestus habet ratio comitiorum?* [for what strait, what Euripus, do you think has so many eddies so great and so variable disturbances and changes of current, as are the turmoils and surges in the system of elections?][57]

One must beware of mixing metaphors; many, says Quintilian, begin with a storm and end with fire or collapse. The *riddle*, a short, very obscure allegory, is not permitted in a speech. The appropriate grammar-book example: *mater me genuit, autem mox gignitur ex me* [My mother gave birth to me but soon she is born of me] (Water—Ice—Water).

Irony (illusio): the words say exactly the opposite of what they seem to say. Quintilian distinguishes *sarcasmos (plena odio atque hostilis irrisio)* [sarcasm (full of hatred and hostile derision)] *meta sesērotos tou prosōpou legomenos*, with the face distorted into a grinning laugh (Latin: *exacerbatio*), *asteismos* [wit, ironical self-deprecation, mock modesty] (a witty self-irony), *myktērismos* [sarcasm] and *chleuasmos* [mockery, scoffing], irony aimed at someone else. In the form of a gentle mockery one has *charientismos* [wit]. Then *antiphrasis*: a *lexis dia tou enantiou ē parakeimenou to enantion paristōsa chōris hypokriseōs* [word that by means of the opposite of reality presents the opposite of what the speaker says].[58] Homer (*Iliad*, 15,

ἐπεὶ οὔ μιν ἀφαυρότατος βάλ' 'Αχαιῶν. Dazu gehört der *Euphemismus*. Dann die λιτότης (der Kunstausdruck nur bei Servius Virg. Georg. 1, 125 und bei Horaz Scholiasten (ungefähr identisch mit der ἀντίφρασις). *Oxymoron*, Verbindung eines Subjekts mit einem sein Wesen negirenden Prädikat. ἄχαρις χάρις, ἀπόλεμος πόλεμος, ἄπολις πόλις. Die περίφρασις circumlocutio circuitio circuitus loquendi gehört besser zu den rhet. Figuren und nicht zu den Tropen. Nur zum Schmuck z.B. in βίη 'Ηρακληείη, μένος Ατρείδαο, ἴς Τηλεμάχοιο.

Das ὑπέρβατον, verbi transgressio, die Hervorhebung eines bedeutsamen Wortes durch seine Stellung an Anfang oder Schluss des Satzes. Die ἀναστροφή bei bloss zwei Worten z.B. die Nachstellung der Praeposition: meorum quibus de rebus. *Diacope* oder *Tmesis*, Trennung eines Compositum durch ein dazwischen geschobenes Wort: septem subjecta trioni, bei Virg. Georg III 381. *Dialysis* oder *Parenthesis*, Einschaltung eines anderen Satzes in einen Satz. Auch das *Hyperbaton* ist eigentlich kein Tropus. Die ὑστερολογία sensuum ordo praeposterus das, was man zuerst sagen müsste, sagt man später. Virg. Aen II 353: moriamur et in media arma ruamus. Oder τροφὴν καὶ γένεσιν. Die ὑπερβολή Übertreibung der Wahrheit, um eine Sache zu vergrössern oder zu verkleinern. Verschiedene Weisen: man sagt entweder mehr als geschehen kann oder geschehen ist, Hor. od 1,1, 36: sublimi feriam sidera vertice. Oder wir heben die Dinge durch eine Vergleichung, Il. A 249: τοῦ καὶ ἀπὸ γλώσσης μέλιτος γλυκίων ῥέεν αὐδή. Die Hyperbol sucht sich durch andere Tropen zu stärken. Die Gefahr der κακοζηλία sehr gross.

VIII. DIE RHETORISCHEN FIGUREN

Bei den Tropen handelt es sich um Übertragungen: Wörter statt anderer Wörter gesetzt: an Stelle des Eigentlichen das Uneigentliche. Bei den Figuren giebt es keine Übertragungen. Es sind kunstmässig geänderte Formen des Ausdrucks, Abweichungen vom Usuellen, doch keine Übertragungen. Doch ist die ganze Bestimmung sehr

ll): *epei ou min aphaurotatos bal' Achaiōn* [For not the weakest of the Achaeans was it who had smitten him]. *Euphemism* belongs here. Then *litotēs* (the technical term only in Servius: Virgil [*Georgics*, l, 125] and the *Scholiasts* of Horace, approximately identical with *antiphrasis*).

Oxymoron, combination of a subject with a predicate that negates its essence: *acharis charis* [unlovely loveliness],[59] *apolemos polemos* [unwarlike war],[60] *apolis polis* [a city that is no city, i.e. a ruined city].[61] *Periphrasis*: *circumlocutio, circuitio, circuitus loquendi* should be classified among the rhetorical figures rather than among the tropes. Only decoratively, e.g. in *biē Heraklēeiē*,[62] *menos Atreidao*,[63] is *Tēlemachoio*.[64]

Hyperbaton, *verbi transgressio* [transposition of a word], is the emphasis given to a significant word by its position at the beginning or end of a sentence. It is called *anastrophē* if only two words are involved, e.g. the placing back of a preposition: *meorum quibus de rebus* [concerning which things of my friends]. *Diacope* or *tmesis*, separation of a *compositum* by an interjected word; *septem subjecta trioni* [beneath the Northern Bear], in Virgil (*Georgics*, 3, 381). *Dialysis* or *parenthesis*, insertion of one sentence into another sentence. Even the *hyperbaton* is not really a trope. *Hysterologia, sensuum ordo praeposterus* [inverted order of meanings], what would have to be said first is said later. Virgil (*Aeneid*, 2, 353): *moriamur et in media arma ruamus* [So let us die and rush into arms]. Or *trophēn kai genesin* [the care and birth].[65] *Hyperbolē*, exaggeration of the truth to magnify or minimize a thing. Different ways: one either says more than can or has happened, Horace (*Odes* 1, 1, 36): *sublimi feriam sidera vertice* [My forehead will clang against the stars].[66] Or we enhance a thing by a comparison, *Iliad* (A 249): *tou kai apo glōssēs melitos glykiōn rheen audē* [he from whose tongue flowed speech sweeter than honey]. The hyperbole tends to be strengthened by other tropes. The danger of *kakozēlia* [affectation] is very great.[67]

VIII. THE RHETORICAL FIGURES

Tropes deal with transferences: words are used instead of other words: the figurative is used instead of the literal. The figures of rhetoric involve no transference. They are artistically changed forms of expression, deviations from the usual, but not transferences. But the

schwer. Figura (σχῆμα) sit arte aliqua novata forma dicendi. Formae et lumina, sagt Cicero orat. 181, luminibus, quae Graeci quasi aliquos gestus orationis σχήματα vocant. Varianten von Satzformationen, die eher ein wesentlicher Unterschied in der Bedeutung nach ihrer Form theils als Vermehrung, theils als Verminderung, theils als Umänderung derjenigen Ausdrucksmittel erscheinen, welche sonst regelmässig und usuell sind. Mehreren Lautbildern und Lautfigurationen kommt dieselbe Bedeutung zu und die Seele wird zur Bildung derselben Vorstellung angeregt. Mehr will "Bedeutung" nicht sagen: *kein* Ausdruck bestimmt und umgränzt eine Seelenbewegung ganz fest, dass er als die *eigentliche* Darstellung der Bedeutung angesehen werden könnte. Jeder Ausdruck ist nur Symbol, nicht die Sache; und Symbole können sich unter einander vertreten. Es bleibt eine *Wahl* möglich. Eine Häufung von Ausdrucksmitteln (Pleonasmus) will die Vorstellung gleichsam zum Verweilen einladen, die Weglassung von Wörtern (Ellipse) zeigt ein Streben nach Beschleunigung an und erregt das Gemüth. Die Vertauschung von Wortformen (Enallage) und Stellungsveränderungen (Hyperbaton) zieht eine Erhöhung der Aufmerksamkeit nach sich.

Schwer ist zu bestimmen, ob es eine grammatische oder eine rhetorische Figur ist: eine feste Grenzlinie zwischen der Art, wie der Redende den Seelenmoment darstellt, und dem allegoricus usus kann oft nicht gezogen werden. Die Sprache gestaltet ja auch individuelle Formationen, und nun hängt es von dem schwankenden Urtheil über das mehr oder minder Gebräuchliche ab, ob wir eine Figur für grammatisch oder rhetorisch achten.

Pleonasmus (1) Überflüssige Ausdrücke im Satz, weil entweder das, was sie bezeichnen seinem Inhalt nach in diesem Satz schon genugsam bezeichnet ist (Pleonasmus im engeren Sinn) oder weil sie eines bestimmt angebbaren Inhalts ermangele (Parapleroma). Der Grammatiker Tryphon verglich die Expletiv-Conjunktionen δὲ ῥα νυ που τοι θην ἄρ δῆτα περ πω μεν ἂν αὖ οὖν κεν γε mit dem Stroh, welches beim Einpacken zerbrechlicher Gefässe verwandt wird. In sorgfältiger Rede wirken sie meistens rhythmisch als complementa numerorum. Isocrates gefällt sich in Herbeiführung musikal. Wirkungen durch Verwendung von Füllwörtern. Mancherlei wird im Laufe der Zeit zu Pleonasmen multo usu ἴδμεν ἐνὶ φρεσὶ, λευκὸς ἰδεῖν, ἀνὴρ ῥήτωρ, novos adolescentulos. Es sind unbeabsichtigte

entire determination is very difficult. *Figura (schēma) sit arte aliqua novata forma dicendi* [We shall then take a figure *(schēma)* to mean a form of expression to which a new aspect is given by art].[68] *Formae et lumina* says Cicero, (*Orator*, 181), *luminibus, quae Graeci quasi aliquos gestus orationis schemata vocant* [figures and embellishments ... which the Grecks call schemata, as it were some gestures of speech].

Variants of sentence formations [convey] an essential difference in meaning by their form. Some seem to be an increase, some a diminution, some a change of the means of expression that otherwise are regular and usual. Several phonetic spellings (*Lautbilder*) and sound-configurations have the same meaning; and the soul is stimulated to form the same idea. "Meaning" means no more than that: *no* expression determines and delimits a movement of soul with such rigidity that it could be regarded as the *actual* statement of the meaning. Every expression is just a symbol and not the thing; and symbols can be interchanged. A *choice* always remains possible. An accumulation of means of expression (*pleonasmus*) seeks as it were to invite the idea to tarry; the omission of words (*ellipsis*) shows a striving to accelerate and stimulates the mind. Substitution of word forms (*enallage*) and changes of position (*hyperbaton*) result in heightened attention.

It is hard to determine whether it is a grammatical or a rhetorical figure; a solid boundary often cannot be drawn between the way the speaker represents the content of his mind and the *allegoricus usus*. For the language also shapes individual formations, and whether we consider a figure to be grammatical or rhetorical depends on the uncertain judgment of the more or less customary.

Pleonasm: (1) superfluous expressions in the sentence, because either what we designate in the sentence is already sufficiently designated (pleonasm in the narrower sense) or because it lacks a specifically statable content (*parapleroma*). The grammarian Tryphon compared the expletive conjunctions *de, rha, nu, pou, toi, thēn, ar, dēta, per, pō, men, an, au, oun, ken, ge* with the straw that is used in packing fragile porcelain. In polished discourse they usually have a rhythmic effect as *complementa numerorum* [fillers in poetry]. Isocrates delights in creating musical effects by using filler words (*Füllwörter*). Some terms become pleonasms in the course of time by a great deal of use: *idmen eni phresi, leukos idein, anēr rhētor, novos adolescentulos* ["we know in our minds," "white, to look at," "a man

Pleonasmen, überflüssige Genauigkeit, während die eigentlich rhetorischen Pleonasmen, über die genügende Feststellung des Sinnes hinaus, Wirkungen individueller Art beabsichtigen. Ursprünglich rhetorisch ist der Pleonasmus des Dativus ethicus. Oder wenn Substantive durch ein folgendes Pronomen wieder aufgenommen werden (epanalepsis). Dann wenn ein Wort desselben Namens dem Verbum beigefügt wird οἰκεῶ τὴν οἰκίαν, σοφὸς τὴν σοφίαν. (2) Die zweite Art des pleonastischen Ausdrucks ist Perissologia, nur wie ein längeres Verweilen der Seele bei dem dargestellten Moment auszudrücken. Wenn sich ein bestimmter Begriff nicht einfach mit seinem Worte bezeichnet findet, sondern umschrieben wird, so oft durch Periphrasis. λέξις περιττή keiner wagt nur eine wegen Wortaufwand tadelswerthe Rede, sondern eine durch Fülle ausgezeichnete. Eine gewisse behagliche Ruhe, sinngewisseres Abwägen, aber auch Würde und Majestät finden durch die Perissologie ihren Ausdruck. Dazu Epitheta oder Epexegesen, die sich von selbst verstehen—das epitheton ornans. Dann Häufung von synonymen Ausdrücken, die Seele kann sich (wie beim Zorn) nicht gleich von einer Sache freimachen. (3) Die Tautologie, das Gesagte nicht nur mit demselben Sinn sondern denselben Worten wiederholt. πάθος ποιοῦσι οἱ διπλασιασμοί z.B., Corydon Corydon in Vergil. Ecl. 2, 69. παλιλλογία quamvis sint sub aqua, sub aqua maledicere temptant, von den in Frösche verwandelten Bauern, Ov. Hist VI 376. Mit Nachdruck fangen mehrere Glieder der Rede mit demselben Wort an in den Epanephora. Cic. Philipp XII, 12: sed credunt improbis, credunt turbulentis, credunt suis. Das Gegentheil der Antistrophe. Cic. Philipp. I, 10, de exilio reducti a mortuo, civitas data a mortuo, sublata vectigalia a mortuo. Wiederholung desselben Anfangs- und Schlussworts, Symploke, Cic., pro Milone II, 22: quis eos postulavit? Appius. Quis produxit? Appius. Dann kann das Schlusswort eines

who is an orator," "youthful twelve-year-olds"]. These are unintentional pleonasms, superfluous precision, whereas the genuinely rhetorical pleonasms intend effects of an individual kind, beyond the adequate statement of the meaning. The pleonasm of the ethical dative was originally rhetorical. Or when nouns are taken up again by a subsequent pronoun (*epanalepsis*). Then when a word of the same name is added to the verb, *oikeō tēn oikian, sophos tēn sophian* ["I am housing in the house," "being wise as far as wisdom is concerned"].

(2) The second kind of pleonastic expression, *perissologia*, is used to express merely a longer sojourn of the soul with the depicted factor. When a certain concept is not simply designated by a word but told in a roundabout way, that is often *periphrasis*. *Lexis peritte* [redundant speech]: no one dares to give a speech which can be criticized for verbosity rather than one characterized by abundance. A certain casual calmness, deliberation to be more certain of meaning, but also dignity and majesty are expressed by *perissologia*. In addition, [there are] epithets or epexegeses which are self-evident—the *epitheton ornans*. Then [there is] an accumulation of synonymous expressions, the soul can (as in anger) not immediately detach itself from the subject.

(3) *Tautology*, the statement is repeated not just with the same meaning but in the same words. *Pathos poiousi hoi diplasiasmoi* [doubling inflicts suffering].[69] E.g. *Corydon Corydon*, in Virgil (*Eclogues*, 2, 69). *Palillogia: quamvis sint sub aqua, sub aqua maledicere temptant* ["repetitions": although they are underwater, even underwater they try to curse], said of the farmers metamorphosed into frogs (Ovid, *Histories*, 6, 376).

Emphasis is created by *epanaphora*, in which phrases begin with the same word. Cicero (*Philippics*, 12, 12, 29): *sed credunt improbis, credunt turbulentis, credunt suis* [but they believe the dishonest, they believe the turbulent, they believe their friends]. [This is] the opposite of *antistrophe*. Cicero (*Philippics*, 1, 10): *de exilio reducti a mortuo, civitas data . . . a mortuo, . . . sublata vectigalia a mortuo* [called back from exile by a dead man, the right of citizenship given . . . by a dead man, . . . exemption of taxes by a dead man]. *Symploke* is repetition of the same initial and final words. Cicero (*Pro Milone*, 2, 22): *quis eos postulavit? Appius. Quis produxit? Appius* [who demanded them? Appius. Who led them forth? Appius]. Then the last word of a sentence can serve as the first word of the following

Satzes als Anfangswort des folgenden dienen Cic. Catil. 1,1. hic tamen vivit. Vivit? Immo vero etiam in senatum venit. Die *Ellipse*. Im allgemein Auslassung von Worten in einem Satze, so dass das Fehlende aus dem Zusammenhange ergänzt werden kann. Die grammatische Ellipse ist so zum usus geworden, dass die ausgefüllte Rede missfällt, "er hat den kürzeren (Halm) gezogen." Entstanden einmal aus phonetischen Gründen, damit der Lautkörper gedrängter erscheine. Jungfr. v. Orl. II,2 "ich liebe (den) wer mir Gutes thut und hasse (den) wer mich verletzt und ist es der eigne Sohn, den ich geboren (welcher mich verletzt, so ist er) desto hassenswerther." Dann ist [es] des Satzes Veranlassung, welche nicht vollständig bezeichnet werden soll "Wenn er (doch) [mit ruchlos frechem Übermuth / Den eigenen Schoss] verletzt, [der ihn getragen]," unbestimmte Ergänzung, Aposiopesis. Dann das Asyndeton "ich darf ihn hassen, (denn) ich hab' ihn geboren" Mit ἔλλειψις bezeichnen die Alten auch die Auslassung eines Buchstaben oder einer Silbe. Quintilian bezeichnet einmal damit ein vitium detractionis, dann stellt er sie mit der Synecdoche zusammen, da auch bei ihr ein Wort aus anderen ergänzt wurde: endlich IX 3, 58 bespricht er die figurae quae per detractionem fiunt. (1) cum subtractum verbum aliquod satis in ceteris intelligitur, (2) in quibus verba decenter pudoris gratia subtrahuntur, (3) per detractionem figura, cui conjunctiones eximuntur. (ἀσύνδετον), (4) das sogenannte ἐπεζευγμένον, in qua unum ad verbum plures sententiae referuntur, quarum unaquaeque desideraret illud, si sola poneretur, z.B. Cic pro Cluentio 6,15, vicit pudorem libido, timorem audacia, rationem amentia. Sehr verworrene Unterscheidung, grammatisch und rhetorisch verwechselt. Ellipse im einfachen Satz νίφει ὕει βροντᾷ ἀστράπτει es fehlt Ζεύς oder ὁ θεός. σημάνοει ἐσάλπιγξε (ὁ σαλπιγκτής), ἐκήρυξε (ὁ κήρυξ). Dann fehlt die copula Cicero, Milo.

one, Cicero (*Catilina*, 1,1): *hic tamen vivit. Vivit? Immo vero etiam in senatum venit* [This man, however, lives. Lives? In fact he even comes into the Senate].

Ellipsis. Generally, the omission of words in a sentence so that what is missing can be inferred from the context. Grammatical ellipsis has become so customary that fully explicit speech is displeasing, "*er hat den kürzeren (Halm) gezogen*" [he drew the short end (of the straw)]. It once originated for phonetic reasons so that the utterance (*Lautkörper*) would appear more compact. Schiller (*Jungfrau von Orleans*, 2, 2): "I love (the one) who is good to me and hate (the one) who harms me, even if it is my own son, to whom I gave birth (who injures me, for then he is) all the more hateful." Then there is the sentence's occasion which is not supposed to be characterized completely. "But if [with impiously insolent arrogance] / he injures [the very womb that bore him]!" with an unspecified completion, *Aposiopesis.* Then *asyndeton:* "I may hate him, (for) I gave birth to him." The ancients also called the omission of a letter or a syllable *elleipsis.* Quintilian once so labeled a *vitium detractionis* [defect of omission], then he groups [it] together with synecdoche, since with it too a word is supplied from others; finally (in 9, 3, 58) he discusses the *figurae quae per detractionem fiunt, (1) cum subtractum verbum aliquod satis in ceteris intelligitur, (2) in quibus verba decenter pudoris gratia subtrahuntur, (3) per detractionem figura, cui conjunctiones eximuntur (asyndeton)* [figures produced by omission: (1) when the word omitted may be clearly gathered from the context, (2) in which words are decently omitted to spare our modesty, (3) by omission, when the connecting particles are omitted].[70] (4) The so-called *epezeugmenon, in qua unum ad verbum plures sententiae referentur, quarum unaquaeque desideraret illud, si sola poneretur, e.g. Cicero. (Pro Cluentio, 6, 15), vicit pudorem libido, timorem audacia, rationem amentia* [*epezeugmenon*, in which a number of clauses are all completed by the same verb, which would be required by each singly if they stood alone, e.g. Cicero (*Pro Cluentio*, 6, 15), "Lust conquered shame, boldness fear, madness reason"].[71]

Very confusing distinction, confuses grammatical and rhetorical. Ellipsis in a simple sentence: *niphei huei brontai astraptei* [He snows, rains, thunders, and emits lightning] (missing is *Zeus* or *ho theos* [god]); *sēmanoei esalpinxe (ho salpinktēs), ekēryxe (ho kēryx)* [(the trumpeter) trumpeted, (the herald) heralded "upon a signal"]. Then the copula is missing, Cicero (*Pro Milone*, 14): *summum ius summa iniuria, nihil per vim Milo* [The highest law (is) the greatest injury.

14 summum ius summa iniuria; nihil per vim Milo. Ellipsen, die ersten Bestimmungen des einfach erweiterten Satzes treffend quae cum dimisserat, finem ille (fecit), nihil ad rem, dextra sinistra (manu) παῖσον διπλῆν Soph. El. 1415. Im Latein lässt man die einen Nachsatz einleitenden Worte "so sage ich" "so wisse" aus. Cic. ad Att. 3,18: quod scribis te audire me etiam mentali errore ex dolore affici—mihi vero mens integra est. Das Fehlen des Nachsatzes im Griechischen heisst ἀνανταπόδοτον. Mit ἐπεφευγμένον ζεῦξις oder ἀπὸ κοινοῦ bezeichnet man die Weglassung von Worten, die beim zusammengezogenen Satz eintritt; für Reihenbezüge hatte man den terminus σύλληψις. "was einem von jenen zukommt, wird auch auf den anderen übertragen." Von diesen Ausdrücken ist das Zeugma in Gebrauch geblieben, hat aber die Bedeutung der σύλληψις bekommen. Tacit. Annal. II, 20: Germanicus quod arduum sibi, cetera legatis permisit, zu sibi "er behielt sich vor." (Zeugma verwechselt, wie arsis und thesis) Cic. Tusc. 5,40: nostri graece fere nesciunt, nec Graeci latine (sciunt).

Die *Enallage*. In der Sprache erscheinen viele Synonym-Schöpfungen, der logische Verstand würde vieles ausschieden. Die Wissenschaft der Synonymik sucht das Wesen der sinnverwandten Sprachbilder mit einer Schärfe festzustellen, die das Wesen der Sache nicht trifft. Um dieselben Bezeichnungen der Begriffe auszudrücken durch verschiedenartige Mittel, sind Synonyme die Bezeichnungsform. Das ist die Enallage—sofern die angewandten Ausdrucksmittel sich vom usus entfernen. Die lateinische Sprache kann die Causalität durch Conjunktion ausdrücken: nam, enim, etenim, oder eo, ideo, idcirco, propterea; durch Adverbia: cur, quae, quam, obviam; durch Präpositionen: propter; durch Casus: Ablativ, Genitiv; durch modi; durch Partizipien; usw.—alles dem usus gemäss, also keine *Figur*. Aber wenn bei laetus statt quod oder Ablat. sich Genit. findet Dido—laeta laborum Än XI, 73, so ist durch eine Vertauschung Enallage. Beispiele, das Adjektiv für das Adverbium Αἰδὼς οὐρανία ἀνέπτη. Hor. Ars poet. 268: vos exemplaria Graeca nocturna versate

Milo did nothing by violence]. Ellipses pertaining to the first assertions of a simple extension of a sentence: *quae cum dimiserat, finem
ille (fecit), nihil ad rem, dextra sinistra (manu), paison diplēn*
["although he had sent these things out, he put an end to them,"
"nothing pertaining to the matter at hand," "with right and left
hand," "gave a blow in return"] (Sophocles, *Electra*, 1415). In Latin
one omits the words introducing a secondary clause: "then I say,"
"then know." Cicero (*ad Atticum* 3, 18):

> *quod scribis te audire me etiam mentali errore ex dolore affici—mihi
> vero mens integra est* [What you write namely: that you heard that I am
> affected, resulting from my mourning, also with a wandering mind—
> indeed my mind is sound].

The omission of the secondary clause is called in Greek *anantapo-
doton*. The omission of words in a contracted sentence is called
epepheugmenon zeuxis or *apo koinou*. *Syllēpsis* was the term for
series-references: What applies to one of them is transferred also to the
others. Of these expressions zeugma has remained in use, but has
taken the meaning of *syllēpsis*. Tacitus (*Annals*, 2, 20): [*Germanicus*]
quod arduum sibi, cetera legatis permisit, As to "sibi": "he reserved
for himself." [The difficult part of the enterprise he reserved for himself, the rest he left to his deputies].[72] Zeugma is interchanged like
arsis and thesis. Cicero (*Tusculan Disputations*, 5, 40): *nostri graece
fere nesciunt, nec Graeci latine (sciunt)* [Our countrymen hardly
know Greek, nor do the Greeks (know) Latin].

Enallage. In language many synonymic constructions appear; logical reason would eliminate many. The science of synonymics seeks
to determine rigorously the essence of synonymous language structures rather than touching the reality of the thing itself. Synonyms
are the terms used to express the same concept-designations by different means. This is enallage—insofar as the terms used depart from
usage. The Latin language can express causality by conjunctions:
nam, enim, etenim, or *eo, ideo, idcirco, propterea*; by adverbs: *cur,
quae, quam, obviam*; by prepositions: *propter*; by case: ablative, genitive; by moods; by participles; etc.—all according to usage, hence
not a *figure*. But when *laetus* is used with the genitive instead of *quod*
or the ablative (*Dido—laeta laborum* [Dido—glad of the tasks],
Aeneid 11, 73), then that is enallage because of the substitution.
Examples are: the adjective for the adverb, *Aidōs ourania aneptē*
[Shame flew up to heaven (lit: Heavenly shame flew up)]; Horace
(*Ars Poetica*, 268), *vos exemplaria Graeca nocturna versate manu,*

manu, versate diurna. Wenn statt Präposition nur der casus steht: Ovid, Met. III, 162, verba refers aures non pervenientia nostras. Oder Präposition statt des casus: de potione gustare. Enallage in bezug auf das Genus ὦ φιλ᾽ Αἰγίσθου βία. Dann Vertauschung von Dual und Plural, bei Homer sooft δύο Αἴαντε zu δὺ᾽ Αἴαντες. Il. II 278: ὣς φάσαν ἡ πληθύς. Für den Vocativ häufig Nominativ ὦ φίλτατ᾽ Αἶας. Soph. Aj. 977. Vertauschung des Casus ἀντίπτωσις. Dann Vertauschung von Comparativ und Superlativ und Positiv. Od. 11, 483: σεῖο δ"Ἀχιλλεῦ οὔ τις ἀνὴρ προπάροιθε μακάρτατος. (für μακάρτερος). In Bezeichnung der Person [illegible] 2. Pers. Imperativ bei πας, ἄκουε πας. Seume im *Leben* erzählt: wo haben wir unsere Präparation? fragte mich einmal der Rektor. "Hier," antwortete ich und zeigte auf die Stirne. "Wir sind etwas keck; wir werden ja sehen." So einmal zu einem anderen Schüler, "wir sind ein Esel." Aoristformen vertreten im Griech. oft das Präsens wie in den Homer. Gleichnissen. Imperativ für Indikativ οἴσω · ὣς ποίησον für ποιήσεις, ein Atticismus. Aktiv und Passiv gegeneinander, z.B., κακῶς ἀκούειν male audire getadelt werden, blinder Schuss, blinder Lärm, eine traurige Gegend, eine "betrübte Erfahrung."—Das σχῆμα πρὸς τὸ σημαινόμενον Construktion nach dem Sinn, constructio κατὰ σύνεσιν modern. Il. 5, 382 τέτλαθι, τέκνον ἐμόν, καὶ ἀνασχεο κηδομένη περ. Plato, Apol. p. 29. ᾽Αθηναῖος ὤν, πόλεως τῆς μεγίστης καὶ εὐδοκιμωτάτης. 2. Programmen von F. Grüter, In Synesis Münster, 1855 und 1867. Das ἕν διὰ δυοῖν Zweimaleins bei Servius zu Virgil Georg. II, 192. Aeschylos Eumen. 238 αἷμα καὶ σταλαγμός für αἵματος στ. Dann die ὑπαλλαγή es treten solche Satztheile grammatisch in Beziehung, weil sie dem Sinn nach zu anderen gehören. Soph. Oed. rex 1235 τέθνηκε θεῖον ᾽Ιοκάστης κάρα. νεῖκος ἀνδρῶν ξύναιμον. Antig. 793. Ov. Met. VIII 676 de purpureis collectae vitibus uvae.

versate diurna [Peruse the Greek models by night, peruse them by day]. When case is used instead of a preposition: Ovid (*Metamorphoses*, 3, 162): *verba refers aures non pervenientia nostras* [You are saying words that do not reach my ears]. Or a preposition instead of case: *de potione gustare* [to taste of the beverage]. Enallage in relation to gender, *ō phil' Aigisthou bia* [dear Aegisthus]. Then substitution of dual and plural, so often in Homer, *duo Aiante* to *du' Aiantes*. *Iliad* (2, 278): *ōs phasan he plēthus* [Thus spoke the multitude]. Frequently, the nominative instead of the vocative: *ō philtat' Aias* [O beloved Ajax] (Sophocles, *Ajax*, 977). Substitution of case [is called] *antiptōsis*. Then [there is] substitution of comparative and superlative and positive. *Odyssey* (11, 483): *seio d' Achilleu ou tis anēr proparoithe makartatos* [Whereas than thou, Achilles, no man was more blessed] for *makarteros*. In designating person [?] the second person imperative with *pas*: *akoue pas* [totally: listen totally]. Seume told in his *Life*: "Where do we have our preparation?" the director once asked me. "Here," I answered, pointing to my forehead. "We are somewhat bold, we shall see." Then once to another pupil, "We are an ass." Aorist-forms in Greek often replace the present, as in the Homeric comparisons. Imperative for indicative: *oisō; ōs poiēson* for *poiēseis*, an Atticism. Active and passive replace one another, e.g.: *kakōs akouein* (*male audire*) [literally: to hear badly], "to be blamed," *blinder Schuss* [a shot in the dark], *blinder Lärm* [false alarm], a "sad region," a "dismal experience." The *schēma pros to sēmainomenon*, construction according to the meaning, *constructio, kata synesin*, [is] modern. *Iliad* (5, 382): *tetlathi, teknon emon, kai anascheo kēdomenē per* [Be of good heart, my child, and endure for all thy suffering].[73] Plato (*Apology*, p. 29): *Athēnaios ōn, poleōs tēs megistēs kai eudokimōtatēs* [You are a citizen of Athens, the greatest of cities and the most famous]. 2 programs of F. Grüter, *In Synesis* (Münster, 1855 and 1867). The *hen dia duoin* [Hendiadys, "One through two"]. 2 x 1, in Servius on Virgil's *Georgics* (2, 192). Aeschylus (*Eumenides*, 238) [uses] *haima kai stalagmos* for *haimatos stalagmos* [blood and a drop; drop of blood]. Then the *hypallagē*: such phrases enter into grammatical relationship because in their meaning they relate to others. Sophocles (*Oedipus rex*, 1235): *tethnēke theion Jokastēs kara* [the divine head of Jocasta died]. *neikos andrōn xynaimon* [hatred among men nourished by the same blood], *Antigone*, 793. Ovid (*Metamorphoses*, 8, 676): *de purpureis collectae vitibus uvae* [grapes gathered from purple vines].

Hieher gehört die sog. *comparatio compendiaria* im Latein. Hor. Od. III 1,42: quod si dolentem nec Phrygius lapis nec purpurarum sidere clarior delenit usus (statt clariorum). Od. II. 14, 28: tinget pavimentum superbis (mero) pontificum potiore coenis (für potiore quam esse solet in pontificum coenis)—Die *Prolepsis*, wenn einem Wort eine Eigenschaft beigelegt wird, welche erst in Folge der im verbum bezeichneten Thätigkeit ihm zufällt. Soph. Aj. 70: ἐγὼ γὰρ ὀμμάτων ἀποστρόφους αὐγάς ἀπείργω. Der Terminus ist nicht antik. Dort bedeutet prolepsis (1) Vorwegnahme und Abwehr der Einwürfe des Gegners (2) so viel wie Anachronismus (3) ungrammatischen Sinn, wenn durch ein Ausdruck im Allgemein vorher bezeichnet wird, was nachher im Einzeln folgt. z.B. Virg. Aen. 12, 161: interea reges, ingenti mole Latinus—bigis it Turnus—tum pater Aeneas. Die Attraction. J. Grimm "über einige Fälle der Attraktion," Abh. d. Ak. 1858 sagt z.B. "Attr., Bächen, ja Wassertropfen ähnlich, die wo sie sich nähern in einander rinnen, gewährt die ungehemmte Rede der Griechen am meisten, weniger schon die lateinische, beide jedoch werden sie vorzüglich im Element der Volkssprache, manche fast nur bei Comikern aufzuweisen haben, von Cicero darf man eben keine Beispiele dafür verlangen. Deutsche Zunge, der von jeher, soweit ihre geschriebene Denkmäler reichen, Zwang angethan wurde, sei es durch Steifheit der Übersetzungen, sei es durch Verwahrlosung oder beschränkte Regel der Grammatiker, kann oft nur Spuren dessen, was dennoch nicht ganz in ihr untergieng, zeigen"— R. Förster quaestiones de attractioni enuntiationum relativorum 1868. Hor. Od. III 27, 73: uxor invicti Jovis esse nescis. Aen. Virg. I, 573, Urbem quam statuo vestra est. Herod. 2, 15, τὸ πάλαι, αἱ

Here belongs the *comparatio compendiaria*, as it is called in Latin. Horace (*Odes*, 3, 1, 42): *quod si dolentem nec Phrygius lapis nec purpurarum sidere clarior delenit usus* [and so if Phrygian marble will not relieve / distress, nor wearing purples more lustrous than / a star][74] instead of *clariorum. Odes* (2, 14, 28): *tinget pavimentum superbis (mero) pontificum potiore coenis* [The haughty wine will stain bright floors at / Suppers more lavish than pontiffs' banquets] (for *potiore quam esse solet in pontificum coenis* [stronger than is customary at pontiffs' banquets].[75] *Prolepsis*, when a word is ascribed a quality which it acquires only as a result of the activity designated by the verb. Sophocles (*Ajax*, 70): *ego gar ommatōn apostrophous augas apeirgō*[76] [for I shall turn aside his vision]. The term is not ancient. In antiquity prolepsis means: (1) anticipation and repulsion of the opponent's objections; (2) the same as anachronism; (3) an ungrammatical meaning, when an expression first designates generally what will follow later in detail, e.g. Virgil (*Aeneid*, 12, 161): *interea reges, ingenti mole Latinus—bigis it Turnus—tum* [sic] *pater Aeneas* [Meanwhile the kings (were riding forth) Latinus / Imposing. . . . and Turnus coming behind a (snow-white) team. . . and on this side Aeneas, father (of Rome)].[77]

Attraction. J. Grimm ("Über einige Fälle der Attraction," in *Abh. d. Kgl. Acad. d. Wissenschaften zu Berlin*, 1858) says, for example: "Attraction, like brooks, indeed water-drops, which flow together when they approach one another, is displayed by the unrestrained discourse of the Greeks most of all, Latin discourse already less, but both have it appear primarily in the element of the vernacular, some almost only among comedians; of course, one must demand no examples of it from Cicero. The German language which has been constrained from the remote past, as far back as its written documents reach, whether because of the stiffness of the translations, or because of the neglect or limited rules of grammar, can often show just traces of what nonetheless did not vanish completely from it." —R. Förster, *quaestiones de attractioni enuntiationum relativorum* (1868). Horace (*Odes*, 3, 27, 73): *uxor invicti Jovis esse nescis* [Jove Unconquered makes you his wife without your / Knowledge]. Virgil (*Aeneid*, 1, 573): *Urbem quam statuo vestra est* [The city I am building is yours]. Herodotus (2, 15): *to palai, ai Thēbai Aigyptos ekaleeto* [In old times, Thebes was called Egypt].

θῆβαι Αἴγυπτος ἐκαλέετο.—Die Anocoluthie. Die Construktion des zusammengesetzten Satzes ist Ausdruck des besonnenen Denkens: ist Unfähigkeit zu dieser Besonnenheit da, bei zu starkem Andrang verschieden aber doch verwandter Vorstellungen, oder bei Lässigkeit, so tritt diese Figur ein. Hermogenes sagt, der λόγος ἀληθής dürfe, um die Natur starker Erregungen darzustellen, auch die Verlegung der ἀκολουθία nicht scheuen. Letzteres bei Plat. Apol. p. 19. zeigt die erhabene Unbekümmertheit des Sokrates. Die Enallage in der Wortstellung ist das Hyperbaton, schon besprochen. Chiasmus, moderner terminus, die Alten sagen προϋπάντησις praeoccursio. Hermogenes nennt [es] χιασμός wenn bei vier Satzgliedern das vierte dem ersten, das dritte dem zweiten [entspricht]. Gegensatz der περίοδος διαφυμένη ist die ἀναστρεφομένη, das dritte dem ersten, das zweite dem vierten Glied entsprechend. Wir reden dann von Parallelismus oder Continuität des Ausdrucks. Latein heisst χιασμός decussatio (decussis = ioas, mit einem x bezeichnet). Wird durch Inversionen die Deutlichkeit des Sinns und die Harmonie des Ausdrucks beschädigt, so ist das σύνχυσις, id est, hyperbaton ex omni parte confusum.

Alle Arten von Klanggebilden mit Ähnlichkeiten und Gegenüberstellungen. παρανομασία annominatio. Früher unter dem Begriff der ἴσα σχήματα gefasst (einer der Sophisten). Dahin gehört das σχῆμα ἐτυμολογικόν pugna pugnata est. Dann die Wiederholung desselben Worts mit verschiedener Bedeutung. Dann Gleichklang oder Conformität ganzer Satzglieder, das ἰσόκωλον eine Periode, deren Glieder im Ganzen aus gleich vielen Silben bestehen. Bei dem πάρισον überragt ein Glied, gewöhnlich das letzte, die anderen etwas. Die παρομοίωσις ist die gesteigerte παρίσωσις, nicht nur gleiche κῶλα, sondern noch ähnlicher Klang der Wörter, besonders am Anfang und Ende der κῶλα. Cicero pro Milo. 4,20: est enim, iudices, haec non scripta, sed nata lex, quam non didicimus accepimus legimus, verum ex natura ipsa arripuimus hausimus expressimus; ad quam non docti, sed facti, non instituti sed imbuti sumus. Das

Anakoluthia: the construction of the complex sentence [is] the expression of deliberate thought. This figure occurs when there is incapacity to deliberate because of an excessively strong crowding of different but related ideas, or carelessness. Hermogenes says that even the *logos alēthēs* [truthful thought], in order to portray the nature of strong emotions, does not avoid the displacement of the *akoluthia* [correct sequence]. The latter, in Plato (*Apology*, p. 19), shows Socrates' sublime nonchalance. The enallage in word order has already been discussed under the *hyperbaton*. Chiasmus is a modern term; the ancients say *prohypantēsis, praeoccursio*. Hermogenes calls [it] *chiasmos* when of four sentence-parts the fourth [corresponds] to the first, and the third to the second. The opposite of the *periodos diaphymenē* is the *anastrephomenē*, in which the third part corresponds to the first, and the second to the fourth. We then speak of parallelism or continuity of expression. In Latin *chiasmos* is called *decussatio* (*decussis* = *ioas*, marked with an x). If the clarity of meaning and the harmony of expression are damaged by inversions, that is called *synchysis*, i.e., *hyperbaton ex omni parte confusium*.

All kinds of phonetic structures with similarities and contrasts— *paranomasia, annominatio* [were] formerly classified under the concept of *isa schēmata* (by one of the Sophists). To this category belongs the *schēma etymologikon*: *pugna pugnata est* [the battle has been fought]. Then the repetition of the same word with different meaning. Then the homophony or conformity of entire clauses, the *isokōlon*, a period whose clauses consist of broadly the same number of syllables. In the *parison* one clause, generally the last, is somewhat longer than the rest. The *paromoiōsis* is an intensified *parisōsis*, [however] not just the same *kōla*, but also a similar sound of the words, especially at the beginning or end of the *kōla*. Cicero (*Pro Milone*, 4, 20):

> *est enim, iudices, haec non scripta, sed nata lex, quam non didicimus accepimus legimus, verum ex natura ipsa arripuimus hausimus expressimus; ad quam non docti, sed facti, non instituti sed imbuti sumus* [There does exist therefore, gentlemen, a law which is a law not of the statute book, but of nature; a law which we possess not by instruction, tradition, or reading, but which we have caught, imbibed, and sucked in at Nature's own breast; a law which comes to us not by education but by constitution, not by training but by intuition].[78]

ὁμοιόπτωτον besteht in der mehrfachen Wiederholung desselben casus innerhalb einer Periode. Es ist eine Art des ὁμοιοτέλευτον. Aristoteles soll einmal geschrieben haben ἐγὼ ἐκ μὲν ᾿Αθηνῶν εἰς Στάγειρα ἦλθον δεὰ τὸν βασιλέα τὸν μέγαν, ἐκ δὲ Σταγείρων εἰς ᾿Αθήνας διὰ τὸν χειμῶνα τὸν μέγαν. Polus, Licymnius, Gorgias und seine Schüler, auch noch Isocrates in seiner ersten Periode, gefielen sich in ἀντίθετα, παρόμοια und παρισώσεις. Später galten diese Figuren als μειρακιώδη und θεατρικά. Die kunstvolle Gegenüberstellung entgegensetzter Wörter ἀντίθετον, ἀντίθεσις. Man unterscheidet den Worten nach oder dem Gedanken. Grosses Beispiel bei Cornificius: in otio tumultuaris, in tumultu es otiosus; in re frigidissima cales, in ferventissima friges; tacito cum opus est, clamas, cum tibi [sic] loqui convenit obmutescis; ades, abesse vis; abes, reverti cupis; in pace bellum quaeritas, in bello pacem desideras; in contione de virtute loqueris, in proelio prae ignavia tubae sonitum perferre non potes.

Das alles bezeichnen die Alten als Wortfiguren, nun kommen noch die Sinnfiguren figurae sententiarum σχήματα διανοίας (und σχήματα ᾿λέξεως, fig.verb.). Dahin wird die προσωποπαιία gerechnet fictio personarum (Rede einer fingierten oder wirklich vorhandenen Person in den Mund gelegt). Gedanken der Gegner als Selbstgespräche ans Licht gebracht. Götter und Unterwelt, Städte und Völker dürfen reden. Dann die ἠθοποιία oder μίμησις imitatio personae aliorum. H Monse veterum rhetorum de sententiarum figuris doctrina, Breslau 1869. Dann die ὑποτυπωσις genaue und deutliche Schilderung einer Sache, dass man sie zu sehen glaubt, selbst bei zukünftigen Dingen. Was Milo gethan haben würde, wenn er zur Prätur gelangt wäre. Dann die rhetorische Frage. Man erwartet keine

The *homoioptōton* consists of the multiple repetition of the same case within a period. It is a kind of *homoioteleuton*. Aristotle is said to have once written:

> *ego ek men Athenōn eis Stageira ēlthon dia ton basilea ton megan, ek de Stageirōn eis Athēnas dia ton cheimōna ton megan* [I travelled from Athens to Stagira on account of the great king, from Stagira to Athens on account of the great winter].[79]

Polus, Licymnius, Gorgias and his disciples, and Isocrates in his first period delighted in *antitheta* [contrasts], *paromoia* [assonance, words that are nearly the same], and *parisōseis* [giving different parts of a sentence the same length]. Later these figures were considered *meirakiōdē* [affected, childish figures] and *theatrika* [theatrical].[80]

The artful counterposing of contrasting words is called *antitheton* or *antithesis*. The distinction can be between the words or the thought. A great example in Cornificius:

> *In otio tumultuaris, in tumultu es otiosus, in re frigidissima cales, in ferventissima friges; tacito cum opus est, clamas; ubi loqui convenit, obmutescis; ades, abesse vis; abes, reverti cupis; in pace bellum quaeritas, in bello pacem desideras; in contione de virtute loqueris, in proelio prae ignavia tubae sonitum perferre non potes* [When all is calm, you are confused; when all is in confusion, you are calm. In a situation requiring all your coolness, you are on fire; in one requiring all your ardor, you are cool. When there is need for you to be silent, you are uproarious; when you should speak, you grow mute. Present, you wish to be absent; absent, you are eager to return. In peace, you keep demanding war; in war, you yearn for peace. In the Assembly, you talk of valor; in battle, you cannot for cowardice endure the trumpet's sound].[81]

The ancients called all these things "figures of diction"; next come the figures of thought, *figurae sententiarum*, *schēmata dianoias* (and *schēmata lexeōs*, *figurae verborum*). Numbered among these is *prosōpopoiia*, *fictio personarum*, in which discourse is put into the mouth of a fictional person or one really present or the opponent's thoughts are brought to light as a monologue. Gods and underworld, cities and nations may speak. Then the *ēthopoiia* or *mimēsis*, *imitatio morum alienorum* [imitation of the behavior of other persons]. H. Monse, *veterum rhetorum de sententiarum figuris doctrina* (Breslau, 1869). Then the *hypotypōsis*, precise and clear depiction of a thing so that one believes one sees it, even of future things. What Milo would have done, had he obtained the praetership. Then the

Antwort, aber auch die Antwort kann zur Frage werden. Die Verbindung nennt man den διαλογισμός. Mann richtet an sich oder jemand die Frage and schiebt selbst die Antwort unter, die ὑποφορά, besonders häufig bei Lysias. Oft noch verstärkt durch die Anaphora (also gleicher Anfang der gleichen Satzglieder). Das Vorwegnehmen gegnerischer Einwürfe ist oft πρόληψις oder προκατάληψις. Der Zweifel διαπόρησις ἀπορία wo anfangen, wo aufhören, was wir hauptsächlich sagen, ob wir überhaupt sprechen sollen. Dann die ἀνακοίνωσις communicatio wenn der Redner z.b. den Richter auffordert, es ihm zu sagen, wenn er etwas nicht ausreichend gefragt oder etwas übergangen habe: Man kann der Rede dadurch den Eindruck des Unvorbereiteten geben. Nach der communicatio fügt man wohl noch etwas Unerwartetes παράδοξον bei. Dann die ἐπιτροπή permissio man überlasst den Richtern die Entscheidung: sehr geeignet um Mitleid zu erwecken. Wenn man den Gegenstand einräumt, von dem man weiss, dass er es doch nicht gebrauchen wird, so ist dies ἀπολογισμός. Die Figuren, welche geeignet sind, die Affekte zu vergrössern beruhen nicht auf simulatio. Dahin die ἐκφώνεσις exclamatio z.b. ὦ γῆ καὶ θεοὶ καὶ δαίμονες καὶ ἄνθρωποι. Dann die παρρησία licentia, z.b. die achte catilinarische Rede hat sie. Dann die ἀποστροφή aversus iudice sermo. Dann die παράλειψις occultatio, eine Figur bei der man unter dem Schein etwas zu verschweigen es doch nennt (auch παρασιώπησις). Mitunter führt man Dinge an, ohne weiter auf sie einzugehen, weil man daran verzweifelt es in gebührende Weise zu thun: nun sehr wirksam Amplifikation.—Die ἀποσιώπησις das plötzliche Abbrechen der Rede, z.b., im Zorn oder weil es ein anderer schon gesagt hat, oder bei etwas Anstössigem.

IX. NUMERUS DER REDE

Cic. orat. c. 56.—quod versus saepe in oratione per imprudentiam dicimus: quod vehementer est vitiosum—senarios vero et Hipponacteos effugere vix possumus. magnam enim partem ex iambis nostra constat oratio. Sed tamen eos versus facile agnoscit auditor: sunt enim usitatissimi. Inculcamus autem per imprudentiam saepe etiam minus usitatos sed tamen versus; vitiosum genus et longa animi provisione fugiendum. Elegit ex multis Isocrati libris triginta fortasse Hieronymus, Peripateticum in primis nobilis, plerosque senarios sed etiam anapaestos.—Sit igitur hoc cognitum in solutis

rhetorical question. One expects no answer, but even the answer can be asked about. The combination is called *dialogismos.* One asks oneself, or someone else, the question and interpolates the answer oneself, *hypophora,* especially frequent in Lysias. Often further intensified by *anaphora* (i.e. the same beginning of the same sentence parts). The anticipation of the opponent's objections is often *prolēpsis* or *prokatalēpsis.* Doubt, *diaporēsis,* or *aporia,* where to begin, where to stop, what we should say as our main point, whether we should speak at all. Then the *anakoinōsis, communicatio,* when the speaker asks, for example, the judge to tell him whether he has not asked something adequately or has overlooked something: this can give the speech the impression of being unprepared. After the *communicatio* one probably adds something else that is unexpected, *paradoxon.* Then the *epitropē, permissio,* one leaves the decision to the judges. When one concedes the object, of which one knows that it will nonetheless not be used, that is the *apologismos.*

The figures which are suited to magnify the emotions are not based on *simulatio.* In this category are *ekphōnesis, exclamatio,* e.g.: *ō gē kai theoi kai daimones kai anthrōpoi* [O earth and gods and demonic powers and men]. Then the *parrēsia, licentia,* e.g. in the 8th Catilinarian Speech. Further: the *apostrophē, aversus iudice sermo,* addressing someone else than the judge. Then the *paralepsis, occultatio,* a figure whereby one pretends not to mention something but does so (also *parasiōpēsis*). Sometimes one cites things without going into any further details, because one despairs of being able to do it in a suitable manner, amplification is very effective at this point. The *aposiōpēsis,* the sudden breaking off of discourse, e.g. in anger, or because another has already said it, or when the subject is obscene.

IX. THE RHYTHM OF DISCOURSE

Cicero (*Orator,* c. 56) [writes]:

quod versus saepe in oratione per imprudentiam dicimus: quod vehementer est vitiosum . . . senarios vero et Hipponacteos effugere vix possumus. Magnam enim partem ex iambis nostra constat oratio. Sed tamen eos versus facile agnoscit auditor: sunt enim usitatissimi. Inculcamus autem per imprudentiam saepe etiam minus usitatos sed tamen versus; vitiosum genus et longa animi provisione fugiendum. Elegit ex multis Isocrati libris triginta fortasse Hieronymus, Peripateticum in primis nobilis, plerosque senarios sed etiam anapaestos. . . . Sit igitur

etiam verbis inesse numeros eosdemque esse oratorios qui sint poetici. Cf. Dionys. de comp. verborum c. 25. Die Rede gegen Aristocrates fängt gleich mit einem homerischen Hexameter an, der aus anapestischen Takten besteht. Der letzte Fuss fehlt. Das macht, dass er nicht gemerkt wird μηδεὶς ὑμῶν ὦ ἄνδρες ᾽Αθηναῖοι νομίσῃ με (παρεῖναι). Umgekehrt erscheinen die Lyriker als reine Prosa, wenn man den Gesang hinwegnimmt. Orat. 55. maximeque id in optimo quoque eorum poetarum, qui λυρικοί a Graecis nominantur, quoscum cantu spoliaveris, nuda paene remanet oratio. Quorum similia sunt quaedam etiam apud nostros, velut ille in [sic] Thyeste

quemnam te esse dicam? qui tarda in senectute

et quae sequuntur, quae nisi cum tibicen accessit, orationis sunt solutae simillima. Comicorum senarii propter similitudinem sermonis ita saepe sunt abjecti, ut nonnunquam vix in eis numerus et versus intellegi possit.

Isocrates gilt als der erste qui verbis solutis numeros primus adiunxerit. Seine Schüler, Ephorus und Naucrates. Aristoteles sonst Gegner des Isokrates, stimmt bei, versum in oratione vetat esse,

*hoc cognitum in solutis etiam verbis inesse numeros eosdemque esse ora-
torios qui sint poetici* [that we often make verses unintentionally in
delivering a speech. This is very reprehensible, . . . as a matter of fact it
is almost impossible to avoid senarii and Hipponacteans, for our speech
consists largely of iambi. The listener, however, recognizes these verses
readily; for they are of the commonest sort; but we often unwittingly
insert other verses, of less common type, but verses all the same—a
vicious practice, which is to be avoided by looking far ahead. The eminent Peripatetic philosopher Hieronymus culled from the numerous
works of Isocrates some thirty verses, mostly senarii, but also anapaests
. . . We may put it down as certain, then, that there are rhythms even in
prose, and that those used in oratory are the same as those in poetry].

Cf. Dionysius *De Compositione Verborum*, c. 25. The speech against
Aristocrates begins immediately with a Homeric hexameter, consisting of anapaestic beats. The last foot is missing. This causes it to go
unnoticed. *mēdeis hymōn ō andres Athēnaioi nomisēi me (pareinai)*
[let no one of you, men of Athens, take it for granted that I am
present]. Vice versa, the lyric poets seem like pure prose if their mel-
ody is removed. *Orator* (55):

> *maximeque id in optimo quoque eorum poetarum, qui lyrikoi a Graecis
> nominatur, quoscum cantu spoliaveris, nuda paene remanet oratio. Quo-
> rum similia sunt quaedam etiam apud nostros, velut ille in Thyeste*
> > *quemnam te esse dicam? qui tarda in senectute*
> *et quae sequuntur, quae nisi cum tibicen accessit, orationis sunt solutae
> simillima. Comicorum senarii propter similitudinem sermonis ita saepe
> sunt abjecti, ut nonnunquam vix in eis numerus et versus intellegi possit*
> [this is particularly true of the best of the poets whom the Greeks call
> "lyric"; deprive them of the musical accompaniment and almost noth-
> ing but bare prose remains. We have something like this at times in
> Latin poetry; this, for example, from the *Thyestes*:
> > *quemnam te esse dicam? qui tarda in senectute*
> and the rest of the passage; unless accompanied by the pipe, it is exactly
> like prose. But the senarii of comedy are often so lacking in elevation
> of style because of their resemblance to ordinary conversation that
> sometimes it is scarcely possible to distinguish verse and rhythm in
> them].[82]

Isocrates is considered to be the first *qui verbis solutis numeros primus adiunxerit* [to add rhythm to unrhythmical words]. His students
were Ephorus and Naucrates. Aristotle, otherwise an opponent of
Isocrates, agrees, *versum in oratione vetat esse, numerum iubet* [he

numerum iubet, Theodectes ausführlicher, Theophrastus am genauesten. Ephorus empfiehlt Paean und Daktylus, verwirft Spondeus und Trochaeus; Aristoteles hält den Daktylus für zu feierlich, den Iambus für zu gewöhnlich, empfiehlt den Päan. Auch der Trochaeus ist nicht recht, als κορδακικώτερος. Bei Cicero folgt nun eine ausführliche Lehre (ebenfalls bei Quintilian im Orat.). Zunächst allgemeiner Gesichtspunkt—Beispiel des Dochmius: amicos tenes (nicht zu lesen "amícóstenés"). Dann "missos faciant patronos: ipsi prodeant" ("nisi intervallo dixisset: sensisset profecto se fudisse senarium"). Berüchtigt ist Hegesias aus Magnesia, den Dionys. de comp. c. 18 und Cicero de orat 68 lächerlich macht.

Besondere Regeln über den Ausgang und den Anfang der Periode. Kurz zusammengefasst ist

erlaubt	fehlerhaft	zu empfehlen	zu vermeiden
∪ – / – –	– – / ∪ –̆	– ∪ / – – ᵁ	– – / – – ∪̆
∪ – / – ∪	∪ – / ∪ –̆	ᵁ ᵁ – / ∪ – –	∪ ∪ / – – ᵁ
– ∪ / – ∪	– ∪ / ∪ –̆	ᵁ ᵁ – / ∪ ∪ – –̆ ᵁ	– ∪ / ∪ – –
– ∪ / – –	∪ ∪ / ∪ ∪	ᵁ ᵁ ∪ / – ∪ ∪ –	– – / ∪ ∪ – –

zu empfehlen	fehlerhaft
– ∪ / –	– / –
∪ – / ∪	∪ / ∪
∪ ∪ – / ∪	

Der Redner muss wissen, wo jede Art der Composition anzuwenden ist, sowohl hinsichtlich der Füsse als der aus Füssen bestehenden Reihen (Kommata, Kola, Perioden), wo man heftig und drängend zu reden hat, viele Glieder und Einschnitte, mit rauhen Rhythmen. Perioden für die Proemien bei wichtigeren Sachen, rauh wenn man klagt, fliessend wenn man lobt. Für Ernstes und Erhabenes mehr lange Silben, für alles, was dem Gespräche gleicht, mehr kurze Silben. Die Erzählung will sehr gemischte Füsse. Die raschen und scharfen Berichte müssen entsprechende Füsse haben, nur nicht Trochäen, die rasch aber kraftlos sind. Das Erhabene liebt Daktylus und Päan. Das Rauhe tritt durch Iamben hervor. Im ganzen ist eine rauhe Composition immer einer weichlichen vorzuziehen.—Die

forbids meter to be in a speech—he does order rhythm]. Theodectes more at length, Theophrastus most precisely. Ephorus recommends the paeon and dactyl, rejects the spondee and trochee; Aristotle considers the dactyl too solemn, the iamb too common, he recommends the paeon. Nor is the trochee acceptable, as *kordakikōteros* [too much like the cordax, i.e. a low-class, voluptuous dance]. In Cicero then follows an extensive theory (also in Quintilian [9]).[83] First a general viewpoint—an example of the *dochmius*: *amicos tenes* (not to be read *amícóstenés*). Then *"missos faciant patronos: ipsi prodeant"* [let them dismiss the patrons: let them do the backing themselves] (*nisi intervallo dixisset: sensisset profecto se fudisse senarium*) [If he had not spoken with intermissions, he would have noticed, surely, that he had produced a senarius (six-footer)]. Notorious is Hegesias of Magnesia, whom Dionysius (*De Compos.*, c. 18) and Cicero (*De Oratore*, 68) ridicule.

Special rules on the beginning and end of the period. Briefly summarized,[84] the following rhythms are

permitted	wrong	recommended	to be avoided
∪ – / – –	– – / ∪ –̆	– ∪ / – – –̆	– – / – – –̆
∪ – / – ∪	∪ – / ∪ –̆	∪̆ ∪̆ – / ∪ – –	∪ ∪ / – – –̆
– ∪ / – ∪	– ∪ / ∪ –̆	∪̆ ∪̆ – / ∪ ∪ – –̆ ∪̆	– ∪ / ∪ – –
– ∪ / – –	∪ ∪ / ∪ ∪	∪̆ ∪̆ ∪ / – ∪ ∪ –	– – / ∪ ∪ – –

recommended	wrong
– ∪ / –	– / –
∪ – / ∪	∪ / ∪
∪ ∪ – / ∪	

The speaker must know where each kind of composition is to be used, both as regards the feet and the sequences of feet (*kommata*, *kōla*, periods), where one must speak forcefully and urgently, with many parts and pauses, with rough rhythms. Periods [should be used] in *prooemia* for more important matters; rough when one complains, smooth when one praises. For a serious and sublime topic, [use] longer syllables; for anything that resembles conversation, more short syllables. Narration calls for more mixed feet. Swift, sharp reports must have the corresponding feet, but not trochees which are swift but weak. The sublime loves dactyls and paeons. The rough is stressed by iambs. In general, a rough composition is always preferable to a weak one.

Rede hat drei Formen κόμματα incisa κῶλα membra und περίοδοι. Kommata sind kleine κῶλα, das κῶλον hat in sich einen abgeschlossenen Sinn, das κόμμα nicht (wie bei den zusammengezogenen Sätzen). Die κῶλα entsprechen den Versen, sie dürfen nicht zu lang sein, wie ja auch in der Poesie der Vers selten über die Länge des Hexameters hinausgeht, auch nicht zu kurz, so hat man die ξηρὰ σύνθεσις. Andernseits hat eine kurze kommatische Rede den Eindruck der σφοδρότης Hitzigkeit. Aus der Verbindung von κῶλα und κόμματα entsteht die Periode. Die unperiodische Rede ist die λέξις εἰρομένη, davon sich die Alten und noch Herodot bedienten, ohne Ruhepunkt, bis die Sache selbst zu Ende ist. Gegensatz die λέξις κατεστραμμένη, ἡ ἐν περιόδοις. Die einfache ἀφελής hat nur ein Glied, μονόκωλος, aber auch sie wird eine gewisse Länge und Abründung zum Schlusse haben und sich dadurch von der λέξις εἰρομένη unterscheiden. Mit περίοδος μονόκωλος identisch περίοδος ἁπλῆ. Über vier κῶλα darf die Periode nicht hinausgehen. In der Rede ist theils die λέξις εἰρομένη, theils ἡ ἐν περιόδος am Platz: ganz periodisch darf die epideiktische Rede (Isocrates) sein. In der periodischen Erzählung ist die λέξις εἰρομένη nöthig, wie immer bei Lysias. Innerhalb der periodischen Reihe ist auf Ordnung, Verbindung und numerus zu achten: über letzten schon gesprochen. Ordnung: bei Aufeinanderfolge einzelner Worte (namentlich asyndetisch) immer Steigerung nöthig. Auf das weniger Deutliche muss das Deutlichere folgen, auf das Kleinere das Grössere. So weit möglich muss man den Satz mit einem verbum schliessen. Bei irgend welchem Nachdruck das Hyperbaton. Auch wohl zu Gunsten des Rhythmus. Verbindung: Schlusssilbe eines Wortes mit der Anfangssilbe des folgenden [dürfen] nie ein obscenum [bilden]. Dann der Hiat, der zum Eintreten einer Pause zwingt, wo eine solche sinnstörend ist. Am wenigsten nimmt man noch Anstoss am zusammentreffen zweier kurzen Vokale. Isocrates und Theopomp vermeiden ihn mit der grössten Angst. Demosthenes und Cicero haben es nicht so genau genommen. Mitunter kann er sogar einzelnen Wörtern Nachdruck verleihen: auch macht er den Eindruck der gefälligen Nachlässigkeit. Polybius und Plutarch vermeiden ihn. Hauptschrift: Benseler *de hiatu in scriptoribus Graecis*, 1841. Auch den Zusammenstoss härterer Consonante hat man zu vermeiden: sx, ss. Dann das ὁμοιοπρόφορον zu vermeiden (Alliteration): "o Tite, tute, Tati, tibi tanta, tyranne, tulisti." Ennius. Iotacismus, häufige Wiederholung des i, Labdacismus, Mytacismus, Polysigma. Das sind freni: Solche Parechesen bei Dich-

Speech has three forms: *kommata* (*incisa*), *kōla* (*membra*), and *periodoi*. *Kommata* are small *kōla*; the *kōlon* has a complete meaning, the *komma* does not (as in complex sentences). The *kōla* correspond to verses; they must not be too long, just as in poetry the verse seldom is longer than a hexameter; nor too short, otherwise one has the *xēra synthesis* [dry, frustrated composition]. On the other hand, a brief *komma*-rich speech gives the impression of *sphodrotēs* (violence, vehemence). The period originates from the combination of *kōla* and *kommata*. Unperiodic discourse is the *lexis eiromenē* [continuous, running style, lit. strung together], which the ancients and even Herodotus used without a resting point until the subject matter itself is finished. The opposite is the *lexis katestrammenē hē en periodois* [periodic style]. The simple period *aphelēs*[85] has just one part, *monokōlos*; but it too will have a certain length and rounding off at the end and thus differs from the *lexis eiromenē*. Identical with the *periodos monokōlos* is *periodos haplē* [the simple period]. The period must not be longer than four *kōla*. In a speech a mixture of *lexis eiromenē* and *hē en periodois* is suitable: the epideictic speech (Isocrates) may be completely periodic. Periodic narrative always needs *lexis eiromenē*, as is always the case in Lysias.

Within the periodic sequence, order, combination, and rhythm (*numerus*) must always be observed: the latter has already been discussed. Order: in a sequence of individual words (especially asyndotal), intensification is always necessary. The less clear must be followed by the more clear, the smaller by the greater. As much as possible, the sentence must end with a verb. With any emphasis [use] the *hyperbaton*. Probably also for the sake of rhythm. Combination: the final syllable of a word and the initial syllable of the following one must never [form] an obscenity. Then the hiatus, which compels an insertion of a pause where it is disruptive of meaning. Least offensive is the meeting of two short vowels. Isocrates and Theopompus avoid it most fearfully. Demosthenes and Cicero did not take it so seriously. Sometimes it can even give emphasis to individual words: it also gives the impression of a pleasant nonchalance. Polybius and Plutarch avoid it. Main source: Benseler *Hiatu in Scriptoribus Graecis* (1841).

The collision of harder consonants must also be avoided: sx, ss. *Homoioprophoron* (alliteration) must also be avoided: "*ō Tite, tute, Tati, tibi tanta, tyranne, tulisti*" [Thyself to thyself, Titus Tatius the tyrant, thou tookest those terrible troubles].[86] Ennius. Iotacism, frequent repetition of i; labdacism, mytacism, polysigma. These are

tern nicht selten: Soph. Aj. 866. πόνος πόνῳ πόνον φέρει Il. IV 526: χύντο χαμαὶ χολάδες; Aesch. Pers. 1041: δόσιν κακὰν κακῶν κακοῖς. Besonders häufig bei πᾶς, ἕτερος, ὅσος, οἷος, πολύς. Haufig der Negationen-Schluss in der Prosa, z.B. Plat. Phaed. p. 78 D: οὐδέποτε οὐδαμῇ οὐδαμῶς ἀλλοίωσιν οὐδεμίαν ἐνδέχεται; Parm. 166 B: οὐδενὶ οὐδαμῇ οὐδαμῶς οὐδεμίαν κοινωνίαν ἔχει. Zu den freni gehören Häufungen von Wörtern mit gleichen Flexionen, z.B. gen. plur., also die Homoioptota. Fehlerhaft, die rasche Wiederholung desselben Wortes (ausser einer Wortfigur). Auch so etwas wie das ciceronische: o fortunatam natam me consule Romam, gehört hierher. Oder Cicero, orat. 3, 11: ea quae quaerimus. Reihe einsilbiger Wörter ist fehlerhaft. Bei Oed. rex 370 ein τραχεῖα σύνθεσις: − ἀλλ᾽ ἔστι πλὴν σοί. σοὶ δὲ τοῦτ᾽ οὐκ ἔστ᾽ ἐπεὶ τυφλὸς τά τ᾽ ὦτα τόν τε νοῦν τά τ᾽ ὄμματ᾽ εἶ. (auch die τ zu beachten). Öfter benützt, die Stilarten und ihre modifizirende Kraft. Die Dreitheilungen, von den Isocratern erfunden, von Theophrast περὶ λέξεως adoptiert: sie passt eigentlich nur auf die ältere Entwicklung der attischen Beredsamkeit von Gorgias bis Isocrates und ist aus Betrachtung des Thucydides Lysias und Isocrates hervorgegangen. Gravis, mediocris, extenuata (gesteigert: sufflata, dissoluta, exile). So bei Cornif. Bei Quintil. genus subtile ἰσχνόν, genus grande atque robustum ἀδρόν, medium (floridum) ἀνθηρόν. Unter den Historikern ist Thucydides Vertreter des χαρακτὴρ ὑψηλός, Herodot des χαρακτὴρ μέσος, Xenophon des ἰσχνός. So unterscheidet Dionysus v. Halicarnassus. Thucidides und Lysias zusammengestellt, χαρ. ὑψηλος und ἰσχνος

freni ["reins"]: such *parecheses* [accumulations] are not infrequent in the poets: Sophocles (*Ajax*, 866): *ponos ponōi ponon pherei* [toil, toil, and toil on toil]; *Iliad* (4, 526), *chynto chamai cholades* [and forth upon the ground gushed all his bowels]; Aeschylus (*Persians*, 1041): *dosin kakan kakōn kakois* [a wretched offering from the wretched to the wretched]. Especially frequent is *pas, heteros, hosos, hoios, polus*. The negation-ending is frequent in prose, e.g. Plato (*Phaedrus*, p. 78 D): *oudepote oudamēi oudamōs alloiōsin oudemian endechetai* [never, anywhere, in any way, does he accept any change]; Parmenides (166 B): *oudeni oudamēi oudamōs oudemian koinōnian echei* [He does not have any contact with anyone, anywhere, in any way]. To the *freni* belong clusters of words with the same inflections, e.g. genitive plural, i.e. the *homoioptota*.

One error is the rapid repetition of the same word (except for a word-figure). Even something like the Ciceronian *ō fortunatam natam me consule Romam* [O fortunate Rome to be born under my consulship] falls under this prohibition. Or Cicero (*Orator*, 3, ll): *ea quae quaerimus* [the things we are investigating]. A series of monosyllabic words is wrong. In *Oedipus Rex* (370) there is a *tracheia synthesis* [harsh composition]:

> *all' esti plēn soi. soi de tout' ouk est' epei typhlos ta t'ōta ton te noun ta t' ommat' ei* [With other men, but not with thee, for thou / In ear, wit, eye, in everything art blind].[87]

Note also the "t." Rather often used, the kinds of style and their modifying power.

The tripartite division was invented by the Isocrateans, then adopted by Theophrastus *peri lexeōs*; in reality it was appropriate only for the older development of Attic eloquence from Gorgias to Isocrates, and it arose from the study of Thucydides, Lysias, and Isocrates. *Gravis* [grand], *mediocris* [middle], *extenuata* [simple] (defective equivalents: *sufflata* [swollen], *dissoluta* [slack], *exile* [meager]: this is Cornificius' terminology.[88] Quintilian uses the terms *genus subtile* [plain style] (*ischnon*), *genus grande atque robustum* [grand and forcible] (*hadron*), *medium* (*floridum*) [intermediate (flowery)] (*anthēron*). Among the historians, Thucydides is the representative of the *charaktēr hypsēlos* [grand style], Herodotus of the *charaktēr mesos* [middle style], Xenophon of the *ischnos* [simple style]. This distinction is made by Dionysius of Halicarnassus. Thucydides and Lysias are grouped together. *Charaktēr hypsēlos* and *ischnos* are

verhalten sich wie Grundton zur Oktave. Kunstmässiger Begründer des μέσος ist Thrasymachos von Chalcedon, dann der Sokrates; Plato, dem die Stellen besser glücken, wo er den χαρ. ἰσχνός sucht, als den ὑψηλός. Fehler: die dithyrhambische Überschwenglichkeit. Demosthenes hat das Eigenthümliche aller drei Stilarten vermischt, wie Proteus, darin ruht sein δεινότης, jede Stilart zu gebrauchen, wenn sie am Platze ist.

Entsprechend dieser Stilarten giebt es eine dreifache Composition—(1) ἁρμονία αὐστηρὰ καὶ φιλάρχαια καὶ σεμνὴ καὶ φεύγουσα ἅπαν τὸ κομψόν;—(2) ἁρμονία γλαφυρὰ καὶ λιγυρὰ καὶ θεατρική, καὶ πολὺ τὸ κομψὸν καὶ αἱμύλον ἐπιφαίνουσα;—und drittens die gemischte. Als Vertreter der αὐστηρὰ ἁρμονία Antimachus, Empedocles, Pindar, Aeschylus, Thucydides, Antiphon. Der γλαφυρὰ καὶ ἀνθηρὰ σύνθεσις Hesiod, Sappho, Anachreon, Simonides, Euripides, Isocrates, von Historikern etwa Ephorus und Theopomp, der κοινὴ ἁρμονία Homer, Stesichorus, Alcaeus, Sophocles, Herodot, Demosthenes, Democrit, Plato, Aristoteles. Es entsprechen sich die drei Stilarten und die drei Compositionsarten nicht, wo ist die Composition, die zu χαρ. ἰσχνός gehört? Allmählich kommt als weitere Stilart der δεινότης hinzu (zu ἰσχν. μεγαλοπρεπής γλαφυρός). Zur σύνθεσις μεγαλοπρεπής gehört päonischer Rhythmus zu Anfang oder Ende der κῶλα. Vor δυσφωνία (freni oder δυσπρόφορα) vor Hiat und harten Wörtern nicht zu scheuen. Metaphern. Kurz. . . .Gleichnisse, mächtige Composita, ὀνόματα πεποιημένα mässig poetische Färbung, Thucydides als Meister des grandiosen Stils. (Gegensatz χαρ. ψυχρός, Haschen nach Geist, Symbole, usw.).—Der χαρ. γλαφυρός anmüthig, harmlosen Witz, Kürze, Sprichwörter, Fabeln, Wahl der λεῖα ὀνόματα, die ganz oder überwiegend aus Vocalen bestehen. Rhythmus in der Rede. (Gegensatz das κακόζελον, manierirt albern;—Der χαρ. ἰσχνός die gewöhnliche Umgangssprache [als] Richtschnur. Er verwendet auffallende Composition (διπλᾶ ὀνόματα) πεποιημένα, sagt gern eine Sache zweimal. ἐνάργεια und πιθανότης, Hauptsache. (Gegenstück ξηρός χαρ.)—Die δεινότης liebt nachdrückliche Dinge, Kommata statt Kola, liebt das gewaltige in der Komposition, verschmäht Antithesen und παρόμοια, meist zweigliedrige Perioden, Paraleipsis, Prosopopoiia, Anadiplosis, Anaphora, bes. διάλυσις (Weglassung der Conjunktionen), also

related as basic tone to the octave. Artistic founder of the *mesos* is Thrasymachos of Chalcedon, then Socrates; Plato, who has better luck with passages where he seeks the *charaktēr ischnos* rather than the *hypsēlos*. Dithyrambic exuberance is a mistake. Demosthenes mixed the peculiarity of all three styles, like Proteus; that is where his *deinotēs* [natural ability] lies, in using each kind of style in the right place.

Corresponding to these styles, there are three kinds of composition: (1) *harmonia austēra kai philarchaia kai semnē kai pheugousa hapan to kompson* [the harmony which is austere, traditional, solemn, entirely avoiding brilliance]; (2) *harmonia glaphyra kai ligyra kai theatrikē, kai poly to kompson kai haimulon epiphainousa* [the harmony which is dainty, clear, intent on making an impression, and showing much brilliance and flattery]; and (3) the mixed. Representatives of *austēra harmonia* are Antimachus, Empedocles, Pindar, Aeschylus, Thucydides, Antiphon. Of the *glaphyra kai anthēra synthesis*: Hesiod, Sappho, Anacreon, Simonides, Euripides, Isocrates; among historians, for instance Ephorus and Theopompus. Of the *koinē harmonia*: Homer, Stesichorus, Alcaeus, Sophocles, Herodotus, Demosthenes, Democritus, Plato, Aristotle. The three kinds of style and the three kinds of composition do not match perfectly; where is the composition that belongs to *charaktēr ischnos*? Gradually an additional style (*deinotēs*) is added (to *ischnos, megaloprepēs,* and *glaphyros*, a fourth: *deinos* [clever, skillful]).

Synthesis megaloprepēs has paeonic rhythm at the beginning or end of the *kōla*. It has no fear of *dysphōnia* (*freni* or *dysprophora*) or of hiatus and hard words. Metaphors. In brief . . . similes, huge composita, *onomata pepoiēmena*, a moderately poetic coloration, Thucydides as master of the grandiose style. (Opposite: *charaktēr psychros*, grasping for intellect, symbols, etc.). *Charaktēr glaphyros* is charming, with innocent joking, brevity, proverbs, fables, choice of the *leia onomata*, which consist entirely or predominantly of vowels. Rhythmic speech. (Opposite: *kakozēlon*, affectedly stupid).

Charaktēr ischnos uses ordinary colloquial language as its guideline. It uses noticeable composition (*dipla onomata*), *pepoiēmena*, and likes to say a thing twice. *Enargeia* and *pithanotēs* [are] the main thing. (Opposite: *xēros charaktēr*).

Deinotēs loves emphatic things, *kommata* instead of *kōla*, it loves powerful composition, despises antitheses and *paromoia*, uses mostly periods with two clauses, *paraleipsis, prosopopoiia, anadiplosis, anaphora*, especially *dialysis* (omission of conjunctions).

Asyndeton, Klimax. Gegenstück χαρ. ἄχαρις. Cynizismus des Ausdrucks, unverhüllte Nacktheit usw. Ende der elocutio oder lexis.

X. DIE LEHRE VON DER STASIS

Die inventio ist die *Auffindung* des Stoffes. Wichtige Begriffsbestimmungen gehen vorher. Gegenstand der νόησις intellectio der Stoiker. (νόμος, εὕρεσις, διάθεσις). Sie wird so beschrieben. Sulpitius Victor, p. 315: intelligendum primo loco est thesis sit an hypothesis. cum hypothesin esse intellexerimus i.e. controversiam, intelligendum erit an consistat, tum ex qua specie sit, deinde ex quo modo, deinde cuius status, postremo cuius figurae. Also θέσεις quaestiones infinitae allgemeiner Art (philosophisch), ὑποθέσεις auf bestimmte Fälle quaestiones finitae. Die allgemeinen zerfallen in theoretische Thesen (quaestiones cognitionis) und praktische (quaestiones actionis, auch θ. πολιτικαί genannt) (z. B. ob einer sich mit dem Staat zu befassen habe, ob man Handel treiben solle). Die Thesen kommen für den Redner nur als Vorübungen in Betracht. Eigentlich gehen ihn nur die speziellen Fälle an (Begebenheiten, Personen, Zeiten bestimmt) caussae controversiae. Die einzelnen Fragen der περίστασις sind quid, quando, ubi, cur, quemadmodum, quibus adminiculis (ἀφορμαῖς). Hat der Redner in der νόησις erkannt, dass er mit einer ὑπόθεσις zu thun hat, so sucht er, ob sie in sich Bestand hat, an consistat, oder ob sie ein ἀσύστατον ist. Eine Frage ist durch verschiedene Urtheile bedingt, ja oder nein, κατάφασις affirmatio, ἀπόφασις negatio (im genus iudiciale spezielle accusatoris intentio oder insimilatio und defensoris depulsio oder deprecatio). Sagt der Ankläger, du hast einen Menschen getödtet, der Beklagte, ich habe ihn nicht getödtet, so entsteht die Frage, ob er ihn getödtet hat. Der status prima deprecatio defensoris cum accusatoris insimulationis coniuncta, status στάσις quod in eo caussa consistat, "Bestand." Die

Hence: *asyndeton, climax.* (Its opposite is *charaktēr acharis*: cynicism of expression, unconcealed nakedness, etc.) End of *elocutio* or *lexis.*

X. THE DOCTRINE OF STASIS

Inventio is the *discovery* of material. Important definitions of terms precede it. The Stoics' object of *noēsis intellectio* (*nomos, heuresis, diathesis*) is so described. Sulpitius Victor, p. 315:

intelligendum primo loco est thesis sit an hypothesis. cum hypothesin esse intellexerimus, i.e. controversiam, intelligendum erit an consistat, tum ex qua specie sit, deinde ex quo modo, deinde cujus status, postremo cujus figurae. [In the first place it must be understood whether it is a thesis or a hypothesis. Once it has been determined to be a hypothesis, i.e. a controversial point, it will have to be understood whether it exists, then on what idea it rests, then of what kind it is, then of what status, and finally of what figure].

Thus *theseis* [general propositions] apply to *quaestiones infinitae* of a general nature (philosophically), *hypotheseis* (the case) [applies] to certain cases, *quaestiones finitae* [definite questions]. The general questions are divided into theoretical theses (*quaestiones cognitionis*) and practical ones (*quaestiones actionis*), also called *theseis politikai* (e.g. whether one must bother with the state, whether one should engage in trade). The theses come in question for the speaker only as preliminary exercises. Actually he is concerned only with specific cases (particular incidents, persons, times), *caussae controversiae.* The individual questions of the *peristasis* [circumstance] are *quid, quando, ubi, cur, quemadmodum, quibus adminiculis (aphormais)* [what, when, where, why, to what extent, and with what instruments (means or resources)]. Once the speaker has recognized in the *noesis* that he is dealing with *hypothesis*, he studies whether it exists (*an consistat*) or whether it is an *asystaton.* A question is conditioned by various judgments, yes or no, *kataphasis (affirmatio), apophasis (negatio)* (in the *genus iudiciale* [there is] a special *accusatoris intentio* or *insimilatio* [accuser's charge] and *defensoris depulsio* or *deprecatio* [defender's rebuttal]). If the accuser says, "You killed a man," while the accused says, "I did not kill him," then the question arises whether he did kill him. The *status prima deprecatio defensoris cum accusatoris insimulationis coniuncta, status, stasis, quod in eo caussa*

Theorie der ἀσύστατα richtig für die Deklamation schätzen. Eine στάσις kommt nur aus κατάφασις und ἀπόφασις zu stande, beide müssen ein Grund für sich haben: das, womit der Kläger seine κατάφασις begründet, heisst αἴτιον (propter quod res in iudicium devocatur), das womit der Gegner seinen ἀπόφασις begründet heisst συνέχον, firmamentum, / quo continetur omnis defensio. Aus αἴτιον und συνέχον resultiert τὸ κρινόμενον, der Gegenstand richterlicher Entscheidung. Es giebt nur vier Arten von ἀσύστατα 1. ὑπόθεσις ἐλλείπουσα κατ᾽ ελλιπές. Hier fehlt einer der notwendigen Bestandtheile der ὑπόθεσις, wenn ein Vater seinen Sohn ohne jeden Grund verstösst. Ebenso wie für den Grund, kann auch die Person, der Ort oder sonst ein μόριον περιστάσεως fehlen. 2. ὑπόθεσις ἰσάζουσα ἰσομερής. Zwei junge Leute, Nachbarn, haben beide schöne Frauen. Sie sehen sich beide des Nachts aus ihren Wohnungen heraustreten und klagen sich gegenseitig des Ehebruchs an: verisimile est te adulterium voluisse committere quia adolescens es.— "te quoque verisimile est voluisse quia adolescens es." verisimile est quia speciosam uxorem habeo. "te quoque verisimile est, quia et ego speciosam uxorem habeo." facultatem tibi vicinitas praebuit. "et tibi eadem vicinitas praebuit facultatem." cur nocte in me? "cur tu autem in me incidisti?" 3. ὑπόθεσις μονομερής: es fehlt an einem συνέχον, es ist keine Vertheidigung möglich. 4. ὑπόθεσις ἄπορος. Hier fehlt es an αἴτιον und συνέχον, und in Folge dessen kann der Richter zu keinem κρινόμενον kommen. Ein Beispiel aus dem genus deliberativum: Jemand träumt, er solle den Träumen keinen Glauben schenken. Was soll er nun beim Erwachen thun? Glaubt er dem Traum, dann folgt, dass er ihm nicht glaubt, glaubt er ihm nicht, dann folgt, dass er ihm glaubt.

consistat (Bestand) [the first basis, the defender's denial coupled with the accuser's charge].

The theory of *asystata* [cases impossible of proof] [must be] correctly estimated for declamation. A *stasis* [arguable case] comes about only from *kataphasis* [accusation] and *apophasis* [denial], both must have a reason supporting them: the one on which the accuser bases his *kataphasis* is called *aition (propter quod res in iudicium devocatur* [the grounds (on which a case is taken to court]), the one on which the opponent bases his *apophasis* is called *synechon, firmamentum, quo continetur omnis defensio* [the central argument, in which the entire defense is contained]. From *aition* and *synechon* results *to krinomenon*, the object of judicial decision.

There are only four kinds of *asystata*: (1) *hypothesis elleipousa, kat' ellipes.* Here one of the necessary components of the *hypothesis* is missing, when a father disinherits his son without any reason. Like the reason, the person, place or any other *morion peristaseōs* [part of the circumstances] can be missing. (2) *hypothesis isazousa isomerēs.* [An argument that cuts equally in either direction]. Two young men, neighbors, both have beautiful wives. They see each other leaving their apartments at night and accuse one another of adultery:

> *verisimile est te adulterium voluisse committere quia adolescens es.—* *"te quoque verisimile est voluisse quia adolescens es." verisimile est quia speciosam uxorem habeo. "te quoque verisimile est, quia et ego speciosam uxorem habeo." facultatem tibi vicinitas praebuit. "et tibi eadem vicinitas praebuit facultatem." cur nocte in me? "cur tu autem in me incidisti?"* [It is probable that you wanted to commit adultery because you are a young man. "It is also probable that you wanted to because you are young too." It is probable because I have a beautiful wife. "It is probable in your case too, because I too have a beautiful wife." Proximity gave you the opportunity. "It also gave you the same opportunity." Why did you enter my place at night? "Why did you enter my place?"]

(3) *hypothesis monomerēs*, one *synechon* is missing, no defense is possible. (4) *hypothesis aporos.* Here *aition* and *synechon* are missing, and as a consequence, the judge can come to no *krinomenon* [decision]. An example from the *genus deliberativum*: someone dreams that he should give no credence to dreams. What should he do on awakening? If he believes the dream, then it follows that he does not believe it; if he does not believe it, then it follows that he believes it.

Die einzelnen στάσεις. Gegen eine Anschuldigung kann sich der Redner auf eine vierfache Art vertheidigen. Er kann die That erstens leugnen. Dann sagen es sei nicht das geschehen, was behauptet wird. Drittens, er kann sie vertheidigen, indem er sie als eine unschuldige Handlung hinstellt. Viertens, bleibt ihm übrig zu sagen, die Klage sei nicht richtig erhoben, er kann die Competenz des Klägers oder des Gerichtshofs angreifen: also Absicht, die Entscheidung hinausschieben. (1) status coniecturalis, (2) status definitivus, (3) status qualitatis, (4) translatio.

Also: (1) status conjecturalis, στοχασμός, Frage an sit, der Thatbestand steht nicht fest, es findet controversia de facto statt, und durch Conjektur wird der Thatbestand ermittelt. Ajax stürzt sich, bewusst geworden über die Thaten des Wahnsinns, in einem Wald ins Schwert. Ulysses kommt und zieht die blutige Waffe heraus. Teuker kommt, sieht den getödteten Bruder, zugleich seines Bruders Feind, und klagt ihn des Mordes an. Die meisten antiken Gerichtsreden gehören zum status conjekturalis. Man unterscheidet conjectura plena στοχασμὸς τέλειος und non plena ἀτελής. Bei ersterer wird Person und That vermittelt, bei zweiterer bloss die That. Beide sind entweder ἁπλοῖ oder διπλοῖ, je nachdem es sich um eine Person und Sache oder mehrere handelt.

(2) status definitivus, ὅρος ὁρισμός, quid sit, es wird nicht die Thatsache sondern die vom Kläger gewählte Bezeichnung erstritten. controversia criminis. C. Flaminius bringt als Volkstribun gegen den Willen des Senats und der Optimaten in seinem Aufstande beim Volke ein Ackergesetz in Vorschlag. Als er eine Volksversammlung abhält, führt ihn sein Vater aus dem Tempel weg. Er wird der Majestätsverletzung angeklagt. Behauptung: Du hast die Majestät verletzt, weil du einen Volkstribun aus dem Tempel fort hingeführt. Antwort: Ich habe nicht verletzt. Frage: Hat er die Majestät verletzt? Begründung: Ich habe von der mir zustehenden väterlichen Gewalt Gebrauch gemacht. Entgegnung. Wer auf Grund einer Privatgewalt eine Volksgewalt angreift, verletzt die Majestät. κρινόμενον: ob derjenige die Majestät verletze, der gegen die tribunarische Gewalt von seiner väterlichen Gebrauch mache.

Einteilung wieder in ἁπλοῖ und διπλοῖ, Letztere zerfallen in 5 Klassen: ὅρος ἀντονομάζων, ὅρος κατὰ σύλληψιν, ὅρος κατὰ πρόσωπα διπθοῦς, ὅρος ἐμπίπτων und δύο ὅροι.[11] Bei (1) wird eine That vom Kläger unter diesen, vom Verklagten unter jenen Begriff gebracht. (2) Bei 2 geschieht dies in der Art, dass beide Bezeich-

The individual *staseis* [basic lines of argument]. The speaker can defend himself against an accusation in four different ways. First of all, he can deny the deed. Secondly, he can say that what is claimed never happened. Thirdly, he can defend it by making it appear as an innocent action. Fourthly, he can still resort to saying that the charge has not been made correctly, he can attack the competency of the plaintiff or the court: hence the intention of postponing the decision. (1) *status conjecturalis*; (2) *status definitivus*; (3) *status qualitatis*; (4) *translatio*.

To begin with: (1) *status conjecturalis, stochasmos*, the question *an sit*, the facts of the case are not certainly established, a controversy *de facto* takes place and the facts are determined by conjecture. Having become aware of the deeds he has committed in madness, Ajax throws himself on his sword in the forest. Ulysses comes and pulls out the bloody weapon. Teucer arrives, sees his dead brother, and at the same time his brother's enemy, and accuses him of murder. Most ancient forensic orations belong to the *status conjecturalis*. A distinction is made between *conjectura plena* (*stochasmos teleios*) and *non plena* (*atelēs*). In the first one, the person and deed are established, in the second merely the deed. Both are either *haploi* or *diploi*, depending on whether one person and cause or several are involved.

(2) *Status definitivus* (*horos horismos*), *quid sit*, not the fact but the term chosen by the plaintiff is denied, *controversia criminis*. During his revolt C. Flaminius, as a tribune of the people, proposes to the people a land reform law against the will of the Senate and the *optimati*. While he is holding a popular assembly, his father leads him out of the temple. He is accused of *lèse majesté*. Statement: you violated protocol by leading a tribune of the people out of the temple. Answer: I did not. Question: Did he commit *lèse majesté*? Reason: I made use of my rightful authority as a father. Reply: Whoever attacks a popular power on the basis of a private one is guilty of *lèse majesté*. *Krinomenon*: Whether a person who makes use of his fatherly authority against the tribune's power is guilty of *lèse majesté*.

A further division is made into *haploi* and *diploi*. The latter are subdivided into five classes: *horos antonomazōn, horos kata syllēpsin, horos kata prosōpa diplous, horos empiptōn*, and *duo horoi*.[89] In (1) a deed is brought under one concept by the accuser, under another by the accused. In (2) this happens in such a way that the

nungen zu einander sich verhalten wie Species zum Genus. Der Kläger adoptiert die Definition des Angeklagten, aber subsümiert sie
unter einen höheren Begriff. (3) Beim ὅρος κατὰ πρόσωπα διπλοῦς
vindizieren sich zwei Personen eine That oder streiten sich um ein
und dieselbe Sache. (4) Beim ὅρος ἐμπίπτων fällt in die constitutio
finitiva noch eine andere Frage dazwischen; z.B. ein nicht in die
Mysterien Eingeweihter sieht sie im Traum und fragt einen Einge-
weihten, dem er das, was er gesehen mittheilt, ob es sich so verhalte.
Der bejaht es und wird als Verräther der Mysterien angeklagt. Hier
fragt sich erst: was heisst die Geheimnisse verrathen? Das [ist] die
constitutio finitiva, dann kommt die Frage: was ist ein Uneingeweih-
ter? (5) Es wird bei einer Person nach zwei Definitionen gefragt: das
Gesetz lautet: τὸν καθαρὸν καὶ καθαροῦ ἱερᾶσθαι. Jemand wird von
der Priesterwürde ausgeschlossen, weil er seinen ehebrecherischen
Vater getödtet hat.

3. status qualitatis: der ποιότης oder iuridicialis mit der Frage:
quale sit. es handelt sich um Beschaffenheit der That, ob sie zulässig
oder nicht, gesetzlich oder ungesetzlich, nützlich oder unnütz sei. Als
die Thebern die Lacedämonier überwunden hatten, so errichteten sie
eine eherne Trophäe: Sitte, dass die Sieger zum Zeichen des augen-
blicklichen Sieges eine Trophäe auf Feindesgebiet errichten, sie woll-
ten aber für alle Zeiten den Sieg manifestieren. Deshalb werden sie
beim Amphityonen-Gericht verklagt. Behauptung: es durfte nicht
geschehen. Antwort: es durfte geschehen! Frage: ob es geschehen
durfte? Begründung: wir haben durch unsere Tapferkeit im Kriege
einen solchen Ruhm gewonnen, dass wir ewige Abzeichen desselben
unseren Nachkommen lassen wollen. Entgegnung: Griechen dürfen
über Griechen kein ewiges Denkmal ihrer Feindseligkeiten errichten.
Gegenstand der Beurtheilung: wenn Griechen über Griechen zur
Feier ihrer ausserordentlichen Tapferkeit ein ewiges Denkmal ihrer
Feindseligkeiten errichten, ob sie darin recht oder unrecht han-

two designations are related to one another as species to genus. The plaintiff adopts the defendant's definition, but subsumes it under a higher concept. (3) In *horos kata prosōpa diplous* two persons clear themselves of one deed or quarrel over one and the same matter. (4) In *horos empiptōn* an additional question is interjected into the *constitutio finitiva*: e.g. a person not initiated into the mysteries sees them in a dream and asks an initiate to whom he tells what he has seen whether that is the way they are. He assents and is accused of betraying the mysteries. The first question is: what does it mean to betray the secrets? That [is] *constitutio finitiva*, then comes the question: what is a noninitiate? (5) In regard to one person, two definitions are sought: the law states *ton katharon kai ek katharou hierasthai* [Only the pure and offspring of the pure are eligible for the priesthood]. Someone is excluded from the priestly dignity because he has killed his adulterous father.

(3) *Status qualitatis*: the *poiotēs* or *iuridicialis* with the question *quale sit*. It deals with the nature of the act, whether it is permissible or not, legal or illegal, useful or useless. When the Thebans had conquered the Lacedaemonians, they erected a bronze trophy according to the custom that the victors set up a trophy on enemy territory as a symbol of the victory of the moment. Therefore they were sued before the Amphictyonian Court. Assertion: It was not permissible. Answer: It was permissible! Argument: We acquired such fame through our courage in war that we want to leave an eternal memorial of it to our descendants. Counterargument: Greeks should not erect an eternal memorial to their hostilities with Greeks. Object of judgment: If Greeks set up an eternal memorial of their hostilities with Greeks to celebrate their extraordinary bravery, are they acting rightly or wrongly?

deln?—Unterarten der Qualitätsstatus:

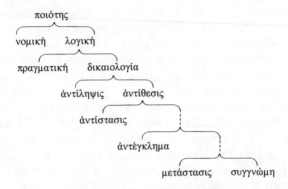

Die Qualität fragt entweder auf Grund einer That oder einer gesetzlichen Urkunde. Im letzten Falle die στάσις νομική genus legale. Im ersteren die στάσις λογική genus rationale. Die That entweder zukünftig oder bereits geschehen: die zukünftige gibt die στάσις πραγματική constitutio negotialis. Die geschehene die δικαιολογία constitutio juridicialis (oder der eigentl. Qualitätsstatus). Nun giebt der Angeklagte seine That als Vergehen zu oder nicht. Erklärt er die Handlung für erlaubt, so haben wir die ἀντίληψις, die constitutio iuridicialis assumptiva. Giebt er die That als Vergehen zu, sucht sie aber durch Herbeiziehung von Nebenumständen zu rechtfertigen, so haben wir die ἀντίθεσις.

Die constitutio iuridicialis assumptiva. Der Verklagte nimmt nun die als Vergehen eingestandene That ganz auf sich—ἀντίστασις compensatio: er zeigt, dass das Gesetzwidrige weit durch sein andersweitigen Nützen überwogen wird. Auch die Vertheidigung einer That, weil im Unterlassungsfalle sich etwas Schlimmeres zugetragen hätte.—Oder der Angeklagte überträgt die als Vergehen eingestandene That auf etwas Äusseres: die allgemeine Bezeichnung fehlt. Unterabtheilungen: Der Beklagte überträgt das Vergehen auf den durch ihn Beeinträchtigte selbst, ἀντέγκλημα, relatio criminis, die

Subdivisions of the quality—status:[90]

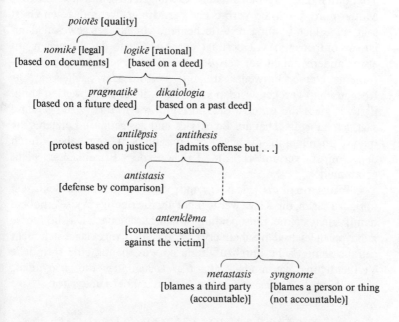

Quality asks either on the basis of a deed or of a legal document. In the latter case it is *stasis nomikē, genus legale*. In the former, the *stasis logikē, genus rationale*. The deed is either future or has already happened: the future one gives *stasis pragmatikē, constitutio negotialis*; the one that has already happened, the *dikaiologia, constitutio juridicialis* (or the quality status in the strict sense). Now the accused admits that his deed is an offense or not. If he declares the action to be legal, we have the *antilēpsis*, the *constitutio iuridicialis absoluta*. If he admits that the deed is an offense, but tries to justify it by citing attendant circumstances, then we have *antithesis*.

The *constitutio iuridicialis assumptiva*: the accused now accepts responsibility for the crime which is admittedly an offense.—*Antistasis, compensatio*: he shows that the violation of the law is far exceeded by its benefits in other regards. This includes the defense of a deed because if omitted something worse would have happened.—Or the accused transfers the admittedly wrongful deed to something external: there is no general term for this. Subdivisions: the accused transfers the offense to the victim himself, *antenklēma*,

stärkste Unterart der const. iurid. assumptiva. Man erklärt zu der That durch das Vergehen anderer gezwungen zu sein, wie Orest zum Muttermord durch die Verbrechen der Mutter (wenn dagegen Orest sagt, seine That sei für ganz Griechenland von Nutzen gewesen, dann ist es compensatio).—Überträgt der Angeklagte das Vergehen auf etwas anderes, nicht auf den Beeinträchtigten, fehlt wieder der allgemeine Name. Entweder auf eine Person oder Sache, die zur Rechenschaft gezogen werden kann, oder die es nicht werden kann. Ersteres giebt die μετάστασις die remotio criminis (wenn jemand sagt, ich habe die That auf Befehl des und des gethan). Letzteres die συγγνώμη purgatio: die angeklagten zehn Strategen haben, durch den Sturm verhindert, die Leichen der Ertrunkenen nicht gesammelt.

4. Translatio μετάληψις oder παραγραφή. Es bleibt dem Beklagten übrig, zu sagen, die Klage werde nicht auf die richtige Weise erhoben: damit sucht er die Entscheidung hinauszuschieben. Da die blosse παραγραφή leicht den Schein erweckt, dass der Angeklagte sich nicht getraue seine Sache durchzuführen, so wird häufig eine förmliche Vertheidigung verbunden ὡς τῆς εὐθυδικίας τοῦ πράγματος εἰσηγμένης. Die εὐθυδικία ist das Gegentheil der παραγραφή.

XI. GENERA UND FIGURAE CAUSARUM

Diese bilden den nächsten Gegenstand der intellectio. ex qua specie sit, ex quo modo, cuius figurae. Die Bezeichnungen der Rhetoren schwanken: die Ausdrücke genera figurae (σχήματα) und modi werden bald von der einen, bald von der anderen Eintheilung gebraucht. *Erste Eintheilung* der caussae (species). γένος ἔνδοξον, ἄδοξον, ἀμφίδοξον, παράδοξον, δυσπαρακολούθητον. Der Gegenstand erscheint der Behauptung oder Vertheidigung werth oder unwerth. Die Personen oder die streitige Sache erscheinen kaum der Beachtung werth (Diebstahl eines Schankmädels). Der Gegenstand kann gemischter Natur sein, anständige Person, unanständige Sache, ἀμφίδοξον. Er kann der Art sein, dass man sich wundert, wie ihn jemand vertheidigen kann, παράδοξον. Endlich sehr complizirt und obscurum. *Zweite Eintheilung* der Hypothesen (modus). Die causa entweder simplex oder iuncta ex pluribus quaestionibus. *Dritte Eintheilung* (figura) in Bezug auf eine gewisse Beschaffenheit der caussa, die für die Art der Darstellung von Wichtigkeit ist. genus ethicum, Person und Sache sind beklagenswerth. Der Redner hat sich in das

relatio criminis; this is the strongest subtype of *constitutio iuridicialis assumptiva.* One claims to have been forced to do the deed by someone else's misconduct, as Orestes committed matricide due to his mother's crimes (if, on the contrary, Orestes says that his deed was beneficial to all of Greece, then that is *compensatio).*—If the accused transfers the offense to something other than the victim, again a general term is missing. Either to a person or thing which can be called to account, or which cannot be called to account. The first results in *metastasis* or *remotio criminis* (when someone says I did the deed at the command of this or that person). The latter is *syngnōmē, purgatio:* the accused ten admirals failed to gather the corpses of the drowned because they were prevented by the storm.

(4) *Translatio, metalēpsis* or *paragraphē.* The accused still has the recourse of saying that the suit was not filed properly: he tries thus to postpone the decision. Since the mere *paragraphē* easily arouses the appearance that the accused does not dare to plead his cause, often a formal defense is combined *hōs tēs euthydikias tou pragmatos eishēgmenēs* [on the grounds of proposed immediate acceptance by defendant of the process]. The *euthydikia* is the opposite of the *paragraphē.*

XI. GENERA AND *FIGURAE CAUSARUM*

These comprise the next object of *intellectio: ex qua specie sit, ex quo modo, cuius figurae* [on what idea it rests, what it consists of, and what form it has]. The rhetoricians' terms vary: the expressions *genera figurae* (*schēmata*) and *modi* are used now for one, now for another classification. *First classification* of the *caussae* (*species*): *genos endoxon* [*honestum*], *adoxon* [*humile*], *amphidoxon* [*dubium*], *paradoxon* [*admirabile*], *dysparakolouthēton* [*obscurum*].[91] The object seems worthy or unworthy of assertion or defense. The persons or the disputed matter seem hardly worth attention (theft by a barmaid). The object can be of mixed nature, a decent person, an indecent act, *amphidoxon.* It can be of such a kind that one wonders how anyone can defend it, *paradoxon.* Finally, very complicated and obscure. *Second classification* of hypotheses (*modus*). The cause is either simple or *iuncta ex pluribus quaestionibus* [a combination of many questions]. *Third classification* (*figura*), in relation to a certain nature of the *caussa* which is important for the manner of presentation. In the *genus ethicum* the person and cause are deplorable. The

ἦθος der von ihm vertretenen Person zu versetzen. Beim genus
patheticum kommt die Leidenschaft der Person in Betracht, die sie
zu einer gewaltsamen Handlung veranlasst hat. Beim genus apodicticum handelt es sich nur um den beizubringenden Beweis. Beim
genus diaporeticum ist die Sache selbst ungewiss und muss sehr
behütsam angefasst werden. Beim genus mixtum kommen mehrere
der genannten Arten in Betracht. Eine andere Eintheilung über den
ductus caussae (oder den genus figuratum, ductus est agendi per
totam caussam tenor sub aliqua figura servatus. Ductus simplex, die
Absicht des Redners ist von den Worten nicht verschieden. Beim
ductus subtilis verfolgt der Redner zunächst eine andere Absicht als
in seinen Worten liegt. Beim ductus figuratus wird der Redner durch
eine schamhafte Nachsicht verhindert, seine Meinung gerade heraus
zu sagen. Er giebt seine Absicht verhüllt zu verstehen. Beim ductus
obliquus dasselbe, nur wird der Redner durch Furcht verhindert.
Der ductus mixtus, gemischt. Wird der ductus nicht in der ganzen
Rede durchgeführt spricht man von color χρῶμα. Die griech. Termini σχηματισμὸς ἐναντίος (ductus subtilis), σχ. πλάγιος (ductus
obliquus), σχ. κατ' ἔμφασιν (ductus figuratus).

XII. DIE THEILE DER GERICHTSREDE

Fünf Theile: prooemium προοίμιον exordium, narratio διήγησις,
probatio πίστις, ἀπόδειξις, κατασκευή, refutatio λύσις auch
ἀνασκευή, peroratio ἐπίλογος. Dann schliessen sich auch partitio
und propositio an die probatio an: endlich ist die egressio oder excessus kein Theil, sondern ein Zusatz zu den Theilen, von denen es
abschweift. Zusammenfassung bei Cicero orator 35, 122: quid iam
sequitur, quod quidem artis sit, nisi ordiri orationem, in quo aut
concilietur auditor aut erigatur, aut paret se ad discendum; rem breviter exponere et probabiliter et aperte, ut quid agatur intelligi possit:
sua confirmare, adversaria evertere eaque efficere non perturbate,
sed singulis argumentationibus ita concludendis, ut efficiatur quod
sit consequens eis, quae sumentur ad quamque rem confirmandam:
post omnia perorationem inflammantem restinguentemve con-
cludere?

Prooemium:[12] Cicero, de orat. 77, pflegt oft zuletzt an den Eingang
der Rede zu denken; wollte er den Anfang zuerst aussinnen, so "ver-
mochte ich nur Dürftiges und Alltägliches zu finden." Das prooemium, sehr wichtig als erste Wahrnehmung und Empfehlung des

speaker must put himself into the *ēthos* [character] of the person he represents. In the *genus patheticum* the passion which led a person to commit a violent act is considered. In the *genus apodicticum* it is a matter only of the proof that must be presented. In the *genus diaporeticum* the matter itself is uncertain and must be dealt with very carefully. In the *genus mixtum* several of the aforementioned types come into consideration. Another classification for the *ductus caussae* (or the *genus figuratum*): *ductus est agendi per totam caussam tenor sub aliqua figura servatus* [The 'conducting' of an argumentation is the course, uninterrupted throughout the trial, kept up under any one of the *figurae*].[92] *Ductus simplex*, the speaker's intention is not different from the words. In the *ductus subtilis*, the speaker first pursues a different intention than his words state. In the *ductus figuratus* the speaker is prevented by a shameful consideration from speaking his mind openly. He lets his intention be known cryptically. In the *ductus obliquus* the same thing except that fear is what prevents the speaker. The *ductus mixtus*, mixed. If the *ductus* is not carried out throughout the speech the term used is *chrōma*. The Greek terms are *schēmatismos enantios (ductus subtilis), schēmatismos plagios (ductus obliquus),* and *schematismos kat' emphasin (ductus figuratus).*

XII. THE PARTS OF THE FORENSIC SPEECH

Five parts: *prooemium (prooimion, exordium), narratio (dihēgēsis), probatio (pistis, apodeixis, kataskeuē), refutatio (lysis,* also *anaskeuē) peroratio (epilogos).* Then *partitio* and *propositio* are also added to the *probatio*: finally *egressio* or *excessus* is not a part, but an addition to the parts, from which it digresses. Summary in Cicero (*Orator,* 35, 122):

> *quid iam sequitur, quod quidem artis sit, nisi ordiri orationem, in quo aut concilietur auditor aut erigatur, aut paret se ad discendum; rem breviter exponere et probabiliter et aperte, ut quid agatur intelligi possit: sua confirmare, adversaria evertere eaque efficere non perturbate, sed singulis argumentationibus ita concludendis, ut efficiatur quod sit consequens eis, quae sumentur ad quamque rem confirmandam: post omnia perorationem inflammantem restinguentemve concludere?* [For what remains that is subject to the rules of art, except to begin the speech in such a manner as to win the favor of the audience or to arouse them or to put them in a receptive mood; to set forth the facts briefly, clearly, and reasonably, so that the subject under dispute may be understood; to prove

Redners: er muss augenblicklich die Zuhörer einnehmen. Der Consul L. Marcius Phillippus pflegte zwar zu sagen: er pflege dann zu kämpfen, wenn ihn der Arm erst warm geworden sei. Cicero sagt dagegen, dass selbst die Fechter anfangs ihre Lanzen sanft schwingen, um ihre Kräfte für das Folgende aufzusparen und um eine schöne Stellung zu zeigen. Der Inhalt nicht von aussen her, sondern aus dem Inneren der Sache entnommen. Mann muss oft die ganze Sache erforscht und durchschaut haben und alle Beweisgründe gefunden und geordnet haben. Der Eingang wird am besten aus dem innersten Mark der Vertheidigung entlehnt, aus den Materien, welche an Beweisgründen am reichsten sind. Die Eingänge müssen zu der Sache in Verhältniss stehen wie die Vorhöfe und Eingänge zu den Häusern und Tempeln. Bei ganz geringfügigen Dingen ist es das Beste gleich mit der Sache anzufangen. Der Eingang soll auf das Engste mit der nachfolgenden Rede verbunden sein, dass er nicht wie das Vorspiel des Zitharöden angedichtet, sondern als ein Glied des ganzen Körpers erscheine. Die Gedanken des Eingangs sind entweder von dem Angeklagten oder vom Gegner oder von der Sache oder von den Zuhörern herzunehmen. Vom Angeklagten, indem man ihn als einen redlichen, von Missgeschick verfolgten, des Mitleidens würdigen Mann schildert: vom Gegner indem man das Umgekehrte sagt. Von der Sache, indem sie grausam, unnatürlich, unerwartet, unverschuldet, unersetzlich, unheilbar geschildert wird. Von den Zuhörern, indem man ihr Wohlwollen zu gewinnen sucht. Jetzt sind die Zuhörer am gespanntesten: er soll benivolus, attentus, docilis gemacht werden. Um das Wohlwollen des Richters zu erlangen, spricht der Redner von sich wenig und mit Mass. Es kommt darauf an, dass der Redner für einen vir bonus gehalten wird, damit dass auch die Glaubwürdigkeit gewinne, seine Parteilichkeit als Anwalt zurücktrete. Er gewinnt an Ansehen, wenn er von seinem Anbieten den Verdacht von schmutzigem Gewinn, von Gehässigkeit, von Ehrgeiz fern zu halten weiss. Demosthenes sagt in der Einleitung der Reden gegen Androtion und Timokrates: "Fast immer finden wir, dass die συνήγοροι sich bemühen, den Richtern ihr Auftreten gleichsam zu vertheidigen, indem sie entweder ihre Freundschaft mit dem, für welchen sie sprechen, oder ihren Hass gegen den Gegner, oder irgend einen anderen triftigen Grund angeben, um dem Verdacht zu begegnen, als hätten sie sich für Geld dazu dingen lassen."—Eine Empfehlung liegt darin, dass er sich als schwach, unvorbereitet, dem Gegner nichtgewachsen bezeichnet: vor allem hat man seine Bered-

one's case and demolish the adversary's, and to do this not confusedly, but with arguments so conclusive as to prove what is the natural consequence of the principles laid down to prove each point; finally to pronounce a peroration either to inflame or to quench the passion of the audience].[93]

Prooemium.[94] Cicero (*De Oratore*, 77) often tends to think of the beginning of the speech last; if he wanted to think of the beginning first, then "I would be able to find only something scanty and banal." The *prooemium* is very important as the speaker's first perception and recommendation: he must win the audience instantly. The Consul L. Marcius Phillippus used to say: he tended to fight only after his arm was warm. Cicero says, on the contrary, that even fencers at the beginning swing their lances gently, in order to save their strength for later and to show a beautiful stance. The content is not taken from the outside, but from the heart of the matter. One must have studied and examined the whole case often and found and classified all proofs. The opening is best taken from the innermost core of the defense, from the materials which are richest in proofs. The openings of speeches must stand in relation to the cause as the porticoes and lobbies to houses and temples. In very trivial things it is best to get right to the point. The opening should be very closely connected with the following speech, so that it does not seem like a prelude but like part of the whole edifice. The thoughts of the opening must be taken either from the defendant, from the plaintiff, from the case, or from the audience. From the defendant, by describing him as an honest man, pursued by bad luck and worthy of pity; from the plaintiff, by saying the opposite. From the case, by describing it as cruel, unnatural, unexpected, undeserved, irreparable, and irremediable. From the listeners, by wanting to win their favor. Now the audience is most intent: it must be made *benivolus, attentus, docilis* [favorably disposed, attentive, docile].

To obtain the judge's favor, the speaker talks little and moderately about himself. What matters most is for the speaker to be considered a *vir bonus* so that he gains credibility and his partisanship as advocate falls to the background. He gains repute if he manages to keep his pleading far from the suspicions of mercenariness, hatefulness, ambition. Demosthenes says in the introduction to the speeches against Androtion and Timocrates: "We almost always find that the *synhēgoroi* [advocates] strive to defend their appearance in the eyes of the judges by citing either their friendship for their client, or their

samkeit sorgfältig zu verbergen: *artis est artem tegere.* Man kann so
thun, als fürchte man sich vor dem Anwalt der Gegenpartei, vor
seine Beredsamkeit, seinen persönlichen Einfluss und macht ihn
damit den Richtern verdächtig. Die Anwendung von 1000 kleinen
Kunstgriffen richtet sich natürlich nach den genera causarum. Beim
ἀμφίδοξον muss man den Richter hauptsächlich wohlwollend
machen. Beim δυσπαρακολούθητον vor allem gelehrig, beim
ἄδοξον aufmerksam. Das ἐνδοχον genügt schon an sich, den Richter
zu gewinnen. Beim παράδοξον besondere Mittel, bes. die insinuatio,
das sich Einschleichen in den Geist des Zuhörers. Im allgemein solle
man von dem, was an der Sache verletze, seine Zuflucht zu dem nehmen, was an derselben nütze. Wenn es zuvorderst am wünschens-
wertheste ist, sich möglichst viel Gunst zu erwerben, so ist das näch-
ste, sich möglichst wenig Hass zuzuziehn. Bei dem, was sich nicht
leugnen lässt, muss man darauf hinzeigen, dass es kleiner ist, als
gesagt wurde oder in anderer Absicht geschehen. Dann dass es zu
vorliegender Frage keinen Bezug habe oder dass es schon hinlänglich
bestraft sei. Wenn die Darstellung des Gegners die Richter einge-
nommen hat, ist insinuatio nöthig. Wir werden sofort unser Beweiss
in Aussicht stellen und auf die kommende Widerlegung hinweisen.
Sind die Richter ermüdet, werden wir Hoffnung auf Kürze erregen,
auch einen Witz machen.—Die Form des prooem. anlangend, darf
kein ungewöhnlicher Ausdruck, kein kühner Metapher darin sein.
Steckenbleiben und Stolpern ist uns im ganzen am bedenklichsten:
das ist der schlechteste Steuermann, der sein Schiff gleich beim Aus-
laufen aus dem Hafen auffahren lässt. Fehler des Prooemium: es
darf nicht vulgare sein, nicht zu mehreren Fällen passen. Nicht
commune, der Gegner darf sich desselben nicht auch bedienen können. Nicht commutabile, der Gegner darf es nicht zu seinem Nutzen ausbeuten können. Nicht separatum, ohne Zusammenhang mit der Sache. Nicht translatum, nicht anderswo hergeholt,
und darf nichts anderes zu Wege bringen als die Sache verlangt, es
darf den Zuhörer nicht gelehrig machen, wenn es gilt, sein Wohlwollen zu erwecken. Es darf kein principium sein, wenn die Sache
eine insinuatio verlangt. Es darf nicht *lang* sein.

   Narratio, διήγησις. Es braucht nicht immer erzählt zu werden. Die
Erzählung fällt weg, wenn es sich um keine Begebenheit, sondern um
eine Rechtsfrage handelt, ποιότης νομική genus legale. oder wenn
bereits alles früher auseinandergesetzt wurde, in einer Deuterologie.
Dann tritt wohl eine κατάστασις ein, d.h. ein ψιλὴ ἔκθεσις
πραγμάτων. Verschiedene τόποι der Erzählung. προδιήγησις erzählt

hatred for the opponent, or some other suitable reason, to counter the suspicion of having hired themselves out for money."

It is also commendable to present himself as weak, unprepared, no match for his opponent: above all, one must carefully conceal one's eloquence: *artis est artem tegere* [it is the mark of art to conceal art]. One can pretend to be afraid of the opposite party's lawyer, of his eloquence, his personal influence, and thus to cast suspicion on him in the eyes of the judges. The use of a thousand little tricks depends, of course, on the *genera causarum* [kinds of cases]. In the *amphidoxon*, one must primarily dispose the judge favorably. In the *dysparakoloutheton* mainly [keep him] informed; and in the *adoxon*, attentive. The *endoxon* already suffices by itself to win over the judge. The *paradoxon* uses particular means, especially insinuation, by which it sneaks into the mind of the listeners. Generally, one should escape from what harms the cause to what helps it. If the first priority is to acquire as much goodwill as possible, the next is to attract as little hatred as possible. As to what cannot be denied, one must point out that it is of less consequence than was said or that there was a different intention behind it. Then that it is irrelevant to the present question or that it has already been punished sufficiently. When the opponent's presentation has convinced the judge, *insinuatio* is necessary. We will immediately hold our proof in prospect and allude to the coming refutation. If the judges are tired, we will arouse hope of brevity, and also tell a joke.

As regards its form, the *prooemium* should contain no unusual expression, no bold metaphor. Halting and stumbling are generally most dubious: the worst helmsman is the one who smashes his boat while leaving the harbor. Errors of the *prooemium*: it must not be *vulgare*, fitting many cases. Not *commune*, the opponent must not be able to use it. Not *commutabile*, the opponent must not be able to exploit it to his advantage. Not *separatum*, without connection with the case. Not *translatum*, not farfetched and achieving something else than the case requires; it must not instruct the listener when what is necessary is to arouse his goodwill. It must not be a *principium* when the case calls for an *insinuatio*. It must not be *long*.

Narratio (*dihegesis*). It is not always necessary to narrate. The narrative is omitted when one is dealing not with an incident but with a legal question, *poiotes nomike* (*genus legale*), or when everything has already been explained before in a deuterology. Then a *katastasis* [presentation] probably occurs, i.e. a *psile ekthesis pragmaton* [short exposition of the facts]. Various *topoi* of the narrative. *Prodihegesis*

dessen, was der Darlegung des Sachverhalts vorausliegt; auch προκατάστασις genannt. ὑποδιήγησις die Art, welche mit der That zugleich auch Motive, Pläne und Veranlassungen der Thaten erzählt. Die παραδιήγησις eigentlich extra causam, aber trägt bei, die Richter für unsere Darlegung des Sachverhalts zu gewinnen, theils eine Digression, nur angenehm, theils zur Steigerung. Also zu Parallelgeschichten, Gegenstücke. ἀντιδιήγησις gegen die Erzählung des Gegners gerichtet. καταδιήγησις die Erzählung dient mit als Beweis. Die ἐπιδιήγησις findet ihre Stelle nach dem Beweis, repetita narratio.— Anforderungen deutlich, σαφής, lucida, aperta; kurz, σύντομος brevis; wahrscheinlich, πιθανή, verisimilis [sic], probabilis, credibilis. Cicero, de orat. II 80, kämpft gegen die Kürze. Versteht man darunter soviel Worte als schlechterdings nothwendig, so schadet sie, nicht nur weil sie Dunkelheit bewirkt, sondern weil sie nicht unterhält und interessiert. Zuweilen muss man stehenbleiben: Die Personen müssen belebt einander gegenüber gestellt werden. Deutlichkeit ist hier wichtiger als irgendwo: eine dunkle Erzählung macht die ganze Rede dunkel. Zur Wahrscheinlichkeit gehört, dass man die περιστάσεις richtig giebt und vollständig: Person, Sache, Ort, Zeit, Ursache (μόρια περιστάσεως). Die Hauptereignisse muss man aus ihren Gründen, also pragmatisch, erzählen. Wichtig, dass manches wahr und doch nicht wahrscheinlich ist. Oft ist das Falsche wahrscheinlich. Die Erzählung der Sache ist entweder ganz für uns, oder ganz für den Gegner oder gemischt. Im zweiten Fall kommt es dann sehr auf das genus caussae und die στάσεις an. Beweis status definitio, wo es sich um die Art der Handlung handelt, kann man die That eingestehen, also gleich mit der nöthigen Beschränkung. Fragt es sich, ob die That, oder wie sie geschehen ist, status conjecturalis und qualitatis, so kann man die Erzählung nicht umgehen: denn dann würde der Richter glauben, man räume die übertriebene Darstellung des Klägers als wahr ein. Mitunter werden Erdichtungen nöthig. Die müssen höchst wahrscheinlich sein. Man darf es auch nicht wieder vergessen, im Verlauf der Rede.

Die egressio παρέκβασις, ἐκδρομή. παρέκβασις δέ ἐστι λόγος ἐξαγώνιος μέν, συναγωνιζόμενος δὲ πρός ἀγῶνα. Vor der confirmatio gewöhnlich ein angenehmer Excurs. Er ist nur dann statthaft, wenn er gleichsam das Ende der Erzählung oder der Anfang des Beweises ist. Dahin gehört das Lob von Menschen und Orten, Beschreibung von Gegenden, Mittheilung interessanter Fabeln. (Lob Siciliens und Erzählung von dem Raub der Proserpina in den Verrinen. In der Rede pro Archia, über den Werth der Dichtkunst. (Die

tells about what preceded the portrayal of the facts of the case; also called *prokatastasis*. *Hypodihēgēsis*, the art of telling, together with the deed, at the same time the motives, plans, and occasion of the deeds. *Paradihēgēsis* actually *extra causam*, but contributes to winning over the judges to our portrayal of the facts; in part it is a digression, a pleasant one, however, in part for intensification. Hence, for parallel stories and precedents. *Antidihēgēsis* is directed against the opponent's narrative. In *katadihēgēsis*, the narrative serves as part of the proof. *Epidihēgēsis* finds its place after the proof, *repetita narratio*.

Requirements [are that the narrative be] clear, *saphēs*, *lucida*, *aperta*; brief, *syntomos*, *brevis*; probable, *pithanē*, *verisimile*, *probabilis*, *credibilis*. Cicero (*De Oratore*, 2, 80), opposes brevity. If one understands by it only as many words as absolutely necessary, it is harmful, not only because it causes obscurity but because it does not amuse and interest. At times one must stop: the persons involved must be contrasted vividly. Clarity is more important here than anywhere: a vague narrative makes the whole speech vague. Part of probability is to give the *peristaseis* rightly and completely: person, thing, place, time, cause (*moria peristaseōs*). The main events must be told with their causes, i.e. pragmatically. Important that some things are true and yet not probable. Often the false is probable. The narration of the case is either completely for us, or completely for the opponent, or mixed. In the second case, it depends on the *genus caussae* and the *staseis*. Proof, *status definitio*, when it is a question of the kind of action, one can admit the deed, i.e., with the necessary reservation. If the question is whether the deed took place, or how it took place, *status conjecturalis* and *qualitatis*, then the narrative cannot be avoided: for then the judge would believe that one were conceding that the plaintiff's exaggerated description is true. Sometimes fabrications are necessary. They must be extremely probable. Nor must one forget them in the course of the speech.

The *egressio, parekbasis, ekdromē* [digression]. *parekbasis de esti logos exagōnios men, synagōnizomenos de pros agōna* [digression is a statement which, though beside the point, is a fellow combatant in the struggle].[95] Generally a pleasant digression before the proof is presented. It is permissible only when it is, as it were, the end of the narrative or the beginning of the proof. Here belong praise of persons and places, description of regions, communication of interesting fables. (Praise of Sicily and narration of the rape of Proserpina in the *Verrine* speeches. In the speech *Pro Archia*, on the value of litera-

Episoden der Historiker der παρενθῆκαι fallen mit unter dem Begriff der παρέκβασις). Formeln, durch welche der Redner wieder zurückkehrt, longius evectus sum, sed redeo ad propositum. Mitunter andere Stellung der egressio, vor dem Schluss, auch gleich nach dem Prooemium. Die *Propositio ad partitio*, πρόθεσις giebt das ζήτημα, das eigentliche Thema von der Rede. Schliesst sich an die Erzählung an, kann ihr auch vorher gehen, selbst mitten hineingenommen werden. Sehr nützlich beim status finitivus, damit der Richter einsieht, seine Aufgabe sei ganz allein zu untersuchen, welche Bezeichnung der That die richtige sei. Es können dem Angeklagten ein, zwei, oder mehrere Punkte zur Last gelegt werden. Darnach ist die propositio einfach, zweifach, mehrfach. Man legt dem Richter genau dar, worüber er zu entscheiden hat. Die geordnete Aufzählung unserer Propositionen, oder deren des Gegners, oder beides ist partitio. Bei jeder Eintheilung ist immer ein Punkt der wichtigste; wenn der Richter dieses hört, pflegt er die anderen für überflüssig zu halten. Wenn wir also Mehreres vorzuwerfen haben, ist eine partitio ganz angemessen. Wenn wir ein Vergehen auf verschiedene Weise vertheidigen, ist sie unnütz. Wenn man eintheilt: "ich werde sagen, dass mein Klient nicht der Mann ist bei dem ein Mord glaublich scheinen könnte; ich werde sagen, dass er keine Veranlassung zum Tödten gehabt hat; ich werde zeigen, dass er zu der Zeit, als der Mensch getödtet wurde, über See war"—so wird alles, nach dem letzten Punkt, überflüssig. Gutes Beispiel giebt Cicero de invent. 1, 23: ostendam adversarios, quod arguimus, et potuisse facere et voluisse et fecisse: das letzte zu zeigen ist genug. Viele verwerfen eine solche Vertheidigung: "wenn ich getödtet habe, so habe ich recht gehandelt, aber ich habe nicht getödtet." Wozu das Erste, wenn das zweite sicher ist! Aber wenn es nicht so ganz fest steht, wird es gut sein, wenn der Redner beides benützt, das eine als pars absoluta, das andere als pars assumptiva. Eine sichere Hand kann sich mit einem Stoss begnügen: eine unsichere muss mehrere besitzen. Eine zur rechter Zeit angewandte Partition wirkt angenehm: der Richter merkt, dass ein Theil zu Ende ist: wie die Inschrift auf den Meilenzeigern, wenn man eine lange Reise macht. Hortensius war berühmt dadurch: doch macht sich Cicero über das Pedantische mitunter lustig.

Probatio argumentatio πίστεις κατασκευή κεφαλαίων, später ἀγῶνες. Manche ziehen ihn mit der Widerlegung zusammen. so ist der wichtigste Theil, der nie fehlen darf. Nach Aristot. theilt man die πίστεις in ἄτεχνοι und ἔντεχνοι. Die ausserhalb der Kunst liegenden

ture.) The episodes of the historians of the *parenthēkai* [insertions] fall under the concept of *parekbasis* [deviation, digression]. Formulae by which the speaker returns to the subject, *longius evectus sum, sed redeo ad propositum* [I have digressed very long, but now I am returning to the subject]. Sometimes the *egressio* is located elsewhere, before the ending or right after the *prooemium*.

The *propositio ad partitio* (*prothesis*) presents the *zētēma* [thing sought], the actual theme of the speech. It is appended to the narrative, but can also precede, or even be inserted within it. Very useful for the *status finitivus* so that the judge will realize that his task is simply to investigate what term correctly designates the deed. One, two, or several charges can be made against the accused. Accordingly, the *propositio* is simple, double, or plural. One spells out precisely for the judge what he must decide on.

The orderly enumeration of our propositions, or the opponent's, or both, is *partitio* [division]. In every division, one point is always the most important one; when the judge hears this, he usually considers the others to be superfluous. If we have several points to make, a *partitio* is quite appropriate. But when we defend one offense in different ways, it is useless. When one divides: "I will say that my client is not the kind of man of whom the commission of a murder would seem credible: I will say that he had no reason to kill; I will show that at the time when the man was killed he was overseas"— after the last point everything else is superfluous. Cicero (*De Inventione*, 1, 23) cites a good example: *ostendam adversarios, quod arguimus, et potuisse facere et voluisse et fecisse* [I will show that the opponents both were able to and wanted to do and did what we claim]: to show the last is enough. Many reject such a defense: "If I killed, then I acted right, but I did not kill." Why the first point, if the second one is certain! But when it is not quite sure, it will be good for the speaker to use both, the one as *pars absoluta*, the other as *pars assumptiva*. A sure hand can settle for one push: an unsure one must use several. A *partitio* used at the right time makes a pleasing impression: the judge notices that one part is over: like the mileage on road signs when one makes a long journey. Hortensius was famous for this: but sometimes Cicero makes fun of this pedantry.

Probatio, argumentatio, pisteis kataskeuē kephalaiōn, later *agōnēs*. Some combine it with the refutation, so it is the most important part, which must never be missing. According to Aristotle, the *pisteis* [probable as opposed to demonstrative proofs] are divided into *atechnoi* [not invented by the orator] and *entechnoi* [skillfully

Beweise werden nicht vom Redner herbeigeschafft, sondern liegen
ihm vor, sie sind bloss anzuwenden; die innerhalb der Kunst liegenden sind aufzufinden. 1. Der unkünstliche Beweis: Gesetze, Zeugen,
Verträge, Foltergeständnisse, Eidschwüre. An die Gesetze schliessen
sich Senats- und Volksbeschlüsse, richterliche Entscheidungen, usw.
an. An die Zeugenaussagen, die testimonia divina: Orakelsprüche,
Vorzeichen. Hinzuzufügen zu den fünf Arten bei Aristoteles: die
προκλήσεις provocationes. Aufforderung der einen Partei an die
andere, irgend eine Handlung zu leisten, um durch sie den Rechts-
streit zu erledigen: Eid, Herausgabe eines Dokuments, Sklaven zur
Tortur zuzulassen. Die Annahme oder Verweigerung der provocatio
wird aktenmässig festgestellt: als moralischen Beweis für die Schlech-
tigkeit der Sache gilt die Verweigerung. *Gesetze*. Ist das geschriebene
Gesetz entgegen, so muss der Redner an das allgemeine Gesetz und
die Billigkeit appellieren: schon die Eidesformel der Richter γνώμῃ
τῇ ἀρίστῃ drückt aus, nicht ohne Unterschied durchaus nur das
geschriebene Recht zur Anwendung zu bringen. Der Richter sei eine
Art Münzwart um das Ungerechte vom Gerechten zu unterscheiden.
Spricht das geschriebene Gesetz für den Redner, so sagt der, der Ausdruck "nach bestem Wissen und Gewissen" besage nicht, dass der
Redner gegen das Gesetz entscheiden solle, sondern sei nur da, damit
der Richter, falls er nicht wisse, was das Gesetz besage, keinen Meineid begehe. Ein Gebot nicht anzuwenden, sei aber so gut, als wäre es
nicht da. Es sei verderblich, es besser wissen zu wollen als der Arzt:
ein Fehlgriff des Arztes sei lange nicht so schlimm als die dauernd
hervorgehende Gewöhnung, den Oberen nicht zu gehorchen: klüger
sein wollen als die Gesetze, werde ja ausdrücklich in anerkannt guten
Gesetzen verboten. *Praeiudicia*. Erstens, Urtheile, die aus gleichen
Rechtsgründen gefällt sind, res quae aliquando ex paribus caussis
sunt iudicatae. Zweitens, schon gefällte Urtheile, die auf die Sache
selbst Bezug haben. Drittens, Urtheile, die bereits über die Sache
selbst gefällt sind, in niederen Instanzen. *Gerüchte* gelten der einen
Partei als öffentliche Meinung, als öffentliches Zeugniss! Der anderen
als Resultat der Bosheit, vergrössert durch Leichtgläubigkeit. *Foltergeständnisse* dagegen, Cicero, pro Sulla c. 28. quaestiones nobis ser-
vorum accusator ac tormenta minitatur: in quibus quamquam nihil
periculi suspicamur, tamen illa tormenta gubernat dolor, moderatur
natura cuiusque cum animi tum corporis, regit quaesitor, flectit
libido, corrumpit spes, infirmat metus, ut in tot rerum angustiis nihil
veritati loci relinquatur. Dagegen sagen, dass Foltergeständnisse

wrought].[96] The proofs located outside art are not procured by the speaker, they are ready at hand, he need only use them; those within art must be discovered.

1. The natural proof [is based on]: laws, witnesses, contracts, confessions under torture, oaths. Under laws fall senate decrees and popular referenda, judicial decisions, etc. Under eyewitness statements are divine testimonies, oracular sayings, omens. Aristotle adds a sixth category: *proklēseis* (*provocationes*). One party challenges the other to perform some act in order to thereby settle the legal dispute: an oath, surrender of a document, submission of slaves to torture. The acceptance or rejection of the *provocatio* becomes a matter of record: refusal is considered a moral proof for the badness of the case. *Laws.* If the written law is against him, the speaker must appeal to universal law or fairness: even the judge's oath of office, *gnomēi tēi aristēi* [to the best of one's judgment], expresses that he should not apply the written law indiscriminately. The judge is a kind of custodian (*Münzwart*) to distinguish justice from injustice. If the written law is in the speaker's favor, then he says that the expression "according to one's best knowledge and conscience" does not mean that the judge should decide contrary to the law, but is only there so that the judge should not commit perjury, in case he did not know what the law says. But not to apply a precept was the same as if it did not exist. It is ruinous to want to know better than the doctor: but a doctor's mistake is far less disastrous than the increasing tendency to disobey the authorities: to want to be more clever than the laws is expressly forbidden in admittedly good laws. *Praejudicia* [preliminary decisions]: First, judgments which were made on the same legal grounds, *res quae aliquando ex paribus caussis sunt iudicatae.* Secondly, judgments already passed which have some relation to the case itself. Thirdly, judgments already passed on the case itself, in lower courts. *Rumors* are considered as public opinion, as public testimony, by one party. For the other, they result from malice magnified by credulity. *Confessions under torture.* Cicero opposes them in *Pro Sulla* (c. 28):

> *quaestiones nobis servorum accusator ac tormenta minitatur: in quibus quamquam nihil periculi suspicamur, tamen illa tormenta gubernat dolor, moderatur natura cuiusque cum animi tum corporis, regit quaesitor, flectit libido, corrumpit spes, infirmat metus, ut in tot rerum angustiis nihil veritati loci relinquatur* [The prosecutor threatens us with an examination of the slaves by torture. Although no danger threatens us from this, still in examinations by torture pain is the guiding motive,

zuverlässiger sind als Zeugen, denn den Zeugen nützt es oftmals die Unwahrheit zu sagen, den Gefolterten dagegen, die Wahrheit zu sagen, um sobald als möglich ihrer Pein frei zu sein. *Eidschwur.* Liegt es in unserem Interesse, einem Eide Gewicht beizulegen, so sagt man: niemand wird einen Meineid schwören aus Furcht vor der Strafe der Götter und der Schande bei den Menschen. Vor den Göttern kann man ihn nicht verbergen. Nimmt der Gegner zum Eide seine Zuflucht, wollen wir seine Bedeutung herabsetzen, sagen wir: Menschen die Schlechtes thun, scheuen sich auch vor einem Meineide nicht. Man bezieht sich auf Beispiele von Meineiden. Seinen Eid, ohne Bedingung, dass mindestens auch der Gegner schwören solle, anbieten, gilt fast für gottlos. Wer einen angebotenen Eid zurückweist, wird auf die ungleiche Lage hinweisen, dass er selbst mit einem Aufwand von Beweismitteln seine Sache führt, und jener so leichten Kaufs davon kommen will: von vielen werde die Furcht vor einem Eide verachtet, zumal als [es] auch Philosophen giebt, die lehren, dass die Götter sich gar nicht um die Menschen bekümmern. Man wolle lieber beweisen, was man behaupte, als einen Zweifel lassen, ob man falsch geschworen. *Zeugenaussagen.* Entweder zu Akten gegeben oder persönlich vorgebracht. Gegen die ersteren lässt sich leichter ankämpfen: vor einem zahlreichen Gerichtshofe würde der Zeuge weniger wagen, falsch zu zeugen. Seine Abwesenheit kann als Misstrauen ausgelegt werden. Gegen anwesende Zeugen verfährt man (1) durch actio: (2) interrogatio, d.h. in zusammenhängender Rede oder Fragen vorlegend. Bei der actio liegt das Material der Zeugenaussagen schon vor, bei der interrogatio wird es erst genommen. Letztere gehört nicht zur Aufgabe des Redners, sondern des Anwaltes, ebenso wie die altercatio, dem römischen Gerichtsverfahren eigenthümlich: vor dem Spruch des Urtheils dringen die Anwälte noch einmal mit kurzen Fragen aufeinander ein.

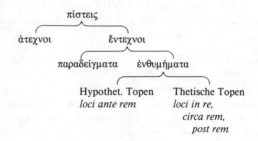

each one's qualities of mind and body control it, the inquisitor directs it, passion diverts it, hope vitiates it, fear weakens it, so that in such straits there is no place left for truth].[97]

Against this one can say that confessions under torture are more reliable than witnesses, for the witnesses often find it to their advantage to lie, but the tortured tell the truth in order to be freed from their pain as soon as possible. *Oaths.* If it is in our interest to include an oath, then one says: no one will commit perjury out of fear of the punishment of the gods and disgrace before men. One cannot hide the perjury from the gods. If the opponent resorts to an oath, we want to minimize its significance by saying: men who do wrong are not afraid of committing perjury. Then one cites examples of perjury. To offer one's oath without the condition that the opponent too should swear is considered almost atheistic. Whoever rejects an offered oath will point out the unequal situation that he pursues his case with a great quantity of proofs, and the other party wants to get off so cheaply: many make little of the fear of perjury, especially since there are philosophers who teach that the gods do not concern themselves with men at all. One should prove what one states rather than leave any doubt whether one swore falsely. *Witnesses' testimony* is either placed on record or presented in person. The former is easier to attack: the witness would be less likely to give false testimony before a numerous jury. His absence can be interpreted as a lack of confidence. Against witnesses in person one proceeds: (1) by *actio*, (2) by *interrogatio*, i.e. in a coherent speech, or by cross-examination. *Actio* is used when the testimony of the witnesses is already available; *interrogatio* when it still remains to be elicited. The latter is not the speaker's task, but the lawyer's, as is the *altercatio*, which is peculiar to the Roman trial system: before the judgment is pronounced, the lawyers bombard one another with short questions.

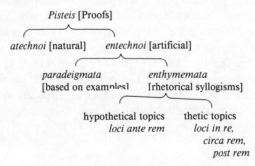

Pisteis [Proofs]

atechnoi [natural]   *entechnoi* [artificial]

paradeigmata   *enthymemata*
[based on examples]   [rhetorical syllogisms]

hypothetical topics   thetic topics
loci ante rem   *loci in re,*
                         circa rem,
                         post rem

Der *künstliche Beweis*, eine logische Operation, durch die das Ungewisse mittelst des Gewissen oder Wahrscheinlichen Glaubwürdigkeit bekommt, πίστις argumentum argumentatio. Dagegen ist ἀπόδειξις kein rhetorischer Terminus. Jeder Beweis durch Induction (durch Beispiele) oder durch Syllogismus (durch Schlüsse) zu Rede gebracht. Die πίστεις zerfallen also in ἐνθυμήματα und παραδείγματα. Die ἐνθυμήματα zerfallen in δεικτικά und ἐλεγκτικά. Ist der erste Schluss vollständig aus Obersatz, Untersatz, Schlusssatz bestehend, so heisst er Epicheirem. Dionysus v. Halic. bemerkt, dass Lysias nur in Enthymenen, Isaeus und Hyperides auch in Epicheiremen beweisen. Alle τόποι für einzelne Beweise zerfallen in loci ante rem, in re, circa rem, post rem. Denn sind die loci ante rem hypothetische loci, solche also die sich mit den Peristasen befassen, dem complexus rerum personarumque durch welche das ζήτημα zur Hypothesis wird: die anderen, loci in re, circa rem, post rem, sind thetische Topen, die sich mit der nach Abzug der Peristasen in jeder Hypothesis befindlicher Thesis befassen. Die Topen der ersten Gruppe sind konkret persönliche und sachliche, die der zweiten abstrakt logische. Zu den loci ante rem gehören Name, Natur (Geschlecht, ob Mann oder Frau, Nation, Vaterland, Verwandtschaft, Alter, natürliche Eigenschaften des Körpers und der Seele) Lebensweise (Erziehung, Unterricht, Lehrer, Freunde, Beruf, Verwaltung des Vermögens, häusliche Gewohnheit) Glück (Sklave oder Freier, reich oder arm, Privatmann oder in öffentlicher Stellung, glücklich oder unglücklich, berühmt oder unberühmt, was er für Kinder hat; bei einem Todten, welche Todesart er gehabt hat), geistige und körperliche Stimmung, Studien, Pläne, Absichten, Thaten, Zufälle, Reden. Dann die Sache betreffend: Ort, Zeit, Gelegenheit, Art und Weise, die zur Ausführung vorhandenen Mittel und Werkzeuge. Dann *Ursachen*: der Grund unsers Thuns dreht sich einmal um Erhaltung, Vermehrung, Erlangung von Gütern oder Vermeidung, Befreiung, Verminderung von Übeln. Das Böse kommt aus den falschen Meinungen, den Irrthümern und Leidenschaften, Zorn Hass, Begierde, Furcht; dann einiges Zufälliges: Trunkenheit, Unwissenheit. Die thetischen Topen (die abstrakten): 1. *loci in re*, zunächst der Schluss von dem Ganzen auf die Theile, oder umgekehrt. Beispiel: si totam rem publicam prodidit, quod ex multis rebus ostenditur, non est incredibile eum classem et equitatum prodidisse.

The *artificial proof*, a logical operation, by which the uncertain is given credibility by means of the certain or probable, *pistis, argumentum, argumentatio. Apodeixis* [proof], on the other hand, is not a rhetorical term. Each proof is examined by induction (through examples) or syllogism (deduction). The *pisteis* thus are divided into *enthymēmata* [enthymemes, rhetorical syllogisms based on probable premises] and *paradeigmata* [proof by examples, historical or fictitious; rhetorical induction]. The *enthymēmata* are divided into *deiktika* [positive proofs] and *elengtika* [refutations]. If the first conclusion is complete, consisting of major and minor premise and conclusion, it is called *epicheireme* [attempted or dialectical proof, opposite of a demonstrative syllogism]. Dionysius of Halicarnassus remarks that Lysias proved only by means of enthymemes, while Isaeus and Hyperides also used epicheiremes.

All *topoi* for individual proofs can be divided into *loci ante rem, in re, circa rem, post rem* [commonplaces prior to the fact, during the fact, around the fact, after the fact]. For the *loci ante rem* are hypothetical loci, i.e. such as deal with the *peristases*, the *complexus rerum personarumque* [complex of facts and persons] through which *zētēma* becomes a hypothesis: the others, *loci in re, circa rem, post rem*, are thetic topoi, which deal with the thesis located in each hypothesis after withdrawal of the *peristases*. Topoi of the first group are concretely personal and objective, those of the second abstractly logical. Among the *loci ante rem* are name, nature (sex, man or woman, nation, fatherland, relatives, age, natural qualities of body and soul), way of life (education, instruction, teachers, friends, profession, administration of wealth, domestic habits), fortune (slave or free, rich or poor, civilian or in public office, happy or unhappy, famous or unknown, what kind of children he has; for a deceased person what kind of death he had), psychological and physical mood, studies, plans, intentions, deeds, accidents, speeches. Then concerning the case: place, time, opportunity, circumstances, means and instruments used to carry out the deed. Then *causes*: the basis of our action is centered first on the preservation, increase, or attainment of goods or avoidance, deliverance, lessening of evils. Evil stems from false opinions, errors and passions, anger, hatred, desire, fear; then some accidental things: drunkenness, ignorance.

The thetic topoi (abstract ones) are:

1. *loci in re*, first the deduction from the whole to the parts, or vice versa. Example: *si totam rem publicam prodidit, quod ex multis rebus ostenditur, non est incredibile eum classem et equitatem prodidisse*

Dann werden Beweise aus der definitio entlehnt, bei einer Def. kommt es auf genus, species, und differentia (Artunterschied) an und endlich proprium das spezifische Merkmal. Lebendes Wesen ist genus, sterbliches lebendes Wesen, species, auf dem Lande lebendes, differens: endlich, rationale, dann ist dies das proprium. Einen Beweis a genere: quoniam argentum omne mulieri legatum est, non potest ea pecunia, quae numerata domi relicta est. non esse legata; forma enim a genere, quoad suum nomen retinet, numquam seiungitur, numerata autem pecunia nomen argenti retinet: legata igitur videtur. Die Zerlegung eines genus in seine species heisst divisio: Beispiel: "Du willst Geld verliehen haben, dann hast du es entweder selbst gehabt, oder von Jemand empfangen, oder gefunden, oder gestohlen. Wenn du es aber weder zu Hause gehabt usw., so hast du keines verliehen." Das ist der Beweis ex remotione: "Dieser Sklave, den du beanspruchst, ist entweder in deinem Hause geboren, oder gekauft, oder geschenkt, oder testamentarisch vermacht, oder dem Feinde abgenommen, oder fremd"—jetzt werden alle Möglichkeiten, ausser der letzten, beseitigt. Häufig diese Manier in Form des Dilemmas. διλήμματον σχῆμα: man legt dem Gegner zwei Fragen vor, die beide ihm gleich verhängnisvoll sind. 2. loci circa rem laufen auf Vergleichung hinaus: "Wer einen Tempelraub begeht, der wird auch einen Diebstahl begehen." "Wer leicht und öffentlich lügt, der wird auch falsch schwören." "Wer sogar seinen Vater schlägt, schlägt auch seinen Nebenmenschen."

3. Loci post rem, die Beweise ab eventu (ἀπὸ τῆς ἐκβάσεως) und ab iudicatu, z.B. quodsi ex eo, quod hi naves reliquerunt et ad pedestrem exercitum transierunt, victoriam paraverunt, desertores eos appellare non possumus. Vom zweiten sagt Quintilian: utimur iudicatu tum omnium, tum plurimorum, tum optimorum, praeterea

[If he betrayed the entire republic, which is shown by many things, it is not incredible that he betrayed the knightly class].[98] Then proofs are borrowed from the definition; in a definition it is a matter of *genus, species,* and *differentia* (specific difference), and finally *proprium,* the specific trait. "Living being" is genus; "mortal living being" is species; "living on land," specific difference; finally, "rational" is a property. A generic proof:

> *quoniam argentum omne mulieri legatum est, non potest ea pecunia, quae numerata domi relicta est, non esse legata; forma enim a genere, quoad suum nomen retinet, numquam seiungitur, numerata autem pecunia nomen argenti retinet: legata igitur videtur* [Because a woman inherits all the money, she cannot fail to inherit that money which is counted and left in the house; for the species is never separated from the genus, insofar as it retains its name; but counted money retains the name of money: therefore she seems to inherit it].[99]

The division of a genus into its species is called *divisio.* Example: "You claim to have lent money; then either you had it yourself, or you received it from somebody, or you found or stole it. But if you neither had it at home nor . . . etc., then you lent none." That is the proof *ex remotione* [by elimination]: "This slave, whom you claim was either born in your house, or bought, or given as a present, or bequeathed to you, or captured from the enemy, or belonged to someone else"—now all possibilities except the last one are eliminated. Frequently this approach is used in the form of a *dilemma, dilēmmaton schēma*: one poses two questions to the opponent, each as damaging as the other.

2. *loci circa rem* run in the same direction: "Whoever robs a temple will also commit a theft." "Whoever lies easily and publicly will also swear falsely." "Whoever beats even his father, will also beat his fellowman."

3. *loci post rem,* the proofs *ab eventu (apo tēs ekbaseōs)* and *ab iudicatu,* e.g. *quodsi ex eo, quod hi naves reliquerunt et ad pedestrem exercitum transierunt, victoriam paraverunt, desertores eos appellare non possumus* [but if these men by abandoning the ships and going over to the infantry prepared the victory, we cannot call them deserters].[100] Of the second one Quintilian says:

> *utimur iudicatu tum omnium, tum plurimorum, tum optimorum, praeterea eorum, qui in unaquaque arte peritissimi sunt* [we use the judgment now of all, now of the majority, now of the best, moreover of those who are most expert in an art].[101]

eorum, qui in unaquaque arte peritissimi sunt. Die παραδείγματα. Anaximenes sagt: παραδ. ἐστί πράξεις ὅμοιαι γεγενημέναι καὶ ἐναντίαι τοῖς νῦν ὑφ' ἡμῶν λεγομένοις. (wie man auch ἐνθυμήματα ex sequentibus—ex pugnantibus unterscheidet). Man hat Beispiele anzuwenden, um dem Gegenstand grössere Klarheit zu schaffen, falls dieser durch Beweisgründe noch nicht glaublich geworden ist. Als Beweise wendet man sie an, wo man keinen Enthymeme hat: als Zeugnisse, wo man Enthymeme hat, denen sie zum Nachwort dienen. Es giebt zwei Arten π. κατὰ λόγον und παρὰ λόγον, d.h. solche welche den Anschauungen der Zuhörer entsprechen oder welche nicht entsprechen. Erstere sollen einer Sache Glauben bringen, letztere der Sache die Glaubenswürdigkeit nehmen. "Die Reichen sind gerechter als die Armen," zum Beispiel, entspricht der allgemeinen Überzeugung. Führt man Beispiele von ungerechten Thaten der Reichen an, so widerspricht das den Anschauungen der Zuhörer und erschüttert den Glauben an ihre Richtigkeit. Es giebt wirkliche, es giebt erfundene Beispiele, letztere wieder theils vom Redner neuerfunden, theils von anderen bereits erfunden (Mythen, aesopische Fabeln.)

Refutatio, λύσις das vierte Theil oder mit der tractatio verbunden. Der schwierigste Theil der Rede. Die Widerlegung gegnerischen Behauptungen und Beweise. Die Rolle der Widerlegung ist nun ganz verschieden bei Ankläger und Vertheidiger. Letztere findet Behauptungen vor. Erstere muss sich solche Behauptungen erst künstlich schaffen. Er muss sich klar machen, was der Gegner alles zu seiner Vertheidigung vorbringen wird: er ist auf ὑποφορά und προκατάληψις angewiesen. Die στάσεις sind dabei von grösster Wichtigkeit. Der Ankläger muss dem Verklagten die Möglichkeit entziehen, sich unter einen anderen status zu flüchten. Alles was der Gegner aufgestellt hat oder aufstellen kann, ist ἀντίθεσις. Sie bedarf der λύσις. Man widerlegt durch einen Gegenschluss ἀντισυλλογισμός oder durch Vorbringung von Instanzen ἐνστάσεις. Diese werden auf viererlei Arten erhoben, aus der Sache selbst, oder aus einem Ähnlichen, oder aus dem Entgegengesetzten, oder aus einer vorhandenen Entscheidung. Sagt jemand, die Liebe sei etwas treffliches, so wendet man aus der Sache ein, dass jedes Bedürfniss ein Übel ist und dass man nicht von Καύνιος ἔρως (der Cariër Kaunos verliebt in seine Schwester) reden würde, wenn es nicht auch eine schlechte Liebe gebe. Sagt man: "der gute Mann thut allen Freunden Gutes," so entgegnet man aus dem Entgegengesetzten: "Auch der

The *paradeigmata*. Anaximenes says: *paradeigmata esti praxeis homoiai gegenēmenai kai enantiai tois nyn hyph' hēmōn legomenois* [Examples are when things happen that are similar but other than what is under our discussion][102] (as one also distinguishes *enthymē-mata ex sequentibus—ex pugnantibus* [syllogisms on the basis of one thing following from another, and those on the basis of things opposed to each other].[103] Examples must be used to give the subject greater clarity if it has not been made credible by arguments. They should be used as proofs, where one has no enthymemes: as witnesses, where one has enthymemes, to which they can serve as comment. There are two kinds, *paradeigmata kata logon* and *para logon*, i.e. such as correspond to the listeners' views or such as do not. The first are to lend credence to a matter, the second to detract from its credibility. "The wealthy are more just than the poor," for example, corresponds to the general conviction. If one adduces examples of unjust acts of the wealthy, that contradicts the views of the listeners and undermines their belief in their rightness. Examples can be real or invented, the latter in turn partly newly invented by others (myths, Aesopian fables).

Refutatio (*lysis*), the fourth part, or combined with the *tractatio*. The most difficult part of the speech. The refutation of the opponent's assertions and proofs. Now, the role of refutation is completely different for the accuser and the defender. The latter finds statements in existence. The former must first artfully discover such statements. He must make clear to himself everything that the opponent will present in his defense: he must rely on *hypophora* [purging of the opponent's statements] and *prokatalēpsis* [anticipation of the adversary's arguments]. The *staseis* are of the greatest importance in this. The accuser must block off any possibility for the accused to flee under another status. Everything that the opponent has established or can establish is *antithesis*. It needs *lysis* [refutation]. One refutes by a counterdeduction (*antisyllogismos*) or by citing precedents (*enstaseis*). These are raised in four ways: from the thing itself, or from a similar one, or from the opposite, or from an existing decision. If someone says that love is something excellent, then one objects, based on its nature, that every need is an evil and that one would not speak of *Kaunios erōs* (the Carian Kaunos in love with his sister), if there were not also a bad love. If someone says: "The good man does good to all his friends," then one replies from the opposite:

schlechte Mann thut ihnen kein Übles." Gegen die Behauptung "Leute, denen es schlecht gegangen ist, hassen immer," entgegnet man aus dem Ähnlichen: "Leute, denen es gut gegangen, lieben nicht immer." Gegen das Enthymem, den Betrunkenen muss man verzeihen, denn sie fehlen unbewusst, wendet man aus einer vorhandenen Entscheidung ein, dann ist Pittacus nicht zu loben, denn er hat auf Vergehen im Trunke grössere Strafen gesetzt.—Die Widerlegung geschieht entweder direkt, durch einfaches in Abredestellen oder indirekt. Letzteres, z.B., wenn man das, worauf zumeist der Gegner sich stützt, ihm unter den Füssen wegzieht od. es gegen ihn wendet. Iphikrates fragte den Aristophon, ob er wohl die Flotte um Geld verrathen würde: als Aristophon es verneinte, sagte er, Du, ein Aristophon würdest sie nicht verrathen, und ich ein Iphikrates sollte es thun? Das ist die μέθοδος κατὰ περιτροπήν. Zweitens, die μέθοδος κατὰ σύγκρουσιν. Man stellt die Behauptungen des Gegners einfach zusammen und zeigt, dass sie sich widersprechen. Drittens, die μέθοδος κατὰ μείωσιν. Was man durch die Rede nicht widerlegen kann, wirft man verächtlich bei Seite, ut quae dicendo refutare non possumus, quasi fastidiendo calcemus. Ist die gegnerische Antithese nicht eigentlich dem vorliegenden Falle entnommen, sondern von anderen herbeigezogen, so bedient man sich dieses locus: er gehöre nicht zur Sache, man dürfe sich nicht dabei aufhalten, es sei nicht so schlimm als der Gegner behaupte, auch wohl Stillschweigen. 4. μέθοδος κατ' αὔξησιν, wenn der Gegner die Sache als geringfügig darstellt. 5. λύσις κατ' ἀντιπαράστασιν, reichen die Mittel zur Beseitigung der Antithese nicht aus, so stellt man ihr etwas anderes entgegen. Man zeigt, dass die Antithese in ihren Folgen grausam, unehrenhaft, usw., sei. Oder man setzt Autorität gegen Autorität, Vorschlag gegen Vorschlag. Kräftig oft, die Verbindung von ἔνστασις und ἀντιπαράστασις. Behauptet der Gegner, es sei schwierig dies zu thun, so ist es ἔνστασις, es ist nicht schwierig. ἀντιπαράστασις, gesetzt es wäre schwierig, so muss es doch gethan werden, etwa weil es die Rechtlichkeit gebietet. Beruft der Gegner sich auf Gesetze und Urkunden (ἀντίθεσις ἄτεχνος ἀπὸ ῥητοῦ), so wird ἐξέτασις διανοίας angewendet. Die eigentliche Absicht des Gesetzgebers sei eine andere gewesen. Gegen ἀντιθέσεις παραδειγματικαί wendet man die λύσις ἐκ διαφορᾶς an: das angezogene Beispiel passt nicht her. Dann die ἀπαγωγὴ εἰς ἄτοπον deductio ad absurdum, sehr wirksam. Nach Abzug dieser Fälle bleiben noch genug ἀντίθεσις ἄλυτοι übrig, gegen die sich im Gemüth nichts

"The bad man also does them no evil." Against the statement "People who have had it bad always hate," one replies from the similar: "People who have had it good do not always love." Against the enthymeme that one must pardon drunks for they err unconsciously, one objects from an existing precedent, then Pittacus should not be praised, for he imposed greater penalties on offenses committed while drunk.

The refutation occurs either directly, through simple denial, or indirectly. The latter, for example, by pulling the opponent's main argument out from under him or turning it against him. Iphicrates asks Aristophon whether he would betray the fleet for money: when Aristophon answered negatively, he said, "You, an Aristophon, would not betray it, and I an Iphicrates would be expected to do it?" That is the *methodos kata peritropēn* [turning the opponent's argument against himself]. Secondly, the *methodos kata synkrousin*. One simply gathers together the opponent's arguments and shows that they contradict one another. Thirdly, the *methodos kata meiosin* [disparagement, minimizing]. What one cannot refute by speech, one casts aside contemptuously, *ut quae dicendo refutare non possumus quasi fastidiendo calcemus*. If the opposing antithesis is not really taken from the present case, but dragged in from another one, then one uses this *locus*: it was irrelevant, one should not waste time on it, it was not as bad as the opponent claimed, or else one can simply pass over it in silence. Fourthly, *methodos kat' auxēsin* [amplification], when the opponent describes the case as paltry. Fifthly, *lysis kat' antiparastasin*, if the means are inadequate to eliminate the *antithesis*, then one sets up something else against it. One shows that the *antithesis* is cruel, dishonorable, etc. in its consequences. Or one sets authority against authority, proposal against proposal. The combination of *enstasis* and *antiparastasis* is often strong. If the opponent says that it is difficult to do this, that is *enstasis*, it is not difficult, *antiparastasis*; assuming that it were difficult, still it must be done, for instance because the law requires it. If the opponent appeals to laws and documents (*antithesis atechnos apo rhētou*) [appeal deriving naturally from an accepted warrant], the *exetasis dianoias* [exposition of insight] is used. The lawgiver's real intention had been a different one. Against *antitheseis paradeigmatikai* one uses the *lysis ek diaphoras*: the cited example does not fit this case. Then the *apagōgē eis atopon*, *deductio ad absurdum*, very effective. After the removal of these cases enough *antitheseis alutoi* are still left against which no objections can be brought to mind.

sagen lässt. List und Sophismen: (1) Unter dem Schein, den Gegner zu widerlegen, klagt man ihn an: die Aufmerksamkeit der Richter [wird] auf einen ungünstigen Punkt abgelenkt. (2) Man schiebt die Widerlegung als vorläufig nicht zur Sache gehörig hinaus. (3) Man geht scheinbar auf die Behauptung ein, kehrt sie aber zu einer Anklage um. (4) Man giebt die Richtigkeit zu, stellt den Gesichtspunkt des Nutzens des Staatsinteresses dagegen. Dann zerlegt man die Behauptung und sucht die Theile zu entkräften. Man geht der Antithese aus dem Wege oder um sie herum. Man redet dem Gegner freundlich zu von seinen Ansprüchen abzusehen und erweckt den Schein, als ob es damit nichts sei. Man ändert die gegnerische Antithese, in dem man etwas leicht Widerlegbares hineinlegt und sich jetzt den Schein giebt, als habe man sie selbst widerlegt. Man übergeht eine Antithese ganz mit Stillschweigen, wenn man hofft, die Richter werden es nicht merken. Man giebt die Antithese zu, aber verdächtigt die Gesinnung des Gegners und gibt sich den Schein als wäre die Sache erledigt.

Peroratio, ἐπίλογος (cumulus oder conclusio) Nach Arist. Rhet. III. 19 mit 4 Bestandtheilen ὁ δ' ἐπίλογος σύγκειται ἐκ τεσσάρων· ἔκ τε τοῦ πρὸς ἑαυτὸν κατασκευάσαι εὖ τὸν ἀκροατὴν καὶ τὸν ἐναντίον φαύλως, καὶ ἐκ τοῦ αὐξῆσαι καὶ ταπεινῶσαι, καὶ ἐκ τοῦ εἰς τὰ πάθη τὸν ἀκροατὴν καταστῆσαι καὶ ἐξ ἀναμνήσεως. Meist enumeratio, amplificatio, commiseratio. Schlussformel, dass man fertig sei: οὐκ οἶδα ὅτι δεῖ πλείω λέγειν· οἴομαι γὰρ ὑμας οὐδὲν ἀγνοεῖν τῶν εἰρημένων. Oder: σχεδὸν εἴρηκα ἃ νομίζω συμφέρειν· ὑμεῖς δ' ἔλοισθε, ὅτι καὶ τῇ πόλει καὶ ἅπασι συνοίσειν ὑμῖν μέλλει. Die *enumeratio* lässt exord. und narratio unberührt, fängt bei der partitio an, und geht den Beweis und die Widerlegung kurz durch. Sie hilft dem Gedächtnisse des Richters. Man muss dasselbe mit Nachdruck enden. Die *amplificatio* regt die Zuhörer mittelst eines Gemeinplatzes auf, κοινὸς τόπος locus communis, zunächst Aufstellung des Gegentheils, soll z.B. ein Verräther angeklagt werden,

Deceit and sophistries: (1) pretending to refute the opponent, one accuses him: the judges' attention is diverted to an unfavorable point; (2) one postpones the refutation as irrelevant for the moment; (3) one pretends to discuss the statement but turns it into an accusation; (4) one admits its rightness, but counters it from the standpoint of usefulness to state interest. Then one analyzes the statement and seeks to refute its parts. One avoids the antithesis or goes around it. In a friendly tone one urges the opponent to desist from his claims and arouses the impression as if they were without foundation. One changes the opponent's antithesis by inserting something easily refutable into it and one pretends to have refuted it itself. One passes over an antithesis with complete silence, hoping that the judge will not notice it. One admits the antithesis but casts suspicion on the opponent's attitude and pretends to have settled the matter.

Peroratio (*epilogos*) (*cumulus* or *conclusio*). According to Aristotle (*Rhetoric*, 3, 19), it has four components:

> *ho d' epilogos synkeitai ek tessarōn; ek te tou pros heauton kataskeuasai eu ton akroatēn kai ton enantion phaulōs, kai ek tou auxēsai kai tapeinōsai, kai ek tou eis ta pathē ton akroatēn katastēsai kai ex anamnēseōs*
> [to dispose the reader favorably towards oneself and unfavorably towards the adversary; to amplify and deprecate; to excite the emotions of the hearer; to recapitulate].[104]

Generally *enumeratio, amplificatio, commiseratio*. Concluding formula, that one is finished:

> *ouk oida hoti dei pleiō legein; oiomai gar hymas ouden agnoein tōn eiremenōn* [I know of nothing more that I need say; for I think that no part of my argument has escaped your attention].[105]

or

> *schedon eirēka ha nomizō sympherein. humeis d'heloisthe, hoti kai tēi polēi kai hapasi synoisein humin mellei* [I have said approximately what I deem is contributing. You, please, grasp also what is of advantage to the city and to you all].[106]

The *enumeratio* leaves the *exordium* and *narratio* untouched, and begins with the *partitio*, and briefly reviews the proof and refutation. It helps the judge's memory. One must end emphatically. The *amplificatio* excites the listeners by means of a commonplace, *koinos topos, locus communis*; first, establishing the opposite, for example,

lobe man die Treue gegen das Vaterland. Dann Mittheilung der Thatsachen, aber μετὰ δεινώσεως καὶ αὐξήσεως, man zeigt, dass es einer der schlimmsten und ausserordentlichsten Fälle ist. Dann σύγκρισις, hellere Beleuchtung durch Contrast. Dann γνώμη verdächtigt die Gesinnung des betreffenden Übelthäters. Die παρέκβασις verdächtigt sein voraufgegangenes Leben. Die ἐλέου ἐκβολή beseitigt das Mitleid. Dafür dient auch ὑποτύπωσις, lebhafte, anschauliche Schilderung der That.

Ein Epilog, in dem nicht die Affekte für und wider aufgeregt werden ist undenkbar. (Recapitulation und Amplifikation können schon fehlen.) Die mehr prüfende Haltung der Zuhörer ist in eine aufgeregte, leidenschaftliche zu verwandeln. Cicero, orat. c. 37: est faciendum ut irascatur iudex, mitigetur, invideat, faveat, contemnat, admiretur, oderit, diligat, cupiat, satietate afficiatur, speret, metuat, laetetur, doleat. Er muss bei der Sache persönlich betheiligt werden. Wie Liebende über die Schönheit des Geliebten nicht urtheilen können, weil der Wille den Eindruck der Augen zuvorkommt, so verliert auch der von Leidenschaften fortgerissene Richter die vernünftige Überlegung. Ebenso wichtig als das παθος ist aber auch das ἦθος, generell verschieden, wo das πάθος entritt, hört das ἦθος auf; keineswegs aber fängt das ἦθος dort an, wo das πάθος aufhört, es giebt lange Partien der Rede, in denen [es] keine Gelegenheit hat, sich zu äussern. Ethos: ruhige Haltung des Gemüths, Ausdruck der edlen Gesinnung. Sie haben mit einem menschenfreundlichen, anspruchslosen Mann zu thun. Das ἠθικῶς λέγειν bewirkt niemals πάθος, aber ruhiges Aufmerken und williges Glauben. Das blosse Wort und der Blick eines rechtschaffenen Menschen nimmt es oft mit zahllosen Enthymemen in Bezug auf Glaubwürdigkeit auf. Das πάθος momentane Störung der Seele, des Willens oder des Begehrungsvermögens drängt sich vor. Arist. Rhet III 7 sagt: συνομοιοπαθεῖ ἀεὶ ὁ ἀκούων τῷ παθητικῶς λήγοντι. Die rhetorische Theorie hat sich frühzeitig mit der künstlichen Erregung von Affekten befasst. Das ἦθος berührte sie beiläufig, denn [es] ist nicht zu erregen. Um πάθη beim Zuhörer zu erregen, muss man selbst ergriffen sein: dies erregt die Phantasie und daraus wieder folgt ἐνάργεια, illustratio, cridentia. Nächst dem Epilog ist im Exordium Stelle für Affekte: doch hier zu gewinnen conciliare, dort zu concitare. Der Vertheidiger braucht stärkere Affekte als

if a traitor is supposed to be accused, one praises loyalty to the fatherland. Then the communication of the facts, but *meta deinōseōs kai auxēseōs* [with exaggeration and amplification], one shows that it is one of the worst and most extraordinary cases. Then *synkrisis*, clearer illumination by contrast. Then *gnōmē* casts suspicion on the attitude of this particular culprit. The *parekbasis* casts suspicion on his previous life. The *eleou ekbolē* eliminates pity. *Hypotypōsis*, lively, vivid description of the deed, also serves this purpose.

An epilogue in which the emotions are not stirred *pro* and *con* is unthinkable. (Recapitulation and amplification can be omitted.) The relatively critical attitude of the listeners must be transformed into an excited, passionate one. Cicero (*Orator*, c. 37):

> *est faciendum ut irascatur iudex, mitigetur, invideat, faveat, contemnat, admiretur, oderit, diligat, cupiat, satietate afficiatur, speret, metuat, laetetur, doleat* [The juror must be made to be angry or appeased, to feel ill will or to be well disposed, he must be made to feel scorn or admiration, hatred or love, desire or loathing, hope or fear, joy or sorrow].[107]

He must become personally involved with the case. As lovers cannot judge the beauty of the beloved, because the will anticipates the visual impression, so the juror who is carried off by passions also loses rational reflection. As important as *pathos*, however, is *ēthos*. [They are] generally different; where *pathos* enters in, *ēthos* ceases; but *ēthos* by no means begins where *pathos* ends; there are long sections of the speech in which [it] has no opportunity to express itself. *Ethos*: a calm attitude of mind, the expression of a noble mentality. You are dealing with a friendly and modest man. This *ēthikēs legein* never produces *pathos*, but a calm attention and willing belief. The mere word and look of a decent man often outweighs countless enthymemes as regards credibility. *Pathos*, momentary disturbance of the soul, the will, or the appetitive faculties, comes to the fore. Aristotle (*Rhetoric*, 3, 7), says: *synhomoiopathei aei ho akouōn tōi pathetikōs legonti* [and the hearer always sympathizes with one who speaks emotionally].[108] Rhetorical theory dealt very early with the artificial arousal of emotions. It treated *ēthos* only casually, for [it] cannot be aroused. To excite *pathē* in the listener, one must oneself be moved: this arouses the imagination and that in turn produces *enargeia*, *illustratio*, *cridentia*. Besides the epilogue, another place for emotions is in the *exordium*: but the goal in the former is *concitare*, in the latter *conciliare*. The defendant needs stronger emotions

der Ankläger. Aber Erregung des Mitleids darf nicht zu lang sein. Der Rhetor Apollonius sagt (Cicero, de inventione, I, 55), nichts trocknet und versiegt so schnell als Thränen. Nicht nur durch Worte, auch durch gewisse Handlungen kann man Thränen erregen. Das schmutzige Trauergewand, Kinder, Angehörige vorführen (παραγωγή oder παράκλησις) oder der Ankläger zeigt ein blutiges Schwert, Knochen aus den Wunden, blutige Kleider. Cicero, orator 38, sagt: miseratione nos ita dolenter uti solemus, ut puerum infantem in manibus perorantes tenuerimus. Quintilian erzählt, einmal sei das Bild des Angeklagten öffentlich ausgestellt worden, um durch sein schreckliches Aussehen auf die Richter Eindruck zu machen. Übrigens kann bei gleichgültiger Stimmung der Richter ein zu grosser Affekt leicht lächerlich werden. Aber es ist nicht nur die Aufgabe des Epilogs, Mitleid zu erregen (ἐλέου εἰσβολὴ oder αἴτησις) sondern auch zu beseitigen (ἐκβολή). Schon Gorgias sagt, man müsse den Ernst der Gegner durch Lachen, ihr Lachen durch Ernst zerstören. So müsste jeder Redner auch die Gabe haben, die traurigen Affekte aufzuheben oder das Lachen der Richter zu erregen: wer den Geist von der scharfen Betrachtung der Dinge abzieht, erquickt ihn. Die Gabe des Witzes sehr selten, keine Spur bei Demosthenes. Cicero war darin berühmt. Alle Scherze der Hauptstadt gingen auf sein Namen. Aristoteles bemerkt, nicht jede Art des Lächerlichen schicke sich für den gebildeten Mann, die Ironie ist edler als die βωμολοχία das Possenmachen. In der Poetik eine Definition des Lächerlichen: τό γὰρ γελοῖόν ἐστιν ἁμάρτημά τι καὶ αἶσχος ἀνώδυνον καὶ οὐ φθαρτικόν· οἷον εὐθὺς τὸ γελοῖον πρόσωπον αἰσχρόν τι καὶ διεστραμμένον ἄνευ ὀδύνης. Von den Arten ist nicht gehandelt, doch scheint Cramer Anecd. Paris, I p. 403, sie zu haben (alte Handschrift des 10. Jahrhunderts). Das Lächerliche entsteht aus Form ἀπὸ τῆς λέξεως oder ἀπὸ τῶν πραγμάτων Wort- und Sachwitz. Zu (1) κατὰ ὁμωνυμίαν auf Zweideutigkeit eines Ausdrucks ruhendes Wortspiel. (2) κατὰ συνωνυμίαν, (3) κατ' ἀδολεσχίαν, dasselbe Wort widerholt gebraucht. (4) κατὰ παρωνυμίαν, komische Verstümmelungen. Dann γελοῖον ἀπὸ τῶν πραγμάτων (1) ἐκ τῆς ὁμοιώσεως und zwar προς

than the accuser. But the arousal of pity must not be too long. The rhetor Apollonius says (Cicero, *De Inventione*, 1, 55), nothing dries and stops flowing as fast as tears. Tears can be aroused not only by words, but also by certain actions. To display the dirty mourning garment, children, dependents (*paragōgē* or *paraklēsis*); or the plaintiff shows a bloody sword, bones from the wounds, bloody clothing. Cicero (*Orator*, 38), says:

> *miseratione . . . nos ita dolenter uti solemus, ut puerum infantem in manibus perorantes tenuerimus* [we are wont to use it (the appeal for sympathy) so piteously that we have even held a babe in our arms during the peroration].[109]

Quintilian tells that once the picture of the accused was displayed in public in order to impress the jury with his horrible appearance. Incidentally, if the jurors' mood is indifferent, excessive emotion can easily become ridiculous.

But to arouse pity (*eleou eisbolē* or *aitēsis*) is not the only goal of the epilogue, but also to eliminate it (*ekbolē*). Gorgias already says that one must destroy the opponents' seriousness by laughter, their laughter by seriousness. So each speaker also had to have the talent of abolishing sad emotions or exciting the jurors to laughter: whoever withdraws the mind from the sharp observation of things, refreshes it. The talent of wit is very rare, not a trace in Demosthenes. Cicero was famous for this. All jokes in the capital were ascribed to him. Aristotle remarks that not every kind of ridiculous joke is appropriate for the educated man, irony is nobler than *bōmolochia*, buffoonery, ribaldry. In his *Poetics* he gives a definition of the ridiculous:

> *to gar geloion estin hamartēma ti kai aischos anōdynon kai ou phthartikon, hoion euthys to geloion prosōpon aischron ti kai diestrammenon aneu odynōs* [The causes of laughter are errors and disgraces not accompanied by pain or injury; the comic mask, for instance, is deformed and distorted, but not painfully so].[110]

There is no treatment of the kinds of humor, but Cramer (*Anecd.*, Paris, 1, p. 403), seems to have them (an old tenth-century manuscript). The ridiculous stems from the form (*apo tēs lexeōs*), or *apo tōn pragmatōn* (from word- and thing-jokes). On the first type (1) *kata homōnymian*, a word-play based on ambiguity of expression; (2) *kata synōnymian* [from synonyms]; (3) *kat' adoleschian*, the same word used repeatedly; (4) *kata parōnymian*, comical detruncations. Then *geloion apo tōn pragmatōn: (1) ek tēs homoiōseōs*,

τὸ χεῖρον oder πρὸς τὸ βέλτιον, wenn Dionysus in den "Fröschen" sein Herakleskostüm mit Xanthion vertauscht: für Xanthion die ὁμοίωσις πρὸς τὸ βέλτιον (προς Ἡρακλέα). (2) ἐκ τῆς ἀπάτης, wenn Strepsiades sich die ungereimten Lehren über die Rede als wahr aufbinden lässt. (3) ἐκ τοῦ παρὰ προσδοκίαν usw. Die Norm für Witze: urbanitas, venustum, salsum, facetum, iocus, dicacitas, oder ἀστϊσμός, χαριεντισμός, διασυρμός, μυκτηρισμός.

Sehr zu vermeiden, dass der Witz auch den Richter trifft. Cicero, de orat II 60: pusillus testis processit. 'Licet,' inquit, 'rogare?' Philippus. Tum quaesitor properans, 'modo breviter,' hic ille, 'non accusabis. perpusillum rogabo.' ridicule. Sed sedebat iudex L. Aurifex brevior ipse quam testis: omnis est risus in iudicem conversus, visum est totum scurrile ridiculum.

XIII. DIE BERATHENDE BEREDSAMKEIT

Das γένος συμβουλετικόν genus deliberativum, vor Senat und Volk: entweder überredend oder abredend. Eine Rede der Art δημεγορία (im Gegensatz zu κατηγορία, nicht sehr üblich—und συνηγορία, beide genus δικανικόν) consultatio, deliberatio, später suasoria (gewöhnlich Schulübung), die wirklich gehaltene bei Quintilian contio oder sententia. Siebenfacher Inhalt: Religionssachen, Gesetze, innere Staatseinrichtung, Bündnisse, und Verträge, über Krieg, Frieden, über Staatseinkünfte. Die wirkliche suasoria hat dieselbe Eintheilung wie die Gerichtsrede. 5 Theile, also exordium, narratio, partitio, probatio, refutatio adversariorum, Epilog. Im ganzen treten exordium und narratio sehr zurück oder fallen weg. Der Epilog wird selten die Aufgabe haben, Mitleid zu erregen (ausser wenn es gilt, Belagerten Hülfe zu bringen oder Abgesandte um Hülfe bitten). Häufig ist Zorn, Furcht, Begierde, Hass zu erregen. Besonders wich-

namely *pros to Xeiron* or *pros to Beltion*, when Dionysos in *The Frogs* exchanges his Heracles costume with Xanthion: for Xanthion the *homoiōsis pros to Beltion* (*pros Heraklea*) [comparison for the better (towards Heracles)]; (2) *ek tēs apatēs* [from immunity from punishment], when Strepsiades falls for the nonsensical teachings on speech; (3) *ek tou para prosdokian* [from the unexpected], etc. The norm for jokes: *urbanitas* [urbaneness], *venustum* [charm], *salsum* [wit], *facetum* [grace], *iocus* [humor], *dicacitas* [glibness],[111] or *asteismos* [witty self-irony], *charientismos* [cheerful irony], *diasyrmos* [mockery], *mykterismos* [thinly veiled mockery].

Very much to be avoided, that the joke also apply to the judge. Cicero (*De Oratore*, 2, 60):

> *pusillus testis processit, 'Licet,' inquit, 'rogare?' Philippus. Tum quaesitor properans, 'modo breviter,' hic ille, 'non accusabis. perpusillum rogabo.' ridicule. Sed sedebat iudex L. Aurifex brevior ipse quam testis: omnis est risus in iudicem conversus, visum est totum scurrile ridiculum* [A very small witness once came forward. 'May I examine him?' said Philippus. The president of the Court, who was in a hurry, answered, 'Only if you are short.' 'You will not complain,' returned Philippus, 'for I shall be just as short as that man is.' Quite comical; but there on the tribunal sat Lucius Aurifex, and he was even tinier than the witness: all the laughter was directed against Lucius, and the joke seemed merely buffoonish].[112]

XIII. DELIBERATIVE ELOQUENCE

The *genos symbouleutikon* (*genus deliberativum*) before Senate and people, can be either to persuade or dissuade. A speech of the kind *dēmēgoria* (in contrast to *katēgoria*), not very usual—and *synēgoria*, both belonging to the *genos dikanikon* (*consultatio, deliberatio*), later *suasoria* (generally a school-exercise); in Quintilian those which were really given are called *contio* or *sententia*. Seven kinds of content: religious matters, laws, internal city management, alliances and treaties, or war, peace, government income. The real *suasoria* has the same divisions as a forensic speech: five parts, namely *exordium, narratio, partitio, probatio, refutatio adversariorum* (the epilogue). On the whole, the *exordium* and *narratio* are very diminished or completely missing. The epilogue will seldom have the task of arousing pity (except when its objective is to bring help to the besieged or to ask emissaries for help. Often anger, fear, desire,

tig die auctoritas und das ἦθος des Sprechers. Quint. III, 8, 13: nam et prudentissimus esse haberique et optimus debet, qui sententiae suae de utilibus atque honestis credere omnes velit: in iudiciis enim vulgo fas habetur indulgere aliquid studio suo: concilia nemo est qui neget secundum mores dari. Das prooemium von der Sache aus ist nicht nöthig, diese ist den Zuhörern bekannt. Prooemium von der Person aus mitunter erforderlich, oder vom Gegner aus, wenn dieser den Gegenstand nicht für so wichtig hält als der Redner (oder für wichtiger). Dann muss die Rede verdächtigen, entkräften, vergrössern oder vermindern. Dann ist das Prooemium des Schmuckes wegen da, da die Rede sonst leichtfertig angelegt erscheint (αὐτοκάβδαλος, Aristoteles). Im Epilog ist Amplification und locus communis überflüssig, bloss Rekapitulation genug. Gewöhnlich direkte Aufforderung, im Sinne des Antragsstellers ihre Stimmen abzugeben. Einige Redner nahmen den Status eigentlich für die δημηγορία an, den status negotialis πραγματική. Die Suasorien sind einfach oder doppelt, conjunctae, oder vergleichend, comparativae, concertativae. Einfach: ob die Soldaten Sold bekommen sollen. Doppelt: Caesar berathet, ob er darauf bestehen soll nach Germanien zu gehen, da die Soldaten alle ihr Testament machen (er berathet einmal wegen der Bestürzung, sodann überhaupt, ob man, auch ohne sie, nach Germanien gehen solle). Vergleichend: welcher von zwei Anträgen der bessere sei.

Von Wichtigkeit die διαίρεσις der στάσις πραγματική. Sie giebt die Topen an die Hand, nach welchen der Stoff gesucht werden muss, also die partes suadendi. Anaximenes sagt, der Rathgeber muss zeigen, dass das, wozu er räth, δίκαιον, νόμιμον, συμφέρον, καλόν, ἡδύ, ῥάδιον, weiter sei wenn er zu etwas schwer Ausführbaren auffordert δυνατόν und ἀναγκαῖον. Der Abrathende umgekehrt. Aristo-

hatred must be aroused. The speaker's *auctoritas* and *ēthos* are especially important. Quintilian (3, 8, 13):

> *nam et prudentissimus esse haberique et optimus debet, qui sententiae suae de utilibus atque honestis credere omnes velit: in iudiciis enim vulgo fas habetur indulgere aliquid studio suo: concilia nemo est qui neget secundum mores dari* [For he, who would have all men trust his judgment as to what is expedient and honorable, should both possess and be regarded as possessing genuine wisdom and excellence of character. In forensic speeches the orator may, according to the generally received opinion, indulge his passion to some extent. But all will agree that the advice given by a speaker should be in keeping with his moral character].[113]

The *prooemium* from the point of view of the case is not required, since the audience is already familiar with it. Sometimes the *prooemium* from the person is necessary, or from the opponent, when he does not consider the matter as important as (or more important than) does the speaker. Then the speech must cast suspicion, refute, magnify or minimize. The *prooemion* can also be there as adornment, since otherwise the speech seems to be frivolously organized (*autokabdalos* [done carelessly, slovenly], Aristotle). In the epilogue, amplification and *locus communis* are superfluous, mere recapitulation is enough. Generally a direct invitation to cast their votes in favor of the appellant. Some speakers, indeed, adopted this *status* for the *dēmēgoria*, the *status negotialis pragmatikē*. The *suasoria* are simple or double, *conjunctae* or *comparativae, concertativae*. Simple: whether the soldiers should receive pay. Double: Caesar deliberates whether he should insist on going to Germany, since the soldiers are all writing their wills (he deliberates first, because of their perplexity, then in general, whether, even apart from that, the journey to Germany should be made). *Comparative*: which of two claims is the better one.

Important is the *diairesis* of the *stasis pragmatikē*. It provides the *topoi* according to which the material must be sought, i.e. the *partes suadendi* [persuasive arguments]. Anaximenes says that the adviser must show that the course he recommends is *dikaion* [just], *nomimon* [legal], *sympheron* [expedient], *kalon* [beautiful], *hēdu* [pleasant], *rhaidion* [easy]. When he recommends something difficult, additional qualities are *dynaton* [possible, practicable] and *anankaion* [necessary]. The dissuader, vice versa. Aristotle depicts

teles stellt [dazu] als der berathenden Beredsamkeit eigentümlich sei συμφέρον und βλαβερόν, die anderen Punkte untergeordnet (δικαιον: Haupt-τέλος der gerichtlichen, καλόν der epideiktischen Beredsamkeit). Hermogenes nennt diese Gesichtspunkte τελικὰ κεφάλαια—Gesichtspünkte, durch deren Anwendung die Rede den Zweck, zu überreden, erreicht. Longinus, Apthonius, Hermogenes. Planudes sagt, an sich gebe es bloss drei κεφ. τελ., nämlich δίκαιον für gerichtliche, συμφέρον für berathende, καλόν für panegyrische Beredsamkeit. δικαιόν eingetheilt in νόμιμόν, δίκαιον, ἔθος, das συμφέρον in χρήσιμον, ἀναγκαῖον, δυνατόν, ῥάδιον ἐκβησόμενον, und das καλόν in πρέπον und ἔνδοξον.

Interessant, die Divisionen der römischen Deklamation, die Seneca in den Suasorien aufbewahrt hat, z.B. die Fünfte: deliberant Athenienses, an tropaea Persica tollant Xerxe minante rediturum se nisi tollerentur. Argentarius sagt: entweder wird Xerxes nicht kommen, oder, wenn er kommt, ist er nicht zu fürchten. Fuscus: selbst wenn Xerxes, im Falle dass wir die Trophäen nicht wegnehmen, kommen wird, dürfen wir sie nicht wegnehmen: Befohlenes zu thun ist ein Geständniss der Knechtschaft: wenn er kommt, werden wir ihn besiegen: wir werden den besiegen, den wir schon besiegt haben. Aber er wird auch nicht kommen. Wollte er wirklich kommen, so würde er es uns nicht ankündigen, er ist gebrochen an Kräften und Geist. Gallio räth den Athenern, die Trophäen wegzunehmen, ihr Ruhm werde nicht darunter leiden, das Andenken an den Sieg wird ewig bleiben. Die Trophäen selbst würden durch die Zeit zerstört, man habe einen Krieg übernehmen müssen für Freiheit, Weib und Kind: für etwas Überflüssiges dürfe man sich nicht in den Krieg begeben. Xerxes, der im Zorn selbst gegen Götter vermessen sei, werde kommen: weder habe er alle Truppen nach Griechenland geführt, noch alle in Griechenland verloren. Man müsse die Veränderlichkeit des Glücks fürchtern. Die Kräfte Griechenlands seien erschöpft und könnten keinen Krieg aushalten. Quintilian III 8, 35 sagt, jede Suasoria sei überhaupt eine Vergleichung: man müsse zusehen, was man verrichten wolle und wodurch man es verrichten wolle, sodass sich abschätzen lässt, ob in dem, was man erstrebt, mehr Nützen oder in dem, wodurch man es erstrebt, mehr Nachtheil enthalten sei. est utilitatis et in tempore quaestio, expedit sed non nunc. et in loco, non hic: et in persona, non nobis sed [sic] contra nos [sic]. et in genere agendi, non sic: et in modo, non [sic] tantum.

as peculiar to deliberative oratory *sympheron* [expedient] and *bla-beron* [harmful], the other points being subordinate: (*dikaion*: the main *telos* of forensic, *kalon* of epideictic eloquence). Hermogenes calls these points of view *telika kephalaia* [topics pertaining to supreme principles][114]—points of view by use of which the speech attains its purpose of convincing. Longinus, Apthonius, Hermogenes. Planudes says that actually there are only three *kephalaia telika*, namely *dikaion* for forensic, *sympheron* for deliberative, *kalon* for panegyric eloquence. *Dikaion* is divided into *nomimon, dikaion, ethos; sympheron* into *chrēsimon, anankaion, dynaton, rhaidion, ekbēsomenon;* and *kalon* into *prepon* and *endoxon*.

Interesting are the divisions of Roman declamation which Seneca preserved in the *suasoria*, e.g. the Fifth:

> *deliberant Athenienses, an tropaea Persica tollant Xerxe minante rediturum se nisi tollerentur* [The Athenians are deliberating whether to remove the Persian trophies, since Xerxes is threatening to return unless they are removed].

Argentarius says, "Either Xerxes will not come, or, if he does come, there is no need to fear him." Fuscus: "Even if Xerxes is going to come unless we remove the trophies, we should not remove them, for to do what is commanded is an admission of slavery; if he does come we will defeat him; we will defeat a man whom we have already defeated. But he will not even come; if he really wanted to come, he would not have announced it to us; he is broken in powers and mind." Gallio advises the Athenians to remove the trophies: their reputation will not suffer from it, the memory of the victory will remain. The trophies themselves would be destroyed by time; they [the Athenians] have had to wage a war for freedom, wife, and child: one must not enter a war for something superfluous. Xerxes, who in anger was outrageous even toward the gods, would come: he had neither led all his troops to Greece nor lost all in Greece. The mutability of fortune had to be feared. Greece's forces were exhausted and could not endure a war.[115]

Quintilian (3, 8, 35), then says that every *suasoria* is a comparison: one had to examine what one wanted to achieve and how one wanted to achieve it, in order to estimate whether one's objective contained greater usefulness or the means to attain it greater disadvantage:

> *est utilitatis et in tempore quaestio, expedit sed non nunc; et in loco, non hic; et in persona, non nobis, sed [sic] contra nos [sic]; et in genere*

Hier haben wir Anwendung der Topen mit Zuhülfenahme der Peristasen. Nach Cicero hat der Redner am meisten Rücksicht auf honestas zu nehmen, demnächst auf incolumitas (persönliche Sicherheit),
endlich auf commoditas, etwaigen Vortheil und Nachtheil.

XIV. DIE EPIDEIKTISCHE BEREDSAMKEIT

Das γένος ἐπιδεικτικόν (πανηγυρικόν) oder ἐγκωμιαστικόν
demonstrativum, auch laudativum. Kleinerer Kreis von Zuhörern,
oft nur Beurtheiler der angewendeten Kunst, doch auch bei grossen
Festversammlungen, bei Leichenfesten. Mit öffentlichem Geschäfts-
charakter noch mehr in Rom als in Griechenland: Leichenrede oft
durch ein öffentliches Amt bedingt, an Magistratspersonen durch
Senatsbeschluss übertragen. Was der junge Redner bei diesem genus
gelernt hat, kommt jedenfalls den anderen Gattungen zu Gute. Cornificius III 8, 15: nec hoc genus caussae, eo quod raro accidit in vita,
neglegentius commendandum est, neque enim id, quod potest accidere, ut faciendum sit aliquando, non oportet velle quam commodatissime posse facere; et si separatim haec caussa minus saepe tractatur in iudicialibus et in deliberativis causis saepe magnae partes
versantur laudis aut vituperationis, quare in hoc quoque genere caussae non nihil industriae consumendum putavimus. Schon Isocrates
hat gelehrt, dass Lob und Tadel überall vorkommt. In der späteren
Kaiserzeit beschränkte sich die praktische Beredsamkeit fast ganz
auf die epideiktische Gattung. Erstaunliche Mannigfältigkeit der
Gegenstände: Götter, Helden, Menschen, Thiere, Pflanzen, Berge,
Länder, Städte, Flüsse, Berufsarten, Künste, Tugende, Zeitab-

agendi, non sic: et in modo, non [*sic*] *tantum* [The question of usefulness applies to time, it is expedient, but not now; and to place, but not here; to persons, not to us but against us; and to the way of acting, not thus; and in quantity, not so much].[116]

Here we have the use of *topoi* with the help of the *peristases* [circumstances]. According to Cicero, the orator must take most in consideration *honestas*, then *incolumitas* (personal safety), and finally *commoditas*, possible advantage and disadvantage.

XIV. DECLAMATORY ELOQUENCE

The *genos epideictos (panēgyrikos)* or *enkōmiasticon* (*demonstrativum*), also *laudativum* [is addressed to] a smaller circle of listeners, often only judges of the applied art, but also to large festive assemblies, or at funerals. Even more in Rome than in Greece [it is associated] with public affairs and purposes: funeral oration often conditioned by a public office, or assigned to magistrates by a Senate decree. What the young orator has learned in this *genus* is, at any rate, useful for the other types of speeches. Cornificius (3, 8, 15).

nec hoc genus caussae, eo quod raro accidit in vita, neglegentius commendandum est, neque enim id, quod potest accidere, ut faciendum sit aliquando, non oportet velle quam commodatissime posse facere; et si separatim haec caussa minus saepe tractatur in iudicialibus et in deliberativis causis saepe magnae partes versantur laudis aut vituperationis, quare in hoc quoque genere caussae non nihil industriae consumendum putavimus [Nor should this kind of cause be the less strongly recommended just because it presents itself only seldom in life. Indeed when a task may present itself, be it only occasionally, the ability to perform it as skillfully as possible must seem desirable. And if epideictic is only seldom employed by itself independently, still in judicial and deliberative causes extensive sections are often devoted to praise or censure. Therefore let us believe that this kind of cause also must claim some measure of our industry].[117]

Isocrates already taught that praise and blame occur everywhere. In the later Imperial period practical oratory was limited almost exclusively to the epideictic genre. [It displays an] astounding multiplicity of subject matter: gods, heroes, men, animals, plants, mountains, countries, cities, rivers, kinds of professions, arts, virtues, periods of

schnitte, usw. Auch viele im Grunde nicht zu Lobende. Menander: ἰστέον, ὅτι τῶν ἐγκωμίων τὰ μέν ἐστιν ἔνδοξα, τὰ δὲ ἄδοξα, τὰ δὲ ἀμφίδοξα, τὰ δὲ παράδοξα. ἔνδοξα μὲν τὰ περὶ ἀγαθῶν ὁμολογουμένων, οἷον θεοῦ ἢ ἄλλου τινὸς ἀγαθοῦ φανεροῦ, ἄδοξα δὲ τὰ περὶ δαιμόνων καὶ κακοῦ φανεροῦ· ἀμφίδοξα δὲ ὅσα πῆ μέν ἔνδοξά ἐστιν, πῆ δὲ ἄδοξα, ὃ ἐν τοῖς παναθεναϊκοῖς εὑρίσκεται καὶ 'Ισοκράτους καὶ 'Αριστείδου. (Lobrede auf die Geschichte Athens: auch minder löbliche Partien, z.B. Verhalten der Athenern gegen die Meliern gelobt), τὰ μὲν γάρ ἐστιν ἐπαινετά, τὰ δὲ ψεκτὰ ὑπὲρ ὧν ἀπολογοῦνται. παράδοξα δὲ οἷον 'Αλκιδάμαντος τὸ τοῦ θανάτου ἐγκώμιον, ἢ τὸ τῆς Πενίας Πρωτέως τοῦ κυνός (des Peregrinus Proteus des Cynikers). Polycrates, Schüler des Gorgias, schrieb Lob der Mäuse, Töpfe, Steinchen. Andere Hummeln, Salz, das sind die Adoxographen. Dio Chrysost. hat ein Lob der Mücken, der Papageien und des Haares. Lucian, Lob der Fliege. Isocrates tadelt die Richtung im Lob der Helena und sagt: καὶ περὶ μὲν τῶν δόξαν ἐχόντων σπάνιον εὑρεῖν ἃ μηδεὶς πρότερον εἴρηκε, περὶ δὲ τῶν φαύλων καὶ ταπεινῶν ὅτι ἄν τις τύχῃ φθεγξάμενος ἅπαν ἴδιόν ἐστιν. Der Redner Fronto schrieb laudes fumi et pulveris und laudes negligentiae; bis dahin, nichts Lateinisches.—Überwiegend das Lob von Göttern und Menschen, dann von Ländern und Städten.—Jede Lobrede mit Prooemium zu eröffnen, vereinzelt Gorgias der mit Ἦλις πόλις

time, etc. Also many things that were really not praiseworthy. Menander:

> *isteon, hoti tōn enkomiōn ta men estin endoxa, ta de adoxa, ta de amphidoxa, ta de paradoxa. endoxa men ta peri agathōn homologoumenōn, hoion theou ē allou tinos agathou phanerou, adoxa de ta peri daimonōn kai kakou phanerou. amphidoxa de hosa pē men endoxa estin, pē de adoxa, ho en tois Panathenaikois heurisketai kai Isokratous kai Aristeidou* [It is to be known that of the laudatory speeches some are conventional, others not, others partly. The conventional ones are about those who are generally considered to be good, e.g.: a god or someone else who is evidently good. The nonconventional ones are about demons and apparent evil. The part-conventional ones are all those that are conventional in one respect, nonconventional in another—which are found in the Panathenaics of Isocrates and Aristides].[118]

(Eulogy on the history of Athens: even less praiseworthy parts, e.g. the Athenians' behavior toward the Melians, are praised),

> *ta men gar estin epaineta, ta de psekta, hyper hōn apologountai. paradoxa de hoion Alkidamantos to tou thanatou enkōmion, ē tō tēs Penias Prōteos tou kunos* [Indeed some are praising, others loathing those of whom they speak. The anticonventional are, e.g., the encomium of Death by Alkidamas, or the one of Poverty by Proteus the Cynic] (Peregrinus Proteus the Cynic).[119]

Polycrates, disciple of Gorgias, wrote in praise of mice, pots, pebbles. Others of bees, salt, those are the Adoxographs. Dio Chrysostomos has a praise of mosquitoes, parrots, and hair. Lucian, praise of the fly. Isocrates criticizes this tendency in his *Praise of Helen*, saying:

> *kai peri men tōn doxan echontōn spanion heurein ha mēdeis proteron eirēke, peri de tōn phaulōn kai tapeinōn hoti an tis tychēi phthengxamenos hapan idion estin* [and while on famous subjects one rarely finds thoughts which no one has previously uttered, yet on trifling and insignificant topics whatever the speaker may chance to say is entirely original].[120]

The rhetor Fronto wrote *laudes fumi et pulveris* [praises of smoke and dust] and *laudes negligentiae* [praises of negligence]; until then there was no such thing in Latin. Preponderant [topics were] praise of Gods and men, then of countries and cities.

Every eulogy has to open with a *prooemium*; only Gorgias sometimes began with *Hēlis polis eudaimōn* [fortunate town of Elis]. A

εὐδαιμων anfieng. Man bewegte sich sehr frei darin, Aristoteles sagt, man könne alles anbringen, was einem in den Sinn komme, das Exordium der Helena des Isocrates spricht von den eristischen Sophisten und Philosophen. Im Panegyr. des Isocrates: dass man den Vorzügen des Körpers mehr Ehre erweist, als denen des Geistes. Von einer narratio kann nicht die Rede sein, doch lässt sich irgendeine That der Person besonders hervorheben. Propositio und partitio ist anzuwenden, um anzugeben, was man loben oder tadeln will. Auch das epideiktische Lob hat mitunter einen Beweis, wenn die Handlungen, die wir angeben, unglaublich sind oder wenn ein anderer als Urheber der That gilt. Quintilian: ut qui Romulum Martis filium educatumque a lupa dicat, in argumentum coelestis [sic] ortus utatur his, quod abiectus in profluentem non potuerit extingui, quod omnia sic egerit, ut genitum praeside bellorum deo incredibile non esset, quod ipsum quoque coelo [sic] receptum temporis eius homines non dubitaverint. Eine refutatio kann nur vorkommen, wenn man das ἄδοξον oder ἀμφίδοξον durch seine Beschönigung zum Loben verwandelt. Am Schluss ist eine eigentliche ἀνακεφαλαίωσις unstatthaft. Die Hauptaufgabe ist die Gegenstände amplificare und explicare, αὔξησις. Es soll ja keine unparteische Charakteristik sein, also ist das Mangelhafte weg zu lassen. Daher gehört auch die Wahl der Ausdrücke; Tugend und Laster sind oft nahe oder verwandt, Verwegene tapfer, Verschwender freigebig, der Geizige sparsam.—Ein Beispiel: das Lob der Helena von Isokrates, eine falsche Lobrede eines Sophisten entgegengestellt. Zuerst Lob ihrer Herkunft: die einzige Halbgöttin, die Zeus zum Vater hat. Er hat sie noch mehr ausgezeichnet als den Herakles, da er diesem Stärke ihr aber Schönheit verlieh, die ja sogar die Stärke überwindet. Da nicht Ruhe, sondern Krieg und Kampf zum Ruhm verhilft, so machte er ihre Schönheit zum Gegenstande des Kampfes. Theseus entführte sie schon in zarter Kindheit mit Gewalt und Gefahren. Dem Pirithous aber, der ihn dabei unterstützte, wusste er so grossen Dank, dass er ihn zum Raub der Proserpina in die Unterwelt begleitete. Die Liebe des Theseus fällt zu Günsten der Helena ins Gewicht, als dieser in jeder Hinsicht vortrefflich ist. Sein Lob (mit Herakles Vergleich) hier eingeschaltet. Als Helena das jungfräuliche Alter erreicht, versammeln sich aus

great deal of freedom was exercised in this. Aristotle says that one was free to say whatever came to mind; the *exordium* of Isocrates' *Helen* speaks of the eristic Sophists and philosophers. Isocrates' panegyric gives greater honor to physical than to spiritual prerogatives. No *narratio* is used, but any deed of the person can be particularly stressed. *Propositio* and *partitio* are used to state what one wants to praise or criticize. Even epideictic praise sometimes has a proof, when the actions we list are incredible or when another person is considered author of the deed. Quintilian:

> *ut qui Romulum Martis filium educatumque a lupa dicat, in argumen-*
> *tum caelestis ortus utatur his, quod abiectus in profluentem non potuerit*
> *extingui, quod omnia sic egerit, ut genitum praeside bellorum deo*
> *incredibile non esset, quod ipsum quoque caelo receptum temporis eius*
> *homines non dubitaverint* [For example, a speaker who tells how Romu-
> lus was the son of Mars and reared by the she-wolf, will offer as proofs
> of his divine origin the facts that when thrown into a running stream he
> escaped drowning, that all his achievements were such as to make it
> credible that he was the offspring of the god of battles, and that his con-
> temporaries unquestionably believed that he was translated to
> heaven].[121]

A *refutatio* can occur only when the *adoxon* or *amphidoxon* is changed into praise by extenuation. A real *anakephalaiōsis* [summary] is impermissible at the closing. The main task is *auxēsis* (*amplificare* and explicare) to amplify and explain the objects. It is not supposed to be impartial characterization, i.e., defects must be left out. Hence the choice of expressions also is pertinent here; virtues and vices are often closely related: rash men are courageous; spendthrifts generous; misers thrifty. An example: Isocrates' *Praise of Helen*[122] compared with a false eulogy by a Sophist. First praise of her origin: the only demigoddess whose father is Zeus. He favored her more than Heracles, since he gave him strength but her beauty, which conquers even strength. Since not peace, but war and struggle lead to fame, he made her beauty the object of struggle. Even in tender childhood she was kidnapped by Theseus with violence and dangers. He was so grateful to Pirithous, who assisted him in the deed, that he accompanied him to the underworld to capture Proserpina. Theseus' love weighs in Helen's favor, since this man is excellent in every way. Praise of him (compared with Heracles) is inserted here. When Helen reached maidenly age, the noblest suitors in all

ganz Griechenland die edelsten Bewerbern, indem sie sich verbünden, den bevorzügten Freier zu schützen. Das Urtheil über Helenas Schönheit bald durch Aphrodite bestätigt, die sie dem Paris anbot. Mit Recht erschien ihm die Verwandtschaft mit Zeus und der Besitz eines solchen Weibs werthvoller als der Besitz von ganz Asien und Kriegsruhm. Es ist thöricht, dem Paris das Urtheil wegen der Folgen zum Vorwurf zu machen. Die Göttinnen haben ihn hoch geehrt, dadurch dass sie den Streit durch ihn schlichten liessen. Der Trojanische Krieg bekündet den Werth, den Asien und Europa auf den Besitz dieses Weibes legten. Auch die Götter betheiligten sich am Kampfe und schickten nicht nur ihre eigenen Söhne in den Kampf. Es ist ja auch die Schönheit das ehrwürdigste und Göttlichste, was es gibt, das, dem sie fehlt, wird verachtet. Selbst die Tugend wird nur so gepriesen, weil sie die schönste von allen Bestrebungen ist. Selbst Götter sind der Liebe unterthan und von menschlichen Frauen sind mehr durch Schönheit berühmt geworden als durch alle andere Eigenschaften zusammen. So ist auch Helena unsterblich geworden und hat die Unsterblichkeit ihren Brüdern und ihrem Gemahl verschafft, der von den Lakedämoniern als ein Gott verehrt wird. Stesichorus zeigt ihre Macht: auch Homer verdankte, wie einige Homeriden sagen, ihrer Huld den Liebreiz und Ruhm der Gedichte. Deshalb gebührt ihr Verehrung und Lob: ja es lässt sich viel mehr sagen, denn der Trojanische Krieg ist der erste Sieg des vereinigten Griechenlands über die Barbaren. Seit jenem Kriege bricht ein Umschwung ein, die Macht der Griechen nimmt zu, den Barbaren wird viel Land weggenommen.

Ausser wirklicher Lob- und Tadelreden gehört hierher jede epideiktische Gelegenheitsrede, Lob- und Danksagungsrede an, die Kaiser-, Festreden, Einladungsreden, begrüssende Ansprache-, Antritts-, und Abschiedsreden, Geburtstagsreden, Leichenreden, Hochzeitsreden, Trostreden, Ermahnungsreden, λογόι προτρεπτικοί. Hier fordert der Redner zu etwas auf, dessen Vorzüge nicht erst zu ermitteln sind, sondern feststehen, zum Frieden, zur Tugend, zur Philosophie, usw. Erinnern an das γένος συμβουλευτικόν. Die meisten Arten der Gelegenheitsreden hat Menander in seiner Schrift περὶ ἐπιδεικτικῶν. Er beginnt mit λόγος βασιλικός, einer Amplificatio seiner guten Eigenschaften. Wie das Auge nicht vermag den schrankenlosen Ozean zu messen, so die Rede nicht den ganzen Kaiser. Eigentlich verlangend die Hand eines Homer oder Orpheus. Verlegenheit von welchem Punkte beginnen: dies alles ein prooemium.

Greece assembled and formed an alliance to protect the preferred suitor. The judgment of Helen's beauty was soon confirmed by Aphrodite, who offered her to Paris. Paris rightly believed her relationship with Zeus and the possession of such a woman to be more valuable than the possession of all Asia and of military fame. It is foolish to reproach Paris by condemning the consequences [of his action]. The goddesses honored him highly by selecting him to settle their dispute. The Trojan war proclaims the value which Asia and Europe set on the possession of this woman. Even the gods took part in the struggle and did not merely send their sons to battle. Beauty is, indeed, the most noble and divine thing there is; whatever lacks it is despised. Even virtue is praised only because it is the most beautiful of strivings. Even gods are subject to love, and more human women have become more famous for beauty than for all other qualities put together. So Helen too has become immortal and obtained immortality for her brothers and her husband, who is honored as a god by the Lacedaemonians. Stesichorus shows her power: even Homer, as some Homer commentators say, owed the charm and fame of his poem to her graceful presence. She therefore deserves honor and praise: indeed much more can be said, for the Trojan war marks the first victory of united Greece against the barbarians. Since that war a drastic change has taken place, the power of the Greeks has been increasing and a great deal of land has been taken away from the barbarians.

Besides real speeches of praise or criticism, every epideictic occasional speech or speech of praise or gratitude belongs to this category: speeches about emperors, festive speeches, invitational speeches, speeches of greeting, inaugural addresses and farewell addresses, birthday speeches, funeral orations, wedding speeches, speeches of condolence and admonitory speeches, *logoi protreptikoi* [hortatory speeches]. Here the speaker recommends something whose advantages do not first have to be discovered, but are already established: e.g., peace, virtue, philosophy, etc. It reminds one of the *genos symbouleutikon* [deliberative genre].

Menander treated most kinds of occasional speeches in his book *peri epideiktikōn* [*On Declamation*]. He begins with *logos basilikos* [speech in honor of the emperor], an amplification of his good qualities. As the eye cannot measure the boundless ocean, so the speech not the whole emperor. It would really require the capacity of a Homer or an Orpheus. One expresses bewilderment as to where to

Dann kurz die Vaterstadt des Kaisers oder das Volk, Lob des kaiserlichen Geschlechts, Geburt des Kaisers, etwaige prodigia, der Redner darf hier getrost erdichten. Erziehung, Anlage, Talente, Studien. Dann Haupttheil: die Thaten des Kaisers: zu theilen in Krieg- und Friedensthaten. Dann Betrachtung des Glückes, das ihm zur Seite steht (Kinder, Freunde, Minister), zum Schluss Schilderung des blühenden Reiches, Sicherheit des Handels, zunehmende Religiosität. Segenswünsche für sein Wohlergehen.—Das glänzendste Denkmal ist der Panegyricus des jüngeren Plinius auf Trajan. Die Erweiterung einer wirkl. gehaltenen (im Senat) gratiarum actio. λόγοι χαριστήριοι und εὐχαριστήριοι. Dann giebt es den στεφανωτικὸς λόγος, kurze Ansprache an den Kaiser bei Überreichung eines Ehrenkranzes. 150 bis 200 Zeilen [illegible]. Dann der πρεσβευτικὸς λόγος, Gesandtschaftsrede mit der Bitte einer Stadt zu Hülfe zu kommen. Panegyricus bezeichnet uneigentlich jede längere Lobrede. Eigentlich bei einer πανήγυρις, grossem nationalem Festspiel vor freudig gestimmter Festversammlung. Diese stehen im Zusammenhang mit dem Kultus einer Gottheit und beginnen damit. Dann das Lob der Stadt. Dann das Festspiel, Entstehung, Einsetzung, Jahreszeit. Art des Spiels, ob gymnastisch oder musisch. Der Kranz. Eiche, Oelbaum, Lorbeer, Ährenkranz, Fichte. Der κλητικὸς λόγος Einladungsrede an einen ἄρχων, zugegen zu sein.—Kaiserliche Beamte werden mit einer Ansprache geehrt, wenn sie in eine Stadt kommen oratio compellatoria προσφώνησις, λόγος προσφωνητικός oder ἐπιβατήριος. Gegensatz λόγος προπεμπτικός, προπεμπτήριος, bei einem Abschied. Im λόγος συντακτικὸς oder συντακτήριος verabschiedet sich der Redende. Dann die γαμικὸς oder ἐπιθαλάμιος. Der λόγος γενεθλιακός am Geburtstag oder natalitia. Endlich λόγος ἐπιτάφιος und λόγος παραμυθητικός an die Hinterlassenen. F. Hubner hat vermuthet dass der Agricola des Tacitus eine ausgearbeitete laudatio funebris ist.—Alle kürzere Vorträge, λαλιαί nicht ἐπιδείξεις, mit freier ungezwungener Form. Eine λαλιά zur Eröffnung einer Reihe von Vorträgen heisst προλαλιά. Alle künstgerecht ausgearbeiteten Reden über fingirte Themata heissen in der Sophistik μελέται oder ἀγῶνες, wenn sie zum γένος δικανικόν oder συμβουλευτικόν gehören. Controversia und suasoria.

begin; all this a prooemium. Then follows a brief discussion of the emperor's native city or people, praise of the imperial ancestors, the emperor's birth, perhaps also *prodigia* [omens]; the speaker may go ahead and invent some. Education, temperament, talents, studies. Then the main section, the emperor's deeds: to be divided into his actions in war and in peace. Then consideration of the fortune which stands at his side, his children, friends, ministers, concluding with a description of the prosperous realm, the safety of commerce, increasing religiosity. Best wishes for his prosperity. The most brilliant document of this type of oratory is Pliny the Younger's panegyric to Trajan, [which is] the expansion of a *gratiarum actio* [speech of gratitude] that was actually delivered (in the Senate).

Logoi charistērioi and *eucharistērioi* [speeches of affection and gratitude]. Then there is the *stephanōtikos logos*, a brief address to the emperor while presenting him with a wreath of honor. 150 to 200 lines [?]. Then the *presbeutikos logos*, an emissary speech with a plea to come to a city's assistance. Panegyric in the broad sense meaning any relatively long eulogy. In the strict sense, a speech given at a *panēguris*, a great national festival before a joyous holiday crowd. These ceremonies are associated with the cult of a god and begin with praise of this deity. Then praise of the city. Then explanation of the holiday, its origin, institution, season. The nature of the ceremony, whether gymnastic or artistic. The wreath. Oak, olive, laurel, sheafs of grain, spruce. The *klētikos logos*, invitation speech to an *archōn*, requesting his presence.

Imperial officials are honored with a speech when they come to a city *oratio compellatoria, prosphōnēsis* [public oration or address], *logos prosphōnētikos* or *epibatērios* [speech given on disembarking]. Opposite of *logos propemptikos* is the *propemptērios*, at a farewell. In the *logos syntaktikos* or *syntaktērios* the speaker says farewell. Then the *gamikos* or *epithalamios*. The *logos genethliakos* on the birthday or *natalitia*. Finally *logos epitaphios* and *logos paramythē-tikos* to the bereaved. F. Hubner suspects that Tacitus' *Agricola* is an elaborated *laudatio funebris*.

All shorter speeches [are called] *laliai*, not *epideixeis*, with a free unconstrained form. A *lalia* at the opening of a series of lectures is called *prolalia*. All artfully elaborated speeches on fictive themes are called by the Sophists *meletai* or *agōnes*, if they belong to the *genos dikanikon* or *symbouleutikon. Controversia* and *suasoria*.

XV. DIE DISPOSITIO

Ausserordentliche Armut der Vorschriften. τάξις dispositio, auch οἰκονομία. So zuerst Dionysios von Halik. Nach ihm ist οἰκονομία die Verwendung des durch die εὕρεσις zusammengebrachten Stoffes. ἡ χρῆσις τῶν παρεσκευασμένων, so dass παρασκευή gleich εὕρεσις ist. Die Hauptregeln sind fast überall bei der inventio mitabgehandelt. Ursprünglich gab es ja nur eine Zweitheilung εὕρεσις, φράσις inventio, elocutio. Sowohl bei Anaximenes als bei Aristoteles ist von τάξις die Rede, doch nur nebenbei. Allein wesentlich bei Arist. Rhet III, c 17. Sowohl in der berathenden als [in der] gerichtlichen Beredsamkeit muss wer zuerst das Wort hat, zuerst seine Beweisgründe vorbringen, dann dem ihm Entgegenstehenden widerlegend entgegentreten oder indem er es im voraus wirkungslos macht. Ist aber die Entgegnung sehr umfangreich, so bringt man sie zuerst vor, und lässt darauf seine Beweisgründe folgen. Wer dagegen an zweiter oder späterer Stelle spricht, der hat immer mit der Widerlegung des Gegners zu beginnen, um dadurch seiner eigenen Rede erst Platz zu machen.—Die Stoiker welche νόεσις, εὕρεσις, διάθεσις als die drei ἔργα bezeichneten, theilten die letztere in τάξις, οἰκονομία, λέξις, ὑπόκρισις. Ordnung der Rede, oder dann die innere Verbindung und Gliederung der Gedanken: dahin gehört auch die geeignete Behandlung der κεφάλαια, also die ἐχεργασία, die eigentliche Ausführung oder expositio und ἐπιχείρημα. Cornif. III 9, 16 unterscheidet natürliche und künstliche Disposition: dispositionis genus ab institutione artis profectum und genus ad casum temporis accommodatum. Für die natürliche Ordnung (die angebrachte) verweist er auf die Lehre von den Theilen der Rede; für die dispositio der argumentationes auf die Angaben der Erweiterung der Epicheireme. Das wäre τάξις und ἐξεργασία. Für die dispositio ad usum temporis accommodata hat er nur wenige Sätze. Bei Quintil. nimmt die dispositio das ganze siebte Buch ein: er theilt sein eigenes Inventionsverfahren bei Behandlung der Controverse und Suasoria mit. Sodann die διαιρέσεις στάσεων, die Angabe der Spezialtropen für den status. Die οἰκονομία nach Dionys. von Halic., behandelt διαίρεσις, τάξις, ἐξεργασία. Wenig nachzutragen: von der constanten Reihenfolge der Theile kann der Redner abweichen, er kann die Rede gleich mit der narratio eröffnen, oder mit ganz sicherem Beweis, oder dem Verlesen eines Schriftstückes. So kann man auch nach der Einleitung die confirmatio anbringen und die Erzählung an dritte Stelle. Für die Ordnung der Epicheireme im Beweise wird die Regel empfohlen, die

XV. DISPOSITIO

Extreme scantiness of rules. *Taxis* (*dispositio*), also *oikonomia*, as Dionysius of Halicarnassus first called it. According to him *oiko-nomia* is the use of material collected by *heuresis*. *Hē chrēsis tōn pa-raeskeuasmenōn*, so that *paraskeuē* is the same as *heuresis*. The main rules are treated almost everywhere along with *inventio*. Originally there was just a twofold division, *heuresis, phrasis* (*inventio, elocu-tio*). Both Anaximenes and Aristotle speak of *taxis*, but only curso-rily. [It is treated as] essential, however, only in Aristotle (*Rhetoric*, 3, 17). Both in epideictic and in forensic oratory, the first speaker must present his proofs, then refute his opponent's anticipated reply or nullify his arguments in advance. But if the refutation is very long, then it is presented first and one's own proofs follow. But whoever speaks second or later, must always begin by refuting the opponent in order thereby to make place for his own speech.

The Stoics, who designated *noēsis, heuresis, diathesis* as the three *erga*, divided the last one into *taxis, oikonomia, lexis, hypokrisis*. Arrangement of the speech, or then the inner combination and artic-ulation of the thoughts: to this belongs also the suitable treatment of the *kephalaia*, i.e. the *exergasia*, the actual elaboration or *expositio* and *epicheirema*. Cornificius (3, 9, 16), distinguishes between natural and artificial disposition: *dispositionis genus ab institutione artis pro-fectum* [a kind of arrangement arising from the principles of the art] and *genus ad casum temporis accommodatum* [a kind accommo-dated to particular circumstances].[123] For the natural order (the proper one) he refers to the doctrine of the parts of speech; for the *dispositio* of the *argumentationes* to the data obtained by expansion of the epicheireme. That would be *taxis* and *exergasia*. He has only a few sentences on the *dispositio ad usum temporis accommodata*. In Quintilian *dispositio* takes up the entire seventh book: he presents his own process of invention in his treatment of *controversia* and *suasoria*. Then the *diaireseis staseōn*, the listing of the special tropes for *status*. According to Dionysius of Halicarnassus, *oikonomia* treats of *diairesis, taxis, exergasia*. There is little to add: the orator can deviate from the constant sequence of the parts; he can open the speech immediately with the *narratio*, or with a completely certain proof, or by reading a written document. Or he can also insert the introduction after the *confirmatio* and place the narrative in the third position. For the arrangement of the epicheiremes in the proof, the

stärksten Beweismittel am Anfang und Ende zu nehmen, die unbe-
deutendsten in der Mitte. Cornif: firmissimas argumentationes in
primis et in postremis caussae partibus collocare: mediocres et neque
inutiles ad dicendum neque necessarias ad probandum, quae si separatim ac singulae dicantur, infirmae sunt cum ceteris conjunctae fir-
mae et probabiles fiunt, in medio collocari oportet. Gleich nach der
Erzählung erwartet der Zuhörer, wodurch wohl die Sache begründet
werden könne, deshalb muss man einen starken Beweisgrund
anbringen: weil aber das, was wir zuletzt sagen, sich am leichtesten
einprägt, muss zuletzt ein recht fester Beweis kommen. Bei der
Widerlegung soll man das Leichtzuwiderlegende zuerst nehmen und
zu dem Schwierigen aufsteigen.

Diaeresis des status conjecturalis. Cornif. II, 2,3, stellt auf, bei der
causa conj. müsse die Erzählung des Anklägers darauf aus sein, überall Verdächtigungen anzubringen, die des Vertheidigers klar und
schlicht sein mit Milderung der verdächtigen Umständen. Er theilt
die ratio dieses status ein: probabile, collatio, signum, argumentum,
consecutio, approbatio. Durch das probabile wird erwiesen, dass es
dem Angeklagten genützt habe, das Verbrechen zu begehen und dass
er von einer schlechten Handlung nie fern gewesen (probabile ex
caussa und probabile ex vita) Gefragt: (1) Was für Vortheile bei der
That, oder Nachtheile vermeiden? (2) Hat er etwas Ähnliches gethan
oder giebt es ein Verdacht?—Durch die collatio wird das Allgemeine
der bisherigen Beweisführung beschränkt, in dem man zeigt, dass
Niemandem ausser dem Verklagten durch die That Vortheil
erwürbt, dass Niemand ausser ihm sie habe thun können. Das signum weist nach, dass der Angeklagte eine günstige Gelegenheit zur
Ausführung seiner That gesucht habe, betrachtet Ort, Zeit, Zeit-
dauer, Hoffnung, die That zu vollbringen oder zu verheimlichen.—
Das argumentum giebt festere Indicien, und stichhaltige Beweise.—
Die consecutio betrachtet das Benehmen des Angeklagten nach der
That, die approbatio giebt eine amplificatio des Bisherigen durch loci
communes zur ἐκβολή ἐλέου. Probabile entspricht den Topen
βούλησις und δύναμις collatio der μετάληψις (diese ist gerichtet
gegen die ἀντίληψις, welche die Indizien des Anklägers als unver-

recommended rule is to put the strongest proofs at the beginning and at the end, the most insignificant ones in the middle. Cornificius:

> *firmissimas argumentationes in primis et in postremis caussae partibus collocare: mediocres et neque inutiles ad dicendum neque necessarias ad probandum, quae si separatim ac singulae dicantur, infirmae sunt, cum ceteris conjunctae firmae et probabiles fiunt, in medio collocari oportet* [(1) the strongest arguments should be placed at the beginning and at the end of the pleading; (2) those of medium force, and also those that are neither useless to discourse nor essential to the proof, which are weak if presented separately and individually, but become strong and plausible when conjoined with the others, should be placed in the middle].[124]

Immediately after the narrative the listener expects to hear how the case can be proven; therefore one must present a strong proof: but because what we say last is most easily remembered, a very solid proof must come last. In the refutation one first takes what is easy to refute and advances to the difficult.

Diaeresis of the status conjecturalis. Cornificius (2, 2, 3) asserts that in the *causa conjecturalis* the plaintiff's narrative must aim to cast suspicions everywhere, while the defense's must be clear and simple with mitigation of the suspicious circumstances. He divides the *ratio* of this *status* into *probabile, collatio, signum, argumentum, consecutio, approbatio.* The *probabile* proves that the accused benefited from committing the crime and that he was never averse to a bad action (*probabile ex caussa* and *probabile ex vita*). Questions: (1) What advantages "did he derive" from the deed, or what disadvantages avoid? (2) Has he ever done anything similar, or is there a suspicion? Through the *collatio* the generalness of the preceding line of proof is restricted by showing that no one except the accused draws advantage from the deed, that no one but he could have done it. The *signum* proves that the accused sought a favorable opportunity to perform his deed; it examines place, time, duration, and hope of carrying out the deed or of keeping it secret. The *argumentum* gives more solid evidence and cogent proofs.—The *consecutio* examines the defendant's behavior after the deed; the *approbatio* gives an *amplificatio* of the previous material through *loci communes* for the *ekbolē eleou* [removal of pity]. *Probabile* corresponds to the *topoi boulēsis* and *dynamis, collatio* to *metalēpsis* (this is aimed against the *antilēpsis,* which portrays the plaintiff's evidence as harmless, as

fänglich darstellt, als solche für die man keine Rechenschaft zu geben braucht: dagegen wird geltend gemacht das, was im Allgemein erlaubt ist, so doch nicht auf diese Weise unter diesen Umständen. Also Beseitigung der allgemeinen bisherigen Beweisführung.) signum argumentum und consecutio geben τὰ ἀπ᾽ ἀρχῆς ἄχρι τέλους. approbatio entspricht der κοινὴ ποιότης. Quintilian sagt, bei der Conjektur sind der Reihe nach drei Fragen zu beantworten, ob der Angeklagte die That hat thun wollen, ob er sie hat thun können, ob er sie gethan hat. 1. intuendum ante omnia qualis sit, de quo agitur. Der Ankläger hat darauf zu sehen, dass das, was er dem Angeklagten vorwirft, nicht nur an sich schimpflich sei, sondern auch zu dem betreffenden Verbrechen passe. Wenn er einen des Mordes angeklagten Menschen unzüchtig nennt, so ist dies weniger zur Sache, als wenn er zeigt, dass er frech und grausam war. Wird nichts vorgeworfen, muss der Vertheidiger darauf aufmerksam machen. Im Ganzen ist es besser, keine Angriffe auf das frühere Leben zu machen als nichtige oder falsche: es schadet der Glaubwürdigkeit. Dann der Beweis aus den Ursachen: Leidenschaften, Zorn, Hass, Begierde, Furcht, Hoffnung: jedes hat zum Schlimmsten führen können. Ist dies nicht der Fall, so muss er sagen, es seien vielleicht geheime Ursachen, es thue nicht weiter zur Sache, warum er es gethan hat, wenn er es nur gethan hat. Der Vertheidiger muss darauf bestehen, dass nichts ohne Grund geschehe. Bei den Absichten kommen mancherlei Fragen: konnte der Angeklagte glauben, die That könne von ihm vollbracht werden: oder verborgen bleiben? oder konnte er Freisprechung hoffen? ob er durch Gewohnheit zu sündigen verführt sei? warum er gerade an jenem Orte, zu jener Zeit angegriffen habe: ob er sich habe überrascht fortreissen lassen? 2. Hat er die That thun können? Lässt sich erweisen, dass keine Möglichkeit zur Ausführung der That da war, so ist die Sache erledigt, z.B. bei absentia. War die Möglichkeit vorhanden, so fragt [man] nach 3. hat er sie gethan? Schall, Geschrei, Geseufze, Verbergen, Flucht, Furcht, Worte und Handlungen des Angeklagten nachher, usw.

Diaeresis des Definitionsstatus. Cornif. II, 12, 17 man hat von einer kurzen Definition des streitigen Begriffs auszugehen. Primum igitur vocabuli sententia breviter et ad utilitatem caussae accommodate describetur: deinde factum nostrum cum verbi descriptione coniungetur. deinde contrariae descriptionis ratio refelletur si aut falsa erit, aut inutilis, aut turpis, aut iniuriosa. Letztere Widerlegung

such for which one need give no accounting: to refute one tries to prove what is permitted in general, but not in this way and under these circumstances, i.e., the elimination of the general line of proof up to this point). *Signum, argumentum,* and *consecutio* present *ta ap' archēs achri telous* [the entire cause—from beginning to end]. *Approbatio* corresponds to the *koinē poiotēs* [common quality].

Quintilian says that in *conjectura* three questions must be answered in sequence, whether the accused wanted to commit the act, whether he was able to, and whether he did commit it. (1) *intuendum ante omnia qualis sit de quo agitur* [the first thing we must know is what kind of case we are dealing with].[125] The plaintiff must see to it that what he charges the accused with is not only damnable in itself, but fits the crime in question. When a person accused of murder is called unchaste, that is less pertinent to the case than when it is shown that he was impudent and cruel. If no reproach is made, then the defense must call attention to that fact. On the whole it is better to make no attacks on previous life than flimsy or false ones: this damages credibility. Then the proof from causes: passions, anger, hatred, greed, fear, hope: each was sufficient to lead to the worst outcome. If that is not the case, then he must say that there are perhaps secret motives, why he did it, as long as he did do it. The defense must insist that nothing happens without a reason. Concerning motives there are various questions: could the defendant believe that he could do the deed? Or remain hidden? Or could he hope to be found innocent? Or could he have been seduced to sin by force of habit? Why did he attack precisely in that place, at that time: whether he let himself get carried away by surprise? (2) Was he able to commit the deed? If it can be proven that there was no possibility of his committing the deed, then the case is closed, e.g. by *absentia.* If the possibility existed, then one asks concerning (3) Did he do it? Noise, screaming, groaning, concealment, flight, fear, words and actions of the accused afterwards, etc.

Diaeresis of the definition-status. According to Cornificius (2, 12, 17), one must start with a short definition of the disputed concept:

Primum igitur vocabuli sententia breviter et ad utilitatem caussae accommodate describetur: deinde factum nostrum cum verbi descriptione conjungetur. Deinde contrariae descriptionis ratio refelletur si aut falsa erit, aut inutilis, aut turpis, aut iniuriosa [Thus the meaning of the term is first explained briefly, and adapted to the advantage of our

also durch Anwendung der τελικὰ κεφάλαια. Locus communis gegen die Bosheit, dessen der sich nicht nur willkürliche Handlungen sondern auch willkürliche Benennungen anmasst. Dagegen der locus communis des Vertheidigers, dass der Gegner, um ihn in Gefahr zu bringen, nicht nur die Thatsachen sondern auch die Bezeichnungen zu entstellen sucht. Cicero hält übrigens die strenge rein wissenschaftliche Definition für pedantisch und unpassend: er verlangt nur Widergabe des Begriffs in weitere Umschreibungen. Quintilian sagt, es ist schwieriger die Definition zu begründen, als sie auf dem gegebenen Fall anzuwenden. Streng inne zu halten die Reihenfolge quid sit? und an hoc sit?

[Widerlegung in der gerichtlichen Rede:]

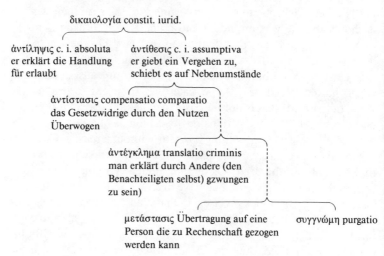

δικαιολογία constit. iurid.

ἀντίληψις c. i. absoluta
er erklärt die Handlung
für erlaubt

ἀντίθεσις c. i. assumptiva
er giebt ein Vergehen zu,
schiebt es auf Nebenumstände

ἀντίστασις compensatio comparatio
das Gesetzwidrige durch den Nutzen
Überwogen

ἀντέγκλημα translatio criminis
man erklärt durch Andere (den
Benachteiligten selbst) gzwungen
zu sein)

μετάστασις Übertragung auf eine
Person die zu Rechenschaft gezogen
werden kann

συγγνώμη purgatio

Die deprecatio gibt die Absichtlichkeit der That zu, legt sich aber aufs Bitten. In der Praxis des Gerichts kann sie nicht vorkommen, nur [?] im Senat, vor dem princeps.

Diaeresis des status qualitatis. Nach Cornif. wird bei der constitutio iuridicialis absoluta nach Mittheilung des Sachverhalts gefragt, ob die Sache mit Recht geschehen sei. Man muss wissen, aus welchen Theilen das Recht besteht constat igitur ex his partibus: natura, lege, consuetudine, iudicato, aequo et bono, pacto, his igitur partibus iniuriam demonstrari, ius confirmari convenit. Dann die constitutio iuri-

cause; then we shall connect our conduct with the explanation of the term; finally, the principle underlying the contrary definition will be refuted, as being false, inexpedient, disgraceful].[126]

The latter refutation, thus, by applying the *telika kephalaia* [principal topics, drawn from the supreme ends]. *Locus communis* against the malice of the one who not only indulges in arbitrary actions but also in arbitrary nomenclature. Against this the defense's *locus communis* that the opponent, in order to bring him into danger, seeks to distort not just the facts but also the terminology. Cicero, incidentally, considers strict, purely scientific definition to be pedantic and inappropriate: he requires just the rendition of the term in broader paraphrases. Quintilian says that it is more difficult to establish the definition than to apply it to the current case. The sequence *quid sit?* and *an hoc sit?* must be observed strictly.

[Refutation in the juridical oration:]

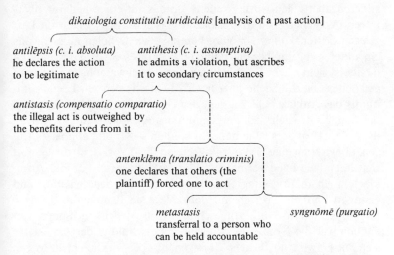

dikaiologia constitutio iuridicialis [analysis of a past action]

antilēpsis (c. i. absoluta)
he declares the action
to be legitimate

antithesis (c. i. assumptiva)
he admits a violation, but ascribes
it to secondary circumstances

antistasis (compensatio comparatio)
the illegal act is outweighed by
the benefits derived from it

antenklēma (translatio criminis)
one declares that others (the
plaintiff) forced one to act

metastasis
transferral to a person who
can be held accountable

syngnōmē (purgatio)

The *deprecatio* admits the intentionality of the deed, but resorts to pleas for mercy. It cannot occur in court practice, only [?] in the Senate, before the emperor.

Diaeresis of the status qualitatis. According to Cornificius, in the *constitutio iuridicialis absoluta*, after presentation of the content of the case, it is asked whether the thing was rightfully done. One must know of what parts the right consists:

constat igitur ex his partibus: natura, lege, consuetudine, iudicato, aequo et bono, pacto, his igitur partibus iniuriam demonstrari, ius confirmari

dicialis assumptiva. Bei der comparatio muss zuerst gefragt werden, welche von beiden Handlungen die ehrenvollere leichtere und vortheilhaftere gewesen sei. Dann ist zu fragen, ob es dem Angeklagten zukam, selbst zu entscheiden, welche die nützlichere war oder ob er die Entscheidung darüber anderen überlassen musste. Dann sucht der Ankläger durch Conjektur zu erweisen, dass das Bessere dem Schlechteren nicht mit Überlegung vorgezogen sei, sondern dabei dolus malus im Spiel gewesen sei. Der Angeklagte hat dieses Conjekturalbeweis zu widerlegen. Zum Schluss locus communis des Anklägers gegen den, der ohne Berechtigung darüber zu entscheiden, das Unnütze dem Nützlichen vorzieht. Locus communis des Angeklagten gegen diejenigen, welche verlangen, das Gefährliche dem Nützlichen vorzuziehen. Frage an den Ankläger und Richter, was sie an seiner Stelle gethan haben würden, mit lebhafter Schilderung von Zeit, Sache, Ort, und seiner Überlegung.—Bei translatio criminis ist zu fragen, ob die Anschuldigung der Wahrheit gemäss auf einen anderen übertragen wird; zweitens, ob das auf einen anderen übertragene Vergehen eben so gross sei als das dem Angeklagten zur Last gelegte; drittens, ob er ein Vergehen habe wiederholen müssen, was ein anderer vor ihm begangen und ob über das Vergehen des anderen nicht erst richterliche Entscheidung einzuholen war; ob, da dies nicht geschehen sei, die Sache jetzt noch zu entscheiden sei. Locus communis des Anklägers gegen den, der Gewalt vor Recht gehen lässt, der Angeklagte sucht sich durch amplificatio zu helfen und zu zeigen dass er nicht anders habe handeln können.—Bei purgatio ist zu fragen: ob wirklich eine Nothwendigkeit zur That vorlag: ob die Gewalt sich irgendwie habe vermeiden oder mildern lassen, ob der Angeklagte auch in Erwägung gezogen, was er habe dagegen thun und ersinnen können: ob sich auf dem Wege der Conjektur erweisen lässt, dass da, wo Noth vorgeschützt wird, Absicht im Spiele war: endlich war die Noth eine zwingende? Entschuldigt der Angeklagte sich mit Unwissenheit, so ist zu fragen, ob er es wirklich nicht wissen konnte; ob er sich bemüht, sich Kunde zu verschaffen; ob er aus Zufall es nicht gewusst oder Schuld an seinem Nichtwissen habe; endlich, ist Nichtwissen ein ausreichender Entschuldigungsgrund? Loci communes auf Seiten des Klägers gegen den, der die That eingesteht und doch noch Weitläuftigkeiten machen will. Der Angeklagte appellirt an Humanität und Mitleiden, überall müsse man auf die Absicht sehen: wo diese fehle, liege auch kein Vergehen vor.—

convenit [The constituent departments, then, are the following: Nature, Statute, Custom, Previous Judgments, Equity, and Agreement].[127]

Then the *constitutio iuridicialis assumptiva* [argumentation based on likelihood]. In the *comparatio* it must first be asked which of the two actions was the more honorable, easier, and more advantageous. Then one must ask whether the accused was authorized to decide which was more beneficial or whether he had to leave the decision to others. Then the plaintiff tries to prove by conjecture that the better course was chosen over the worse not deliberately, but that *dolus malus* played a role. The accused must refute this conjectural proof. At the end *locus communis* of the plaintiff against the person who, without justification to make that decision, prefers the useless to the useful. *Locus communis* of the accused against those who demand that the dangerous be preferred to the useful. Question to the plaintiff and judge, what they would have done in his place, with a vivid description of time, thing, place, and his deliberation.

In *translatio criminis* the question is raised whether the accusation is truthfully transferred to another person; secondly, whether the offense transferred to another person is as great as the one the accused is charged with; thirdly, whether he had to repeat an offense which another committed before him, or whether a juridical decision did not first have to be obtained on the other's offense, whether, since this did not happen, the matter still had to be decided. *Locus communis* of the plaintiff against the person who gives priority to might over right; the accused tries to help himself through *amplificatio* and to show that he could not have acted otherwise.

In the *purgatio* it must be asked whether necessity for the deed existed: whether violence could somehow have been avoided or diminished, whether the defendant also considered what he could have done or thought up against it; whether it can be proven by way of conjecture that intention was really at work where necessity is being used as pretext; finally was the necessity a compelling one? If the accused pleads ignorance, then one must ask whether he really could not have known it; whether he tried to inform himself; whether he failed to know by chance or was guilty of his ignorance; finally, is ignorance a sufficient excuse? *Locus communis* on the plaintiff's part against the one who admits the deed but wishes to make long-winded excuses. The defendant appeals to humaneness and pity; one must always consider intent: where it is missing, there is no crime.

Bei deprecatio wird der Angeklagte in Erwägung geben, die Zahl seiner sonstigen Verdienste, dann was man im Falle seiner Freisprechung für Vortheile zu erwarten habe: dass seinem Vergehen keine
unedle Absicht zu Grund gelegen, dass in ähnlichen Fällen bereits
andere Verzeihung erlangt haben, dass aus seiner Freisprechung kein
Nachtheil und keine üble Nachrede bei Mitbürgern und fremden
Staaten erwachse. Umgekehrt der Ankläger.—Bei remotio criminis
wird die Schuld auf eine Sache oder Person zurückgeschoben: im
letzten Falle gefragt: ist die Person wirklich so einflussreich? Wie hat
er ihr auf ehrenwerthe und gefahrlose Weise widerstehen können:
Conjecturalbeweis trotzdem der Absichtlichkeit der That. Wird die
Ursache der That auf eine Sache geschoben, dann tritt das Verfahren
ein, wie bei purgatio aus Nothwendigkeit.

XVI. ÜBER MEMORIA UND ACTIO[13]

Von den Sophisten, seit Gorgias, wird ein ausserordentlichen
Werth auf das Extemporieren αὐτοσχεδιάζον gelegt, im ganzen aber
werden in der gerichtlichen und berathenden Beredsamkeit die
Reden ausgearbeitet und auswendig gelernt. Diejenigen, die grossen
Beifall fanden, würden zur Veröffentlichung nochmals überarbeitet.
Die erste Rede nach seiner Rückkehr las Cicero übrigens, weil sie zu
lang war, im Senat vor. Es war höchst wichtig die Gedächtniskraft
zu stärken. Wunderbare Leistungen antiker Mnemoniker. Der Rhetor Seneca sagt von sich: memoriam aliquando in me floruisse, ut
non tantum ad usum sufficeret, sed in miraculum usque procederet,
non nego. Nam duo milia nominum recitata, quo ordine erant dicta,
referebam et ab iis qui ad audiendum praeceptorem nostrum convenerant, singulos versus a singulis datos, cum plures quam ducenti
efficerentur, ab ultimo incipiens usque ad primum recitabam. Nec
ad complectenda tantum quae vellem, velox erat mihi memoria, sed

In *deprecatio* the accused will call into consideration his other merits, then the advantages that could be expected from his exoneration: that no ignoble intention was at the basis of his offense; that others had, in similar cases, already obtained pardon; that no disadvantage and no malicious slander would result from his release among fellow citizens or other states. The accuser does the opposite.

In *remotio criminis* the blame is pushed back onto a person or thing: in the former case the question is asked: is the person really so influential? How could he resist that person honorably and safely: conjectural proof despite the intentionality of the deed. If the cause of the deed is pushed upon a thing, then the procedure used is like *purgatio* from necessity.

XVI. ON *MEMORIA* AND *ACTIO*[128]

The Sophists since Gorgias placed extraordinary value on the extemporaneous *autoschediazon*, but generally in forensic and deliberative oratory the speeches were composed in writing and learned by heart. Those which met with great approval were revised again for publication. Incidentally, Cicero *read* to the Senate, his first speech after his return because it was too long. It was extremely important to strengthen one's memory. Marvelous achievements by ancient mnemonicists. The rhetor Seneca says of himself:

memoriam aliquando in me floruisse, ut non tantum ad usum sufficeret, sed in miraculum usque procederet, non nego. Nam duo milia nominum recitata, quo ordine erant dicta, referebam et ab iis qui ad audiendum praeceptorem nostrum convenerant, singulos versus a singulis datos, cum plures quam ducenti efficerentur, ab ultimo incipiens usque ad primum recitabam. Nec ad complectenda tantum quae vellem, velox erat mihi memoria, sed etiam ad continenda, quae acceperat [I do not deny that my own memory was at one time so powerful as to be positively prodigious, quite apart from its efficacy in ordinary use. When two thousand names had been reeled off I would repeat them in the same order; and when my assembled schoolfellows each supplied a line of poetry, up to the number of more than two hundred, I would recite them in reverse. My memory used to be swift to pick up what I wanted it to; but it was also reliable in retaining what it had taken in].[129]

etiam ad continenda, quae acceperat. Als Erfinder der Künst gilt Simonides von Keos, Distichen von ihm

μνήμη δ' ὀὔτινά φημι Ζιμωνίδη ἰσοφαρίζειν
ὀγδωκονταέται παιδὶ Λεωπρέπεος.

Gastmahl des Scopaden in Krannon fabelhaft. Der Sophist Hippias (bei Plato, Hippias 97E) rühmt als besonderen Vorzug, dass er fünfzig Worte wieder aufsagen könne. Anaximenes und Aristoteles berühren die μνήμη nicht. Der Freund des Aristoteles, Theodectes war ein grosser Mnemoniker semel auditos quamlibet multos versus protinus dicitur reddidisse. Cornificius fand über diese Sache schon allerlei Schriften vor. Der Redner hat weniger Regeln in diesem Punkte zu beachten: Gedächtnissörter. Er merkt sich z.b. ein Haus mit allen darin befindlichen Zimmern, Räumen, oder einen Saal mit den Gegenständen, oder eine Strasse mit den wichtigsten Häusern. Das muss absolut fest und sicher sein, ihr vollkommen treues Bild in jedem Augenblick zu reproduciren. Gut, wenn die Theile gleichmässig entfernt sind und wenn sie selbst sich deutlich von einander unterscheiden (nicht lauter Säulen oder Bäume). Auf diese Örter wird der zu memorierende Stoff vertheilt, so dass er durch ein mit dem Stoffe in Verbindung stehendes Gedächtnisbild mit dem Ort verbunden wird. Dann wird memoriert, der Blick fest auf Ort und Bild gerichtet. Beim Hersagen des Gelernten giebt die Reihenfolge der Örter die Reihenfolge des gelernten Stoffes an die Hand. Die Erfahrung lehrt, dass je öfter man sich ein und derselben Gedächtnissörter bedient, um so sicherer auf sie Verlass ist. Die Gedächtnisbilder sind hieroglyphische Zeichen: Anker bedeutet Schifffahrt, Schwert Kampf. Man kann auch das Bild für das Anfangswort als Zeichen verwenden, Sonne für solet. Wieviel Stoff man dem Gedächtnissystem anvertrauen will, wieviele Worte oder Sätze man dadurch symbolisieren will, hängt vom Belieben des Einzelnen ab. Ohne Gedächtnisörter kann man memorieren, wenn die Gedächtnissbilder durch irgend welche Vorstellungsassoziation verbunden sind, zu einer Kette.—Vorschriften für solche, die keine Mnemonik anwenden. Eine Rede muss nach kleineren Theilen gelernt werden. Besonders schwierige Stellen kann man immer am Rande durch mnemonische Zeichen ausdrücken. Man thut gut nach dem Concept zu lernen, sich die Seiten zu merken, auf denen eines steht und beim

Simonides of Keos was considered to be the inventor of the art. Distichs of his:

> *mnēmē d'outina phēmi Simōnidēi isopharizein*
> *ogdōkontaetai paidi Leōprepeos*
> [Simonides was able to recite from memory no less than
> eighty words to the child Leoprepeos][130]

The banquet of the Skopades in Krannon is fabulous. The Sophist Hippias (in Plato, *Hippias*, 97E) boasts of it as a special talent that he can recite off fifty words. Anaximenes and Aristotle do not touch upon *mnēmē*. Aristotle's friend, Theodectes, was a great mnemonicist: *semel auditos quamlibet multos versus protinus dicitur reddidisse* [having heard any number of verses he is said to have repeated them at once].

Cornificius found all sorts of writings already existing on this subject. The orator has less rules to observe on this point: memory-places. He notes, for example, a house with all its rooms and halls or a room with its contents, or a street with the most important houses. That must be absolutely firm and certain, to reproduce its perfectly accurate image at any moment. It is good if the parts are equidistant and if they differ clearly from one another (not exclusively pillars or flowers). The material to be memorized is distributed among these places, so that it is connected with the place by a memory-image associated with the material. Then one memorizes with one's gaze fixed firmly on place and image. In reciting what one has learned, the sequence of places provides us with the sequence of the learned material. Experience teaches that the more often one uses the same memory-places, the more securely one can rely on them. The memory-images are hieroglyphic signs: anchor means navigation, sword battle. One can also use the image as a sign for the first word, "sol" [sun] for "solet" [he is accustomed]. How much material one wants to entrust to the mnemonic system, how many words or sentences one wishes to symbolize thereby depends on individual preference. One can memorize without mnemonic places, if the mnemonic images are connected into a chain by some sort of association of ideas.

Rules for those who use no mnemonic system. A speech must be learned in short portions. Especially difficult passages can always be marked in the margin with mnemonic symbols. One does well to learn word for word, noting the pages where something stands and

Hersagen das Ganze fast abzulesen. Stellen, an denen etwas eingeschaltet ist, muss man fester memorieren. Mit halblauter Stimme zu
lernen. Gut Disponiertes und sorgfältig Ausgearbeitetes lernt sich
leichter. Angestrengte Übung nöthig. Erst Stücke von mässigem
Umfang, dann immer grössere, zuerst poetische, dann rednerische
Prosa, dann Kunstlosere. Dem frischen Gedächtniss nicht zu sehr zu
trauen: besser sitzt was Abends vorher gelernt wurde. Je besser man
memorirt hat, umso mehr kann man die Rede den Anstrich des
Unstudierten geben. Wer ein schweres Gedächtnis hat oder wem es
an Zeit fehlt, kann sich mit einem Überblick begnügen und sich Freiheit vorbehalten, im Augenblick den Ausdruck frei zu gestalten: dazu
gehört eine gewisse Fertigkeit, aus dem Stegreif zu reden.

Die ὑπόκρισις. Nach Dionys v. H. zerfallend in πάθη τῆς φωνῆς
καὶ σχήματα τοῦ σώματος. Bei den Römern actio oder pronuntiatio:
nach Cicero die Beredsamkeit des Körpers vocis et motus (gestus)
auf Ohr und Augen der Zuhörer wirkend, sehr wichtig: eine mittel-
mässige Rede, durch kräftigen Vortrag empfohlen, hat mehr Gewicht
als die beste ohne jene Hülfe. Demosthenes gefragt, was bei der ganzen Aufgabe des Redners die Hauptsache sei, hat gesagt, (1) der Vortrag; (2) der Vortrag; (3) der Vortrag. Bei der Stimme kommt es einmal auf die natürliche Beschaffenheit an, dann auf die Art der
Anwendung. Umfang, Grad der Stärke und der Ausdauer, Biegsam-
keit, Klangfarbe. Sorgfältige Übung im täglichen lauten Vortrag von
memorirten Stücken. Die Aussprache vor allem deutlich. Endsilben
nicht verschlucken, auch nicht die einzelnen Buchstaben zu zählen.
Gegliedert nach der Interpunktion, mit Pausen und mit Fallenlassen
der Stimme am Schluss der Perioden. Ein gutes, klangreiches, gleich-
mässiges Organ muss durch die Art des Vortrags Abwechslung
geben, um der Monotonie zu entgehen. Beim Anfang der Rede nicht
zu laut anzusetzen. Promptum sit os, non praeceps, moderatum, non
lentum. Wichtig, die richtige Vertheilung des Athems. Namentlich
am Schlusse der Rede muss man viel in einem Athem sagen können.
Nie singen, was aber die Asianer thaten: bei den griechischen Orphi-
sten weichlich singender Tonfälle. Höchstens im Epilog darf die
Stimme flebilis werden. Im Allgemein: Dionys. von Halic. πάνυ
γὰρ εὔηθες ἄλλο τι ζητεῖν ὑποκρίσεως διδασκάλιον ἀφέντας

almost reading off the whole thing on delivery. Passages into which something is inserted have to be memorized more firmly. One reads in a soft voice. Well-organized and carefully composed material is easier to learn. Intensive practice is necessary. First a section of moderate scope [is memorized], then longer and longer ones; first poetic passages, then oratorical prose, then less artistic ones. Fresh memory should not be relied on too much: what was learned the evening before sticks better. The better one has memorized the more the speech can be given a flavor of improvisation. Whoever has a bad memory or a shortage of time, can settle for an overall view and reserve the freedom to shape the expression at the moment: a certain skill in extemporizing is necessary for this.

The *hypocrisis* [delivery]. According to Dionysius of Halicarnassus, it is divided into *pathē tēs phōnēs kai schēmata tou somatos* [modulation of the voice and gestures of the body]. The Romans called it *actio* or *pronuntiatio*: according to Cicero the eloquence of the body, *vocis et motus (gestus),* acting on the ear and eyes of the listener is very important: a mediocre speech, recommended by a strong delivery, carries more weight than the best one without any help. Demosthenes, when asked what the main thing was in the orator's entire task, said (1) delivery; (2) delivery; (3) delivery. As for the voice, what matters most is its naturalness, and secondly, the way it is used. Range, strength and endurance, suppleness, and timbre. Diligent practice in daily oral delivery of memorized pieces. Enunciation must be especially clear, not swallowing the final syllables but without counting the individual letters. Articulated according to punctuation, with pauses and lowering of the voice at the end of periods. A good, sonorous, smooth vocal apparatus must provide variety by its mode of delivery, in order to avoid monotony. One should not begin too loud at the beginning of the speech. *Promptum sit os, non praeceps, moderatum, non lentum* [The tempo of speech must be fast but not headlong, moderate but not slow]. Especially at the end of the speech, one must be able to say a lot in one breath. Never singsong, which however the Asiatics did: the Greek Orphists used a soft, singing intonation. Only in the epilogue may the voice become *flebilis* [plaintive, doleful]. In general: Dionysius of Halicarnassus:

pany gar euēthes allo ti zētein hypokriseōs didaskalion aphentas tēn alētheian [It is very simple to seek a different method of performing after dismissing the truth].[131]

τήν ἀλήθειαν. Cornif.: scire oportet pronuntiationem bonam id proficere, ut res ex animo agi videatur. Dann Gesten und Körperhaltung. Der Kopf ungezwungen, gerade. Beim Beweis wird er etwas vorgebeugt samt dem Oberkörper. Gesten dürfen nie zu Pantomimen zu lebendiger Plastik der Körperstellungen werden. Merkwürdige Schilderung bei Quintil. Buch XI, Cap. III.

ANHANG: ABRISS DER GESCHICHTE DER BEREDSAMKEIT

Empedocles soll der Gründer sein Ἀριστοτέλης ἐν τῇ σοφιστῇ 2a. VIII 57, wie Zeno der Erfinder der Dialektik: ein grosser Volksredner im höchst bevölkerten Agrigent, der eine Demokratie dort einführt. Der Syracusaner *Corax* hat eine τέχνη hinterlassen: der Redner müsse nach dem εἰκός, dem Wahrscheinlichen, streben: er unterscheidet die Redetheile und bezeichnet das prooemium als κατάστασις. Seine Definition der Rhetorik: πειθοῦς δημιουργός.

Sein Schüler ist *Tisias*, berühmte Geschichte, dass er ihm nach einem Pakt, erst den Lohn zahlen wolle, wenn er den ersten Prozess gewonnen habe (dieselbe Geschichte von Protagoras und Euathlos). Corax verklagt ihn und stellt den Satz auf, dass er jedenfalls das Geld erhalten müsse, im Fall des Sieges nach dem Spruch des Gerichts, in dem des Unterliegens nach dem Pakt. Tisias dreht es um: er habe in keinem Falle zu zahlen: siege er, weil ihn der Richterspruch dann entbinde, siege er nicht, so finde der Contrakt keine Anwendung. Die Richter jagen beide fort mit ἐκ κακοῦ κόρακος κακον ᾠόν.—In Thurii ist er Lehrer des Lysias, in Athen des Isocrates gewesen. c. 480 geb. Herumwandernd, wie ein Sophist. Hinterlässt eine τέχνη. Tisias und Corax waren wesentlich Lehrer des Prozessirens. Anders steht es mit den Sophisten des eigentlichen Griechenlands und der ostlichen Kolonien, bei denen der eigentlicher Name σοφιστής aufkommt. Sie geben eine enzyklopädische Bildung.

Protagoras v. Abdera geb. 485 durchzog etwa von 455 (von wo die Sophistik zu datieren ist) die hellenischen Städte. Auf die attische Beredsamkeit hatte Protagoras viel früher Einfluss als die Sicelioten. Er verheisst zu lehren τὸν ἥττω λόγον κρείττω δοκεῖν: wie man durch Dialektik der schwächeren Sache den Sieg schaffen könne. Diese Dialektik sollte alle anderen Künste und Wissenschaften ent-

Cornificius:

scire oportet, pronuntiationem bonam id proficere, ut res ex animo agi videatur [One must remember: good delivery ensures that what the orator is saying seems to come from his heart].[132]

The gestures and posture. The position of the head should be natural and erect. During the proof it is bowed somewhat forward together with the entire body. Gestures must never become pantomimes or living statues of body positions. A remarkable description [can be found] in Quintilian (Book 11, Chapter 3).

APPENDIX. OUTLINE OF THE HISTORY OF ELOQUENCE

Empedocles is said to be the founder of rhetoric, *Aristotelēs en tēi sophistēi* (2a., 8, 57), just as Zeno was the inventor of dialectics: he was a great popular orator in the highly populated Agrigentum who introduced a democracy there. The Syracusan Corax left behind a *technē*: the orator must strive for the *eikos*, the probable: he distinguishes the parts of a speech and calls the *prooemium* by the name of *katastasis*. His definition of rhetoric: *peithous dēmiourgos* [the producer of conviction].

His disciple was *Tisias*. There is a famous story that Corax signed an agreement with Tisias that he would have to pay him his tuition only if he won his first case (the same story is told of Protagoras and Euathlos). Corax sues him, and argues that he must pay him in either case: if he wins, by judgment of the court; if he loses, according to the agreement. Tisias turns the argument around: he did not have to pay either way. If he won, because then the court's decision released him; if he did not win, then the contract did not apply. The judges chased them both away with the words *ek kakou korakos kakon ōon* [a bad egg from a bad crow]. In Thurii he was the teacher of Lysias, in Athens of Isocrates. Born ca. 480. Wandering around like a Sophist. He left a *technē*. Tisias and Corax were essentially teachers of trial oratory. The situation is different with the Sophists of Greece proper and of the Eastern colonies where the actual name *sophistēs* originated. They provided an encyclopedic education.

Protagoras of Abdera, born in 485, wandered about the Hellenic cities from ca. 455 (from which year Sophism dates). Protagoras' influence on Attic oratory is much earlier than that of the Sicilians.

behrlich machen: wie man den Geometer, ohne Geometer zu sein niederdisputiren könne: so über die Naturphilosophie, den Ringkampf, das praktische Staatsleben. Die Schüler mussten Musterproben auswendig lernen. τέχνη ἐριστικῆς oder ἀντιλογικά (aus dem Plato nach Aristoxenus den Stoff zur Politaia entnommen haben soll, d.h. περὶ τοῦ δικαίου). Auch die anderen grossen Sophisten kommen in Betracht. Als praktisches Ergebnis dieser neuen Bildung nach der Mitte des fünften Jahrhunderts: der grosse *Pericles*. Er disputierte viel mit Protagoras: Plato leitet die höchste Meisterschaft in der Beredsamkeit aus der anaxagorischen Philosophie her: sie verlieh dem Geiste einen erhabenen Flug und verstehenden Blick in das Innere der Natur und des Menschen. Phaedrus p. 269 E. Damals schämten sich noch die wichtigsten Männer in den Städten, Reden zu verfassen und Geschriebenes zu hinterlassen. Es fehlte dem Perikles noch ganz die leidenschaftliche Form der späteren Redner, besonders des Demosthenes. Unbewegt stand er da, der umgewikkelte Mantel bewahrte den gleichen Faltenwurf, der hohe Ernst der Mienen verzog sich nie zum Lächeln, die Stimme behielt dieselbe Höhe und Stärke—alles undemosthenisch, doch wundersam imponierend.

Zuerst bildet *Gorgias* in Sicilien einen künstlerischen Stil für prosaische Rede aus, der freilich seine Anwendung in Lobreden nicht in praktischen Reden fand, und bringt diesen nach Athen. In Athen entwickelt sich nur wenig später, aus der gleichfalls eingeführten Rhetorik des Tisias und der Dialektik der östlichen Sophisten, in Anlehnung an die bestehende Sitte des Advokatenthums, die dem Prozessierenden dienende λογογραφία, deren erster noch alterthümlicher Vertreter Antiphon ist. Auch jener Stil macht den Anspruch, ein künstlerischer zu sein: daher die Veröffentlichung der geschriebenen Reden, als Muster für die Nachahmung.

Weiser bildet der Rhetor *Thrasymachus* den der praktischen Rede angemessenen Stil, indem er an die Stelle von Gorgias' Prunk und Antiphons steifer Würde die gerundete Periode und den gebildeten Ausdruck setzt. Mitten in dieser Bewegung stehen Männer wie Kritias und Andokides, die selbst keine Sophisten sind. Thracymachus, ein Altersgenosse des Lysias, in der Einleitungsszene der platonischen Republik hervortretend als Karikatur, anmasslich, käuflich, unsittlich, dummdreist, oft überwiegend Techniker, er ist der Begründer der mittleren Gattung des Stils, er ist Erfinder der für praktische Zwecke passenden Periode, endlich hat er zuerst den päa-

He promises to teach *ton hēttō logon kreittō dokein*: how by dialectics one can obtain victory for the weaker side. This dialectics was supposed to make all other arts and sciences superfluous: how without being a geometrician one can outargue the geometrician: and likewise on natural philosophy, wrestling, the practical life of the state. The pupils had to learn patterns by heart. *Technē eristikēs* or *antilogika* (from which, according to Aristoxenus, Plato supposedly took the material for his *Republic*, i.e., *peri tou dikaiou* [on the just man]). The other great Sophists also came in question.

A practical result of this new education after the middle of the fifth century: the great *Pericles*. He debated a great deal with Protagoras: Plato attributes Pericles' great mastery in oratory to Anaxagorian philosophy: it gave his mind sublime flight and penetrating insight into nature and man. *Phaedrus* (p. 269E). At that time the most important men in the cities were still ashamed to compose speeches and leave writings behind. Pericles still lacked the impassioned form of the later orators, especially Demosthenes. Impassively he stood there; his encircling cloak kept the same folds, the lofty seriousness of his features never bending into a smile, his voice always maintaining the same pitch and volume—everything unlike Demosthenes, but marvelously impressive.

It was in Sicily that *Gorgias* first developed an artistic style for prose discourse which indeed found its first application in eulogies rather than in practical speeches; and he brought it to Athens. Only a little later, in Athens, *logographia* [speech writing] in the service of trial processes—whose first, still archaic representative is Antiphon—developed from Tisias' rhetoric (also introduced from elsewhere) and from the dialectics of the Eastern Sophists, in imitation of the existing custom of legal practice. That style too claims to be artistic: hence the publication of written speeches as models for imitation.

More wisely, the rhetor *Thrasymachus* forms the style appropriate for practical discourse by replacing Gorgias' splendor and Antiphon's rigid dignity with the rounded period and cultured terminology. At the center of the movement stood men like Critias and Andocides, who themselves are not Sophists. Thrasymachus, a contemporary of Lysias, caricatured in the introductory scene of Plato's *Republic* as arrogant, corrupt, immoral, obtuse, is often predominantly a rhetorical technician. He was the founder of the middle genre of style; he is the inventor of the period suitable for practical

nischen Rhythmus (nach Aristoteles) angewendet. Also er erfindet die περιόδος στρογγόλη oder συνεστραμμένη, die Gorgias und Antiphon noch nicht kennen. Der Gedanke wird zu einer Einheit zusammengedrückt: bei Gorgias reiht sich lose Antithese an Antithese. Nach Cicero hat er fast allzurhythmisch geschrieben. Er ist bahnbrechend für den späteren praktischen Redner bes. Lysias, im Gegensatz zu dem panegyrischen Isocrates.

Der berüchtigte *Critias* ist sehr ausgezeichnet: es muss auffallen, dass er nicht die Stelle des Andocides im Kanon bekam, aber ihm schadet, einen der dreissig Gerufenen zu sein: Würde in den Gedanken, Einfachheit in der Form. Er ist Vertreter des jungen Attizismus. Wenig Sprung und Feuer. Wenig gewinnender Eifer. Darum behauptend ἀλλ᾽ ἔμοιγε δοκεῖ oder δοκεῖ δ᾽ ἔμοιγε.

Also *Antiphon* aus Rhamnus, zur Zeit der Perserkriege geboren, etwas jünger als Gorgias: der erste, der Reden für andere verfasste: er hatte den Beinamen Nestor als Redner, zur Auszeichnung. Völliger Mangel an politischem Ehrgeiz. Grosser Lob, Thucydides 8, 63, vielleicht sein Schüler. Das Alterthum hatte 60 Reden von ihm, Caecilius erklärte davon 25 für unecht, ferner eine angezweifelte τέχνη und eine Sammlung Prooemien und Epiloge. Uns sind 15 erhalten, wovon 4 zu Tetralogien dreimal zusammengestellt sind. Cf. Blass p. 91. Meist sind es λόγοι φονικόι, d.h. in Criminalfällen. nur drei beziehen sich auf wirkliche Fälle. Er gilt neben Thucydides als der Meister der alterthümlich strengen Redekunst, besonders wichtig für den politischen Stil der Rede. Der erste im Canon der 10 attischen Redner, den man vielleicht in Alexandrien anlegte. Die Anordnung der Rede sehr regelmässig. Von Isaeus ab, in raffinirter Zeit, liebt man die Kunst entgegen der Natur anzuwenden. Würdevoller Ausdruck, der öffentlicher Sprecher musste damals gemessen auftreten, eine etwas entfernte Sprache sprechen. Der erhabener Stil ist natürlich dem schlichten des Lysias weit näher als der erhabene Stil in der Geschichte[14] oder der Tragödie. Alterthümlichkeit gesucht als Mittel zur Würde: weiss es schon Perikles: ξύν, ἐς. Dem modernen Dialekt folgt das ältere σσ für ττ, z.B. Die komische Ansicht dass man damals nur πράγτεω sprach. Andokides, Lysias, usw., schliessen sich der neuen Ausprache an, nicht Gorgias und Antiphon. In der Composition folgt er der αὐστηρὰ ἁρμονία entgegen der γλαφυρὰ des Isocrates.

purposes; and finally, according to Aristotle, he was the first to use the paeonic rhythm. Thus, he invented the *periodos strongolē*, or *synestrammenē*, which Gorgias and Antiphon still did not know. The thought is compressed into a unity: in Gorgias one loose antithesis is strung after another. In Cicero's opinion, Thrasymachus wrote almost too rhythmically. He led the way for the later practical orators, especially Lysias, as opposed to the panegyrical Isocrates.

The notorious *Critias* is very outstanding. It must be noted that he did not receive Andocides' position in the canon, but what harmed him was that he had been one of the Thirty Jurors. He has dignity of thought, simplicity of form. He is the representative of neo-Atticism. Not much energy and fire. Not much captivating zeal. Therefore asserting *all' emoige dokei* [but it seems to me] or *dokei d' emoige* [it seems, however, to me].

Another orator is *Antiphon*, from Rhamnus, born at the time of the Persian Wars, somewhat younger than Gorgias. He was the first to write speeches for others. As a speaker he was given the surname "Nestor" as a mark of distinction. He was totally lacking in political ambition. Thucydides (8, 63), who was perhaps his pupil, praised him highly. Antiquity had sixty speeches by him; Caecilius declared twenty-five of them to be inauthentic; in addition, there is a *technē* and a collection of *prooemia* and epilogues. Fifteen are still extant, twelve of them combined into three different tetralogies. Cf. Blass, p. 91. They are mostly *logoi phonikoi*, i.e., in criminal cases. Only three have to do with real cases. Next to Thucydides he is considered to be the master of the archaically strict oratorical art, especially important for the political style of speech. He is the first in the canon of the ten Attic orators, which was perhaps first put together in Alexandria. The arrangement of his speeches is very regular. From Isaeus on, in an elegant age, speakers liked to use art against nature. With a solemn expression, the public speaker had to present himself decorously and speak a somewhat remote language. The elegant style in oratory is, of course, much closer to Lysias' plain style than to the elegant style in history[133] or tragedy. Archaisms are sought as a means to elegance, as Pericles already knew: *xyn, es*. The modern dialect is followed by the older: *ss* instead of *tt*, for example. The strange view that only *pragteō* was spoken at that time. Andocides, Lysias, etc. adopt the new pronunciation, but not Gorgias and Antiphon. In composition he follows the *austēra harmonia* as opposed to Isocrates' *glaphyra*.

Andocides geb. 468. vornehmes Geschlecht, die Würde der Mysterien [illegible] sei die Eleusinien verraten. Bewegtes politisches
Leben während des pelopponesischen Kriegs, als Heerführer und
Gesandter, verwickelt in dem Hemokopidenprozess. Wir haben vier
Reden in eigenen Angelegenheiten, nur zwei περὶ τῆς ἑαυτοῦ
καθόδου und περὶ τῶν μυστηρίων sind echt. Andocides [war] kein
Meister der praktischen Rede, dazu fehlt ihm allerseits Durchsichtig-
keit. Sehr wenig Schmuck, wenig Lebendigkeit. Sein Stil ist nicht
gleichmässig sondern buntscheckig. Mit Entlehnungen von selbst
tragischen Wendungen. Im Allgemein die Sprache des gewöhnlichen
Lebens. In der argumentatio ist er mittelmässig, im Erzählen von
Geschichten [viel besser], weshalb er die Reden auch zumeist mit
Erzählungen füllt. In der Ausprägung des Ethos ist Lysias viel vor-
züglicher, im Pathos beide schwach. Unter den Zehn ist er der
geringste an Talent und Studium; obgleich es eine grosse Ehre ist
überhaupt unter sie aufgenommen zu werden.

Lysias geb. 459 zu Athen, begüterte Eltern, die ihre Heimat Syra-
kus 475 verlassen und als Metöken in Athen sich niedergelassen. Er
nahm an der Gründung von Thurii 444 theil, lernt dort unter Tisias
und Nikias Rhetorik, kehrt 412 nach Athen zurück, stirbt 377. Seinen Ruf begründet die Rede gegen Eratosthenes, den Mörder seines
Bruders Polemarchus, einer der 30. Er stiftet eine wichtige Rede-
schule. Von 425 Reden hielten die Alten 230 für echt. Von diesen
sind 34 erhalten, doch nicht sicher echt. Seine τέχνη verloren. Meister des tenue dia[poreticum] g[enus] in der gerichtlichen Beredsamkeit. Im platonischen Phaedrus wird die lysianische Rede scharf
getadelt, die Sache sei unphilosophisch angefasst: dem Isocrates wird
dagegen eine gewisse philosophische Richtung nachgerühmt: Ver-
schiedenheit der Stoffe beider, da Lysias ausser erotische Kleinig-
keiten nur die von Plato verachteten Prozessreden [und] Isocrates
epideiktische Reden mit politischen Hintergründen schrieb, mit
mehr Idealen als praktischen Gesichtspünkten. Aber er ist nicht
gerechtfertigt die Bevorzugung allein nach dem Stoffe zu begreifen:
Perikles wird als grosser Redner anerkannt. Das Fehlen allgemeiner
Begriffsbestimmungen. Sehr selten allgemeine Prinzipien berührt.
Dann fehlt die richtige Ordnung und logische Folge der Gedanken.
Die kunstvolle Rede dürfe nicht eine Häufung von Argumenten sein,
die beliebig so oder so gestellt werden könnten. Plato lobt allein den
Stil: sowohl klar als abgerundet. Später, bes. bei Dionysius ist er

Andocides, born in 468 of a noble family, betrayed the dignity of the mysteries [?] for the Eleusinian. Active political life during the Peloponnesian War, as a military leader and envoy he got involved in the Hemocopides trial. We have four speeches concerning his own affairs, of which only two, *peri tēs eautou kathodou* and *peri tōn mystēriōn*, are authentic. Andocides was not a master of practical discourse; he lacked the clarity for this in every respect. Very little adornment, very little vitality. His style is not constant, but uneven. He even borrows expressions from the tragedies. Generally he uses the language of everyday life. In argumentation he is mediocre; his narrative ability [is better], for which reason he also generally fills the speech with stories. In the shaping of ethos, Lysias is far superior; in pathos both are weak. Among the ten, Andocides has the least talent and study; although it is a great honor just to be included in the canon at all.

Lysias, born in 459, in Athens, of wealthy parents who had left their native Syracuse in 475 and settled as foreign residents in Athens. He took part in the founding of Thurii in 444, studying rhetoric there under Tisias and Nikias. In 412 he returned to Athens. He died in 377. His reputation is established by the speech against Eratosthenes, the murderer of his brother Polymarchus, one of the Thirty. He founded an important rhetorical school. Of 425 speeches, the ancients considered 230 to be genuine. Of these, thirty-four have been preserved, but are not certifiably genuine. His *technē* has been lost. He is master of the *tenue* (*diaporeticum genus*) in juridical eloquence. In Plato's *Phaedrus*, Lysian oratory is criticized sharply for its unphilosophical approach; Isocrates, on the contrary, is lauded for a certain philosophical penchant. Different materials characterize the two; for, besides erotic trivia, Lysias wrote only the trial speeches despised by Plato, while Isocrates wrote epideictic speeches with political backgrounds more with ideals than practical points of view. But there are no grounds to judge the preference only by the material: after all, Pericles was recognized as a great orator. The lack of a general definition of terms. General principles are touched upon very rarely. Then right order and logical sequence of thoughts are lacking. An artful speech must not be a cluster of arguments which could be arranged arbitrarily in one way or another. Plato praises only one style: a style that is both clear and polished. Later, especially in Dionysius, Lysias is the representative of the *charaktēr ischnos, lexis litē*

der Vertreter des χαρακτὴρ ἰσχνός, λέξις λιτὴ καὶ ἀφελής, συνεσπασμένη. Cicero gebraucht von solchen Rednern die Ausdrücke tenues acuti subtiles versuti humiles summissi. Doch eine straffe Nachbildung der gewöhnlichen Rede, anscheinend für jeden leicht, sei ausserordentlich schwer. Der tenuis kann bloss belehren: die Leidenschaften zu erregen gestattet ihm die Beschränktheit der Mittel nicht. Darum ist Lysias nicht der vollkommene Meister, sondern Demosthenes, der je nach den Umständen bald knapp, bald gewaltig, bald gemässigt spricht. Das Streben nach wahrhaft Grossem ist mit einem Theilweisen Misslingen verbunden, während kein grosses Können dazu gehöre, sich bei niedriger gerichtetem Streben von Fehlern fernzuhalten. Auch so erheben sich nun oft Versuchende, doch kein hohes Ziel Erreichende weit über das Mass: die Grösse der Vorzüge, nicht die Zahl entscheide. So der Autor περὶ ὕπσους bei einem Vergleich von Plato und Lysias. Endlich [ist] Lysias, der zweite grosse Logograph: er geht noch weiter als Thrasymachus und wendet ganz den Ausdruck des gemeinen Lebens an, den Periodenbau und den Schmuck der Figuren wohl kennend, doch nicht überall verwendend. Alles das in einem Zeitraum von 30 Jahren: in denselben entstehen schon neue Richtungen, die des Isocrates.

Isocrates geb. 436 zu Athen, Schüler des Tisias Gorgias Prodikus und Socrates, der grösste Lehrer der Beredsamkeit. Schüchtern, schwache Stimme. Sein Vater hatte Ende des peloponnesischen Kriegs sein Vermögen verloren: er schrieb Reden daher. 392 eröffnet er die Schule, zuerst auf Chius, 388 in Athen, höchst ruhmvoll. Er starb freiwillig (durch Hunger) 338 nach der Schlacht bei Chaeronea aus Schmerz über den Verlust der Freiheit. Mächtiger patriotischer Charakter, ideales Streben. Führt die Schule zur politischen Beredsamkeit. Von 60 Reden erkannte Caecil. 28 als echt, 2l erhalten, 15 panegyrische davon und 6 gerichtliche. Am berühmtesten der Panegyr. 382, in seinem 94. Jahre geschrieben. Nicht sicher die τέχνη. Seine talentvollsten Schüler Theopomp, Ephorus, Phitisous, Androtion, dann Isaeus, Demosthenes, Hyperides, Theodectes, usw. Er ist ein Feind alles Sophistenwesens, z.B. in κατὰ τῶν σοφιστῶν, Ἑλένης ἐνκώμιον, und περὶ ἀντιδόσεως. Erst im hohen Alter wendet er sich der Theorie zu, so tadelt er in κατὰ τῶν σοφιστῶν die Theoretiker, οὖ μεθόδῳ ἀλλ᾽ ἀσκήσει γρήσασθαι war in früheren Zeiten

kai aphelēs, synespasmenē [unadorned genus, with a plain and simple style, compact]. Concerning such orators, Cicero uses the expressions *tenues acuti subtiles versuti humiles summissi* [the orators are subtle, intelligent, direct, clever, plain, restrained]. But the rigid imitation of ordinary speech, apparently easy for everyone, is extraordinarily difficult. The *tenue* can merely instruct; its limited means do not permit it to excite the passions. Therefore, it is not Lysias who is the perfect master, but rather Demosthenes, who speaks now tersely, now powerfully, now moderately, depending on the circumstances. The striving for true grandeur is connected with a partial failure, while no great skill is needed to keep free of errors if one is striving for a lesser goal. Even so, those who try but achieve no high goal still rise far above the average: the greatness of merits, not their number, is decisive. So says the author of *peri hypsous* when comparing Plato and Lysias. Finally Lysias is the second great logograph: he goes even further than Thrasymachus and uses terms from everyday life; he is well acquainted with the construction of periodic sentences and figurative embellishment, but does not use them everywhere. All this in an interval of thirty years: in the same period new directions are already arising, those of Isocrates.

Isocrates, born in 436 in Athens, a pupil of Tisias, Gorgias, Prodicus, and Socrates, is the greatest teacher of eloquence. He was shy and had a weak voice. His father had lost his fortune at the end of the Peloponnesian War: therefore he wrote speeches. In 392 he opened his very famous school, first on Chius, then in 388 in Athens. In 338, after the battle near Chaeronea, in grief over the loss of freedom, he committed suicide (by starvation). A mighty patriotic character, with an idealistic striving. He leads the school to political eloquence. Of sixty speeches, Caecilius recognized twenty-eight as genuine; twenty-one have been preserved, fifteen panegyric and six juridical. Most famous is the Panegyric, written in 382, at the age of ninety-four. The *technē* is not certifiably authentic. His most talented pupils are Theopompus, Ephorus, Phitisous, Androtion, then Isaeus, Demosthenes, Hyperides, Theodectes, etc. He is an enemy of all Sophistry, e.g., in *kata tōn sophistōn* ["Against the Sophists"], *Helenēs enkōmion* ["Ode to Helen"], and *peri antidoseōs* ["About Exchange of Property"]. Only in old age does he turn to theory; thus in *kata tōn sophistōn* he criticizes the theorists; *ou methodōi all' askēsei grēsasthai* [not to use a technique, but elbow grease] was his state-

sein Satz. Er wendet sich zuerst zur grossen politischen Beredsamkeit. Dionys. Laert. sagt πρῶτος ἐχώρησεν ἀπὸ τῶν ἐριστικῶν καὶ φυσικῶν ἐπὶ τὰς πολιτικὰς καὶ περὶ ταύτην σπουδάζων τὴν ἐπιστήμην διετέλεσεν. Reiner Stil; aber nicht wie bei Lysias Ausdruck der Natur, sondern künstlerisch geformt. Dionysius: θαυμαστὸν γὰρ καὶ μέγα τὸ τῆς Ἰσοκράτους κατασκευῆς ὕψος, ἡρωικῆς μᾶλλεν ἢ ἀνθρωπίνης. Er ahmt die μεγαλοπρέπεια σεμνότης und καλλιλογία des Thucydides und Gorgias nach. Aber zu der erhabenen Redegewalt des Demosthenes verhält er sich nur wie ein Athlet zu einem Vaterlandsverteidiger (wie Cleochares aus [illegible] gesagt hat). Er besitzt mehr Eleganz als Grazie, mehr Pracht als Anmuth, Dionysius, Is. 3: πέφυκε γὰρ ἡ Λυσίου λέξις ἔχειν τὸ χαριέν ἡ δ' Ἰσοκράτου βούλεται. Gerundete Periode, viele Figuren, oft durch Überfülle monoton und weitschweifig. Höchst ausgearbeitet und Lysias weit in Anordnung und Vertheilung des Stoffes unterlegen. Er hat daher für sein langes Leben nur wenig geschrieben. Übrigens mehr für den Leser als den Hörer. Wahre Gerichtsreden, nur wenige oder keine, dagegen Gerichtliche Muster- und Übungsstücke.

Isaeus lebt c. 420-348, geb. in Cadris, lernt in Athen, wo er Lysias und Isocrates zu Lehrern hat. Darauf wird er λογογραφ, errichtet eine Schule und erzieht darin bes. Demosthenes. Von 64 Reden hielten die Kritiker 50 für echt; nur elf, alle in Erbschaftsangelegenheiten, haben sich erhalten. Technische Schriften verloren. Er gleicht Lysias in der Reinheit und Deutlichkeit des Vortrags: dagegen nicht so naiv, sondern gekünstelt, gefeilt und geschmückt: doch kräftig im Ganzen. ὅσον τε ἀπολείπεται τῆς χάριτος ἐκείνης, ὑπερέχει τῇ δεινότητι τῆς κατασκευῆς. Besonders feine Zerlegung des Stoffes

ment in earlier times. He is the first to resort to great political eloquence. Dionysius (*Isocrates*, 1):

*prōtos echōrēsen apo tōn eristikōn te kai physikōn epi tas politikas kai
peri tautēn spoudazōn tēn epistēmēn dietelesen* [he was the first to set
oratory on a new course, turning away from treatises on dialectic and
natural philosophy and concentrating on writing political discourses
and on political science itself].[134]

He has a pure style, but not like Lysias, an expression of his nature,
but artfully formed. Dionysius:

*thaumaston gar dē kai mega to tēs Isokratous kataskeuēs hypsos, hē-
rōikēs mallen ē anthrōpinēs* [Indeed, this lofty quality of Isocrates' artistry is a great and wonderful thing and has a character more suited to
demigods than to men].[135]

He imitates Thucydides' and Gorgias' *megaloprepeia* [magnifi-
cence], *semnotēs* [majesty], and *kallilogia* [elegant language]. But he
compares with Demosthenes' supreme oratorical force only as an
athlete compares with a defender of the fatherland (as Cleochares of
[?] has said). He has more elegance than grace, more splendor than
charm. Dionysius (*Isocrates*, 3):

pepsyke gar hē Lysiou lexis echein to charien, hē d' Isokratous bouletai
[Lysias possesses charm naturally, Isocrates is always looking for it].[136]

Rounded periods, many figures, often monotonous and digressive
through excessive fullness. Highly elaborate and far inferior to Lysias
in arrangement and distribution of the material. He therefore wrote
only little, if one considers his long life. Moreover, more for the
reader than for the listener. Real forensic speeches, but only a few or
no juridical model- or practice-speeches.

Isaeus lived ca. 420-348 B.C. He was born in Cadris, studied in
Athens, where he had Lysias and Isocrates as teachers. Then he
became a *logograph*, established a school and trained in it, most
notably Demosthenes. Of sixty-four speeches, the critics considered
fifty to be genuine; only eleven, all on inheritance questions, have
survived. His writings on technique are lost. He resembles Lysias in
purity and clarity of delivery: however, he is not so naive, but artful,
polished, and adorned. On the whole, he is a powerful orator.

*hoson te apoleipetai tēs karitos ekeinēs, tosouton hyperechei tē deinotēti
tēs kataskeuēs* [His style compensates for its lack of Lysianic charm by

und schlaue Verflechtung der Argumente: er galt als verschmitzter Betrüger bei seinen Feinden. Der von Antiphon erfundenen, von Isocrates begründeten politischen Rede gab er schärfere Umrisse. Früher gab es nur 10 Reden. 1785 wurde in einer cod. Laurent. noch eine elfte, περὶ τοῦ μενεκλεοῦς κλήρου gefunden: 1815 fand Mai in einem cod. Ambros. die bisher fehlende grösste Hälfte von περὶ τοῦ Κλεωνύμου Κλήρου. In der macedonischen Periode ist Demagog und Redner fast gleich bedeutend. Die antimacedonische Partei Lycurgus, Demosthenes, Hypocrates, und andere, macedonisch Aeschines, Eubulos, Pentocrates, Demeades, Pytheas.

Lykurgus (der VI) aus dem alten Geschlecht der Eteobutaden c. 396 geb. durch Platon und Isokrates gebildet, früh in der politischen Laufbahn. Gewissenhaft und uneigennützig. Von 15 im Alterthum vorhandene Reden ist eine gegen Leocrates auf uns gekommen. Nach Dionysus ist die moralische Tendenz hervortretend. Darstellung edel und erhaben, aber nicht gefällig. Härte im metaphorischen Ausdruck. Ungenauigkeit in der Vertheilung des Stoffes, häufige Abschweifung. Er sprach wie aus dem Stegreife οὐ μὲν αστεῖο οὐδὲ ἡδὺς ἀλλ᾽ ἀναγκαῖος.

Demosthenes (VII) geb. im Gau Päania zu Athen 385, ist 7 Jahre alt, als der Vater stirbt, Vormünder Aphobos und Onetor, gebildet von Plato, Isaeus und Isokrates, 17 Jahre alt durch Callistratus' Rede zum Studium der Beredsamkeit fortgerissen, ersetzt durch Eifer und Übung, was an ihm von Natur oder durch Erziehung fehlt. 354 trat er öffentlich vor dem Volke auf. Sein eigentlich politischer Charakter entwickelt sich mit Philipps immer deutlicher werdenden Plänen. Als 346 Philipp zum Frieden sich geneigt zeigte, war er es, der unter den 10 Gesandten die von Athen zum König geschickt wurden, fest gegen Geld blieb und den Betrug durchschaute. Die Unterjochung von Phocis enttäuschte die Athener. Demosthenes von zwei Übeln das kleinere wählend stimmte jetzt für den Frieden. Philipp mischt sich bald in die peloponnesischen Händel: die Seele der Gesandschaft war immer Demosthenes, der auch bald gegen die Staatsverräther vorging (de falsa legatione gegen Aeschines). Philipps Gewaltstreiche im Chersones und Demosthenes' Anfeuerung führt den

that brilliant artistic resource (which makes it the real spring from which the rhetorical power of Demosthenes flows)].[137]

An especially fine analysis of the subject matter and clever interweaving of the arguments: he was considered a most clever deceiver by his enemies. He gave sharper contours to the political speech, which had been invented by Antiphon and established by Isocrates. Formerly only ten speeches were extant. In 1785 in a Laurentian codex an eleventh one, *peri tou Menekleous klērou* was found; in 1815, Mai found in an Ambrosian codex the previously missing greatest portion of *peri tou Kleōnymou klērou.* In the Macedonian period, demagogue and orator were almost synonymous. The anti-Macedonian Party consisted of Lycurgus, Demosthenes, Hippocrates, and others; pro-Macedonian were Aeschines, Eubulos, Pentocrates, Demades, Pytheas.

Lycurgus (VI), from the Eteabutades family, born ca. 396, educated under Plato and Isocrates, entered the political arena at an early age. Conscientious and altruistic. Of fifteen speeches which existed in antiquity, one against Leocrates has come down to us. According to Dionysius, the moral tendency is predominant. His use of description is noble and sublime, but not pleasant. Harshness in metaphorical expression. Imprecision in the distribution of material, frequent digressions. He spoke as if improvising, *ou men asteio oude hēdus all' anakaios* [neither urbane nor pleasant, just saying the necessary things].

Demosthenes (VII), born in the Paeania province of Athens in 385, was seven years old when his father died; his guardians were Aphobos and Oneton. He was educated by Plato, Isaeus, and Isocrates. At the age of seventeen he was drawn to the study of oratory by Callistratus' speech; he makes up by zeal and practice for what he lacks by nature or education. In 354 he made his public debut before the people. His real political character develops as Philip's plans become clearer and clearer. In 346 when Philip seemed inclined toward peace, he was one of the ten envoys who were sent to the king by Athens who resisted bribery and saw through Philip's treachery. The subjugation of Phocis disappointed the Athenians. Demosthenes, choosing the lesser of two evils, now voted for peace. Philip soon intervened in Peloponnesian affairs: Demosthenes, who quickly took action against the traitors, was still the leader of the delegation (*de falsa legatione* against Aeschines). Philip's military actions in Chersones and Demosthenes' incitations led to the glorious struggle in

ruhmwürdigen Kampf in Thracien herbei, der mit dem Entsatz von Byzanz 340 endigte. Der letzte phokische König wich Philipp und ging von Griechenland, er besetzte Elatea. Bei dieser Schreckensnachricht verlor nur Demosthenes den Muth nicht. Es gelang ihm Athen und Theben zum Kampfe zu vereinigen. Doch ohne Erfolg und mit Chaeronea 338 ging Athens Unabhängigkeit verloren. Mit Philipps Tode 336 gab es eine neue Hoffnung: überall Empörung. Man kam zur Ruhe als Alexander mit einem Heer erschien. Nur Theben, vor Cadmea in Empörung, wurde von Grund aus zerstört. Athens Antheil zu strafen, verlangt Alexander die Auslieferung der Volkshäupter, darunter Demosthenes, doch liess er sich von Phocion und Demades begütigen. In der folgenden Friedenszeit wird Demosthenes in dem Prozess verwickelt, den Harpalos durch Bestechung anregte 325; ohne überwiesen zu sein wird er verurtheilt. Er entkam und begab sich auf Aegina. Da kam die Nachricht von Alexanders Tode. Leosthenes beginnt den Lamischen Krieg. Freimütig schloss sich Demosthenes der Gesandschaft an, welche Athen zum allgemeinen Aufgebot an alle hellenischen Staaten schickte und wurde ehrenvoll nach Athen zurückberufen und glänzend empfangen. Aber die Schlacht bei Crannon ging verloren 322 und Antipater zwang zum Frieden. Vor ihm, seinem Todfeinde, flog Demosthenes nach Calauria und dort starb er an genommenem Gift unter den Händen der Knechte des Antipater.—Er war von Natur nicht wie Aeschines mit mächtiger Stimme begabt oder wie Demades gewaltiger Stegreifredner. Er musste seine Gedanken sorgfältig zusammensetzen. Seine Stimme war kurz, lispelnd, seine Gesten ohne Grazie. Es waren die gleichen Gründe die Isocrates von der öffentlichen Thätigkeit ausschlossen. In der Geschichte der Selbsterziehung ist er höchst denkwürdig. Er wird der gewaltigste Redner δυνατώτατος ῥητόρων, die δεινότης der Rede hat keiner erreicht (Cic. Brut.) plane cum profectum et cui nihil admodum desit dixeris. Von 65 Reden sind 61 erhalten, mehrere darunter unecht, auch zweifelhaft. 17 συμβουλευτικοὶ, darunter die 12 philippischen. Die siebte περὶ ᾽Αλοννήσου ist von Hegesipp gehalten, früh schon einverleibt da die unechte elfte (πρὸς τὴν ἐπιστολῆν τὴν φιλίππου) sie benutzt. Unecht auch die 42, dagegen der Brief Philipps, der unter den 12 Reden die 12te Stellung

Thrace which ended in 340 with the relief of Byzantium. The last
Phocian king escaped from Philip and fled from Greece; Philip occu-
pied Elatea. On hearing this alarming news, only Demosthenes did
not lose courage. He succeeded in uniting Athens and Thebes for the
struggle. But without success; and as a result of the battle of Chaeronea, Athens lost its independence in 338. With Philip's death in
336 there was a new hope: a general uprising. The revolts were put
down when Alexander appeared with an army. Only Thebes, which
had been in a state of insurrection before Cadmea, was razed to the
ground. To punish Athens for its part, Alexander demanded the
extradition of the popular leaders, among them Demosthenes, but he
let himself be placated by Phocion and Demades. During the following period of peace, Demosthenes was involved in the trial which
Harpalos instigated in 325 by means of bribery; he was sentenced but
not arrested. He escaped and went to Aegina. There the news of Alexander's death arrived. Leosthenes began the Lamian War. Genuinely
patriotic, Demosthenes joined the delegation which Athens sent to
all Hellenian states for the general mobilization and he was called
back to Athens and received splendidly. But the battle of Crannon
was lost in 322 and Antipater imposed peace. Demosthenes fled from
this his mortal enemy to Calauria and there he died from poison
given him by the servants of Antipater.

He was not gifted with a powerful voice like Aeschines nor was he
a great improvisor like Demades. He had to compose his thoughts
carefully. His voice was short-winded and lisping; his gestures were
not graceful. These were the same causes which excluded Isocrates
from public activity. Demosthenes is highly noteworthy in the history of self-education. He became the most powerful orator, *dyna-
tōtatos rhētorōn*, whose *deinotēs* of speech no one has ever attained
(Cicero, *Brutus*); *plane cum perfectum et cui nihil admodum desit
dixeris* [for the perfect orator and the one who lacks absolutely nothing you would without hesitation name Demosthenes].[138] Of sixty-
five speeches, sixty-one are extant, several among them ungenuine,
some also dubious. There are seventeen *symbouleutikoi*, among
them the twelve Philippics. The seventh *peri Halonnesou* was given
by Hegesipp, but incorporated [into Demosthenes' canon] at an early
date because the ungenuine eleventh (*prōs tēn epistolēn tēn philip-
pou*) uses it. The forty-second is also ungenuine, but not Philip's letter which occupies the twelfth position among the twelve orations,

nimmt, usf. Dann 42 δικανικοί,12 davon staatsrechtlich, 30 bürger-liches Recht. Am bedeutendsten darunter gegen die Vormünder, gegen Leptines, gegen Androtion, περὶ στεφάνου, der das vollendet-ste Meisterwerk über Beredsamkeit ist. Z. B. 2 ἐπιδεικτικοι, der λόγος ἐπιτάφιος auf die bei Chaeronea gefallen, und der Ἐρωτικός, beide unecht. Sehr zweifelhaft 56 erhaltene Prooemien und 6 Briefe. A. Schäfer *Demosthenes und seine Zeit* Leipzig. 1856-58, 3 Bände.

Hyperides (VIII) aus Athen, Schüler des Plato und des Isocrates, Freund des Demosthenes, entging mit ihm mit Lykurg und Chari-demus nach der Vernichtung Thebens wegen der Gefahr ausgeliefert zu werden. Nach Alexanders Tode am lamischen Krieg betheiligt, wurde er von der macedonischen Partei zum Tode verurtheilt und entkam nach Aegina, wo er 322 auf Befehl Antipaters hingerichtet wurde. Von 77 Reden hielten die Alten 52 für echt. Wir haben nur Fragmente, darunter drei grössere. 1847 auf Papyrus durch Harris Bruchstücke einer Rede κατὰ Δημοσθένους und drei Fragmente gefunden, durch Arden jene Reden ἀπολογία ὑπὲρ Λυκόφρονος und ὑπερ Εὐξενίππον, endlich 1857 λόγος ἐπιταφιος. Grazie, Scharfsinn, Prunk, poetische Färbung. Libanius giebt ihn für den Verfasser von der dem Demosthenes beigelegten Rede περὶ τῶν πρὸς Ἀλεχανδρον συνθηκῶν. Hyperides [ist] an kein Muster gebunden, Mitte zwischen Anmuth des Lysias und Kraft des Demosthenes. Ausdruck rein attisch, doch mit einiger Manier. Behandlung des Stoffes scharfsin-nig, doch nicht sorgfältig, vortrefflich in Beweisführung. Unnach-ahmliche Eleganz und Grazie.

Aeschines (IX) geb. 391 niederer Geburt, Vorfechter im Gymna-sium, dann γραμματεύς im Dienste des Staatsmanns Aristophon, dann Schauspieler, trat 356 gegen Philipp auf. Grosser Rathgeber. 347 wird er mit Demosthenes zu Philipp geschickt, verräth sein Vaterland und lässt sich bestechen. Jetzt wird er Todfeind des Demosthenes. Er ist jetzt Haupt der macedonischen Partei. κατὰ Τιμάρχου gegen die Anklage auf Hochverrath 345. 343 περὶ παραπρεσβείας. 314 starb er auf Samos, besiegt durch Demosthenes Rede περὶ στεφάνου und für ehrlos erklärt. Reich und klar, gewandt, wortreich, falsches Pathos. Die berühmteste Rede κατὰ Κτεσιφῶ-τος. Man sprach von 3 [?], erhalten 3 Reden, 7 oder 9 Briefe des Aeschines (9 verlorene Briefe). Aeschines [zeigt] Fertigkeit im Nach-weisen, sein Reden der reine Erguss eines übersprudelndes Genies.

etc. Then forty-two *dikanikoi*, twelve of them dealing with constitutional law, thirty dealing with civil law. Most significant among them are: against guardians, against Leptines, against Androtion, *peri stephanou*, which is the most perfect masterpiece on eloquence. Two *epideiktikoi*, the *logos epitaphios*, to the soldiers who fell in the battle of Chaeronea, and the *Eroticos*, both ungenuine. Very dubious are fifty-six *prooemia* and six letters. A. Schäfer, *Demosthenes und seine Zeit* (Leipzig, 1856–58), 3 vols.

Hyperides (VIII) from Athens, a pupil of Plato and Isocrates, and a friend of Demosthenes, escaped with him together with Lycurgos and Charidemus after the destruction of Thebes to avoid the danger of extradition. After Alexander's death, he took part in the Lamian War, he was sentenced to death by the Macedonian party and escaped to Aegina, where he was executed in 322 by command of Antipater. Of seventy-seven speeches, the ancients considered fifty-two to be genuine. We have only fragments, among them three larger ones. In 1847 Harris discovered portions of an oration, *kata Dēmosthenous,* and three fragments; and Arden, two orations, *apologia hyper Lykophronos* and *hyper Euxenippon*, and finally in 1857, *logos epitaphios*. He has charm, discernment, splendor, poetic coloration. Libanius names him as the writer of the speech attributed to Demosthenes, *peri tōn pros Alexandron synthēkōn*. Hyperides, bound to no model, stands in the middle between Lysias and the forcefulness of Demosthenes. He uses purely Attic expression with some stylization. His treatment of the material is insightful but not painstaking. He is superb in proof, inimitable in elegance and charm.

Aeschines (IX), born in 391, of lowly origin, was a model wrestler in the gymnasium, then a grammarian in the service of the statesman Aristophon, then an actor. In 356 he opposed Philip. He was a great adviser. In 347 he was sent to Philip together with Demosthenes; he betrayed his fatherland and accepted a bribe. He now became a mortal enemy of Demosthenes. Now he was the head of the Macedonian party. In 345 he wrote *kata Timarchou* against the accusation of high treason; in 343 *peri parapresbeias*. He died on Samos in 314, defeated by Demosthenes' speech *peri stephanou* and declared dishonored. His style is rich and clear, adroit, verbose, with false pathos. The most famous oration is *kata Ktēsiphōntos*. There is mention of three [?]. Three speeches, seven or nine letters of Aeschines have been preserved (nine letters are lost). He is proficient in proof; his speeches are a pure outpouring of his effervescent genius. Power,

Kraft, Glanz, und Fülle. Bei aller Anmuth doch heftig und stürmisch, zeigt mehr Fleisch als Muskel. Sein Einfluss zeigt sich vor allem darin, dass er durch Übersiedelung der Kunst nach Asien der Stifter der verbreiteten und mächtigen asianischen Schule, nach dem Erlöschen der attischen, wurde.

Dinarchus (X) geb. zu Corinth 360, lebte zu Athen und schrieb Reden für andere, besonders für die macedon. Partei. Sehr thätig als Werkzeug Antipaters und während der Herrschaft des Demetrius Phalereus. 307 nach dessen Sturz verbannt. Durch Vermittlung Theophrasti erhält er nach 15 Jahren die Erlaubniss der Rückkehr. Auf Befehl Poliocretes' wurde er 70 Jahre alt getödtet. 160 Reden gab es, nur 64 oder 60 echt, 3 erhalten. Er ist Nachahmer des Demosthenes Δημοσθένες ὁ κρίθινος der "gerstener Demosthenes" genannt. Dinarchus ist, nach Dionysus von Halicarnassus, nicht originell und hat eigentlich gar keinen Charakter, er ahmt bald Lysias, bald Hyperides, bald Demosthenes nach. Eine gewisse Rauhheit, τραχύσης.

Demetrios ὁ Φαληρεύς aus geringem Geschlecht, Zögling des Theophrast, durch glücklichste Naturanlagen zum mächtigen Staatsmann werdend. Beginnt die politische Laufbahn 325 zur Zeit der harpalischen Händel. Nach Phocions Tode verwaltet er 10 Jahre Athen, 317–307, unter Kassanders Regierung, zuerst zur allgemeinen Zufriedenheit (360 Statuen von ihm errichtet), dann bildet sich, bei seinem Übermuth und seinen Ausschweifungen eine Partei Nichtvergnügter. Er entwich nach Theben, von da nach Aegypten: dort fand er gelehrte Kräfte, er lebt in Vertrautem Umgang mit Ptolemaeus Soter. Ihm verdächtigt stirbt er in Oberaegypten 283. Sehr fruchtbarer Autor, Laert. X, 80: ὧν ἐστι τὰ μὲν ἱστορικά, τὰ δὲ πολιτικά, τὰ δὲ περὶ ποιητῶν, τὰ δὲ ῥητορικά, δημηγοριῶν τε καὶ πρεσβειῶν, ἀλλὰ μὴν καὶ λόγων Αἰσωπειων συναγωγαὶ καὶ ἄλλα πλείω. Unecht die vorhandene Schrift περὶ ἑρμηνείας. Seit ihm beginnt die attische Beredsamkeit zu sinken. Der Charakter der Rede war sanft, weichlich, einschmeichelnd. Sein Ausdruck elegant, blühend, ohne richtiges Maass. Der letzte attische Redner. Höchstens noch der Demosthenes-Schüler Eineas zu nennen, der mit Tyrekus 210 nach Italien ging.

splendor, fullness. Despite all his charm, he is forceful and temperamental; but he has more flesh than muscle. His influence is shown especially by the fact that after the demise of the Attic school he became the founder of the widespread and mighty Asian school by the migration of the art to Asia.

Dinarchus (X), born in Corinth in 360, lived in Athens and wrote speeches for others, especially for the Macedonian party; he was very active as an instrument of Antipater and during the reign of Demetrius Phalereus. In 307, after the fall of Phalereus, Dinarchus was banished. Through Theophrastus' mediation he was given permission to return after fifteen years. On Poliocretes' command he was killed at the age of seventy. There were 160 speeches; only sixty-four or sixty are genuine, and only three are extant. He is an imitator of Demosthenes, and was nicknamed *Dēmosthenes ho krithinos* (the barley Demosthenes). According to Dionysius of Halicarnassus, Dinarchus is not original and actually has no character.[139] He imitates now Lysias, now Hyperides, now Demosthenes. He displays a certain crudeness, *tprachysēs*.

Demetrios ho phalereus, of low birth, a pupil of Theophrastus, becomes a mighty statesman by the most favorable natural talents. He begins his political career in 325 at the time of the Harpalian conflicts. After Phocion's death, he rules over Athens for ten years (317–307), under Cassander's government, initially to general satisfaction (360 statues of him were erected). Then a party of dissatisfied citizens was formed in response to his arrogance and excesses. He escaped to Thebes, where he found scholarly colleagues; he lived in friendly association with Ptolemy Soter. Cast under suspicion in Ptolemy's eyes, he died in Upper Egypt in 283. A very fertile author, *Laert.* 10, 80:

> *hōn esti ta men historika, ta de politika, ta de peri poiētōn, ta de rhēto-rika, dēmēgoriōn te kai presbeiōn, alla mēn kai logōn Aisōpeiōn syna-gōgai kai alla pleiō* [among these are his historical and political works, treatises about poets, collections of public speeches and envoy's addresses, even of Aesopian fables and more].

The extant work *peri hermēneias* is ungenuine. After him Attic eloquence begins to decline. The character of his discourse was gentle, somewhat feeble, and ingratiating. His expression is elegant and florid, without real measure. He is the last Attic orator. At most, Demosthenes' pupil Eineas, who went to Italy with Tyrekus in 210, could be mentioned.

Die rhodische Schule, von Aeschines gegründet, der, von Demosthenes überwunden, nach Athen ging und zu Rhodus eine Schule stiftete. Die eigentlich *asianische* von Hegesias aus Magnesia. Die rhodische war die Vermittlerin der attischen und der asianischen, letztere viel stärker und kräftiger, obgleich viel verwerflicher. Cic. Brutus, xcv, 325 unterscheidet in der asianischen zwei Richtungen: genera autem Asiaticae dictionis duo sunt: unum sententiosum et argutum sententiis non tam gravibus quam concinnis et venustis— aliud autem genus est non tam sententiis frequentatum quam verbis volucre et incitatum, quale est nunc Asia tota, nec flumine solum orationis sed etiam exornato et faceto genere verborum. Erstens, die sententische Manier, in Verschlingung anmuthiger Gedanken. Zweitens, die verbose, [?] strömend, mit zierlichen und blümigen Worten. Zur ersten, Hierocles und Menecles aus Alabanda, der zweiten Aeschylus aus Cnidos und Aeschines aus Miletus. Unter den rhodischen Rednern Apollonius, Molon genannt, aus Alabanda, und Hermagoras aus Temnos, berühmt noch mehr als Techniker. Merkwürdig, wie nun Athen von Asien wieder empfängt: es bildet sich in Athen eine asianische Beredsamkeit: Menedemus, Gastfreund des Antonius. Demetrius aus Syrien, den Cicero hörte usw. Cicero selbst ist gebildet einmal durch Philosophen (Arkias, Phaedrus, Diodotus, Posidonius, Philo, Antisteus) dann durch Redner: Xenocles, Dionysius, Menippus, Apollonius, τέλεα sind dabei: Wandlung des römischen Geistes durch griechische Cultur. Das Ereigniss, das Rom der griechischen Beredsamkeit öffnete, war die Gesandschaft der Athener 155 v.C. um die Ermässigung einer wegen der Zerstörung von Oropos aufgelegten Geldstrafe zu erwirken. Der Academiker Corneades, der Richter Diogenes, der Peripatetiker Aristolaus. Die Wirkung war so gross, dass Cato die Betreuung der Gesandten antrug. 161 hatte man senatus consultum de philosophia et rhetoribus Latinis gemacht, uti Romae non essent. Danach aber, sechs Jahre später sagte der Senat Aelian V. H. III 17: ἔπεμψαν Ἀθηναῖοι πρεσβεύοντας οὐ τοὺς πείσοντας ἀλλὰ γὰρ τοὺς

The Rhodian school was founded by Aeschines, who, overcome by Demosthenes, left Athens and established a school in Rhodes. The real *Asian* school was established by Hegesias of Magnesia. The Rhodian school was the mediator between the Attic and the Asian schools, the latter much stronger and mightier, although far more reprehensible. Cicero (*Brutus*, 95, 325) distinguishes two tendencies within the Asian school:

> *genera autem Asiaticae dictionis duo sunt: unum sententiosum et argutum sententiis non tam gravibus quam concinnis et venustis. . . . aliud autem genus est non tam sententiis frequentatum quam verbis volucre et incitatum, quale est nunc Asia tota, nec flumine solum orationis sed etiam exornato et faceto genere verborum* [Of the Asiatic style there are two types, the one sententious and studied, less characterized by weight of thought than by the charm of balance and symmetry. . . . The other type is not so notable for wealth of sententious phrase, as for swiftness and impetuosity—a general trait of Asia at the present time—combining with its rapid flow of speech a choice of words refined and ornate.][140]

First, the sententious manner in a web of charming ideas. Second, the verbose, [?] streaming with delicate and flowery words. Hierocles and Menecles of Alabanda belong to the first school; Aeschylus of Cnidos and Aeschines of Miletus to the second. Among the Rhodian orators were Apollonius, called Molon, of Alabanda, and Hermagoras of Temnos, even more famous as a "technician." It is remarkable how Athens now receives back from Asia: there now develops in Athens an Asian eloquence: Menedemus, guest of Antonius, Demetrius of Syria, whom Cicero heard, etc. Cicero himself was educated first by philosophers (Arkias, Phaedrus, Diodotus, Posidonius, Philo, Antisteus), then by orators: Xenocles, Dionysius, Menippus, Apollonius. *Telea* [goals] in this are: the transformation of the Roman spirit by Greek culture. The event that opened Rome to Greek eloquence was the delegation of Athenians in 155 B.C. to bring about the lowering of a fine imposed for the destruction of Oropos. The Academician Corneades, the judge Diogenes, the Peripatetic Aristolaus. The effect was so great that Cato paid for the delegates' room and board. In 161 there was convened a *senatus consultum de philosophia et rhetoribus Latinis, . . . uti Romae non essent* [a senate council on Latin philosophy and rhetoric, . . . that they no longer can exist]. Then six years later, the Senate said (*Aelian V.H.*, 3, 17):

> *epempsan Athēnaioi presbeuontas ou tous peisontas alla gar tous biasomenous hēmas drasai hosa thelousin* [The Athenians did not send to

βιασομένους ἡμᾶς δρᾶσαι ὅσα θέλουσιν. In der ersten Kaiserzeit ändert sich der Charakter der Beredsamkeit nicht. Die Schulen in Athen verloren etwas, der Zug der römischen Jugend ging nach Massilia oder Asien, wo Tarsus von Rednern wimmelte. Die Redekunst ist die Liebhaberei der studierenden Jugend. Schule zu Mytilena, als Lehrer Timocrates, Lesbonax, Potamon, Lehrer und Freund des Tiberius. In Asien ist Theodorus aus Gadara Stifter der Sekte der Θεοδωρεῖοι, zu Rom mit Palamor im Streit verwickelt. Apollodorus aus Pergamus Stifter der pergamenischen Sekte der 'Απολλοδωρεῖοι.

Berühmter als alle *Dio, Chrysostomus* zubenannt, aus Prusa in Bithynia. In der Heimat verkannt, geht er nach Rom, ist dort Domitian verdächtig (Gell. N.A. XV 11, philosophi Domitiano imprecante senatus consulto ejecti atque urbe et Italia interdicti sunt) entweicht aus Rom und beginnt angeblich auf Rath des delphischen Orakels in Bettlerkleide eine Wanderung durch Thracien, Illyrien, Scythien und das Land der Geten, nichts als Platons Phaedrus und Demosthenes Rede de falsa legatione in der Tasche. Mit Ehren überhäuft kehrt er nach Prusa zurück. Nach Domitians Ermordung 96 a.d. führt er Praetorianer zu Gunsten seines Freundes M. Coccejus Nerva (Sohn des [?] Cocceianus) er ging nach Rom, sehr geehrt, von dort nach Prusa, das ihm bald durch Kleinstädterei verleidet wird. In Rom stirbt er, in hoher Achtung bei Trajan 117 p. C. Es sind 80 Reden erhalten: wenig davon gehört der ersten Periode an; seine Form ist besonders nach Hyperides und Aeschines gebildet, die er als Meister selbst Demosthenes und Lysias vorzog.

Dionys von Halicarnassus, der bedeutendste rhetorische Kunstrichter, in den Schulen Asiens gebildet, kam 25 Jahre alt 29 a. Chr. nach Rom, hauptsächlich um römische Geschichte an der Quelle zu studieren. Es entstehen seine ρωμαϊκὴ ἀρχαιολογία in XX Bänden, die ersten 9 haben wir vollständig, von X und XI nur den grössten Theil und Auszüge der übrigen. Eine Rhetorik unter seinen Namen ist ein Cento aus 4 Hauptpartien, theilweise von Dionysius. Sehr wichtige Schriften verloren, aber erhalten περὶ συνθέσεως ὀνομάτων. Πρὸς Γναῖον Πομπήιον ἐπιστολή über den Vorzug der demosthenischen Schreibart vor der platonischen. 'Επιστολὴ πρὸς

us as envoys those who would persuade us, but those who would force us to do whatever they want].

In the first Imperial age the character of eloquence did not change. The schools in Athens lost somewhat; the stream of Roman youth went to Massilia or Asia, where Tarsus was crawling with orators. Oratory was the favorite subject of young students. Some of the teachers at the school in Mytilene were Timocrates, Lesbonax, Potamon, Tiberius' teacher and friend. In Asia Theodorus of Gadara is founder of the sect of the *Theodōreioi*; in Rome he is involved in a dispute with Palamor. Apollodorus of Pergamon is founder of the Pergamonian sect of the *Apollodōreioi*.

More famous than all of them is *Dio*, surnamed *Chrysostomus*, from Prusa in Bithynia. Unrecognized in his homeland, he goes to Rome, where he falls under Domitian's suspicion. (*Gell. N.A.*, 15, 11, *philosophi Domitiano imprecante senatus consulto ejecti atque urbe et Italia interdicti sunt* [at Domitian's request the Senate was consulted and the philosophers were expelled and forbidden access to Rome and Italy]). He escapes from Rome and, allegedly on the advice of the Delphic oracle, dressed in beggar's clothing, he begins a journey on foot through Thrace, Illyria, Scythia, and the land of the Getes, with nothing in his pocket but Plato's *Phaedrus* and Demosthenes' oration *de falsa legatione*. Showered with honors he returns to Prusa. After Domitian's murder in 96 A.D. he leads the Praetorians in favor of his friend Coccejus Nerva (son of [?] Cocceianus). He went to Rome, where he was honored highly, from there to Prusa, where he soon tired of the small-town mentality. He died in Rome, highly respected by Trajan, in 117 A.D. Eighty orations are extant, few of them belonging to the first period. His form is modeled especially on Hyperides and Aeschines, whom he preferred as masters even over Demosthenes and Lysias.

Dionysius of Halicarnassus, the most important critic of the rhetorical art, educated in the schools of Asia, came to Rome in 29 B.C. at twenty-five years of age, mainly to study Roman history at the source. There he wrote his *rhomaikē archaiologia* in twenty volumes; the first nine are completely extant, as is the greater part of X and XI and extracts from the rest. A rhetoric under his name is a cento with four main parts, partly by Dionysius. Very important works are lost; but extant are *peri syntheseōs onomatōn* and *pros Gnaion Pompēion epistolē*, the *epistolē* on the advantage of the Demosthenian style of writing over the Platonic one. *Epistolē pros*

'Αμμαῖον περὶ τῶν Θουκυδίδου ἰδιωμάτων. Περί τοῦ Θουκυδίδου χαρακτῆρος. περὶ τῶν ἀρχαίων ῥητόρων ὑπομνηματισμοί, auf 6 Abtheilungen berechnet, von denen aber nur die erste Hälfte: 1. Lysias. 2. Isocrates. 3. Isaeus, und von der zweiten nur die erste Hälfte der ersten Abtheilung περὶ τῆς λεκτικῆς Δεμοσθένους δεινότητος vorhanden ist. Leider sind die parallelen Schriften des Rhetor Caecilius aus Κάλη Ἀκτή in Sicilien (daher Καλακτῖνος) verloren. Schrift genannt bei Suidas. Echtheit und Entscheidung über die älteren Reden.

Eine neue Epoche beginnt mit Hadrian: Athen blüht auf. Mark Aurel gründet zwei öffentliche Schulen, eine philosophische und eine rhetorische, die erstere mit 4 Kathedern (nach den 4 Hauptschulen, von jeder zwei Professoren), das Athenern in 2 θρόνοι, in das Sophistische und das politische Fach. Die Professoren erhielten jährlich 10.000 Drachmen. Später stieg für jedes Katheder die Zahl der Lehrer bis auf 6. Kraft kaiserlichen Willens wird der Name Sophist wieder zu Ehren gebracht. Ausserordentlicher Wetteifer bei grosser Entartung, hohe Koketterie der Deklamierenden. Lucian entwirft ein starkes Bild von dieser Entartung.

Berühmt in Athen vor allen, H*erodes Atticus*, in hoher Gunst bei den Antoninen. Grosser Improvisator. Schriften verloren. In Asien berühmt *Aelius Aristides* aus Adrianis in Mysia, geb. 129. Noch 55 Reden und Abhandlungen erhalten, 2 rhetorische Schriften von geringem Masse. *Lucian* aus Samosata 130–200, früher selbst Sophist und Rhetor und wendet sich 40 Jahre alt zur Philosophie; er kämpfend gegen alles Sophistenthum. Ausserordentlicher Darsteller also Kunstschriftsteller ist *Hermogenes* aus Tarsus, ingenium praecox, im 15. Lebensjahr öffentlicher Lehrer, im 17. Jahre Schriftsteller, im 25. unfehlbarer Geist in der Sprache. Erhalten: (I) τέχνη ῥητορικὴ περὶ τῶν στάσεων (de partitionibus) nach Hermagoras' Grundsätzen, (II) περὶ εὑρέσεως (de inventione) in 4 Büchern, (III) περὶ ἰδεῶν (de formis rhetoricis) in 2 Büchern, (IV) περὶ μεθόδου δεινότητος de apto, (V) προγυμνάσματα (praeexercitamenta) et sollerti genere dicendi methodas.

Die drei Philostrati. (1) *Flavius Philostratus*. Sohn des Verus aus Hierapolis, lebt noch unter Severus (II) des *ersteren Sohn*, erst Lehrer in Athen, dann in Rom. Biograph des Apollonius Tyana auf Verlangen der Kaiserin Julia. Verfasser der βίοι σοφιστῶν, Heroica, Imagines (εἰκόνες); (III) des zweiten *Schwester Sohn*, in Gunst bei Caracalla, starb unter Galienus 264. Feiner Kunstkritiker. Dionysius Cassius Longinus (213–273) berichtet περὶ ὕψους Verfasser von vor-

Ammaion peri tōn Thoukydidou idiōmatōn, peri tou Thoukydidou charaktēros, peri tōn archaiōn rhētorōn hypomnēmatismoi, arranged in six sections, of which only the first half: 1. Lysias, 2. Isocrates, 3. Isaeus; and of the second half only the first half of the second section *peri tēs lektikēs Dēmosthenous deinotētos* is extant. Unfortunately the parallel writings of the rhetor Caecilius from *Kalē Aktē* in Sicily (hence *Kalaktinos*) are lost. A work mentioned by Suidas. The genuineness of the older orations is undecided.

A new epoch begins with Hadrian: Athens blossoms forth. Marcus Aurelius founds two public schools, a philosophical and a rhetorical one, the first with four departments (*Katheder*) (after the four main schools, with two professors from each: the Athenian in two *thronoi*, the Sophistic, and the political disciplines). The professors were paid 10,000 drachmas per year. Later the number of teachers for each department rose to six. By the Imperial will, the name "Sophist" is brought back to honor. Extraordinary rivalry is accompanied by great degeneration and much flirtation among the declaimers. Lucian draws a graphic picture of this degeneration.

Herodes Atticus was more famous in Athens than all others, he was held in high favor under the Antonines. A great improviser. His writings are lost. Famous in Asia is *Aelius Aristides* from Adrianis in Mysia, born in 129. Fifty-five orations and treatises are still extant. Two rhetorical writings of slight scope. *Lucian* of Samosata (130–200), earlier himself a Sophist and rhetor who turns to philosophy at the age of forty. He is opposed to all Sophistry. *Hermogenes of Tarsus, ingenium praecox* [a precocious talent], extraordinarily skilled in description and also a writer on rhetorical theory, became a public teacher at the age of fifteen, and a writer at seventeen. By the age of twenty-five he displayed an unfailing wit in language: (I) *technē rhētorikē peri tōn staseōn (de partitionibus)* according to Hermagoras' principles; (II) *peri heureseōs (de inventione)* in four books; (III) *peri ideōn (de formis rhetoricis)* in two books; (IV) *peri methodou deinotētos, de apto*; (V) *progymnasmata (praeexercitamenta) et sollerti genere dicendi methodas.* The three Philostrati. (1) *Flavius Philostratus,* son of Verus of Hierapolis, still living under Severus; (2) his *first son,* a teacher first in Athens, then in Rome. Biographer of Apollonius Tyana at the request of the Empress Julia. Writer of the *bioi sophistōn, Heroica, Imagines (eikones);* (3) a *nephew* of the second, in favor with Caracalla, died under Galienus in 264. A fine art critic. Dionysius Cassius Longinus (213–273) reports in *peri hypous* that

handenen προγυμνάσματα sind *Aphthonius* aus Antiochien und *Aelius Theon* aus Alexandria. *Himarius* aus Prusias und Bithynien c. 315–386 berühmter Lehrer in Athen. Von 71 Reden, die Photius kannte, besitzen wir noch 36 von diesem gemachte ἐκλογαί 24 Reden vollstandig und x in Fragmenten; Prunk und Gelegenheitsreden. Sein Schüler ist der Kaiser *Julianus* 331–363. In Byzanz blüht bis auf Theodosius von Constantin und Julian *Themistius*, wir besitzen 34 Reden. In Asien blüht *Libanius* aus Antiochien, ausserordentlich fruchtbar. Erhalten 60 Reden, 50 Deklamationen. Dann Musterstücke zu rhetorischen Vorübungen. Dann die bekannte Inhaltsanzeige der Reden des Demosthenes und Biographie des Demosthenes; das letzte grosse Talent.

Aphthonius of Antioch and *Aelius Theon* of Alexandria are the authors of extant *progymnasmata*. *Himarius* of Prusias on Bithynia was a famous teacher in Athens ca. 315–386. Of seventy-one orations which Photius knew, we still have thirty-six *eklogai* made by him, twenty-four orations complete and ten in fragments; ceremonial and occasional orations. The Emperor Julian (331–363) is his pupil. *Themistius* flourishes in Byzantium down to Theodosius from Constantine to Julian. We have thirty-four of his speeches. *Libanius* of Antioch flourishes in Asia. He is extremely productive. Extant are 60 speeches, 50 declamations. Then we have models for rhetorical exercises. Then the well-known table of contents of Demosthenes' orations and the biography of Demosthenes. Libanius is the last great talent.

ARISTOTELES' SCHRIFTEN ZUR RHETORIK

Die Dialoge des Aristoteles sind Jugendschriften; spät erst folgen die wissenschaftlichen Werke. Doch verweist er später in diesen oft auf sie zurück. Wie der Dialog περὶ ποιητῶν sich verhält zu der Poetik des Aristoteles, so der Dialog περὶ ῥητορικῆς ἢ Γρύλλος zu den drei Büchern unserer Rhetorik. Der Name bezieht sich auf den in der Schlacht bei Mantinea gefallener Sohn des Xenophon: nach Laert. 2, 55 sagt Aristot dass "unzählige auf Gryllos Lob- und Grabreden verfertigt, zum Theil aus Höflichkeit gegen den Vater." Dieser Wettkampf der Rhetoren war wohl der Anlass des fingirten Gesprächs (ihm sprach Aristoteles selbst als Hauptperson mit, wie das seine Sitte im Gegensatz zu Plato ist). Über den Inhalt erfährt man etwas aus Quintilian 2, 17, 14: Aristoteles, ut solet, quaerendi gratia quaedam subtilitatis suae argumenta excogitavit in Gryllo, sed idem et de arte rhetorica tres libros scripsit, et in eorum primo non artem solum eam fatetur, sed ei particulam civilitatis sicut dialectices assignat. Also die Spitze der Deduktion im Gryllos war dagegen gerichtet, dass die Rhetorik eine Kunst sei.—Diesen Dialog weist Bernays in Die Dialoge des Aristoteles, Berlin 1863, p. 157, und zu Quintil. 3, 1, 13, dass nach Aristoteles Isocrates der Schüler des Gorgias ist. Dann auch Dionysius von Halicarnassus "Über Isocrates." 5, 577 Reiske, dass nach Aristoteles die Buchhändler ganze Bänder von Advokatenreden aus Isocrates Feder feilgeboten hatten "δεσμής πάνυ πολλὰς δικανικῶν λόγων Ἰσοκρατείν περιφέρεσθαί φησω ὑπὸ τῶν βιβλια πωλῶν Ἀριστοτέλης." Damals gehört er noch zur platonischen Schule; wahrscheinlich hat er den Kampf für die Meinungen seines Lehrers Plato im Gorgias aufgenommen. Doch zeigt ebenso die Thatsache, dass er selber zur Rhetorik erzog, eine formliche Abweichung von der Meinung und Schätzung Platos. Dass Isokrates ein ἐνκώμιον Γρύλλου geschrieben, sagt Hermippos (Laert. II, 55). Aristoteles war damals nur 23 Jahre alt.

ARISTOTLE'S WRITINGS ON RHETORIC

Aristotle's dialogues are early writings; the scientific works follow only later. But in his later writings he often refers back to them. Just as the dialogue *peri poiētōn* relates to Aristotle's *Poetics*, so the dialogue *peri rhētorikēs ē Gryllos* relates to the three books of our rhetoric. The name refers to Xenophon's son who died in the battle of Mantinea; according to Laert. (2, 55), Aristotle says that "countless eulogies and funeral orations were composed in Gryllos' honor, partly out of courtesy to his father." This rivalry between the orators was probably the occasion for the fictional conversation (Aristotle himself spoke in the dialogue as the main character, as was his custom in contrast with Plato). One learns something about its content from Quintilian (2, 17, 14): *Aristoteles, ut solet, quaerendi gratia quaedam subtilitatis suae argumenta excogitavit in Gryllo, sed idem et de arte rhetorica tres libros scripsit, et in eorum primo non artem solum eam fatetur, sed ei particulam civilitatis sicut dialectices assignat* [Aristotle, it is true, in his *Gryllus* produces some tentative arguments to the contrary, which are marked by characteristic ingenuity. On the other hand he also wrote three books on the art of rhetoric, in the first of which he not merely admits that rhetoric is an art, but treats it as a department of politics and also of logic]. Thus, the point of the argument in the Gryllos oration was directed against the idea that rhetoric is an art. Bernays includes this dialogue in *The Dialogues of Aristotle* (Berlin, 1863), p. 157. And he refers to Quintilian (3, l, 13), that according to Aristotle Isocrates was a pupil of Gorgias. Then also Dionysius of Halicarnassus, "On Isocrates" (5, 577 Reiske), states that according to Aristotle the bookdealers offered whole volumes of forensic speeches written by Isocrates: *desmēs pany pollas dikanikōn logōn Isokrateiōn peripheresthai phēsō hypo tōn biblia pōlōn Aristotelēs*. At that time he still belonged to the Platonic school; probably he took up the struggle for the opinions of his teacher Plato in the *Gorgias*. But the fact that he himself taught rhetoric also shows a formal deviation from Plato's opinion and estimation. Isocrates wrote an *enkomion Gryllou*, says Hermippos (Laert., 2, 55). Aristotle was only twenty-three years old at the time.[141]

Es gab viele rhetorische Schriften des Aristoteles. τέχνη Θεοδέκτου (erneut citirt ἐν ταῖς ὑπ' ἐμοῦ τέχναις Θεοδέκτῃ γραφαίσαις). Dann erscheint in den Katalogen τέχνη α; ἄκκι τέχνη. Dann Einzelabhandlungen: τέχνη ἐνκωμιαστική. περὶ συμβουλίης. περὶ λεξεις. ἐπιτομὴ ῥητόρων, (sonst ῥητορικῶν). Dann περὶ παθῶς ὀργῆς und πάθη können wenigstens rhetorisch gewesen sein. Dann τεχνων συναγωγή (also eine Art Geschichte der Rhetorik) ἐνθυμήματα ῥητορικά (Musterstücke), περὶ μεγεθους und noch mancherlei. Die ῥητορικὴ πρὸς 'Αλεξανδρον ist, mit Ausnahme des ersten und letzten Kapitels, dem Rhetor Anaximenes von Lampsakus zugewiesen (von Spengel).

There were many rhetorical writings of Aristotle. *Technē theodektou* (cited again in *en tais hyp' emou technais theodektēi graphaisais*). Then the catalogues list *technē a; akki technē*. Then individual treatises: *technē enkōmiastikē, peri symbouliēs, peri lexeis, epitomē rhētorōn* (otherwise *rhetorikōn*). Then *peri pathōs orgēs* and *pathē* can at least have been rhetorical. Then *technōn synagōgē* (i.e., a kind of history of rhetoric), *enthymēmata rhētorika* (models for imitation), *peri megethous*, and several other items. The *rhētorikē pros Alexandron* is, with the exception of the first and last chapter, ascribed to the rhetor Anaximenes Lampsakus (by Spengel).

Anmerkungen zum Deutschen Text

1. Die Abneigung drückt am stärksten Locke aus (Untersuch. über den menschlichen Verstand III 10, 34): " . . . wir müssen zugeben, dass die ganze Redekunst, alle die künstliche und figürliche Anwendung der Wörter, welche die Beredsamkeit erfunden hat, zu nichts weiter dient, als unrichtige Vorstellungen zu erwecken, die Leidenschaften zu erregen, dadurch das Urtheil misszuleiten und so in der That eine vollkommene Betrügerei ist."

2. Ausführliche Sammlungen in diesem Sinne gemacht bei Gustav Gerber, "Die Sprache als Kunst," Bromberg 1871.

3. Solöcismen bei *Lessing* Bd. 20 p. 182: "Seien Sie, wer Sie wollen, wenn Sie nur nicht der sind, der ich nicht will, dass Sie sein sollen," qui nolo ut sis Bd. 8 p. 3: "Die Gelehrten in der Schweiz schickten einen Band alter Fabeln voraus, die sie ungefähr aus den nämlichen Jahren zu sein urtheilten," quas iisdem annis ortas esse iudicabant. *Schiller*, Wallenstein: "gefolgt von einer Heeresmacht," "gehorcht zu sein, wie er, konnte kein Feldherr sich rühmen."

4. Es ist oft schwer zu sagen, was ein Archaismus sei: Adelung tadelt als Archaismen z.B. heischen, entsprechen, Obhut, bieder, Fehde, Heimat, stattlich, lustwandeln, befahren, Rund, Schlacht, Irrsal, als unzulässige Neologismen "sich etwas vergegenwärtigen," liebevoll, entgegnen, Gemeinplatz, beabsichtigen, Ingrimm, weinerlich.

5. Likewise Quintilian I, 5, 1 (quia dicere *apte*, quod est praecipuum [fort. *ego* πρέπον] plerique ornatui subiciunt) fängt so an: iam cum omnis oratio tres habeat virtutes, ut emendata, ut dilucida, ut ornata sit.

6. Die lateinischen Citate sind in dem ganzen Abschnitt am Rande meist vollständiger ausgeschrieben.—MUSARION.

7. Genauer über diese Moden Quintil. VIII 3, 25.

8. ὁ τῆς ἀμπέλου ὀφθαλμός.

9. ἵπποι ἐβουκολοῦντο, "silberne Hufeisen."

10. ἀπο τοῦ γένους ἐπι εἶδος, ἀπὸ τοῦ εἶδος ἐπὶ γένος, ἀπὸ τοῦ εἶδους ἐπι εἶδος, κατὰ τὸ ἀνάλογον [dann Homerstellen].

11. Drei besondere Arten der διπλοῖ: στυχ. ἐμπίπτων, προκατασκευαζόμενος, συνκατασκευαζόμενος. Bei (1) tritt im Verlauf der Untersuchung auf ein Punkt ein, der wieder durch Conjektur erledigt werden muss. Bei (2) ist ein Punkt zu erledigen, ehe die eigentliche Conjektur anfängt. (3) Die Indizien der That werden druch einander begründet und stützen sich gegenseitig.

12. Theodektes: ἔργον ῥήτορος, ὥς φησι Θεοδέκτης, προοιμιάσασθαι πρὸς εὔνοιαν, διηγήσασθαι πρὸς πιθανότητα, πιστώσασθαι πρὸς πειθώ, ἐπιλογίσασθαι πρὸς ὀργὴν ἢ ἔλεον.

13. τέχνη, ἄσκησις, φυσις, die drei Zeugen μνήμη, μελέτη, ἀοιδή.

14. Thucydides erwählte, nach Dionysius, anstatt der gewöhnlichen und schlichten Redeweise die übertragene, alterthümliche, fremdartige: anstatt der glatten Composition die rauhe und kraftvolle: dann vielfache und ungewöhnliche Gestaltung der Worte und Glieder: endlich mit wenig Worten möglichst viel auszudrücken. Als χρώματα Färbungen gebraucht er die [?]keit, die Gedrängtheit, das Gewichtvolle, das Erschreckende, das Pathetische. Dionysius sagt: wenn es ihm gelänge, diesen Charakter nach Wunsch darzustellen, so seien seine Erfolge fast übermenschlich. Doch mehr die Kürze des Rededuktus, und das Künstliche steht nicht immer am rechten Orte und in rechtem Masse. Thucydides erschreckt, wo Lysias und Herodot [?] berühren: Lysias bewirkte ein Nachlassen, er ein Aufschauen, jener schmeichelt sich ein und überredet, dieser zwingt. Denn wie Herodot, Meister im Ethos, er im Pathos. Die schönheit des Herodot ist eine heitere, die des Thucydides eine furchtbare.

Notes to the English Text

1. The aversion is expressed most strongly by Locke (*An Essay Concerning Human Understanding*, 3, 10, 34): "we must allow, that all the Art of Rhetorick . . . all the artificial and figurative application of Words Eloquence hath invented, are for nothing else but to insinuate wrong Ideas, move the Passions, and thereby mislead the Judgment; and so indeed are perfect cheats."—NIETZSCHE, footnote 1.
   See John Locke, *An Essay Concerning Human Understanding*, ed. Peter H. Nidditch (Oxford: Clarendon Press, 1975), p. 508.
2. Kant, *The Critique of Judgement*, trans. James Creed Meredith (Oxford: Clarendon Press, 1961), sec. 51, pp. 184–85.
3. Schopenhauer, *The World as Will and Representation*, trans. E.F.J. Payne (New York: Dover, 1966), vol. 2, p. 118.
4. Nietzsche is referring here to Leonhard Spengel, "Die Definition und Eintheilung der Rhetorik bei den Alten," *Rheinisches Museum für Philologie*, 18 (1863), 481-526, and Richard Volkmann, *Die Rhetorik der Griechen und Römer in systematischer Uebersicht dargestellt* (Berlin: Ebeling und Plahn, 1872; all references are to the later, more available ed. (Leipzig: B. G. Teubner, 1885); reprint, Hildesheim: Georg Ohms Verlag, 1963).
5. See Plato, *Gorgias*, 453a, and Sextus Empiricus, *Adversus Matematicos*, 2, 62, 301.
6. The long passage to which Nietzsche seems to be referring starts at *Phaedrus*, 260.
7. Spengel, "Die rhetorica (des Anaximenes) ad Alexandrum kein Machwerk der spätesten Zeit," *Philologus, Zeitschrift für klassisches Altertum*, 18 (1862): 604-46.
8. The Greek approximation is Nietzsche's, not Quintilian's. See Quintilian, 2, 15, 21.
9. Isocrates, *Against the Sophists*, secs. 19–20.
10. This quotation and the one following (attributed to Quintilian by Nietzsche in the text) are from Sulpitius Victor, *Institutiones oratoriae*, 4. For more on Sulpitius Victor, see the review of the *Institutiones oratoriae* by Michael C. Leff, *Quarterly Journal of Speech*, 63 (1977): 441–43.
11. Sulpitius Victor, *Institutiones oratoriae*, 4.
12. Isocrates, *Against the Sophists*, sec. 16.
13. Dionysius of Halicarnassus, *First Letter to Ammeus*, 3; *On Thucydides*, 24, 2; *Art of Rhetoric*, 4; and *De Composita Verborum*, 1.

14. A detailed collection, in this sense has been made by Gustave Gerber, *Die Sprache als Kunst* (Bromberg, 1871).—NIETZSCHE, footnote 2.

15. Nietzsche's term *Formenlehre* translates as "accidence," that part of grammar dealing with inflection.

16. Solecism in *Lessing*, vol. 20, p. 182. "Be whoever you want to be, provided that you not be precisely that person who I do not want you to be," *qui nolo ut sis*, vol. 8, p. 3: "The learned in Switzerland evaluated a volume of old fables which they judged approximately to be from the same year," *quas iisdem annis ortas esse iudicabant*. Schiller, *Wallenstein*: "no general could boast of being obeyed as he was, when he was followed by a military troop."—NIETZSCHE footnote 3.

17. Dionysius of Halicarnassus, *On Lysias*, 11.

18. It is often difficult to say what an archaism is; Adelung labels the following as archaisms: *heischen* [to command], *entsprechen* [to correspond to], *Obhut* [guardianship], *bieder* [upright], *Fehde* [feud], *Heimat* [homeland], *stattlich* [stately], *lustwandeln* [to stroll], *befahren* [to traverse], *Rund* [globe], *Schlacht* [battle], *Irrsal* [error]; and the following have been labeled inadmissible neologisms: *sich etwas vergegenwärtigen* [to imagine], *liebevoll* [loving], *entgegnen* [to answer], *Gemeinplatz* [commonplace], *beabsichtigen* [to intend], *Ingrimm* [rage], *weinerlich* [inclined to weep].—NIETZSCHE, footnote 4.

19. All of these quotations, including the one attributed (correctly) to Voltaire, are found in Arthur Schopenhauer, *Sämmtliche Werke* (Leipzig: Brodhaus, 1891), vol. 6, text sec. 291, pp. 557-59.

20. The examples here are from Quintilian, 8, 3, 44–45. The errors contained in the examples arise from pronunciation, not from the meanings of the words.

21. This rather cryptic statement may be a reference to sec. 14 of *The Birth of Tragedy*, first published in 1872.

22. Dionysius of Halicarnassus, *On Lysias*, 13.

23. Nietzsche presumably means the substitution of embellished language for typical language.

24. Quoted in Quintilian, 7, 3, 6.

25. Just as Quintilian, 1, 5, 1: *quia dicere apte, quod est praecipuum, plerique ornatui subiciunt* [for many include the all-important quality of appropriateness under the heading of elegance], began: *iam cum omnis oratio tres habeat virtutes ut emendata, ut dilucidata, ut ornata sit* [style has three kinds of excellence, correctness, lucidity, and elegance].— NIETZSCHE, footnote 5.

    Nietzsche inserted the terms *ego* and *prepon* in the above, no doubt referring to the individual character of the quality of appropriateness.

26. Here Nietzsche is referring to Tacitus.

    In this entire paragraph, the Latin quotations are added in the margin, usually in a more complete form.—MUSARION, footnote 6.

27. This reference is to Johann Georg Hamann (1730–88), letter to F. H. Jacobi, January 18, 1776.
28. See Aristotle, *Rhetoric*, 3, 1.
29. Dionysius of Halicarnassus, *On Thucydides*, 2.
30. See Quintilian, 1, 5, 56.
31. For more precise information about this type, see Quintilian, 8, 3, 25. —NIETZSCHE, footnote 7.
32. Quintilian, 8, 3, 30.
33. Quintilian, 8, 3, 37.
34. The reference here is to Christian-August Lobeck, ed., Phrynichus Arabius, *Phrynichi Eclogae Nominum et Verborum Atticorum, Cum Notis* (Lipsiae, 1820).
35. *ho tēs ampelou ophthalmos.*—NIETZSCHE, footnote 8.
36. Cicero's last example, *sitientes agri* [thirsty fields], was apparently added by Nietzsche, for it does not appear in this passage of *De Oratore*. The example is used in the *Orator*, however.
37. Nietzsche does not quote Quintilian here, but since there are significant word omissions in Nietzsche's rendition, I have replaced his wording with that of Quintilian, 8, 2, 3.
38. Jean Paul, *Sämmtliche Werke* (Berlin, 1861), vol. 2, sec. 9, no. 50, p. 179.
39. Quintilian, 8, 6, 4.
40. *hippoi eboukolounto,* "silver horseshoes."—NIETZSCHE, footnote 9.
41. *apo tou genous epi eidos, apo tou eidous epi genos, apo tou eidous epi eidos, kata to analogon* (then passages from Homer).—NIETZSCHE, footnote 10.
42. Nietzsche's attribution to Homer of the examples used here (see n. 41 above) is only partially correct. The first two, as indicated in the text, are from Homer. The third and fourth are from Empedocles.
43. Quintilian, 8, 6, 17.
44. The quotation is from the *Ad Herennium*, 4, 23, 44.
45. Franz Bopp, *Vergleichende Grammatik des Sanskrit. Zend. Griechischen, Lateinischen und Deutschen* (Berlin, 1833).
46. These examples from Sanskrit are taken from Bopp, *Vergleichende Grammatik,* vol. 2, p. 317.
47. David Ruhnken, *Opuscula oratoria philologica critica* (The Hague, 1897).
48. Nietzsche uses the original wording here. The phrase he uses has been removed from more current editions. See *The Institutio oratoria of Quintilian,* trans. H.E. Butler, Loeb Classical Library (Cambridge: Harvard University Press, 1966), vol. 3, p. 312n.
49. The examples used here and in the next two sentences are from Quintilian, 8, 6, 27.

50. Charisius, p. 274, cited in Volkmann, *Rhetorik.*, p. 426. Nietzsche has a question mark after *"vaccas"* [cows]; Volkmann has a different wording, *"valvas"* [folding doors], which seems to accord better with the verb *"stridere"* [to squeak]. Quintilian, 1, 5, 72, refers to *"balare"* and *"hinnire."*

51. Nietzsche has *Iliad*, 2, 127.

52. Quintilian, *The Institutio oratoria*, 8, 6, 37, trans. H.E. Butler, p. 323.

53. Cited in Quintilian, 7, 6, 37.

54. Quintilian, 8, 6, 44.

55. *Ibid.*

56. Cicero, from an unknown speech, cited by Quintilian, 8, 6, 47.

57. Quintilian, 8, 6, 47; translation from Cicero, *The Speeches*, trans. Louis E. Lord, Loeb Classical Library (Cambridge: Harvard University Press,

58. Cf. Volkmann, *Rhetorik*, p. 434.

59. Aeschylus, *Prometheus Vinctus*, 545.

60. Aeschylus, *Prometheus Vinctus*, 904.

61. Aeschylus, *Eumenides*, 457.

62. Homer, *Iliad*, 2, 658.

63. Homer, *Iliad*, 11, 268.

64. *Odyssey*, 2, 409.

65. Xenophon, *Memorabilia*, 3, 5, 10.

66. Quintilian, 8, 6, 67.

67. Quintilian, 8, 6, 73.

68. Quintilian 9, 1, 14.

69. Apsines, *technē rhētorikē*, cited in Volkmann, *Rhetorik*, p. 466.

70. Synopsis of Quintilian, 9, 3, 58 and 62.

71. Cf. Quintilian, 9, 3, 62.

72. Tacitus, *The Histories, The Annals*, 2, 20, trans. by John Jackson, Loeb Classical Library (Cambridge: Harvard University Press, 1962).

73. Homer, *Iliad*, trans. A.T. Murphy (Cambridge: Harvard University Press, 1970), p. 22d.

74. Horace, *The Complete Works*, trans. Charles E. Passage (New York: Ungar, 1983), p. 210.

75. *Ibid.*, p. 199.

76. Original Greek text has *"apeirgo,"* present tense with future meaning. Nietzsche (mis)quotes it in the future tense.

77. Virgil, *Aened*, 12, 161, 164; trans. Rolf Humphries, The Aeneid of Virgil, ed. Brian Willis (New York: Macmillan, 1987), pp. 298–99, ll. 188–95. Nietzsche has *"tum"* [then] rather than *"hinc"* [on, or from this side]; *"tum pater Aeneas"* does occur in other passages, e.g., Virgil, *Aeneid*, 5, 348 and 8, 115.

78. Cicero, *The Speeches*, trans. N. H. Watts, Loeb Classical Library (Cambridge: Harvard University Press, 1908), p. 17.

79. Demetrius, *De Elocutione*, 29.
80. Dionysius of Halicarnassus, 6, 59, 94.
81. [Cicero], *Rhetorica ad Herennium*, trans. Harry Caplan, Loeb Classical Library (Cambridge: Harvard University Press, 1904), pp. 282–83.
82. Cicero, *Orator* 514, 183–84, trans. H. M. Hubbell, Loeb Classical Library (Cambridge: Harvard University Press, 1962), p. 461.
83. Cicero, *ibid.* to the end (circa 50 pages); Quintilian, 9, 4, 85ff.
84. Volkmann, *Rhetorik*, p. 527.
85. Aristotle, *Rhetoric*, 3, 9, 5.
86. [Cicero], *Ad Herennium*, 4, 12, 18.
87. Sophocles, *Oedipus Rex*, trans. F. Storr, Loeb Classical Library (Cambridge: Harvard University Press, 1967), p. 37.
88. [Cicero], *Ad Herennium*, 4, 8, 11 and 11, 16.
89. Three particular kinds of *diploi*: *stych. empiptōn, prokataskeuazyomenos, synkataskeuazomenos*. In the first, the course of investigation reaches a point that must be settled by conjecture. In the second, a point must be settled before the actual conjecture begins. In the third, the evidences of the deed are founded on and support one another mutually.—NIETZSCHE, footnote 11.
90. Cf. Volkmann, *Rhetorik*, p. 75; Quintilian 7, 4, 4–14.
91. [Cicero], *Ad Herennium*, 1, 3, 5; Cicero, *De Inventione*, 1, 15, 20; Quintilian, 4, 1, 40.
92. Cited in Volkmann, *Rhetorik*, p. 112.
93. Cicero, *Orator*, trans. H. M. Hubbell, p. 397.
94. Theodektes: *ergon rhētoros, ōs phēsi Theodektēs, prooimiasasthai pros eunoian, dihegēsasthai pros pithanotēta pistōsasthai pros peithō, epilogisasthai pros orgēn ē eleon* [It is the task of an orator in his introduction to work towards benevolence, then to hold his discourse towards the acceptable, to create trust in his power to convince, and, at the end, to direct his considerations to whether he means to bring about anger or clemency].—NIETZSCHE, footnote 12.
95. Ulpian on Demosthenes, *Midiana*, 77, cited in Volkmann, *Rhetorik*, p. 165.
96. Cf. Aristotle, *Rhetoric*, 1344b35, 1375a22.
97. Cicero, *The Speeches*, trans. Louis E. Lord, p. 337.
98. Julius Victor, p. 397, cited in Volkmann, *Rhetorik*, p. 222.
99. Cicero, *Topics*, 3, 13.
100. Julius Victor, p. 402, cited in Volkmann, *Rhetorik*, p. 231.
101. Volkmann, *Rhetorik*, p. 232.
102. Anaximenes, c. 8, p. 195.
103. Quintilian, 5, 13, 1.
104. Aristotle, *The "Art" of Rhetoric*, trans. John Henry Freese, Loeb Classical Library (Cambridge: Harvard University Press, 1939), pp. 279, 319.

105. *Isaeus*, trans. Edward Seymour Forster, Loeb Classical Library (Cambridge: Harvard University Press, 1907), pp. 279, 319.
106. Demosthenes, *Olynthiacs*, 3, cited in Volkmann, *Rhetorik*, p. 264.
107. Cicero, *Orator*, trans. H. M. Hubbell, p. 405.
108. Aristotle, *Rhetoric*, trans. John Henry Freese, p. 359.
109. Cicero, *Orator*, 38, 131, trans. H.M. Hubbell, p. 403.
110. Aristotle, *Poetics*, c. 5, *On the Art of Fiction*, trans. L. J. Potts (London: Cambridge University Press, 1962).
111. Quintilian, 6, 3, 17–21, trans. H.E. Butler, p. 449.
112. Cicero, *De Oratore*, 2, 60, 16, trans. E.W. Sutton, Loeb Classical Library (Cambridge: Harvard University Press, 1948), pp. 379–81.
113. Quintilian, 3, 8, trans. H.E. Butler, p. 485.
114. Hermogenes, *Prog.* 6.
115. Cf. *The Elder Seneca*, trans. J. M. Winterbottom, Loeb Classical Library (Cambridge: Harvard University Press, 1974), vol. 2, pp. 551–59.
116. Quintilian, 3, 8, 35 reads "*non contra hos*"; "*in*" is omitted by Nietzsche.
117. [Cicero], *Rhetorica ad Herennium*, trans. Harry Caplan, pp. 183–85.
118. Genethlius, 3, p. 346, cited in Volkmann, *Rhetorik*, p. 316.
119. *Ibid.*
120. Isocrates, *In Praise of Helen*, cited in Volkmann, *Rhetorik*, p. 320.
121. Quintilian, 3, 7, 5, trans. H. E. Butler, p. 467.
122. Isocrates, *In Praise of Helen*, pp. 16–48.
123. [Cicero], *Rhetorica ad Herennium*, trans. Harry Caplan, p. 86.
124. [Cicero], *Rhetorica ad Herennium*, trans. Harry Caplan, p. 189.
125. Quintilian, 7, 2, 27ff.
126. [Cicero], *Rhetorica ad Herennium*, trans. Harry Caplan, p. 86.
127. [Cicero], *Rhetorica ad Herennium*, trans. Harry Caplan, p. 91.
128. *technē, askēsis, physis*, the three witnesses *mnēmē, meletē, aoidē* [remembrance, careful treatment, story as product].—NIETZSCHE, footnote 13.
129. *The Elder Seneca*, trans. M. Winterbottom, *Controversiae*, 1, 2 (Cambridge: Harvard University Press, 1974), pp. 3–4.
130. Simonides, 146; cf. Theocritus, 7, 30.
131. Dionysius of Halicarnassus, cited in Volkmann, *Rhetorik*, p. 576.
132. [Cicero], *Rhetorica ad Herennium*, 3, 15, trans. Harry Caplan, p. 205.
133. Thucydides, according to Dionysius, chose, instead of the ordinary and plain mode of speaking, the figurative, archaic, strange; instead of smooth composition, a rough and forceful one; then a variegated and unusual formation of words and phrases; finally the terseness to express as much as possible in few words. As *chromata* (colors) he uses [?]ness, conciseness, impact, shock, pathos. Dionysius says that if he succeeded in portraying this character as he wished, then his successes were almost

superhuman. But this is more a matter of the brevity of the language rhythm, and the artificial is not always in the right place or in the right measure. Thucydides startles, where Lysias and Herodotus [?] move. Lysias brought about a relaxation, Thucyidides arouses attention; Lysias appeals and convinces, Thucydides coerces. For as Herodotus is a master in *ēthos*, he is one in pathos. The beauty of Herodotus is a cheerful one, that of Thucydides is frightful.—NIETZSCHE, footnote 14.

134. Dionysius of Halicarnassus, *Isocrates*, 1, in *The Critical Essays*, trans. Stephen Usher, Loeb Classical Library (Cambridge: Harvard University Press, 1974), p. 105.

135. *Isocrates*, 3, in *Critical Essays*, p. 113.

136. *Isocrates*, 3, in *Critical Essays*, p. 111.

137. *Isaeus*, 3, in *Critical Essays*, p. 179.

138. Cicero, *Brutus*, 8, 32, trans. G. L. Hendrickson, Loeb Classical Library (Cambridge: Harvard University Press, 1962), p. 41.

139. *Dinarchus*, 5, in *Critical Essays*, p. 165.

140. Cicero, *Brutus*, 95, 325, trans. G. L. Hendrickson, p. 283.

141. See Anton-Hermann Chroust, "Aristotle's Earliest 'Course of Lectures on Rhetoric'" and "Aristotle's First Literary Effort: The *Gryllus,* A Lost Dialogue on the Nature of Rhetoric," in Keith V. Erickson, ed., *Aristotle: The Classical Heritage of Rhetoric* (Metuchen, N.J.: Scarecrow, 1974) pp. 22–36, 37–51.

ON THE ORIGIN OF LANGUAGE (1869–70)

An old riddle among the Indians, the Greeks, down to the most recent times was: to say with certainty how the origin of language must *not* be conceived.

Language is neither the conscious work of individuals nor of a plurality.

1. All conscious thought is possible only with the help of language. It is absolutely impossible to have such a clever thought, for instance, with a language consisting of merely animal sounds: the marvelous, intelligent organism. The deepest philosophical insights are already implicitly contained in language. Kant says: "A great part, perhaps the greatest part of the work of reason consists in analyzing the concepts which man finds preexisting in himself."[1] Just think of subject and object; the concept of the judgment is abstracted from the grammatical sentence. The subject and the predicate developed into the categories of substance and accident.[2]

2. The development of conscious thinking is harmful to language. Decadence is caused by advanced culture. The formal element, which has philosophical value, is damaged. Think of the French language: no declension is left, no neuter, no passive; all final syllables are eroded away; the stem-syllables are distorted beyond recognition. A more highly developed culture is even incapable of preserving from decay what was handed down to it complete.

3. Language is much too complex to be the work of a single individual, much too unified to be the work of a mass; it is a complete organism.

The only alternative is to consider language to be the product of an instinct, like among the bees—the anthill, etc.

Instinct, however, is *not* the result of conscious reflection, not a mere consequence of corporeal organization, not the effect of a mechanism located in the brain, not the work of a mechanism acting upon the mind from the outside and alien to its nature, but rather the most proper achievement of the individual, or of a mass, stemming from its very character. Instinct is even one with a being's innermost core. That is the genuine problem of philosophy, the

209

unending purposefulness of organisms and the lack of consciousness in their origin.

Consequently, all earlier naive standpoints are rejected. The Greeks asked whether language was *thesei* or *physei*, i.e., whether the utterance is conditioned by arbitrary formation, by contract and consensus, or by the conceptual content. But even more recent scholars used these same slogans; for example, the mathematician Maupertuis (1697–1759) identified "consensus" as the foundation of language.[3] First, there was supposedly a condition without language, with only gestures and shrieks. Then conventional gestures and shrieks were established. These means could have been perfected into a pantomimed language of shrieks and song. But that would have been precarious. Not everyone is skilled at correct intonation and precise hearing. Then someone got the idea of inventing a new mode of expression. Using the tongue and lips, it was possible to produce a certain amount of articulation. The new language was felt to be advantageous and so it was retained.

Meanwhile the other question came to the fore: namely whether language could have originated from merely human mental power or whether it was a direct gift from God. The Old Testament is the only religious document with a myth about the origin of language, or something of the sort. Two main points: God and man speak the same language, not like among the Greeks. God and man give things their names, which express each thing's relation to man. Thus the myth deals with the naming of the animals, etc.: language itself was presupposed.—The nations are silent about the origin of language: they cannot imagine the world, the gods, and man without language.

That question was justified because of the scanty historical and physiological understanding of the time. Comparative linguistics immediately showed with clarity that the origin of language from the nature of things could not be proven. As early as Plato's *Cratylus*, the arbitrariness of nomenclature was pointed out: for this viewpoint presupposes a language prior to language.[4]

Jean-Jacques Rousseau believed that language could not possibly have originated by purely human means.[5]

An important contribution to the opposite view is the work of de Brosses (1709–1777), which postulates the purely human origin of language, but with inadequate means. According to him, the choice of sounds depends on the nature of things, e.g., [in French] *rude* [crude] and *doux* [sweet], and he asks: "Is not one thing crude and

the other sweet?" But such words are extremely remote from the origin of language; we have grown accustomed to the sounds and imagine that they contain some element of the things.

The next writer of importance on the subject is Lord Monboddo. He accepts a reflexive activity of the mind: language is an invention of man, indeed one that was made rather often. So man needs no primeval language. Monboddo wrote about his theory for twenty-one years; but the difficulties kept increasing. He ascribed the origin of language to the very wisest of men. Even then he still must resort to superhuman help: the Egyptian demon-kings.

In Germany one hundred years ago the Berlin Academy had proposed a prize question: "On the Origin of Language." In 1770, Herder's book was selected. Man was born for language. "Thus the genesis of language is as much an intrinsic urgency as is the embryo's urge to be born the moment it reaches maturity."[6] But Herder shares with his predecessors the view that language is internalized from expressed sounds. He sees exclamation as the mother of language; whereas in actual fact the mother of language is negation.

This right knowledge has become common only since Kant, who in the *Critique of Pure Reason* both recognized teleology in nature and at the same time stressed the remarkable paradox that something can be purposeful without a consciousness. This is the essence of instinct.

In conclusion, a quotation from Schelling (Abt. 2, Vol. 1, p. 82): "Since without language no philosophical consciousness, indeed no consciousness at all, is conceivable, the foundation of language could not be laid with consciousness; and yet the deeper we penetrate into it, the more definitely we discover that its depth far exceeds that of the most conscious product. Language's situation is like that of organic beings; we believe we see them originating blindly and yet we cannot deny the unfathomable intentionality of their formation down to every detail."

NOTES

1. Kant, *Kritik der reinen Vernunft* (1781), #27. Our translation.
2. Schopenhauer, *Die Welt als Wille und Vorstellung*, 1, pp. 566ff. (608 f. Gr.)—Nietzsche.
3. P.L.M. de Maupertuis, *Réflexions philosophiques sur l'origine des langues et la signification des mots* (1747).

4. This is a central theme in the *Cratylus*; see the Loeb Classical Library edition, trans. H. N. Fowler (Cambridge: Harvard University Press, 1920), pp. 7ff.

5. J. J. Rousseau, *Essai sur l'origine des langues* (1749). See John H. Moran, ed. and trans., *On the Origin of Language: Jean-Jacques Rousseau, Essay on the Origin of Languages; Johann Gottfried Herder, Essay on the Origin of Langage.* Trans., with afterwords, by John H. Moran and Alexander Gode (New York: Ungar, 1966).

6. J. G. Herder, *Über den Ursprung der Sprache* (1770), in Moran and Gode, trans., *On the Origin of Language.*

THE HISTORY OF GREEK ELOQUENCE
(1872–73)

To no task did the Greeks devote such incessant labor as to eloquence; the amount of energy they expended on oratory can perhaps
be symbolized by Demosthenes' autodidacticism. Devotion to oratory is the most tenacious element of Greek culture and survives
through all the curtailments of their condition. It is communicable,
contagious, as can be seen from the Romans and the whole Hellenistic world. Again and again in a new age rhetoric blossoms forth; it
does not end even with the great university orators of third- and
fourth-century Athens. The effectiveness of Christian preaching can
be traced back to that element; and indirectly the development of the
whole modern prose style depends on the Greek orators, directly of
course mostly on Cicero. Hellenic culture and power gradually concentrate on oratorical skill [*Reden-können*]; it probably also spells
their doom. Diodorus, in his introduction, says this very naively:
"No one will be able easily to name a higher prerogative than oratory. For it is by virtue of oratory that the Greeks excel the other
nations and the educated person the uneducated; moreover, it is by
oratory alone that one individual acquires authority over many; but
in general everything appears only as the speaker's power represents
it." This was meant quite straightforwardly; for instance, Callis-
thenes says that he held in his hands the fate of Alexander and his
deeds in the eyes of posterity. He had not come to borrow fame for
himself from Alexander, but rather to win the admiration of men for
him, and belief in Alexander's divinity depended not on Olympia's
lies about his birth but on what he, the orator, made known about
his deeds (Arrian 4, c. 10). The most immoderate presumption of
being able to do anything, as rhetors and stylists, runs through all
antiquity in a way that is incomprehensible to us. They control
"opinion about things" and hence the *effect of things upon men*; they
know this. A precondition, to be sure, is that mankind itself was educated in rhetoric. Basically, even today "classical" higher education
still preserves a good portion of this antique view, except that it is
no longer oral speech but its faded image, writing, that emerges as
goal. The most archaic factor in our culture is the view that *action
through books and the press* is what must be learned by education.

However, our public's basic education stands so incredibly lower than in the Hellenistic-Roman world; that is why results can be achieved only by much clumsier and cruder means and everything elegant is either rejected or arouses distrust—or, at best, it has only its own narrow circle.

No one should believe that such an art falls from heaven; the Greeks *worked* at it more than any other people and more than at any other thing (i.e., also so *many* people!). Indeed, from the very beginning there is a *natural eloquence* without compare, namely Homer's; however, that is not a beginning but rather the end of a long cultural development, just as Homer is one of the more recent witnesses concerning religious antiquities. The nation which was educated by means of such a language, the most *speak*able of all languages, spoke insatiably and at an early age found pleasure and a distinctive talent in speaking. There are, indeed, tribal differences, opposite inclinations which erupt almost out of surfeit, such as the *brachologia* [terseness] of the Dorians (especially the Spartans), but on the whole the Greeks feel that they are speakers, in contrast with the *aglōssai*, the [languageless] non-Greeks (Sophocles); they are the ones who speak understandably and beautifully (the opposite is *barbaroi*, the "quackers," cf. *ba-trachoi* [frogs]).

But only with the political forms of *democracy* does the overestimation of oratory begin; it has become the greatest instrument of power *inter pares* [among equals]. Empedocles, the founder of democracy in Agrigentum, is said to be its "inventor": so says Aristotle in the dialogue *sophistēs* (*La.* 8, 57). There it meant the *removal of tyrants*, as it had in Syracuse after the fall of Thrasybulus, Hiero's brother; then a decisive democracy immediately began. Cic. (*Brut.*, 46),

> *itaque ait Aristoteles cum sublatis in Sicilia tyrannis res privatae longo intervallo iudiciis repeterentur, tum primum e controversia natam artem et praecepta Siculos Coracem et Tisiam conscripsisse* [Thus Aristotle says that in Sicily, after the expulsion of tyrants, when after a long interval restitution of private property was sought by legal means, Corax and Tisias the Sicilians, with the acuteness and controversial habits of their people, first put together some theoretical precepts].[1]

Ars technē is the theory of the art of rhetoric *par excellence*, very characteristic among a nation of artists! The famous definition *rhētorikē peithous dēmiourgos* [rhetoric is the maker of persuasion] is

attributed to Corax. He had taken part in political life for many years, was removed by intrigues, and devoted himself to the theory of rhetoric. The goal he set was to strive for *eikos,* the probable; he divided the parts of a speech, e.g., calling the prooemium *katastasis*. His pupil was Tisias, who then taught rhetoric in Syracuse, Thurii, and Athens. He made a famous contract with his teacher: he would pay him his tuition only if he had won his first case. Corax sues him and postulates that he must receive the money in either case: if he wins, by decree of the court; if he loses, according to the contract. Tisias turns the proposition around: in neither case did he have to pay: if he wins, because the court's decision released him from the agreement; if he did not win, then the contract did not apply. The judges chased them both away with the words *ek kakou korakos kakon ōon* [from a bad crow, a bad egg][2] (the same anecdote is told of Protagoras and Euathlos).—In Thurii he was the teacher of Lysias, in Athens of Isocrates; he wandered about like a Sophist. He left behind a *technē,* essentially on the art of conducting a trial.

The actual Sophists, the higher teachers from Greece proper and from the Eastern colonies, presented a much more comprehensive theory; instruction in oratory is just a part of their activity. Sophism originated with Protagoras' journey through the Hellenistic cities, which began ca. 455 B.C. He influenced Attic eloquence much earlier than did the Sicilians. He promises to teach *ton hētto logon kreittō poiein*: how one can by means of dialectics help the weaker case to win out. This dialectics was to make all other arts and sciences superfluous: how without being a geometrician one can outargue the geometrician; and likewise on natural philosophy, wrestling, the practical life of the state. The pupils had to learn model speeches by heart. The other great Sophists also come in question. Despite posing the tasks of dialectics in this manner, the great Sophists were *concentrating* powers of the highest rank, combining various kinds of knowledge and achieving a higher level of education. A practical result of this new education after the middle of the fifth century was the great Pericles: he engaged in many debates with Protagoras. Plato, to be sure, attributes Pericles' great mastery of oratory to philosophy (that of Anaxagoras), not to the Sophists: it gave his mind sublime flight, insight into nature and men, *Phaedr.*, p. 269E. Nevertheless, only the liberation of minds by higher education makes such an association as that between Pericles and Anaxagoras possible in the first place. Otherwise people were still very deficient in their esti-

mation of literature. The mightiest men in the city-states were ashamed to compose speeches and to leave them for posterity, out of the fear of the old "fault" of the Sophists and philosophers: free-thinking. The orator Pericles still completely lacked the impassioned free and bold style of delivery; he stood there motionless, with his arms crossed, his cloak retaining the same pattern of folds; he kept the same pitch of voice, the same seriousness, never a smile—but still he was marvelously impressive. That was the archaic style of oratory.

Innovation already begins with Gorgias; he came adorned festively and magnificently—like Empedocles he appeared in a purple gar-ment—with a worldwide reputation and presented the epideictic oration: in it one wants to display one's ability; there is no intention to deceive; the content is not the issue. Pleasure in beautiful dis-course acquires a realm of its own where it does not clash with neces-sity. It is a refreshing pause (*Athemholen*) for a nation of artists; for once they want to indulge in an exquisite treat in oratory. The phi-losophers, however, have no sense for this activity (for they had no understanding of the art which lived and flourished around them, nor of sculpture), and so their hostility is too vehement.

Artistic prose[3] entered the world with Gorgias, and immediately became victorious, exhilarating; all other kinds of oratory can no longer remain unchanged; stylistic expression becomes a power for itself, whereas until then the arrangement of the speech, the means of proof, the arousal of feelings, etc., were reflected upon and prac-ticed almost exclusively by the rhetors. Now there was in Athens the custom of advocates in the form of *logographoi*. For lawyers in our sense of the word were forbidden; each person *was allowed* to file a lawsuit but everyone *had to* defend himself (only legal assistants were allowed: they could not accept money; *specific grounds* had to be given for their appearance in court). And so the defense was often written up by trained and experienced orators and then read by the defendant. A profitable trade thus arose for men of letters, whose products were *intended to be read aloud from the written page*—this is important! If such a speech was published after a *successful* trial, it served primarily to enhance the writer's reputation and bring him new clients. But soon these speeches took on an absolute interest as clever accomplishments (not to mention, works of art); a discerning public, experienced in law, delighted in *reading* them. This brought consideration of the *reader* into the picture; the logographs revised

their products for publication with an eye to style, just as later political speakers would do; for they were very much aware of the difference between dealing with a listener or with a reader. Arist. (*Rhet.*, 3,1,7):

> *hoi gar graphomenoi logoi meizon ischyousi dia tēn lexin ē dia tēn dianoian* [for written speeches owe their effect not so much to the sense as to the style].[4]

But especially 3, 12:

> The *lexis graphikē* [written style] is completely different from the *lexis agōnistikē* [spoken style]; one must understand both: the one kind (in public oratory) is tantamount to *hellēnizein epistasthai* [knowing good Greek]—what pride in these words, the pride of Hellenic culture!—the other means not to be forced to remain silent when one wishes to communicate something to the public—as it goes for people who do not know how to write.[5]

> The productions of literary speech-artists seem paltry, *stēnoi*, in public presentation, while the real orators, however well they hear themselves read, when one has what they wrote in one's hands, appear *idiōtikoi*, uncultured. . . . The dramatically effective passages appear foolish when oral delivery is missing. For example, asyndeta and frequent repetition of one and the same expression are rightly condemned in the written style, while in public presentation the orators use that sort of thing because they are *hypokritika* [suitable for oral delivery].[6]

The first orator whose juridical *logoi* [speeches] were also read, the *logographos* Antiphon, a real Athenian, in any case revised his speeches; he seems to have been influenced by Gorgias, Tisias, Protagoras. Because of these speeches he was inserted as the first orator in the canon of the ten Attic orators. The structure of his speeches is very regular. Later, starting with Isaeus, a clever sense arose in which art was used contrary to nature. He has a solemn expression; at that time the public speaker still had to speak even more formally, remotely. Thus he is ranked within the genre of the elevated style, except that the elegant style of oratory is closer to the plain style of oratory, e.g. that of Lysias, than the elevated style in historiography stands to the plain one. An archaic tone is part of dignity; Gorgias and Antiphon still have the older Atticism *ss*, *xyn*, *es*, while Pericles already spoke according to modern usage, and likewise Andocides, Lysias, etc. In composition he has the *austēra harmonia* [rough style]

in contrast with Lysias' *glaphyra* [polished style].—He is an aristocrat with a deep mistrust of the *dēmos*, ever active behind the scenes, without apparent political ambition, a famous jurist and adviser, also of Thucydides, it seems, in his trial (praised very highly by him) in 8,18 for *aretē* [excellence] as the foremost man and also the most distinguished mind of Athens at that time, *kratistos enthymēthēnai genomenos kai ha gnoie eipein* [most able both to formulate a plan and to set forth his conclusions in speech].[7] He devised a careful plan to topple the democracy; later he was condemned for installing the Four Hundred and for *prodosia* [treason] (to the Lacedaemonians). His defense speech *peri tēs metastaseōs* ("On Changing the Constitution") was, according to Thucydides, *the best one ever given until his time.* Condemned nonetheless, he is reported to have said to Agathon, who admired the speech: a man with a great soul had to consider more *ti dokei heni spoudaiōi ē pollois tois tynchanousin* [what one virtuous man thinks than what many ordinary people think], Arist. (*Eth. Eudem.* 3, 5, 5).[8] There were sixty speeches; Caecilius contested twenty-five as not genuine. The majority are *logoi dikanikoi dēmosioi* [orations for political trials] rather than *logoi dikanikoi idiōtikoi* [orations in private cases]; he had little use for less important trials. The extant speeches belong to the class of *logoi phonikoi*, criminal matters; he was very famous for these. He should not be confused with Antiphon the Sophist, interpreter of dreams and omens who wrote a two-volume work on natural history, *Alētheia*, in a pompous, artificial style, with poetic, unusual words, utterly lacking in naturalness; his nickname was *logomageiros*, "speech-cook"; our statesman's surname was Nestor.

An important contributor to rhetorical theory (*Techniker*) is Thrasymachus of Chalcedon, the Sophist (also a philosopher, *peri physeōs*), whom Plato caricatures in the introductory scene of *The Republic* as arrogant, corrupt, and impudent. He is the founder of the middle genre of style; he invents the *periodos stroggulē* or *synestrammenē* [well-rounded or terse period], which Gorgias and Antiphon still do not know (in contrast with the *lexis eiromenē*, the "serial" style, he compresses the thought into a unity; no longer like Gorgias' loose antithesis after antithesis). He must, then, be regarded as a magnificent rhythmic nature; for the reproach later made against him, that his style sounds almost too rhythmic (according to Aristotle, he was the first who gave preference to the paeonic rhythm), also shows where his powerful artistry lay. To discover the period

requires a high rhythmic inventiveness; for it is the architectonics of the sentence, the unified mode of construction, where the symmetry or contrast of the individual clauses is measured and felt: an artificial distribution of high, deep, and middle tones over a longer portion of discourse which must be held together by *one* breath. He thereby had a world-historical effect, having discovered a new kind of magic, there can be no doubt. A Sicilian invents artful prose, a Chalcedonian (i.e., a person from a Megaran colony) the period! Among the writings of Thrasymachus there was a *hyperballontes* (means of intensification), *eleoi* (means of arousing pity), etc., also mock laudatory and recriminatory speeches, a kind of *epideixis* [exhibition of examples]. Also once he moderates Gorgias' artistic prose and invents the middle style: this shows a high feeling for moderation and what is typical (his relation [to Gorgias] is like Euripides' to Aeschylus). The "refined" [*gewählt*] style consisting essentially of commonly used words; its charm, *xenon*, consists essentially in the choice. Now, Aristotle (*Rhet.* 3,2) says that Euripides was the *first* to show and find this procedure: thus Thrasymachus seems to be the one who made use of Euripides' discovery *for prose*. (Quintilian, 10, 1, 67f., recommends to orators the study of Euripides more highly than that of Sophocles). Gorgias probably stands in similar relation to the Empedocles-writer-orator style! Empedocles, however, to the Aeschylus-actor style!

The ill-reputed *Critias* is very outstanding as an orator; it is noteworthy that he did not come into the canon in Andocides' place, but he was harmed by having been one of the Thirty. He has dignity in the thoughts, simplicity of form, little verve and fire, a less attractive *ēthos*, and is always asserting *all' emoige dokei* [but it seems to me], also in Xenophon, etc. Herodes Atticus, the talented magnificent Athenian Sophist, preferred him over *all other* Classics and imitated him; the Atticist Phrynichos ranks him lower than the model writers of Atticism.[9] He writes in a polished style, on the whole avoiding poetic diction, but he does use some genuinely Attic words which are relatively rare; he has moderate adornment with figures. He gained such superiority from the most distinguished Athenian education, with training under all the Sophists, especially Socrates, the most exquisite taste, and a wide range of practice in poetry and prose. Yet he is a statesman, a freethinker, astute, relentless, with deep hatreds, in sum, a very classically stamped personality of the aristocratic Athenian, the *anēr agathos*, attractive even in his horrible qualities.

Andocides, the second of the ten canonical orators, an oratorical talent without much prior training and work, not at all a theorist, perhaps the least significant one. As a speaker he is neither a rhetor nor a speech-writer, but only a politician; he was not a Sophist, his knowledge is insignificant and unsure. He represents for us the class of public speakers which was then and is now most numerous: the individual speeches were published as *political pamphlets*; content is absolutely the main thing. The foundation for the form is the most ordinary technique. He was later held in low esteem; Herodes Attikos, who was complimented for being one of the ten, said: "At least I am better than Andocides." His expression is not stylefully mastered, in general common, occasionally with turns of phrase from the tragedies. He shows what an educated Athenian without more advanced rhetorical training could particularly *achieve* at that time: i.e., the preconditions for the specifically *Athenian* talent: great skill and pleasure in narrating, introducing persons who speak directly, concrete depiction even of minor circumstances; *enargeia* [clarity], not much pathos. One sees no antitheses, parisa, homoioleuta; this shows how little he is affected by the rhetorical training of the time; thus also no periodics, or rather a very subordinate one. The enlivening figures such as asyndeton and the question are found in great numbers; Aristotle finds this foolish in written speeches, but on the oratorical platform it prevailed as dramatically effective; one did not first have to be a great "technician" for that.—*Lysias*, the son of the Syracusan, Cephalos, was born in Athens ca. 444; his father had been brought to Athens by Pericles, his host, and lived there for thirty years: he was wealthy, highly cultured, highly honored. He did not need to write speeches for court, but he wrote epideictic master speeches for *reading*, such as the erotic speech, which is treated in Phaedrus. For these things he was very much admired as a writer. That he became a mighty orator brought about the great disaster which struck his family under the Thirty; their whole fortune and his brother Polemarch fell victim to them.

The charm of the Lysian style is first noted at the time of Theophrastus and is revealed by imitation: Dinarchos, Charisius, Hegesias of Magnesia. That is a reaction to the artful Isocratean style and its full tone; simplicity was now appreciated and exaggerated. The reaction was even stronger in Rome, where Lysias was hailed as exemplary in contrast with Asianism. Cicero, violently opposed by these extreme Atticists and Lysians, was, nevertheless, very fair

toward Lysias and calls him an almost perfect speaker, who lacked only the oratorical power to capture the feelings of his audience. He is considered the best representative of the *charaktēr ischnos, lexis litē kai aphelēs* [plain genus, unadorned and simple style], *oratores tenues, acuti, subtiles, versuti, humiles, summissi* [the orators are subtle, intelligent, direct, clever, plain, restrained].

Lysias consciously placed himself in sharpest contrast to Gorgias, retaining *his own* character even in the panegyric orations: i.e., in the choice of words and in expression; he imitates the ordinary man's speech—a great artistic feat! And a most difficult one. Cic. (*Orat.*, c. 76) rightly says: *orationis subtilitas imitabilis illa quidem videtur existimanti, sed nihil est experienti minus* [For that plainness of style seems easy to imitate at first thought, but when attempted nothing is more difficult].[10] Dionys. *Censura vet.*: *hōs anagignōskomenon men eukolon nomizesthai, chalepon d' heuriskesthai zēloun peirōmenois* [for it is easily acknowledged when it is recognized, but for those who try to search for it, it is hard to find]. He refrains from using the *tropikē lexis* [figurative style]; one has to get by with the *kuria* [literal]. There is a genuine Attic word for every object. Brevity without obscurity: the expansion of the thoughts and sentences by unnecessary additions, the *peribolē* [circumlocution] is completely missing; a certain slender thinness. He has the oratorical period (*enagōnios*) but not the epideictic one (he thus depends on Thrasymachus). He has *enargeia* [clarity]. Then *ēthos* [character]; his speakers are felt to be ordinary folk and *they communicate this mood*. The apparent artlessness of composition is the result of the highest art. In sum, there is an inimitable aura of *charis* [grace, beauty] around him, not an adorned Isocratean one, but the *charis* of a natural growth. (How pitifully the Romans with their *polita urbana elegans* [finish, urbaneness, precision] feel this. Cic. (*Brut.*, 285), it sounds almost French!) If he makes much use of the adornment of antithetical and parallel sentence formation, we see that this belonged to the popular way of speaking at the time and was very Athenian: as Euripides also shows. His *letters* were also famous and written with full consciousness (in Antiquity these belonged to the oratorical field).[11] Lysias is one of the finest products of the Athenian artistic spirit: what a course it ran from Gorgias' poetic style to that of Lysias! The combination of consciousness and naiveté is always one of the highest accomplishments and hard to attain; almost never directly, but by long detours and aberrations; common taste despises simplicity as

"boring," while the noblest taste feels a repugnance for the ornate and bombastic; the *genus tenue* always results from a certain reaction; just as admiration of Lysias always presupposes such a feeling.

Isocrates, son of Theodoros, from Athens: he was a citizen from the middle class who owned a flute factory. Isocrates received the finest education and distinguished himself among his fellow pupils (he says himself that he had been more highly regarded among them, *hē nun en tois sympoliteuomenois*, his "fellow citizens"). In addition he was influenced by Prodicus, Socrates, and Theramenes, the orator and statesman. Isocrates himself did not become a statesman and public speaker: he lacked the strong voice and the poise; even in his own house his speech became halting when a stranger entered. When he was in his twenties, his father became impoverished. With the great public catastrophes in Sicily, the maritime war over Athens' allied cities—who wanted to buy flutes? He went to Thessaly to Gorgias, to entrust himself to a master of rhetoric and later become a *logographos*. Toward 400 B.C. he was back in Athens; there were very few forensic speeches written by him. Later, after he had become famous, masses of forgeries were produced; Aristotle tells of entire volumes of Isocrates' forensic speeches which the bookdealers offered for sale, much to the annoyance of both teacher and pupils. He was much too careful and slow a writer to have profited from this; and the common genre resisted him. So he became a *teacher*. Formerly he had denied that theory could make any contribution to oratory; now he changed his opinion: nature and practice are the first thing, theory the second. His program is the speech against the Sophists; in it he is fighting against competitors; he wants to provide the complete education that is necessary for life; thus he rejects the dialecticians and "eristicians,"[12] the disciples of Protagoras; he often accuses his rivals, the rhetors, of promising too much; *his* theory could do no more than make the discovery of thoughts easier for the talented and lead the less gifted somewhat beyond themselves. Now he soon finds his own master-form which he was later so proud of: *logoi* which are at the same time *Hellēnikoi, politikoi*, and *panēgyrikoi* [Hellenic, political, and panegyric], as he himself says, and closer to poetry than the court speeches. Until then, the artistic oration generally had an absurd or paradoxical theme and was a game; just for once the speaker wanted to let himself go and enjoy his art. Only Gorgias shows a higher approach. Isocrates is more perfect. He considers speech to be the cause of all higher culture, including

morals: for "we consider those to be intelligent and wise who best know how to converse about things." Thus for his educational system he lays claim primarily to the words *philosophos* and *sophos*. We pass over his quarrel with the philosophers, especially Plato, already mentioned above. He also was at odds with the poetry explicators and antiquarians. He considers epos and tragedy to be *psychagōgia*, entertainment, based on the injudicious crowd's preference for fables and battle scenes; he despises comedy. Famous poetical works, if presented without meter, would seem much less significant. He is a *fanatical prose-writer*. His pupil Ephorus even said that music had been introduced among men *ep' apatē kai goēteiai* [for fraud and sorcery]. Isocrates himself says of the musician that he did not annoy old men and that he provided a pleasant, useful, and appropriate pastime for the young.

The Isocratean work of art, through which he had this enormous success, seems stranger to us than, say, Demosthenes' discourse; we listen too strongly to the ideas, find them not sufficiently deep, statesmanly, and philosophical; indeed, a bit mediocre! And we do not understand the efficacy which they had. We no longer have a feeling even for their form; the reason may be that we are accustomed to much stronger spices and contrasts and all subscribe to the Asian enjoyment of oratory. But the greatest prose-writer of the century, Leopardi, translated him and learned from him; Leopardi, who could say that excellent prose was much more difficult to write than excellent verse; poetry resembled a magnificently adorned female figure, prose a nude. Pliny, however, says of sculpture: *graeca simplicitas est nihil velare* [Greek simplicity is to hide nothing behind veils]. That is the difficulty. That is probably how Isocrates' style seems to us, with this *simplicitas, quae nihil velat* [simplicity which hides nothing]. For the Greeks' still more sensitive ear he was already adorned and veiled, measured against the Lysian style. It is the epideictic way. This aims to affect the *reader*; the image of the Greek reader from Isocrates' time can be imagined thus: a slow reader, sipping in sentence after sentence with lingering eye and ear, who imbibes a work like a delicious wine, following every detail of the author's art; the type of person for whom it is still a pleasure to write, who does not need to be "stunned, intoxicated, and swept away," but who really has the *reader's natural mood*. The active, the passionate, the suffering person is not a reader. Calm, attentive, carefree, leisurely, a person who still has time—he is matched by the

rounded, smooth, fuller period, the plain harmony, the not overdone means of artistry; but it is a reader who is experienced as the hearer of the practical speech, and who listens even more closely while reading quietly and is not carried away by any dramatic passion of oral delivery; he must not be allowed to hear any more hiatus, he will also relish the rhythmic structures with his ear; he misses nothing. Isocrates' art presupposes that the reader already existed then; now he takes the upper hand mightily, and he is also matched by the *writer* who no longer thinks of oral delivery. Then what we have is the *most delicate, most demanding manner of hearing and the akribestatē lexis* [the most literally accurate word], that of writing. (In our time the reader is almost no longer a listener, and therefore someone who has the oral presentation of art now works more meticulously—what a topsy-turvy world!).

How does Isocrates now achieve the classical reading style? He subtracts the *excess* from the epideictic hearer's style of the masters before him, from Gorgias' ornamentation of figures and bold metaphors, from Thrasymachus' exaggerated rhythm. Thus he *removes* the style one stage further from the *poetic*. He adds something to what is *lacking*, namely Gorgias' and Thrasymachus' composition with its short clauses: he fills the period, makes it rounder and calmer, i.e., he removes the *dramatic liveliness* of the *hypocrisis* [elocution], which had determined the style of the period; that is not proper for the reading style. In both respects he can be called timid and without strong tones, as Dionysius of Halicarnassus says, which, however, does him an injustice, for he had a standard in *his* Athenians. The Athenian of Demosthenes' time was already changed. The most arduous work was necessary, a constantly engaged sensitive hearing and weighing of every word, every rhythmic boundary; the choice of words cost him the most time (as it did Euripides). Then there is the avoidance of the hiatus, taken from the art of tragic and comical dialogue. Then the striving for rhythm and the avoidance of meter. Then again fear of unnatural word-orders. Finally, the structure of the *kōla* and the *periodoi* with their total relations is borrowed from rhythmic theory. All this together forms an art of prose which stands in sharp relief to the poetic, whereas formerly, in Gorgias, prose still learned from poetry. The emotions are excluded; emotional shocks associated with slyness, irony, mockery, all this is missing, as are any enlivening figures—all this does not belong in the reading style; just as, incidentally, Thucydides too, despite his

themes, in principle avoids them. The *ēthos* [character] is dominant throughout. The structure of the orations is very great; the old stiffness of the arrangement has been overcome; a number of contrasting effects have been thought out; the mystery of the episode and retarding motifs, recognized; the artist sometimes alludes to the difficulty of the task of combining diverse elements into a unity.

Later critics exhausted themselves in comparisons between Demosthenes and Isocrates to the latter's disadvantage; but all this amounts to merely the difference between the spoken (*agonistisch*) and the written (*graphisch*) style; it is absurd to blame someone for remaining strictly within the limits of his field of art. He was found to be unvaried and monotonous, after people were already overexcited by dramatic effects and no longer understood the more delicate manifoldness within an *intentional* restriction to one basic color.

Isaeus. Strong similarity with Lysias, except that the latter strives to speak *charientōs* [pleasantly, beautifully], while he does so *deinōs* [forcefully, powerfully]. He begins to form the thought artistically and to color it rhetorically and is the transition to Demosthenes. The forensic speech did not completely escape from the influence of artistic prose, but the emotionality of the political speech also made itself felt. A certain affected simplicity: the clever advocate thinks himself into the good citizen's shoes; the *idiōtēs* [particularity] in Lysias is original, not a copy, as it is here.

Lycurgus. A good solid type, candidly simple, hard on himself, an enemy of all luxury; admiring Aeschylus, Sophocles, Euripides (bronze statues), he defends the old culture which has grown dear to his heart; likewise with the rule against falsifications by actors. A noble reactionary.

Hyperides, in the *Rhodian school's* judgment ranked as superior to Demosthenes.

We come to the *greatest genius of Athenian rhetoric*: Aeschines, not of the most common origin,[13] born in 393 B.C., "he later obtained Athenian citizenship rights only by the most crooked ways," says Demosthenes, but he is lying! He was first a secretary and reader of laws for the political orator Aristophon, then he worked for the demagogue Eubulos, whose convictions he shared. Then he became an actor (a tritagonist[14]), without success, for he was booed off the stage. Then he did military service. He first appeared as a political speaker at the age of thirty-three. A certain pride in his laboriously acquired knowledge and refined morals often emerges;

Demosthenes scolds his *apaideusia* [ignorance], calls him *amousos* [uneducated]. A beautiful voice with rare force and fullness; Demosthenes was terribly afraid of it and its seductive power; he trained it in the extremely meticulous modulation techniques of the contemporary actors. He had the two greatest masters of this art besides himself, Theodorus and Aristodemus (the latter was also, like other actors, used as an emissary in matters of state). Aeschines himself had once stumbled while playing Oenomaus (in pursuit of Pelops) and had to be helped to his feet by the chorus leader. He then toured the land with other bad actors: therefore called *arouraios* [rustic]. Demosthenes was lying terribly when he calumniated Aeschines' significance as an actor. The fact remains: the greatest actors had accepted him as a colleague. He brought his poise with him to the speaker's podium and indeed he appeared dignified, coming closer to the old orators by avoiding gesticulations of the hands; he was somewhat regal in comparison with the completely excited Demosthenes, who was very greatly annoyed by it (he was portrayed as Solon with his hand wrapped in his outer garment). Aeschines ranks the famous political orator Leodamus higher in artistry than Demosthenes. He himself has the lofty tone and solemnity of pathos, *sphodrotēs* [vehemence], *trachysēs* [roughness]; despite his splendid manner of narrating, he gives himself the appearance of the plain and simple, as if he were letting himself be guided only by the facts. All these orators (all practical ones!) strive equally to conceal their art; because, when noticed, it arouses distrust "like toward mixed wines," Aristot. (*Rhet.*, 3, 2).—The Macedonian party in Athens, formed by the negotiations with Philip, consisted of orators who in part sold themselves without further ado to the service of foreign states; of such men as wanted calm and peace at any price because that suited their political system—like Eubulos and Phocion, these were the most upright of men; finally, of men like Aeschines who were at first blinded and deceived but later, when Philip's deceptive game was discovered, remained faithful to him; they had become Philip's guests, had received royal gifts, and believed in the inevitability of the Macedonian policy, like Polybius later concerning the Romans. Naturally they also conceded all means of political procedure, as everyone did at that time. They were not simply corrupted; they regarded Athens' political constitution as a senseless activity which had to be discarded; that is also Plato's view on the subject,

with the difference that they were not thinking of an ideal state, but of the mightiest and most efficient state in their time.

Meanwhile, *forensic oratory reached its peak* because of the many political trials; it is not so oriented for long-range effect as are speeches before the people; it is supposed to act upon shrewd judges. But in important matters, most of the citizens are present, including many Hellenes from elsewhere, e.g., when Aeschines defends himself against Demosthenes concerning his role as emissary, and in the most famous of all trials, that on the coronation of Demosthenes. Here oratory absolutely reaches its supreme height; personal involvement and danger give wings to talent, and the ancients were able to talk about themselves as never before or since. Their profession of opinion, their image, which they wanted to implant in the souls of the listeners, is given with indescribable sharpness and clarity. As far as talent is concerned, Aeschines is the Greeks' greatest orator: yet he represents a policy which received Aristotle's sanction: "an alliance of the Hellenic free states under the tutelage of the Macedonian monarchy," and in this respect he has a deeper insight into the facts than does Demosthenes; one should not decide so easily on the higher or lower degree of moral strength, but one thing is sure: Demosthenes' rhetorical *training* is mightier, more enduring; he himself changed his defects into virtues, while Aeschines seems too richly endowed. Thus Demosthenes discovered the last stage of eloquence, *hypocrisis* [delivery, elocution]—he, who even in the last night of his life dreamed of himself as an actor on the tragic stage— just before it degenerated into mere playacting; and he set it aglow with his *passion*, so that it still appeared *natural*. Aeschines lacked this kind of passion, and so he tended to seek his supreme effects in the pathos of dignity (the ancients also attributed it partly to his lack of training, when they said that he displayed more flesh than muscle). On the other hand, he has the gift of *autoschediazein* [speaking impromptu], which is associated with a *lack* of passion; an *undercurrent* of cool circumspection makes improvisation possible, while an undercurrent of fire counteracts it or ruins its success: obscurity, haste, precipitancy of the themes then result. Generally, thinking about what is called the "natural gift for something" is too easy and premature; often such a natural talent contains a great obstacle to complete development. A great development needs light and shadow, abundance and lack.—His nine letters were called "the nine

muses."—He is still treated as infamous in order to serve as a foil for Demosthenes; and in that case Demosthenes' perfidious calumnies are believed or it is said that although they are exaggerated there was some basis for them, etc.

Demosthenes, son of Demosthenes; his father owned a factory that manufactured knives and ivory racks; he was born about 384. He was a puny lad, unathletic, nicknamed *Batalos*, the reasons for which are unclear. His guardians, Aphobos and Demophon, cheated him of his great fortune. In five long years of struggle, the youth tormented himself in lawsuits, saw himself robbed, and also incurring the enmity of powerful men—a bleak outlook on the world. So he was cheated of his youth; he began his adulthood earlier. He studied rhetoric under Isaeus—who was his lawyer—; his writer was Thucydides, that shows his view of life! Then he became a *logographos* and supported himself so with iron-willed industriousness and precocious skill. Among the orations which are extant, thirty deal with private cases, *logoi dikanikoi idiōtikoi* [speeches for private litigations], and twelve with political trials, *logoi dikanikoi dēmosioi* [speeches for public litigations]. Almost all his forensic orations were written for the plaintiffs. He appeared in person before the court in 354 B.C. as the *synēgoros* [advocate] for Ktesippos against Leptines. He seemed least qualified to be a public speaker. The decisive event which motivated him toward that profession as a boy was the success of the statesman Callistratos, when he emerged victoriously from the Oropian case; even later, at the *acme* of his career he still considered him the better speaker if he was *heard*, and *his* orations better if they were *read*. Here we have a critique of his own *hypocrisis* [delivery]. It had cost him the greatest toil and was not an innate talent; it had been imposed upon his nature by unspeakable labor. The first step was to learn from actors: Neoptolemos and also the comedian Satyros (he is reported to have hired Neoptolemos as teacher for 10,000 drachmas in order to learn to deliver entire periods in *one* breath). It was the time of the highest blossoming of acting (the mightiest expressiveness!); but taste changes swiftly: the more refined minds of the time no longer agreed with his action, nor did Aeschines; he pleased the *crowd* quite extraordinarily, but Demetrios the Phalerian found him

> *hypocritēs hypopoikilos kai perittos, ouch haplous oude kata ton gennaion tropon, all' es to malakōteron kai tapeinoteron apoklinōn*

[somewhat variegated and out of the ordinary as an orator, neither simple nor following the polite way of speech, tending, instead rather to the easygoing and the profane].

Shortly thereafter the reaction in favor of the plain, the archaic began. But now all his eloquence is most closely interwoven with his actor's mode of delivery: the goal is *to make every emotion become visible!* All fear of expressing passion has vanished: he is a Euripides raised to the tenth power. Sobbing, weeping, thundering, scorning, the great scale of tones; he could modulate the tone twice in the same period and let it swell up into a storm. His *deinotēs* is the art of the firm grasp: he seizes and tugs and tears apart. And, nonetheless, he must have had in himself a still higher ideal of the *hypocrisis!* as those words of Callistratus show. Theopompus' judgment that Demosthenes had been very inconstant in his *tropos* [manner] and had not been able to dwell for a long time on the same things and men is very significant. This trait is highly characteristic for the flickering fire of his nature. Theophrastus demands of his ideal public speaker precisely the opposite of the Demosthenean nature; the *sermo* should be *quam maxime remotus ab omni affectione* [as far removed as possible from all emotionality].

Neither Isaeus nor Thucydides must be underestimated in the formation of Demosthenes' *style*; Isocrates was the strongest influence. It is as if he had given himself the task of having the Isocratean prose absorb as much passion and fire as it could bear, so that it now became useful for agonistic delivery; then he believed certainly to have the mightiest prose in the world. Hence the avoidance of the hiatus in favor of the Isocratean eurhythmicality of the period; but naturally a tight concentration of the thought, in contrast with Isocrates' more loosely distended periods; like Isocrates, but with many short sentences and *kommata* interspersed. Precisely such passages are famous for their dramatic power; where question and answer, objection and refutation, cause and effect, and parallel rapid-fire questions follow one after the other in rapid succession without conjunctions, intensification of liveliness reaches its peak. It is absolutely not a reading style, not designed for leisurely contemplation. Aristotle is far from classifying his speeches within Greek "literature" at all. It is as if a soldier had first been trained as an athlete and now, in real combat, applies his art as it were only unintentionally; everything *anankaion* [necessary] will now seem easy, natural, ver-

satile; everything playful and ostentatious that is contained in all purely epideictic art is burned to a crisp by the high earnestness of the cause. One almost forgets that he must have practiced all kinds of eloquence, he must have been at home in all the styles in order to command this seemingly almost naturalistic *polyphony* of style and affective discourse. And precisely because this is easily forgotten, a philosophical Greek, such as Aristotle and Theophrastus, was far from taking him seriously as an *artist*: at that time no one, it seems, spoke of the pinnacle of Attic prose which had been achieved. The great "style" is hard to grasp; it is astonishing how the liberating and perfecting geniuses of an art, because they have stripped from themselves the little traits and "manners" of the genre and taken possession of all the means, easily impress their contemporaries as naturalists or virtuosos, or even dilettantes.[15] Theopompus considered *himself* the greatest prose-writer; he believed that Demosthenes' tremendous temporary influence on Greek politics was disproportionate to Demosthenes' ability; he had not earned it; obviously even this great expert appraised Demosthenes' talent too low.

[On Demosthenes' politics and vicissitudes.]

Of sixty-five speeches, sixty-one are extant, among them seventeen *symbouleutikoi* (among these are twelve Philippics; the seventh is considered to be by Hegesippus, but was incorporated among Demosthenes' works at an early date, since the eleventh, ungenuine one cites it. The fourth is also ungenuine). Then forty-two *dikanikoi*, twelve of them in matters of constitutional law, thirty *idiōtikoi*, on civil law, among them *peri stephanou*, the greatest masterpiece of all eloquence. Civil forensic orations which can be considered genuine beyond doubt are: the four guardianship speeches, for Phormion, against Pantainetos, against Nausimachos, against Boiotos 1, against Conon. They have no particular manner, but show the most complete mastery of all styles and methods, and therefore differ greatly from one another. If simple natures are presented, of course it is not a Lysian simplicity that appears: even there the rhetorical tension can be felt, as the mighty *deinos rhētōr* merely puts on his mask. As in Isaeus, his versatility and shrewdness are remarkable: it has been remarked that even when they are right Demosthenes and Isaeus arouse distrust.

In sum, Demosthenes should be admired as a man inspired by a great passion of noblest rank; but one should beware of believing that he stands completely outside the standard of Athenian morality.[16]

Likewise there should be no exaggeration about his political understanding; his means are, moreover, the means of all contemporary
orators and politicians; he is, in that respect, no idealist. It is quite
wrong to treat Aeschines as a foil to Demosthenes; neither the man
nor the artist justifies this.[17] It is also unjust to envisage the Athenian
people only in contrast to Demosthenes; they still contained a
mighty power of enthusiasm, so that Demosthenes did not have to
see himself as a Don Quixote. The stormy air of Athenian democracy
carries his oratory to the heights; just as it in turn makes this storm
more violent and decisive. The distance from the subsequent servile,
oppressed ages is enormous, since in Athens nothing merged in calm
phases; it is a municipality with an *ēthos diastaltikon* [a distinction-
making character].

The decline of eloquence and of the artful style is very interesting.
Dinarchus, born in 361 in Corinth, lived in Athens and wrote
speeches for others, especially for the Macedonian party; he was very
active as an instrument of Antipater during the reign of Demetrius
Phalereus. He is an *imitator without a style of his own*, who uses now
Hyperides, now Lysias, now Demosthenes as model—it is a usual
process at the height of any art that gifted reproductive talents are
drawn back and forth and achieve great skill between the various
kinds of style—but always a disadvantage for the art, because they
stand outside the various styles; in the great artist the style grows out
of him, with necessity. But here it is as if a style were put on and
taken off like a garment: such artists ruin the judgment and feeling.

Demades, of low birth, a shameless, base character, without culture, equipped by nature with a splendid oratorical talent; he was
ranked above Demosthenes in intellectual brilliance, and often
assumed leadership of the state and rendered it significant services.
He is an *improviser*—in every flourishing period of an art there are
reproductive talents which are astonishing for their instantaneous
quasi-creativity based on a highly developed art and all-pervasive
technique. He was clever enough not to write anything down for publication. He had a great quantity of suitable metaphors and jokes at
his disposal. But he also stole jokes from older orators, e.g. from
Hyperides. When he introduces an illegal *psēphisma* [bill] and
Lycurgus asks him whether he had not consulted the laws, he replies:
"No, they were obscured by the Macedonians' weapons." But Hyperides had already said this before him. He said of Demosthenes that
he resembled the swallows, since his twittering bothered him in his

sleep without being useful when awake (like dogs). He amassed a great fortune through Macedonian bribery, and when asked what he did with it, he lifted his garment, pointed to *koilia* [belly] and *aidoia* [genitals] and said: *ti an toutois hikanon genoito* [what would be befitting to these].

Demetrios of Phaleron, regent of Athens under Cassander, was later one of the cataloguers of the Alexandrian library; his teacher was Theophrastus; he belongs to the peripatetic school. The greatest master of luxury, the most elegant man of the age, the prime authority on clothing, ointments, cosmetics, household furnishings, forms of social intercourse, and honored like a God—but even in all this still an Athenian, not an Egyptian or a Syrian. The *hypocrisis* of the prominent, cultured, and elegant man also shaped a corresponding style of oratory; here Athens is still *productive*. He found Demosthenes too theatrical and not dignified enough; thus his presentation and conduct is calmer, more "dignified," and at the same time more nonchalant and charming: philosophical refinement of thought is now introduced into public speaking as a stimulus. Cicero (*De Off.*, 1, 285), says: *mihi quidem ex illius orationibus redolere ipsae Athenae videntur* [some of these orations seem to me to have the fragrance of Athena herself]—certainly a seductive aroma! He is *parum vehemens* [not vigorous enough], but *dulcis* [pleasant, delightful], the most pleasant and most adorned but the least powerful orator. A highly refined audience, weary of political excitement, an entire municipal community, which now enjoys the audible and visible arts of epideictic prose: a weakly, perfumed Isocrates has now taken over the rhetorical stage. The difference between reader and listener is beginning to be completely blurred, for the listeners are now all accustomed by a great deal of reading to the highest demands of style which make a gourmet's delight. Political passion now is converted into thousands of quarrels about aesthetic fashion. Then the *reactions* first arise, conscious surfeit with the present, an attempt to return to the simple as to a mighty stimulus; rumination on various pasts begins. The Athenian Charisius became a Lysian. Productivity was lost, and soon Athens was overcome as the central location of rhetoric; soon even in Athens oratory was conducted in the *Asian* pattern!

Naturally the art of rhetoric retreated from the Diadochian courts, but it was fostered and transformed in the Hellenic and Hellenized cities of Asia Minor, where it could still prove effective at court or in

the assemblies. From the outset, in conscious contrast with Attic classicism, vulgar and provincial expressions had been adopted in large quantities, and the strict periodic articulation of Demosthenean oratory had been replaced by loose, often choppy sentence structure, while at the same time, weak rhythms, precious word-orders, luxuriant means of expression, and pointed witty aphorisms were preferred. Hegesias, from Magnesia on Sipylos, is the man of doom. He designates as his successor Charisius, according to Demosthenes an affected Lysian (whose orations, moreover, quite characteristically, were ascribed to Menander by the critics).[18] In any case, there is some affinity between Menander's style and Charisius'; and Menander was a forerunner of Asian eloquence in one respect, just as Euripides prepared the way for Lysian eloquence. What was intended with Lysias? Hegesias, in his own opinion, towered far above the Atticists: or, according to Cic. (*Brut.*, 286), he considered himself so much an Atticist that in his eyes they were *paene agrestes* [almost uncouth]. Avoidance of the period, short sentences: thus the *strongest rhythm is felt on a small scale.* Return to what is most effective with the broad masses (as if today a retreat were being made from Beethoven's and Wagner's great periodics back to the four-beat rhythm of song and dance). In these small rhythmic formations, however, everything is refinement and spice. Only when he let himself go, did he write in periods. He prefers rhythms which the non-Attically refined people like: trochees, tribrachs, amphibrachs, ditrochees in the clausula. Thus his style of oratory is for less refined and elegant ears; but *it appealed to the whole Hellenistic mass*, which was enchanted for a few centuries. He also used obtrusive, farfetched imagery, metaphors, strange witty turns of phrase; he was seeking *direct effect* and he attained his goal.[19] His style, compared with the Attic one, is something like Hellenistic culture compared with the Hellenic. He found a tremendous longing everywhere and felt that the Atticists were not meeting this longing sufficiently. His merit is to have discovered and satisfied a universal passion of the whole Hellenistic world; in this regard he stands there mightily, for all ages. Never, down to the present moment, has the Asianism of style ceased; there were very significant countercurrents from refined classes of society and even much coarser and stronger ones from much cruder classes, where only the crudest means of oratory and style are sensed or nothing at all is heard. But insofar as a cultured society is now again expanding, it enjoys Asianism; the French,

schooled in Cicero and the Romanized form of Asianism, have accustomed the whole world to it. So let us beware of scoffing: *de te fabula narratur*. It took approximately one century (the last half of the third and the first half of the second century) for Asianism apparently to be completely victorious and overpowering (in the second half of the second century); indeed, as a sign of its victory, there was even a counterreaction in a place where it had formerly perhaps most strongly taken hold, in Rhodes. The means of instruction in Asianism, completely unknown in Athens, is the *school of declamation*: Aeschines reportedly was the first to establish the *Rhodiakon didaskaleion* [Rhodes School]; its approach was purely practical, with exercises in fictitious legal cases and advisory orations. The difference between the notorious declamation of the Imperial period is that in these schools declaiming was its own purpose, while for the Asians it was a means of practicing for real cases. It is important that no foundation for a general education was being sought (the "philosophical" element, which Dionysius finds in all the Athenians), but the aim was *directly* for oratorical virtuosity. So more time was gained for training and a very specific goal was kept in sight: training to be an *oratorical virtuoso*. That was the *point* of Hellenistic culture; the aim is for immediate effect; the publishing of speeches declines. There were, on the whole, two schools within Asianism, one more intellectual and the other more sensual. Cic. (*Brut.*, 325): "*unum (genus) sententiosum et argutum, sententiis non tam gravibus et severis quam concinnis et venustis*" [the one sententious and studied, less characterized by weight of thought than by the charm of balance and symmetry],[20] [one] a piquant journalistic style packed with elegant and witty ideas; the other genus is verbose, ornate, bombastic, ravishing, stunning—Cicero finds in this school *admirabilis orationis cursus* [a rapid flow of speech]. In more elegant regions this became *opimum quoddam et tamquam adipatae dictionis genus* [a certain rich and unctuous type of diction] [Cic., *Or.*, 25]. Its delivery was with luxuriantly affected facial expressions and gestures, sometimes a veritable singing and howling. Caria is most productive of famous Asians.

A reaction came in Rhodes at the end of the second century. Under Apollonius and Molon (both natives of Alabanda in Caria) oratory went back to *Attic* models and demanded purer diction, strict periodic structure. The unadorned *charis* [grace, beauty] of Hyperides was an especially favored model, with the added ingredient of a cer-

tain Rhodian wittiness and acuity. Demosthenes is not witty. The fragments of Posidonius' historical work, especially the interspersed *demegories* [deliberative speeches] give a picture of this better (?) taste; in which, however, Dionysius of Halic. finds just a wrong kind of imitation. An Atticist *reaction in Athens* itself is represented by Gorgias (who for a time was the young Cicero's instructor). We know him from Rutilius Lupus' excerpt "On the Rhetorical Figures," which condensed Gorgias' four books into one, according to Quint. (9, 2, 102). Mostly, the old classics were used, but then also Charisius, Hegesias, and the Asians; it thus tends to be rather eclectic. At this time all possible fashions are developing; there were extreme Thucydideans (as orators!), Xenophonteans, Platonists, Isocrateans, etc. All have in common that they vaunt the mistakes of the masters. Dionysius of Halicarnassus condemns all this reactionary and fashionable activity *en bloc*: and rightly so.

There is also a kind of reaction in the great rhetorician Hermagoras of Temnos, who invents a highly subtle theory of the art and relies a great deal on the technical education of the ancients; but there is something about him of an age-weary scholastic pedantry which reaches ever more powerfully around itself and which no one can avoid. Thus it seemed to be all over—among the Greeks themselves.

On the foundation of the development of *Roman* eloquence, i.e., of a *powerful new* force, a significant *struggle* between Asianism and Atticism first ensued. Quintus Hortensius in 95 B.C. dared to transplant the Asian mode of oratory completely to Rome and he brought it to dominance. Highly precise and careful, especially in the disposition and in the polishing and cadencing of periods, he combined the *two genres* of the Asian style, and added a very lively theatrical manner of delivery (*motus et gestus etiam plus artis habebant quam erat oratori satis*, Cic. *Brut.*, 303) [his delivery and gesture were even a little too studied for the orator].[21] The older orators were angry and scoffed; the younger generation was enthralled; the masses were enthusiastic. In writing the speeches seemed insignificant. Cicero now has the inestimable merit of having found the classical language of the *Roman world culture*; not un-Roman, not Asian, not Attic, but also not ancient Roman or parochially Roman—an enchanting mixture, which cannot be explained by eclecticism alone, but from a real *ēthos*, a whole spiritual predecision where these various currents converged into one; the genesis of the Ciceronian language is one of the

mightiest cultural feats; it was worthwhile for the artist—that is what he mainly was—to use unspeakable industriousness and in the end to admire himself unspeakably: which Julius Caesar also did. He is one of the greatest rhythmists who have ever lived; we must therefore forgive him a great deal.[22] The Roman Atticists, who may in theory have been right a thousand times over against him, suffered only defeats in the practical field and saw themselves set back; they had a singular "taste," but the deep necessity to speak precisely in this way or that was not on their side. The leader of the Lysians and Hyperideans is Gaius Licinius Calvus, orator and poet; he gave absolutely only forensic speeches, no political speeches in the Senate or before the people. He and his party found Cicero bombastic, verbose, luxuriant in composition, enervated and effeminate, in general an Asian. The Roman palate *wanted* strong stimulants, the provinces all the more so—Cicero had a marvelous instinct for this.

The favoring of Atticism in Rome was a signal for the *Greeks* of that time; their vanity and their nobler nature felt the most violent impulse to also forge ahead and oppose Asianism with the genuine Hellenic prototype. It is not a real *natural force*—backed by necessity—since for the Greeks nothing about their situation changed so that rhetoric would have been in a better, freer state; it is a reaction and a fashion, but quite a strong one. Dionysius and Caecilius are the pioneers; only now is Hegesias despised and mistreated. They did not regard Asianism as a low stage of Hellenic rhetoric, as Cicero did, but as a barbaric corruption; impassioned scolding against the "Phrygians" and "Carians" began. On the other hand, the Atticist quarrels among themselves over their separate masters necessarily led to a more precise scrutiny and estimation of them; and in any case we owe the conscious esteem for Demosthenes to this period. Dionysius brought this about; he purged the canon of Antiphon, Andocides, and Deinarchos, and was quite fair to all others. Both actions are important for questions of the genuineness of the older speeches. Both actions focused the practical and—in this respect they are especially liberating!—they distanced him from the subtleties of the *new technographs*, the Hermagoreans. Attempts were indeed made with special dictionaries to obtain help with the ten orators; Caecilius made the first attempt in this direction. It was, in sum, as much a reaction to bad taste in judgment as to bad taste in education—*against* the *barbaric* and the *scholastic*!

Atticism soon won out everywhere: although countless Asian declaimers still lived on all sides, including in Rome. In the first Imperial period, the nature of eloquence does not change on a vast scale: the schools in Athens lost some ground, and the flow of Roman youth went to Massilia or Asia, where Tarsus was overrun with orators. Also famous was the school in Mytilene (Lesbos), where Timocrates—Lesbonax—Potamon (teacher and friend of Tiberius) succeed one another. In Asia, Theodorus of Gadara is founder of the sect of the *Theodōreioi*;[23] in Rome he is entangled in a quarrel with Potamon. Apollodorus of Pergamon is founder of the Pergamonian sect of the Apollodorei (among them Dionysius Atticus). Dio, surnamed Chrysostomos, from Prusa in Bithynia is more famous than all. Unrecognized in his homeland, he goes to Rome and allegedly on advice of the Delphic oracle, he began a journey on foot through Thrace, Mysia, Scythia, and the land of the Getes, with nothing but Plato's *Phaedo* and Demosthenes' *de falsa legatione* in his pocket. Then again to Prusa, which soon disgusts him with its small-town mentality. After Domitian's murder in 96 A.D. he turns the frontier army in favor of his friend Cocceius Nerva and then goes to Rome, where he is heaped with honors. In Rome he dies, highly respected by Trajan, in 117 A.D. Eighty speeches are extant, few belonging to his first period. His form is modeled on Hyperides and Aeschines, whom he preferred as models even over Demosthenes and Lysias. He is the first of those brilliant Sophist characters who exhilarated the first four centuries, and who are unmatched in the preceding ages. They are separated from the Asians by their taste, their completed general education, their reliance on the best models; they are *reproductive virtuosos* based on reverence for the great ancients as heroes; for them the older Hellenic culture is the guiding light, but not without emulation; they bring this to view again in the greatest decorative splendor, presenting themselves as harmonious, overpowering men. To be sure, their accent in everything lay on *form*; they educated for themselves the most form-conscious public that has ever existed, and it certainly served to undermine antiquity. Common to all of them is a very early development, a changeful, exhausting life, serviceability to princes, abundance of admiration, idolization, mortal enmities; for the most part they were wealthy men; they were not scholars but practicing virtuosos of oratory, and this distinguishes them from the fifteenth-century humanists in Italy, who as impoverished schol-

ars lived even harder lives, but otherwise were very similar to them. There is an excess of antique individualism in them. Their eloquence is one that does not stand on the ground of political, practical life; deeper scientific treatment of things is alien to them; indeed they are hostile to it. However, everything that excites, ravishes, enthralls was studied and practiced most diligently (something incomprehensible to us!); in part, they again count on the most sensitive public with the best rhetorical schooling, which also has a taste for the solution of technical difficulties including diction, which is carried to the point of rapture. The rhetor's self-confidence is in turn intensified by this, and so a state of genial enthusiasm ensues, in which it is no longer possible to distinguish what is ungenuine, affected, feigned, from what is natural—at any rate one's reason was lost in the process. Aristides, for instance, describes his state: "a strange vivacity takes hold of the lips and every part of the body, a rare mixture of sadness and pride, of passion and reflection fills them. The goddess pours out fiery rays from the speaker's head, the only source of speech is the truly sacred flame of Zeus, who then never lets the consecrated person rest." "Then every listener's eyes blur, and he does not know what is happening to him, but as if driven about on the battlefield, he loses all composure," etc. In the rage to appropriate every enthralling and exciting device, they exploited the superstitions and mystical urges of their audience with visions, dreams, prophecies, myths of every kind. Through a long illness, Aristides became associated with the Asclepius-cult and made absolutely a specialty of it. Everything comes to him from Asclepius; he invents a kind of self-praise: it is the god who has spoken out of him; again and again the god appears to assure him that he is like the great ancients, indeed that he has excelled them.

These Greek Sophists once again overpower the favorite Latin inclinations which were modern at the time and take their place. In Italy and in the countries of the West they celebrate triumphs as magnificent as in the old Greek lands; far beyond the success of the old honorable Plutarch in Rome. Native Italians such as Claudius Aelianus mastered the Greek language so thoroughly that one believed one was hearing someone born in Attica.[24] The goal of their ambition was to be director of the Greek chancellory at the Imperial court, then professorships in Athens or the Greek Sophist professorship in Rome at the Athenaeum established by Hadrian; then per-

sonal relations with the princes. Thus the elder Philostratus is a friend of the African emperors and of the Gordian house; he wrote the biography of Apollonius of Tyana at the Empress Julia Domna's request; his *hērōikos* celebrated Caracalla's favorite heroes, Achilles, etc. Especially important is the new flowering of *Athens* from Hadrian on. Marcus Aurelius establishes two public schools, a philosophical one and a rhetorical one, the first with four departments [*Katheder*] (after the four main schools), each with two representatives, and the second with two *thronoi*—the Sophistic and the political disciplines. The professors received 10,000 drachmas per year. Later the number of teachers was raised to six. By the Emperor's will the name Sophist was returned to honor. An extraordinary competition ensues. The main effort of the great rhetors, besides their schoolteaching, was to gain a reputation for brilliant *extemporizing*, in order to move their pupils to stormy applause, for instance in competition with outside visitors. Two school curricula were recognized, a propaedeutic one (it contained an organized training program in style and declamation, study of the ancients, philological or practical-juridical or dialectical exercises, introduction to extemporizing, etc.), then the "acroamatic" [auditory] study, the enjoyment of the professor's regular lectures and master orations; generally a student attached himself to one professor. The rhetoric professors were expected to provide mainly the formal training, but also the positive knowledge (history, literature, political science and law, parts of natural science, mathematics).

[Herodes Atticus. Aelius Aristides.]

Very important as an opponent to all Sophism is Lucian of Samosata, 130–200 A.D., formerly himself a Sophist and rhetor, e.g., in Massilia; at the age of forty he turns to philosophy and writing (later he was procurator of Egypt), the reviver of the philosophical dramatic dialogue, but an Atticist. About eighty works are extant. A classical narrator and extremely witty entertainer; but aglow with the fire of indignation.

[There follows an enumeration of the most important rhetors and Sophists down to Libanius who was called "the last great talent."]

Until 360 A.D. the external history of the University of *Athens* coincides with the series of great *Sophists:* in that year the Neoplatonists established themselves firmly there. At the beginning of the fourth century, a Cappadocian professor, Julian of Caesarea, is the

most important person. His favorite pupil, Proaeresius, is from Armenia; he came to Athens very poor. An imposing figure, intelligent, quick-witted, very diligent; to him Julian bequeathed his magnificent house and classroom and wished him to be his successor. A tumultuous struggle of applicants began; citizenry and students were very excited. As an object and cause of continual disturbances, Proaeresius had to leave Athens on command of the proconsul. Later he fought his way through a huge master oration, which enthralled even his opponents, but the professorship [escaped him]. He now dominated the scene for three decades. The excitement did not subside; it culminated in the famous "battle of the rhetors" under the plantains of the *Lykeion*. The threat was made to depose three Sophists and appoint Libanius (later he became so famous as the pearl of all rhetors in Antioch and an impassioned opponent of Christianity). Then Proaeresius' position became stronger and stronger through the favor of Roman potentates. The Emperor Constans invited him to his Imperial camp in Gaul and on the Rhine. Then he delighted Rome, which honored him with a bronze statue. He used his favor to Athens' advantage; from then on he ruled without any challenging rival until his late end. Libanius shrewdly rejected an appointment. The only person who could compete with the great Armenian was Himerios the Bithynian. Himerios acquired Attic citizenship, bought a farm nearby and had himself initiated into the Eleusinian Mysteries; he became a professor in ca. 345 A.D. His contemporaries knew that in addition to the works of their idolized Aristides he had also studied Demosthenes; they praised the elegance of his oratory more than its strength, "which had reached the sublime dignity of Aristides only now and then." He is a colorful, ornate, luxuriant stylist, with allegorical and mythical pomp. He had very many listeners; he compared his school with that of Isocrates, indeed with Delphi. Himerios enjoyed great favor with the Emperor Julian. After the Emperor's death he withdrew to a life of privacy for quite a long time. Now Proaeresius was again alone in the hegemony. He died in 367, at the age of ninety-one. The following year Himerios returned. It was a bad epoch for the university; a change took place in the great cultural public of the whole world; practical studies pressed to the foreground; enjoyment of the ancient splendor of rhetoric vanished completely; Himerios is the last great Sophist, and soon Athens too is for rhetoric just a seat of dry professional training.

NOTES

1. Cicero, *Brutus*, trans. G. L. Hendrickson, Loeb Classical Library (Cambridge: Harvard University Press, 1962), p. 49.

2. In R. C. Jebb, *The Attic Orators from Antiphon to Isaeos* (New York: Russell and Russel, 1962), p. cxxii, this anecdote is interpreted not as a gauge of the morality or immorality of the early Sophist orators but of their "grotesque unpopularity."

3. At first literary prose (*Kunstprosa*) was poetic (hence it used poetic diction, and it replaced meter with artful figures), according to Aristotle, *Rhet.*, 3, 1, because it was seen how the poets won their fame by using unusual expressions; even to this day the great crowd gives the greatest applause to those who speak such language. Which writers should we have in mind in this regard? The lyric poets and tragedians, in any case; Gorgias imitates their successes; for an actor's delivery of an Aeschylean tragedy may have determined him. He prescribes the *Attic dialect* for the artful speech (*Kunstrede*): a very genial step. In Olympia before all the Hellenes he spoke Attic: on Athens' advantages in this respect as *prytaneion tes sophias* [city hall of wisdom] [Plato, *Prot.*, p. 337D]. Isocr. 15, 295 (Blass [*Geschichte der Beredsamkeit*] I, 52). Simultaneously he discovered the pan-Hellenic idea as the best content for the epideictic oration.—NIETZSCHE.

4. Aristotle, *The "Art" of Rhetoric*, trans. John Henry Freese (Cambridge: Harvard University Press, 1959), p. 349.

5. Translated from Nietzsche's German rendition. Compare with *The "Art" of Rhetoric*, 3, 12, 1, trans. John Henry Freese, p. 419.

6. Aristotle, *Rhetoric* 3,5—he places the mode of expression of the speech before the people (*Volksrede*) on the same level as the *skiagraphia* [painting in light and shadow, rough sketch] of perspectivistic *decorative painting*. The language expression of the epideictic oration is literary, *graphikōtatē*, intended for *reading*. Hence the sequence: (1) epideictic, (2) forensic, (3) popular and ceremonial oration.—NIETZSCHE.

7. *Thucydides*, 8, 68, 1, trans. Charles Forster Smith (Cambridge: Harvard University Press, 1958), vol. 4, p. 307.

8. Aristotle, *The Athenian Constitution. The Eudemian Ethics. On Virtues and Vices*, trans. H. Rackham (Cambridge: Harvard University Press, 1959), p. 341.

9. Plato, who idealized Critias in some respects [Nietzsche, in pencil in a later hand].—MUSARION.

10. *Orator*, 33, 78, trans. H. M. Hubbel Loeb Classical Library ed. (Cambridge: Harvard University Press, 1962), p. 363.

11. Nietzsche is probably thinking of the *logoi epistolikoi*. Dion. Hal., *Lys.* 1, 9 U.-R.—MUSARION.

12. The "*eristikoï*" were philosophers of the Megarean school, who were devoted to dialectics. Cf. Diog. Laertius, *Adv. eristikos*, Plato, *Republic* 454b.

13. For Demosthenes is lying in his speech on the crown and contradicts earlier data (given in the speech on the emissaries); whereas there is no contradiction between these data and Aeschines. He is of *more prominent* origin than Demosthenes, of the priestly family of the Butades. His father Atrometos, who had to flee several times, fought under Thrasybulus for the restoration of democracy; he had lost his property and lived in poverty until the age of ninety-five—as a schoolmaster, naturally without the financial means to finance liturgies for the state. Aeschines' mother was an Athenian and priestess of the mysteries, performing lustrations and dedications (her brother was a capable naval commander); there are disgusting calumnies by Demosthenes in the later speech, not in the earlier one; he transfers to them all the rubbish associated with the secret cults; in enmity even Demosthenes is a lying, malicious culprit.— NIETZSCHE, marginal note.

14. *Tritagōnistēs*, an actor who plays the third part, hence a third-rate performer. This is the name of a play by Antiphanes, cf. *Dem.* 270, 12. Vide Müller, *Literature of Greece* 1, p. 305.

15. Theophrastus finds Demosthenes to be an orator "worthy of the city," but Demades considers him "higher than the city."—NIETZSCHE.

16. He was believed not to be reliable in weapons and not sufficiently proof against bribes (from Persia).—Nietzsche.

17. He excelled the orators of his time in *aretē*, but was not the equal of the ancients.—NIETZSCHE.

18. Quintilian, 10, 1, 70.—MUSARION.

19. Longinus, *peri hyps.*, 3, 2, says of him and his likes: *pollachou gar enthysian heautois dekountes ou bacheuousin alla paizousin* [for, in many places, deeming it a sacrifice, they do not celebrate Bacchus but just play around].—NIETZSCHE.

20. Cicero, *Brutus*, 95, 325, trans. G. L. Hendrickson, p. 283.

21. Cicero, *Brutus*, 88, 303, trans. G. L. Hendrickson, p. 263.

22. In comparison, the Greeks' delicate, deliberative sense of proportion in construction was lost to Roman architecture, which sought the most possible splendor of decorative elaboration. In this area they show real greatness. Many misunderstood and reinterpreted Greek forms are hidden under the Roman ones, but the latter are still admirable for their magnificient effect. According to J[acob] B[urckhardt].—NIETZSCHE.

23. The sectarian disputes dealt with "technical" matters: Atticists are also involved.—NIETZSCHE.

24. In the judgment of Philostratos, *vit. soph.*, 2, 34, whom Nietzsche seems to take seriously.—MUSARION.

ON THE POET (1875)

'divine fury'

How the poet adopts religious sentiments and ideas and preserves them in times of decay (Aeschylus).

The enmity of the poets toward the philosophers contrasts with the philosophers' *friendship* for the poets, for they regard them as bridges from religion to philosophy. The poets, however, regard the philosophers and men of science only as opponents.

How can the madness of *faith in the poet* be explained? The poet *is* the instrument and spokesman not of the gods but of higher opinions; he enunciates these views in such a way that the public does not recognize that the poet has *derived* them from it. The pretense and masquerade as if something completely new were now coming along is the main effect of the poetic artifices (meter, etc., and the accompanying religious excitement). The poets deceive themselves about *their own self*; they do not know where it really comes from— so high has error lifted the opinion that they are inspired. Hesiod Tynnichos (from Plato's *Ion*).

The poet as a deceiver: he imitates being a knower (a general, a cobbler, a sailor); he carries it off with those who do *not* know: finally he himself believes it. Thus he gets the feeling of sincerity. Sensitive people accommodate him and even say that he has the *higher* truth: from time to time they are tired of reality. Sleep and dream for the head—that is what the artist is for men. He makes things *more valuable*: then people *think* that what seems more valuable is also *truer* and more real. Even now poetic men (e.g., Emerson, Lipiner) still seek the limits of knowledge, indeed preferably of skepticism, in order to break free of the spell of logic. They want *uncertainty*, because then the magician, intimation, and the great sentiments become possible again.

vs poets?

243

ON RHYTHM (1875)

How men, even in what they invent for the alleviation of their existence, load new drudgery and labor upon themselves, and how serious life seems when one examines the history of its happiest traits—poetry, and in general the artistic treatment of language, gives a proof of this. The mild gleam which the poet knows how to lay upon the world like dust from a moth's wings did not accrue to life haphazardly. The amount of work which men have applied to just such a thing as rhythm shows how hard life is and how tremendous the urge must be to escape from this feeling of its hardness at least for moments. If life were primarily a problem of cognition and if its difficulty consisted mainly in its being mysterious, then it could, in Schopenhauer's words, "appear almost as high treason against reason to do even the slightest violence to a thought or to its correct and pure expression with the childish intention of having the same sound of words be heard again after a few syllables, or even so that these syllables themselves might have a certain bounce (*Hopsasa*)."[1] But because life arouses feeling so irregularly and hence so painfully, "we mentally follow every sound that recurs regularly and, as it were, agree with it. Rhythm and rhyme thereby become partly an adhesive for our attention, since we follow the reading more willingly, and partly they give rise to a blind agreement with what is read, prior to all judgment; whereby the content takes on a certain emphatic power of conviction independent of all reasons."[2] The magic in rhythm consists in a quite elementary symbolism by which the regular and the orderly imposes itself on our understanding as a higher realm, a life above and beyond this irregular life; that part of us which has the power to move with the same rhythm follows the urging of that symbolic feeling and moves in unison with it or at least feels a strong urge to do so. The more excitable and natural a person is, the more rhythm acts upon him as a *compulsion* to repeat the rhythm and produces that "blind attunement prior to all judgment"; this compulsion is usually associated with pleasure, but it can tear at souls and overpower them so suddenly that it is more like a painful paroxysm. Even this painful following and being-dragged-along may perhaps still be considered an attraction, withdrawal, rapture, oblivion by the

person who stands in the midst of life's distress—the poets and musicians of all ages were aware of this; even when causing pain, they believed they were *alleviating* the pressure of existence. And thus they themselves took life hard, and they grasped their art with an uncommon and consuming earnestness; so that once again the contemplation of their thousand-year-old history admonishes to seriousness and adds the last brush stroke to the picture of life; for nothing is more tragic in life than that precisely those who make life easier and happier had to suffer more deeply from life, to endure a harder life than the world-conquerors and world-destroyers. Perhaps the reason is that they want something that goes against the nature of existence, that they dare to shake at the pillars of dismal necessity; they can deceive themselves and others about the nature of existence only for a short time—this deception is, after all, the essence of art— but the bad conscience and knowledge of all artists avenges itself continually upon them since they want to put on things a mask with purer, freer features, a mask which *must* fall off again and again. What if Plato were right! What if man were only a pretty toy in the hand of the gods! What if life could be arranged as a sequence of games and festivities! What if existence were nothing but an aesthetic phenomenon! Then the artist would become not only the most reasonable, the wisest man; he would not only coincide with the philosopher; but he would also have the easiest life and might with good conscience say with Plato: human affairs are not worth taking very seriously. Whether we would then have such a thing as art? Whether the artist would ever have originated if man himself were a work of art? Whether the very existence of art does not prove that existence is an unaesthetic, evil, and serious phenomenon? Let us consider what a real thinker, Leopardi, says: It would truly be desirable for men not to need art.

NOTES

1. Schopenhauer, *Die Welt als Wille und Vorstellung*, 2, 3, 37, p. 487 (Gr. 2, 502).—NIETZSCHE.
2. Schopenhauer, 1, 3, p. 287 (Gr. 1, 323).—NIETZSCHE.

ON TRUTH AND LYING IN AN EXTRA-MORAL
SENSE (1873)

In some remote corner of the universe that is poured out in count-less flickering solar systems, there once was a star on which clever animals invented knowledge. That was the most arrogant and the most untruthful moment in "world history"—yet indeed only a moment. After nature had taken a few breaths, the star froze over and the clever animals had to die.

Someone could invent such a fable and still not have illustrated adequately how pitiful, how shadowy and fleeting, how purposeless and arbitrary the human intellect appears within nature. There were eternities when it did not exist; and someday when it no longer is there, not much will have changed. For that intellect has no further mission leading beyond human life. It is utterly human, and only its owner and producer takes it with such pathos as if the whole world hinged upon it. But if we could communicate with the gnat, we would learn that it too swims through the air with this same pathos and feels within itself the flying center of this world. Nothing in nature is so contemptible and insignificant that it would not imme-diately be swollen up like a balloon by the slightest touch of that power of knowledge; and just as every cargo-carrier wants to have his admirer, so too the proudest man of all, the philosopher, believes he sees the eyes of the universe focused telescopically from all direc-tions upon his actions and thoughts.

It is remarkable that the intellect manages to do this, for in reality this faculty is given only as a help to the most unfortunate, most delicate, and most perishable creature, in order to preserve it for a moment in an existence out of which it would otherwise, like Less-ing's son, have every reason to flee.[1] The arrogance associated with knowledge and sensation lays a blinding fog over man's eyes and senses and deceives him about the value of existence by instilling in him a most flattering estimation of this faculty of knowledge. Its most universal effect is deception—but even its most specific effects have something of this same deceptiveness.

The intellect, as a means of preserving the individual, develops its

246

main powers in dissimulation; for this is the means by which the weaker, less robust individuals survive, since in the struggle for existence they are denied the horns and the sharp teeth of beasts of prey. This art of dissimulation reaches its peak in man; here deception, flattery, lying and cheating, slander, false pretenses, living on borrowed glory, masquerading, conventions of concealment, playacting before others and before oneself, in sum, the constant fluttering about the flame of vanity, is so much the rule and the law that almost nothing is more incomprehensible than how an honest and pure desire for truth could arise among men. They are deeply immersed in delusions and phantasmagoria; their eye merely glides around the surface of things and sees "forms"; their perception leads nowhere to the truth, but is satisfied with receiving stimuli and, as it were, playing a groping game on the back of things. Moreover, at night, for a whole life long, man lets himself be lied to in dreams, and his moral feeling does not seek to prevent this, although there are said to be men who can overcome snoring by sheer willpower. For what does man really know about himself! If only he could ever see himself perfectly, as if displayed in an illuminated showcase! Does not nature keep nearly everything secret from him, even about his own body, in order to hold him fast under the spell of a proud, delusionary consciousness, unmindful of the windings of his entrails, the swift flow of his bloodstream, the intricate quiverings of his tissues! She threw away the key; and woe to the fateful curiosity that ever succeeded in peering through a crack out of the room of consciousness and downward, suddenly realizing that man is based on a lack of mercy, insatiable greed, murder, on the indifference that stems from ignorance, as it were clinging to a tiger's back in dreams. Given this state of affairs, where in the world does the desire for truth originate?

Since the individual wants to preserve himself against other individuals, in the natural state man uses the intellect mostly for dissimulation. But at the same time, because man, out of necessity and boredom, wants to live socially in the herd, he needs a peace agreement, and he tries to eliminate at least the crudest forms of the *bellum omnium contra omnes* [war of all against all].[2] But this peaceful agreement apparently leads to the first step toward man's acquisition of his mysterious desire for truth. For what "truth" will be from now on is fixed; a uniformly valid and binding terminology for things is invented and the legislation of language also enacts the first laws of truth. For now, for the first time, the distinction between truth and

lying arises. The liar uses the valid terms, the words, to make the unreal appear real; for instance, he says, "I am rich," when "poor" would be the right term. He misuses established conventions by arbitrary substitutions and even reversals of names. When he does this in a selfish and damaging manner, society will no longer trust him and so it will exclude him from its presence. But men flee not so much being deceived as being harmed by deceit. What they hate is really not so much deception as the bad, hostile consequences of certain kinds of deceptions. Man also wants truth in a similar, restricted sense. He longs for the pleasant, life-preserving consequences of truth; he is indifferent to pure, inconsequential knowledge; toward truths which are perhaps even damaging and destructive, he is hostile. And furthermore, what is the situation with those conventions of language? Are they perhaps products of knowledge, of the sense for truth? Do terms coincide with things? Is language the adequate expression of all realities?

Only by forgetfulness can man ever come to believe that he has truth to the above-designated degree. Unless he wants to settle for truth in the form of tautology, i.e., for empty husks, he will perpetually exchange truths for illusions. What is a word? The portrayal of nerve stimuli in sounds. But to conclude from a nerve stimulus to a cause outside ourselves is already the result of a false and unjustified application of the law of causality. What would allow us, if the truth about the origin of language, the viewpoint of the certainty of terms, were alone decisive, what would allow us to say, "The stone is hard," as if "hard" were known to us otherwise than as a subjective stimulation! We arrange things by genders, we designate the tree [*der Baum*] as masculine, the plant [*die Pflanze*] as feminine: what arbitrary transferences! How far-flung beyond the canon of certitude! We speak of a "serpent"; the term applies to nothing but its winding, and so it would apply equally to the worm. What arbitrary delimitations, what one-sided preferences for one trait or another of a thing! The various languages, juxtaposed, show that words are never concerned with truth, never with adequate expression; otherwise there would not be so many languages. The "thing-in-itself" (which would be pure, disinterested truth) is also absolutely incomprehensible to the creator of language and not worth seeking. He designates only the relations of things to men, and to express these relations he uses the boldest metaphors. First, he translates a nerve stimulus into an image! That is the first metaphor. Then, the image must be reshaped into a sound! The second metaphor. And each time there is a com-

plete overleaping of spheres—from one sphere to the center of a totally different, new one. Imagine a person who is completely deaf and never has had a sensation of sound and music. How this person marvels at the Chladnean sound-figures in the sand, identifying their cause as the trembling of the strings, then swearing that now he must know what people call "sound."[3] That is the situation of all of us with language. When we speak of trees, colors, snow, and flowers, we believe we know something about the things themselves, although what we have are just metaphors of things, which do not correspond at all to the original entities. Like sound in the sand-figure, so the mysterious x of the thing appears first as a nerve stimulus, then as an image, and finally as a sound. In any case, the origin of language is not a logical process, and the whole material in and with which the man of truth, the scientist, the philosopher, works and builds, stems, if not from a never-never land, in any case not from the essence of things.

Let us think in particular of the formation of concepts. Every word becomes a concept as soon as it is supposed to serve not merely as a reminder of the unique, absolutely individualized original experience, to which it owes its origin, but at the same time to fit countless, more or less similar cases, which, strictly speaking, are never identical, and hence absolutely dissimilar. Every concept originates by the equation of the dissimilar. Just as no leaf is ever exactly the same as any other, certainly the concept "leaf" is formed by arbitrarily dropping those individual differences, by forgetting the distinguishing factors, and this gives rise to the idea that besides leaves there is in nature such a thing as the "leaf," i.e., an original form according to which all leaves are supposedly woven, sketched, circled off, colored, curled, painted, but by awkward hands, so that not a single specimen turns out correctly and reliably as a true copy of the original form. We call a person "honest." We ask, "Why did he act so honestly today?" Our answer usually goes: "Because of his honesty." Honesty! that means once more: the "leaf" is the cause of the leaves. For we know nothing of an essential quality called honesty; what we know are numerous, individualized, hence dissimilar, actions which we equate by omitting the dissimilar and then referring to them as honest actions. Last of all, we formulate out of them a *qualitas occulta* with the name "honesty."

Overlooking the individual and the real gives us the concept, just as it also gives us the form, whereas nature knows no forms and concepts, hence also no species, but only an x that is inaccessible and

indefinable for us. For even our distinction between individual and species is anthropomorphic and does not stem from the essence of things, although we also do not dare to say that it does *not* correspond to it. For that would be a dogmatic assertion, and as such just as unprovable as its opposite.

What is truth? a mobile army of metaphors, metonyms, anthropomorphisms, in short, a sum of human relations which were poetically and rhetorically heightened, transferred, and adorned, and after long use seem solid, canonical, and binding to a nation. Truths are illusions about which it has been forgotten that they *are* illusions, worn-out metaphors without sensory impact, coins which have lost their image and now can be used only as metal, and no longer as coins. We still do not know where the desire for truth originates; for until now we have heard only of the obligation which society, in order to exist, imposes to be truthful, i.e., to use the customary metaphors, or in moral terms, the obligation to lie according to an established convention, to lie collectively in a style that is mandatory for everyone. Now, of course, man forgets that this is his situation; so he lies in the designated manner unconsciously and according to centuries-old habits—and precisely *by this unconsciousness*, by this forgetting, he arrives at his sense of truth. The sense of being obliged to call one thing "red," another "cold," a third one "mute," gives rise to a moral feeling with respect to truth. By contrast with the liar, whom no one trusts, whom all ostracize, man proves for himself the honorableness, the familiarity, the usefulness of truth. As a "*rational*" being, he now puts his actions under the rule of abstractions; he no longer lets himself be carried away by sudden impressions, by intuitions; he first universalizes these impressions into less colorful, cooler concepts, in order to hitch the wagon of his life and actions to them. Everything that sets man off from the animal depends upon this capacity to dilute the concrete metaphors into a schema; for in the realm of such schemata, something is possible that might never succeed under the intuited first impressions: to build up a pyramidal order according to castes and classes, a new world of laws, privileges, subordinations, boundary determinations, which now stands opposite the other, concrete world of primary impressions, as the more solid, more universal, more familiar, more human, and therefore as the regulatory and imperative world. Whereas any intuitive metaphor is individual and unique and therefore always eludes any commentary, the great structure of concepts displays the rigid regularity

of a Roman columbarium and has an aura of that severity and cold-
ness typical of mathematics. Whoever feels the breath of that cold-
ness will scarcely believe that even the concept, bony and cube-
shaped like a die, and equally rotatable, is just what is left over as
the *residue of a metaphor*, and that the illusion of the artistic transference of a nerve stimulus into images is, if not the mother, then the
grandmother, of any concept. Within this dice game of concepts,
however, "truth" means: to use each die as designated, count its
spots accurately, forming the correct labels, and never violating the
caste system and sequence of rank classifications. As the Romans
and Etruscans carved up the sky into rigid mathematical sectors and
assigned a god to each delimited space as in a temple, so every nation
has such a mathematically divided conceptual sky above it and
understands by the demand for truth that each conceptual god must
be sought only in *his* own sphere. In this respect man can probably
be admired as a mighty architectural genius who succeeds in building
an infinitely complicated conceptual cathedral on foundations that
move like flowing water; of course, in order to anchor itself to such
a foundation, the building must be light as gossamer—delicate
enough to be carried along by the wave, yet strong enough not to be
blown apart by the wind. As an architectural genius, man excels the
bee; for it builds out of wax which it collects from nature, while man
builds out of the much more delicate material of the concepts, which
he must fabricate out of his own self. In this respect he is quite
admirable, but not because of his desire for truth, for pure knowledge
of things. If someone hides an object behind a bush, then seeks and
finds it there, that seeking and finding is not very laudable: but that
is the way it is with the seeking and finding of "truth" within the
rational sphere. If I define the mammal and then after examining a
camel declare, "See, a mammal," a truth is brought to light, but it is
of limited value. I mean, it is anthropomorphic through and through
and contains not a single point that would be "true in itself," real,
and universally valid, apart from man. The investigator into such
truths is basically seeking just the metamorphosis of the world into
man; he is struggling to understand the world as a human-like thing
and acquires at best a feeling of assimilation. Just as the astrologer
observes the stars in the service of men and in connection with their
joys and sorrows, so such an investigator observes the whole world
as linked with man; as the infinitely refracted echo of a primeval
sound, man; as the reproduction and copy of an archetype, man. His

procedure is to hold man up as the measure of all things, but his point of departure is the error of believing that he has these things before him as pure objects. He thus forgets that the original intuitive metaphors *are* indeed metaphors and takes them for the things themselves.

Only by forgetting that primitive metaphor-world, only by the hardening and rigidification of the mass of images that originally gushed forth as hot magma out of the primeval faculty of human fantasy, only by the invincible belief that *this* sun, *this* window, this table is a truth-in-itself, in short, only insofar as man forgets himself as a subject, indeed as an *artistically creative* subject, does he live with some calm, security, and consistency. If he could even for one moment escape from the prison walls of this belief, then his high opinion of himself would be dashed immediately. Even this costs him effort: to admit to himself that the insect or the bird perceives a completely different world than man does, and that the question which of the two world-perceptions is more right is a completely senseless one, since it could be decided only by the criterion of the *right perception*, i.e., by a standard *which does not exist*. Basically the right perception—that would mean the adequate expression of an object in the subject—seems to me to be a self-contradictory absurdity. For between two absolutely different spheres such as subject and object, there can be no expression, but at most an *aesthetic* stance, I mean an allusive transference, a stammering translation into a completely foreign medium. For this, however, in any case a freely fictionalizing and freely inventive middle sphere and middle faculty is necessary. The word "appearance" contains many seductions; and so I avoid it as much as possible. For it is not true that the essence of things appears in the empirical world. A painter who had lost his hands and sought to express the picture he envisaged by means of song, would still reveal more by this exchange of spheres than the empirical world reveals of the essence of things. Even the relation of a nerve stimulus to the produced picture is intrinsically not a necessary one; but when the same image has been produced millions of times and has been passed down through many generations of men, indeed ultimately appearing to all mankind as the result of the same occasion, in the end it has for man the same significance as if it were the only necessary image and as if that relationship of the original nerve stimulus to the produced image were a strictly causal relationship—just as a dream, eternally repeated, absolutely would be felt

and judged as reality. But the hardening and solidification of a metaphor is not at all a guarantee of the necessity and exclusive justification of this metaphor.

Certainly, every person who is familiar with such meditations has felt a deep distrust for that sort of idealism, as often as he has very clearly convinced himself of the eternal coherence, omnipresence, and infallibility of the laws of nature. He drew the conclusion: everything here, as far as we can penetrate, to the heights of the telescopic world or to the depths of the microscopic world, is constructed so securely, endlessly, regularly, and without gaps; science will have to dig successfully in these shafts forever, and everything it finds will coincide and not contradict itself. How little this resembles a product of fantasy; for if it were that, it would surely betray its illusoriness and unreality at some point. Against this reasoning, the following can be said: if we had, each taken singly, a varying sensory perception, we could see now like a bird, now like a worm, now like a plant; or if one of us saw the same stimulus as red, another as blue, while a third heard it even as a sound, then no one would speak of such a regularity of nature, but they would grasp it only as a highly subjective formation. What, then, is for us a law of nature? It is not known to us as such, but only in its effects, i.e., in its relations to other natural laws, which in turn are known to us only as relations. All these relations thus always refer back only to one another and are absolutely incomprehensible to us in their essence; what we add to them—time, space, hence relations of succession and numbers—is all we know about them. Everything marvelous that we admire in the laws of nature and that promotes our explanation and could mislead us into distrusting idealism, consists exclusively of the mathematical stringency and inviolability of time- and space-perceptions. But we produce these perceptions within ourselves and out of ourselves with the same necessity as a spider spins its web. If we are compelled to grasp all things only under these forms, then it is not surprising that in all things we really grasp only these forms: for they all must carry the laws of number in themselves, and number is the very thing that is most astonishing about things. All the regularity which so impresses us about the course of the stars and in the chemical process coincides fundamentally with the properties which we ourselves project into things, so that we impress ourself with it. It follows from this, to be sure, that the artistic metaphor-formation with which every perception begins in us, already presupposed those

forms, and hence is carried out in them. Only the fixed persistence of these original forms explains the possibility that later a structure of concepts was to be constructed again out of the metaphors themselves. For this is an imitation of the time-, space- and number-relations on the ground of the metaphors.

2

Language, as we saw, and later *science* works at the structure of concepts. As the bee simultaneously builds the cells and fills them with honey, so science works incessantly at the great columbarium of the concepts, the sepulcher of intuition, forever constructing new and ever higher levels, buttressing, cleaning, renovating old cells, and striving especially to fill this enormous towering edifice and to arrange the whole empirical, i.e., anthropomorphic, world in it. If even the man of action binds his life to reason and its concepts in order not to be swept away by the current and to lose himself, the researcher builds his hut right next to the towering structure of science in order to help with it and to find shelter himself under the existing fortification. And he does need shelter; for there are terrible powers which constantly press upon him, and which run counter to scientific truth with truths of quite another kind and under a different aegis.

That drive to form metaphors, that fundamental desire in man, which cannot be discounted for one moment, because that would amount to ignoring man himself, is in truth not overcome and indeed hardly restrained by the fact that out of its diminished products, the concepts, a regular and rigid new world is built up for him as a prison fortress. It seeks a new province for its activities and a different riverbed and generally finds it in *myth* and in *art*. It constantly confuses the categories and cells of the concepts by presenting new transferences, metaphors, and metonyms; constantly showing the desire to shape the existing world of the wideawake person to be variegatedly irregular and disinterestedly incoherent, exciting and eternally new, as is the world of dreams. Actually, the wideawake person is certain that he is awake only because of the rigidly regular web of concepts, and so he sometimes comes to believe that he is dreaming when at times that web of concepts is torn apart by art. Pascal is right when he states that if we had the same dream every night we would be as preoccupied with it as by the things we see

every day: "If the craftsman were certain to dream every night for a full twelve hours that he is a king, then I believe," says Pascal, "he would be just as happy as a king who dreamed every night for twelve hours that he is a craftsman." The waking day of a mythically excited nation, the ancient Greeks for instance, is, by the constant action of marvels, indeed more like a dream than like the day of the scientifically sober thinker. When any tree may begin anytime to speak as a nymph, or a god in the guise of a bull can abduct a maiden, when the goddess Athena herself is suddenly seen driving through the marketplaces of Athens on a beautiful team of horses in the company of Pisistratus—as the honest Athenian believed—then at any moment, as in a dream, anything is possible, and all nature crowds around man as if it were only the masquerade of the gods, who only make a joke of deceiving man in all forms.

Man, however, has an unconquerable tendency to let himself be deceived and he is as if enchanted with happiness when the rhapsodist tells him epic legends as true or the actor in a drama plays the king more regally than any real monarch does. As long as it can deceive without harm, the intellect, that master of deception, is free and released from its usual servile tasks, and that is when it celebrates its Saturnalia; never is it more luxuriant, richer, prouder, more skillful and bold. With creative nonchalance it scrambles the metaphors and shifts the boundary-stones of abstraction, so that, e.g., it calls the river a moving road that carries man to where he otherwise walks. Otherwise busy with melancholy business, it has now cast off the mark of subservience in order to show a poor devil who is avid for life the path and the means of attaining it. And like a servant whose master is setting out on a campaign seeking booty and plunder, it has now become the master and can wipe the look of poverty from its features. Which it now does. Compared with its former activities, everything contains dissimulation, just as the former life contained distortion. It copies human life, taking it for a good thing, and seems quite satisfied with it. That enormous structure of beams and boards of the concepts, to which the poor man clings for dear life, is for the liberated intellect just a scaffolding and plaything for his boldest artifices. And when he smashes it apart, scattering it, and then ironically puts it together again, joining the most remote and separating what is closest, he reveals that he does not need the emergency aid of poverty, and that he is now guided not by concepts but by intuitions. From these intuitions no regular road leads to the land

of ghostly schemata, of abstractions. The word is not made for these intuitions; man falls silent when he sees them, or he speaks in sheer forbidden metaphors and unheard of conceptual compounds, in order at least by smashing and scorning the old conceptual barricades to correspond creatively to the impressions of the mighty present intuition.

There are ages in which the rational man and the intuitive man stand side by side, one in fear of intuition, the other with mockery for abstraction; the latter being just as unreasonable as the former is unartistic. Both desire to master life; the one by managing to meet his main needs with foresight, prudence, reliability; the other, as an "overjoyous" hero, by not seeing those needs and considering only life, disguised as illusion and beauty, to be real. Where once the intuitive man, as in more ancient Greece, bore his weapons more powerfully and victoriously than his adversary, in favorable cases a culture can form and the domination of art over life be established. That dissimulation, that denial of poverty, that splendor of metaphorical intuitions and, in general, that immediacy of delusion accompanies all manifestations of such a life. Neither the house, nor the stride, nor the clothing, nor the clay jug betray the fact that need invented them; they seem intended to express an exalted happiness and an Olympian serenity and, as it were, a playing with serious matters. While the man guided by concepts and abstractions merely wards off misfortune by means of them, without extracting happiness for himself from them as he seeks the greatest freedom from pain, the intuitive man, standing in the midst of culture, in addition to warding off harm, reaps from his intuitions a continuously streaming clarification, cheerfulness, redemption. Of course, he suffers more violently when he does suffer; indeed, he also suffers more often, because he does not know how to learn from experience and he falls again and again into the same pit into which he fell before. He is then just as unreasonable in sorrow as in happiness; he cries out loudly and cannot be consoled. How differently stands the stoic person who has learned from experience and controls himself by reason! He who otherwise seeks only honesty, truth, freedom from delusions, and protection from enthralling seizures, now, in misfortune, produces a masterpiece of dissimulation, as the former did in happiness; he does not wear a quivering and mobile human face but, as it were, a mask with dignified harmony of features, he does not scream and does not

even raise his voice. When a real storm cloud pours down upon him, he wraps himself in his overcoat and walks away under the rain with slow strides.

NOTES

1. Lessing, in a letter to J. J. Eschenburg dated December 31, 1777, thus mourns the death of his newborn son.
2. Thomas Hobbes, *Leviathan*, chapter 18.
3. E. F. F. Chladni, the German physicist, used visual means of demonstrating sound. See his *Neue Beiträge zur Akustik* (1817).

Name Index

Subject Index

263